ACKNOWLEDGEMENTS

With grateful th

MARLBOROUGH _ _ _ _ _

For nurturing me for twenty-five years, picking me up when I was down and seeing me on my way with gratitude in my heart for the many kindnesses I received there. It is with the fondest of memories of one of England's great schools that I now write this memoir.

My grateful thanks also to the following for their advice, help and encouragement - much appreciated, particularly in this the Year of the Plague when support of any kind has been most welcome: Jared Armstrong, Jeremy Bourne, Catherine Bromwell, John Tilgate, Kate Goodwin, Jane Green, Graine Lenehan, Angus Maclennen, Chris Newton, Mike Paine, Jan Perrins, Glenys Roberts, Michel Trilles, Louise Wythe and Louise Wickham.

None of the above bear any responsibility for whatever inadequacies this book may contain. All errors and misunderstandings are mine.

John Wilkinson
9 Rue de l'Eglise
31530 Le Castéra
31-12-2020

John Wilkinson

Boy, Beak & Beyond

A Memoir of Public School Life

Mereo Books

2nd Floor, 6-8 Dyer Street, Cirencester, Gloucestershire, GL7 2PF
An imprint of Memoirs Books. www.mereobooks.com
and www.memoirsbooks.co.uk

Boy, Beak and Beyond

First published in Great Britain in 2021
by Mereo Books, an imprint of Memoirs Books.

Copyright ©2021

The address for Memoirs Books can be
found at www.mereobooks.com

Mereo Books Ltd. Reg. No. 12157152

Typeset in 11/15pt Century Schoolbook
by Wiltshire Associates.
Printed and bound in Great Britain

CONTENTS

Acknowledgements

About the author

Chapter

ABOUT THE AUTHOR

John Wilkinson was born in Cranleigh, Surrey in 1942. He went to Cranleigh School, where his father had been a housemaster and the chaplain. He took an honours degree in French and German at Trinity College, Dublin before going on to St. John's College, Cambridge and the Department of Education to take a Diploma in Education. His first and only appointment in 1967 was to the Modern Languages Department, Marlborough College, where he became Senior French master. He took early retirement in 1992 and moved to Gascony, France to create and run his restaurant, Chai John, from his house there in Le Castéra, a village to the west of Toulouse, while at the same time teaching English in the post-baccalauréat Classes Prépas in Toulouse.

He became regional secretary of the Marlburian Club, S W France, and now regularly invites Old Marlburians living in the region to club lunches at Chai John. In 2002 he bought a holiday home in Chefchaouen ('la ville bleue') in the Rif Mountains of North Morocco. He was appointed British Consular Warden there in 2009 and spends up to a third of the year there and in Tangier, where he plays the organ on Sundays at St. Andrew's Anglican church. With regular visits to the UK he now happily bounces back and forth between England, France and Morocco and hopes to be able to continue to do so for the foreseeable future. As he says: "If we were meant to stay in one place, we'd have roots instead of feet."

Chapter One

Desks and Clanging Bells

Time: 6 pm Friday, late November
Michaelmas Term, 1967
Marlborough College
Place: New Court 1 Classroom
Period: Shell (1ˢᵗ year) French Set 6

ZZZi.... i.... ii.... iii.... ing! Ploum! THUD!!! The board-rubber (the heavy old-fashioned variety, half wood, half felt) flew from the raised left hand of the seated beak (schoolmaster) at a velocity worthy of a French Exocet guided missile and found its target sitting in row three at the back of the class, hitting the unsuspecting boy with a glancing blow to the right shoulder – puffs of white chalk dust – before smashing into the wooden panelling at the back of the classroom. ZZZi.... ii.... iii.... ing! Ploum! THUD!! Twenty-three little heads instantly swivel round, relishing the unexpected distraction. Chortles and guffaws all round.

BEAK (SCHOOLMASTER): PONSONBY!! *Réveille-toi!* Wake up! Wake up, you idle child! And sit up straight, will you!

Startled boy straightens himself out of the slumped sleeping position he had so satisfactorily adopted for his ill-judged snooze, his head cradled by arms splayed out on the table before him.

1

BEAK: What the hell do you mean by sleeping your way through my class? *Merde alors!* Get on with your work! Go on! All of you.

PONSONBY: Sorry, sir. Sir I... I...I just couldn't help it.

DIGBY-JONES: (Snooty boy. Thinks he's the cats' whiskers. Also friend of Ponsonby) Sir! Sir! I can assure you he's been doing rugger practice all afternoon. I was there, sir. And then after that he was sent on a Manton run too because....

BEAK: Shut up, Digby! It's none of your business. *Tais-toi!*

PONSONBY: Yes, sir, he's right, sir. I did the rugger practice and then got told by the beak to do the Manton run for a punishment because....

BEAK: Punishment? For what?

PONSONBY: Because I was late for the practice, sir.

BEAK: Then it serves you right for being late for the practice, doesn't it?

PONSONBY: But no, sir. I couldn't get there on time because my violin teacher kept me in late and then I had to go all the way back to Preshute to get changed and then...

BEAK: Well then you should have asked to be let out of your violin lesson on time, shouldn't you?

PONSONBY: I couldn't, sir, because she kept me in because I arrived late and I arrived late because....

BEAK: (volume up) Oh, SHUT UP Ponsonby! Get sorted, can't you?

And here I go again allowing myself to be dragged into yet another of these fatuous sparring bouts, knowing full well how easily these little monsters can wear you down to a point of total exasperation with a litany of excuses, some of them plausible enough, others certainly not. Enough to try the patience of a saint, especially on a horrible dark, wet and windy Friday early evening in late November near the end of a strenuous week and a long term.

To be fair, the poor little mites are indeed probably just as tired as I am, being more or less constantly at the beck and call of a plethora of beaks all fiercely vying with each other for their charges' time and commitment. The more capable the child, the more likely he'll be torn asunder by conflicting calls – his subject beaks will want him in class, sport beaks on the games fields, music beaks at orchestral and choral practices, drama beaks on the stage, beak i/c Debating Society in the debating chamber, and so it goes on and on.

Today, Friday, is a Fag Day, which means two late afternoon classes squeezed in between afternoon activities and supper (Mondays and Wednesdays too). So this is the seventh period of the day for all of us. Personally I don't think there's really much point in actually 'teaching' them in these evening sessions – the kids are just too zonked out, especially in the first-year Shell. Best to give them a task to do which has to be completed and handed in at the end of the forty-minute period. Added advantage – I can then get on with some marking at the same time, unless, of course, distracted by the likes of that idle child Ponsonby.

BEAK: Work, Ponsonby, work!

PONSONBY: (mock-hurt) I am, sir.

Ten minutes into the period with relative calm now established on all fronts. Phew! *Pourvu que ça dure*, as said that wizened old Corsican peasant Napoleon's mother on hearing of yet another of his victories. Provided it lasts, she invariably replied.

A sudden knock at the door.

BEAK: *Oui, entrez!*

Enter Ben Trimble, *trempé jusqu'aux os*. Soaked to the skin and looking like a drowned rat. Twenty-three heads up again in eager anticipation of further distraction.

TRIMBLE (Hesitant) Sorry I'm a bit late, sir.

BEAK: (Volume up again) A BIT late, Trimble? You call 10 minutes late a BIT late? What the devil have you been doing, boy?

TRIMBLE: Sir, I've been doing gym, sir.

BEAK: (mock incredulity) Doing JIM, Trimble? DOING Jim? And what exactly do you mean by that, sir? Nothing improper, I trust. And Jim WHO, might I ask?

The penny suddenly drops and the whole class instantly dissolves into hoots and howls of sheer delight at the double-entendre I have so foolishly thrown out at them. Bang goes my marking. Trimble, still teetering on the doorstep, turns first pink, then rapidly a deep, bright red, contrasting starkly and beautifully with his long, curly blond hair. Laughter redoubles. A veritable riotocracy of merriment and ridicule. They're literally falling about as the poor boy attempts to make himself heard.

TRIMBLE: (Stammering) N... n... no, sir. I m. .m. .mean Gym – Gym in the Sports Hall, sir.

BEAK: (increased mock incredulity) You've been doing him in the SPORTS HALL? Why on earth in the SPORTS HALL, Trimble?

Laughter changes a gear up and turns into a surrealist display of raw, animal noises – grunts, snorts, shrieks, yowls and all. Volume full up. Senior colleague outside, passing by, glances in and turns his head away disapprovingly. *Merde! Tant pis.*

BEAK: (teasing) Surely you can think of better places, can't you? Trimble? Can't you?

He freezes to the spot, totally at a loss as to know what to do or say. General hilarity with no prospect of it abating.

MOLESWORTH: (Screaming above the din) Sir! Sir! Ask him Jim WHO again, sir!

BEAK: Shut up, Molesworth.

Trust Molesworth to milk this one, always the first to pick up the sleazy innuendo, always on the look-out for smut and filth. Big fat lump of lard that he is.

BEAK: (in conciliatory mode) Yes, all right Ben, we understand. You mean gym as in gymnasium, don't you? Not Jim the boy, eh? OK. Now go and sit down and get your books out.

MOLESWORTH: (blurting out) But, sir! Sir! We've ALL been doing Jim, sir. The whole class, sir. It's called a gang-bang, sir.

Mon Dieu! Here we go again. Just typical Molesworth. Never knows when to let go. Another wave of cacophonous delight overtakes the assembled company. A further chorus of cackles and cat-calls erupts.

BEAK: (looks daggers at Molesworth, then turns back to Trimble) Yes. Well, Ben, how come all the others can arrive on time and you not?

TRIMBLE: (regaining his composure): Sir, I couldn't find one of my shoes. Someone had nicked it, sir.

BEAK: Well, how come you've got them both on now?

TRIMBLE: Sir, I found it.

BEAK: Where did you find it?

TRIMBLE: In the loo, sir. The loo next to the gym. (corrects himself hastily) I mean gymnasium, sir.

BEAK: In the LOO, Ben? Actually IN the loo?

TRIMBLE: Yes, sir. Somebody tried to flush it down. I had to fish it out, sir.

Molesworth in a stage whisper the Beak pretends not to hear: "Nasty little sneak." Trimble, of course, hears it and the colour again starts to rise in his cheeks. Poor little fellow.

BEAK: (Surveying the scene from left to right) Well, well, well.

Twenty-three thirteen-year-old little faces are now looking up at him, innocence written all over them, one and all, and yet how cruel and callous they can be when working as a pack.

BEAK: (getting up from sitting behind his desk on the dais. A subtle change of mood in the room. They seem to sense what's coming.) I don't suppose there's any point in my asking the person to own up, is there?... (The noise has subsided)...Well, is there?... (prolonged silence) No, I thought not. Well then, there's someone here who hasn't even got the common decency to apologise for a prank which is in rather poor taste to say the least. In that case, if it's all too difficult to say sorry in public now, I'm asking the person concerned to do so in private. A personal apology to Trimble, please. OK? Before tomorrow morning's period. And if he hasn't received an apology by then, I'll be handing out either detentions or blue chits to the lot of you. Got it? (Volume up) GOT IT?

ALL: (mumbling) Yes, sir.

Then total silence. Just a little shuffling, perhaps from someone who is hopefully inwardly squirming.

BEAK: And now kindly get on with your work, and I'll get on with mine.

Heads down, except Trimble, who's desperately trying to find out what he's supposed to be doing. Ponsonby shows him. Good. Peace and quiet re-established. Little, gentle sighs from time to time. Someone trying to stifle hiccups. Blenkinsop picking his nose, as usual. Weekes sucking his thumb, also as usual. Seems to me a bit strange at his age, I would have thought.

Molesworth suddenly looks up, catches my eye and gives me a great leer. Silly, fat oaf. He sees I'm not amused. So head down again. Poor little Trimble looks up. I send him a discreet wink. He smiles. Good. He's OK then. A nice kid who gets a bit of a hard time, so I'm told. Not always easy being a gentle, well-mannered little boy in this hothouse environment.

Noise of the wind and the sleeting rain beating on the window panes. At least it's fairly warm in here.

What's that? The softest of taps on the back window, hardly discernible from the noise of the rain. Who's that then? Oh, yeah, it's only Hamilton practising his sign-language on me again. I wonder what he wants now. It reads 'Can-I-come-up-for-a-drink-after-Prep-tonight?' In other words, the usual. My reply sign language is brief and to the point: a discreet thumbs up. He flashes an impish smile and disappears into the gloom and over to the Norwood Hall, where, I expect, he's probably trying to get into supper before the queues.

6h 20 pm. Ten minutes to go before the end of the period. The sound of footsteps outside. People sloshing their way over to supper five minutes early, hoping to beat the queues. Followed by a sudden stampede issuing from the classroom next door.

BAVEYSTOCK: (Front row, hand up). Sir?

He's a very polite and well-spoken young man. I know his father and I also know what he's now going to ask me before he even opens his mouth.

BEAK: Yes, what is it, Christian?

BAVEYSTOCK: Please, sir, if we've finished can we go a little early to avoid the queues?

BEAK: You know the answer to that already. Wait till the bell goes.

ALL: (Pleading) Oh, please, sir!

MOLESWORTH: But NC2 have been let out, sir, so why can't we?

BEAK: Because you're not in NC2, my dear Molesworth (a hint

of irony he will have missed, the dolt). You're in NC1 with me. Isn't that just your bad luck?

MOLESWORTH: But, sir, it's not fair, sir.

BEAK: No, it isn't, is it? But that's life, Molesworth. Life just ain't fair. You'll discover that, Molesworth – when, and if, you ever grow up.

Molesworth lets me have one of his sullen stares. A more uncouth youth I never knew. Meanwhile, Ben is loving every bit of this. He's positively beaming at me. If he is thinking that my dig at Molesworth is for his benefit, he's probably not far off the mark.

BEAK: Who's not yet finished?

Trimble's hand goes up.

BEAK: Hardly surprising, is it? Trimble, stay behind and finish. Digby! Collect the books, will you. The rest of you, don't you dare move till that bell goes. (Looking around the class) And by the way would someone kindly tell me why we've not had the pleasure of the company of young Notty this evening? (The Hon. Sebastian Nott-Bower)

DIGBY-JONES: Oh, sir, he's gone to London. Humph has gone too, sir. (The Hon. Humphrey Thompson.) They won't be back till Sunday night, sir.

BEAK: And may I ask what they're doing in London when they're supposed to be here doing French?

DIGBY-JONES: They've been invited to Clarence House, sir. Or is it St James' Palace?

BEAK: And who's invited them there?

DIGBY-JONES: Oh, sir, it's the Prince of Wales, of course, sir. He's godfather to both Notty and Humph. In fact, The Queen goes to stay at Notty's place in Suffolk. He told me, sir. And Humph's mum used to be one of the Prince of Wales' girlfriends.

BEAK: Digby, we don't need a lesson in the Royals from you, thank you. And besides, last time they'd been off cavorting in London I told both of them quite clearly that in future they were to get leave of absence from me. So they're in for the high jump when I see them next on Monday.

DIGBY-JONES: But sir, they had their Housemaster's permission.

BEAK: Digby, I said MY permission.

The last time they'd both been missing from class had in fact been earlier in the term. When I'd asked then where they were, we'd been treated to a classic Molesworth performance. He'd told us that both Notty and Humph were in the House of Lords as Pages of Honour bearing the Queen's train during the State Opening of Parliament. And how Notty had told him that he, Notty, enjoyed dressing up in tight, white britches and buckled black shoes and poncing down the aisle towards the Throne, enclosed and immersed in ermine on all sides. Molesworth had then added in a stage whisper, 'I shouldn't be at all surprised if he doesn't turn out to be a pervy transvestite', much to the amusement of the whole class, myself included, I'm almost ashamed to say. In fact, I'd seen him on TV that evening and he certainly seemed to be enjoying the pantomime of it all. Leave of absence for the House of Lords, fine. And if it's not that, it's weddings, Badminton Horse Trials, Sandhurst passing out parades, the Arc de Triomphe at Longchamp, and so on and so on. And now it's partying in St James' Palace. One sometimes wonders if one is working in a holiday camp.

6.25. Five minutes to go now and already the cramming of books into satchels and all are poised on the edge of their chairs all ears for the ringing of the Porter's Lodge bell. When it does eventually sound they're off, all twenty-three of them making a common dash for the door, forming a tight scrimmage around it and making it virtually impossible for the first one there (that idiot Molesworth, who else?) to open it (it opens inwards). He eventually succeeds by using his great bulk to force the others back. Cries of "ow!" "Get orff, will you!' "Piss off!" "Shut up!" "YOU shut up!' Then they're gone, leaving behind them me, peace and quiet at last, Ben finishing the exercise and Digby-Jones approaching with a pile of exercise books.

BEAK: Just leave them on the side-table, Digby. Thank you.

DIGBY-JONES: Sir, I think I ought to go up a set, at least to Set 5. I'm much better than the rest.

BEAK: I think the End of Term Exam will decide that, don't you?

DIGBY-JONES: Well, I think I deserve to go up for my class work anyway. Sir, were you any good at French at school?

BEAK: Reasonably, I suppose. Why?

DIGBY-JONES: I just wondered. Which school did you go to, sir?

BEAK: Cranleigh.

DIGBY-JONES: Where, sir?

BEAK: Cranleigh School, Near Guildford, Surrey, Digby.

DIGBY-JONES: Never heard of it, sir. Must be a minor public school, I suppose. My father went to Eton. He was a member of Pop, sir, if you know what that is.

BEAK: Yes, Digby, I do actually happen to know what that is.

Almost certainly a collection of the school's most insufferable snobs, if Digby junior is anything to go by. *Tel père tel fils,* as they say. I've never known such an opinionated thirteen-year-old as Digby junior. *C'est moi le meilleur, c'est moi le plus beau, le plus riche.* We know the type. He carries his arrogance in his very gait, displays it whenever he opens his big mouth.

DIGBY-JONES: Why didn't you go to a school like Eton, sir?

BEAK: It wasn't entirely my choice to make, Digby.

If he goes on like this much longer I'm going to thump him one. Already insufferable at the age of thirteen, what on earth is he going to be like in ten years' time? He'll almost certainly be bound for the City, probably then taken into Merchant Banking by his highly influential father. Will be driving his first Porsche at the age of twenty-one (paid for doubtless by his first year's bonus) and to be found in the city champagne bars braying and boasting to all and sundry about how clever he has been. God save us from people like that.

BEAK: Right, off you go, Digby. Finished, Ben?

TRIMBLE: Yes, sir. Finished! Not too difficult, I didn't think.

BEAK: Good. Shall we quickly correct it now?

He comes up, hands me his book and stands behind looking over my shoulder as I wield the red pen. One or two little mistakes, but lots of ticks from top to bottom. 25/30. *Très Bien,* I write, then turn to look up at him, while gently nodding and wearing an expression of agreeable surprise, which he locks on to, a winsome smile dawning over his cherub-like face, a questioning smile as if wanting to say, "So I'm OK then?"

Yes, I think to myself, still looking up at him and slowly nodding, you're certainly OK.

BEAK: Well done, Ben. You're OK, you know. You're going to be just fine.

TRIMBLE: (Pale blue eyes still locked on and still the winsome smile) Thank you, sir. Thank you.

BEAK: Off you go then. See you tomorrow.

TRIMBLE: See you tomorrow, sir. Thank you, sir. Bye, sir.

BEAK: Bye.

What a lovely child. Kids like him suddenly make it all seem so worthwhile. I so much want him to succeed, to get him somehow to find the self-confidence he's going to need to see him through the next testing years. We first met four years ago, when he was just nine years old and I was visiting my friend Nick, a Prep school headmaster, for the weekend. After dinner he took me up to the dormitories for lights-out, and there he had each boy tell me which public school he was headed for – Westminster, Harrow, Winchester, Eton… and then Marlborough.

"Ah, Marlborough," I said, "and what is your name?"

"Ben Trimble, sir" came the reply.

"Well, Ben, I'm going to teach at Marlborough, so maybe we'll meet up there in September."

"Hope so, sir". A prep school Ben, yes, but with that same cherubic face as now, those same pale blue eyes, and oh, that winsome smile. I remember it all so clearly.

I now watch him crossing Court. The rain has stopped and there's an unmistakable spring in his step.

Chapter Two

The End of Another Fag Day

Like many another school of its kind Marlborough College (MC) is tacked on to the edge of a small town, in this case Marlborough, Wiltshire. Geographically this has both advantages and disadvantages, among the former being the fact that my local (pub) is a mere two-minute walk from my classroom, NC1– very handy at the end of yet another Fag day, when batteries tend to need recharging.

Ben's shoe. Ben's shoe. Must remember. Must remember, I remind myself, straightening chairs, retrieving the Exocet board rubber and unable to suppress a faint smile at the thought of the shaken Ponsonby so rudely awakened from the gentle arms of Morpheus. Finish marking. Finish marking. Must remember. Must remember. *Zut! Flute, alors!* That's going to mean another 7 am start tomorrow. Drat Digby, Trimble, Ponsonby, Molesworth and all their like! I really must get them into line, that lot. Trouble is I have so many other irons in so many other fires, both in the Upper School and the Lower School, that a bottom Shell French Set gets pushed into the margins and the poor little things are not really getting the time and attention they need and deserve. Deserve? My foot! They deserve a sharp kick up the arse, half of them... partying with the Prince of Wales, I ask you. Whatever next?

"Have you finished, sir?" Head Porter pushing his head round the door, jangling his huge bunch of keys and wanting to lock up for the night. "Yes, John, going right now." "Down to the Sun then, sir?" "Yes, how on earth did you guess?" He gives me a knowing wink. These porters see, hear and know more than you think. John has clearly got me more or less sussed out, and it's not even the end of my first term!

Out and under the Brad Arches. Into Court with the Norwood Hall opposite going full swing, home to hundreds of hungry youths gobbling down supper before scurrying back to Houses for Prep at 7.30. Down the steps between B and C Houses (couldn't they really have come up with something better than the letters on the architect's plans when choosing names for these Houses?) Past the Master's Lodge on the right (the Master is what most schools call Headmaster). Out and onto the A4. Stop. Look left, right, left before crossing. This is the A4 pre-M4 and the traffic comes swinging round that bend thick, fast and furious, swerving and weaving, dodging and darting, attempting to avoid – and often missing by a whisker – the hundreds of Marlburians who daily cross playfully in their droves and, lemming-like, seem impervious to the dangers of the game, so eager are they to get off Campus and into the so-called normality of the world 'outside.' There have already been near misses, so I'm told. Surely a matter of time before one of them gets winged or worse. Onwards and past St Peter's Church, where Cardinal Wolsey was first ordained priest, finally swinging left into the warmth of the Sun Inn, the oldest public house in town. There to welcome us are the unforgettable landlord and his wife, John and Olly Jones. John, the archetypal English publican, fully bearded and whiskered, genial, convivial, pipe-smoking, firmly anchored to the best of the traditions of the past, regularly riding to hounds with the local hunt, a pair of fiery steeds stabled in the courtyard behind his pub.

I would normally plunge into the public bar. That's where the historical interest lies, what with the low ceiling, the ancient oak beams, the wood panelling, the open wood fire and the steps leading down to the vaulted medieval cellars below. But no, that is Town territory and I'm Gown. In Marlborough, Town is Town and Gown is Gown and any meeting between the two is still liable to misunderstanding. I mean, we can't even pronounce the word Marlborough in the same way! 'They' pronounce it according to the local Wiltshire pronunciation and 'we' in accordance with Received Pronunciation. i. e. as in 'morbid Marlborough', with both first syllable vowels pronounced similarly. Definitely not to be confused with the 'Marlborough Marmalade' pronunciation used by the locals. The difference is palpable, believe you me.

So 'we' head for the Saloon Bar, less atmospheric but it does have the advantage of a bar billiards table, which can be a welcome distraction after a full day at the chalk-face. Fag days are good days to go and in there I find the usual collection of colleagues, between ten and fifteen often, some of them bachelors, some of them married. The married don't tend to stay too long – wives and families waiting impatiently for the return of the breadwinner. We, the bachelors, however (and let's not forget that in 1967 we number around twenty-five in a Common Room – teaching staff – of around eighty), are in no great hurry to move on; as long as we're back in College by 7.45 there'll be a full three-course dinner laid on in Common Room Dining Room for all who require it. So there's time to pass matters in review over a pint or three of Wadworth's excellent 6X, brewed in nearby Devizes. What's more, the company is congenial.

I'll be maybe talking to Robin, the violinist, who'll be telling me about the Yale songs he's chosen for our next Glee Club performance, to Michael who's over from Australia, to Andrew (linguist) and Nick (classicist), both first-rate amateur performing musicians, to David (i/c Woodwork) whose passions are ballroom dancing with the ladies and the making of stringed instruments, principally violins and 'cellos. No lack of talent here, I think to myself, as I try to keep pace with the proceedings. Sometimes we'll be talking 'shop' and about the day's events, sometimes about holidays, girlfriends and the world beyond M.C. – relaxed conversations, usually, after a hard day's work. Then someone will notice the time, 7.40 and the moment to drink up and leave to be back in College in time for Common Room Dinner.

Dinner, too, is usually a merry affair. With seating for forty or so and presided over by the senior in-College bachelor beak (at present Hugh de Weltdon Weldon, Vice-President of Common Room), the Dining Room will feed not only the bachelors but also the married who may have evening duties in College and, indeed, often outside speakers here to address society meetings later in the evening after dinner. In my time I've sat next to bishops, astronauts, novelists, MPs, the local rat-catcher (oops! Rodent Operator) and plenty more besides. Lots to talk about, conversation flowing, aided and ably abetted by the proximity of the Common Room (CR) Wine Cellar so conveniently to be found adjoining and where members may sign for as many bottles as they like knowing nothing need be paid for until the end of term. Not surprisingly these affairs may from time to time become protracted. We dally to the last over coffee and then someone will suggest port and madeira *chez lui*, or a round of croquet in CR garden, depending on the season. But more often there are other matters to be seen to, pupils to be contacted before they finish Prep at 9.15, House play rehearsals to direct, academic reports to discuss individually, tutorials to give – and so on.

On this particular wet, windy and miserable late November evening in 1967, I return to House by 9.15 somewhat cheered by a few pints of Waddys, CR dinner and a half-bottle of claret. House is in my case Turner House (named after a former Master of Marlborough). I'm the Resident House Tutor, which means I have bachelor accommodation within the House and live cheek by jowl with fifty to sixty boys (aged thirteen to eighteen) as well as with the Housemaster, Hugh de Weltden Weldon, (aged forty-two) also a bachelor and whose living quarters, sumptuous and far grander than mine, befitting his exalted position, are at the other end of the building. To arrive in House at 9.15 when all are spilling out of Prep, is to invite disaster. "Please, sir, can I...?" "Sir, can you tell me....?" "When can I see you about...?" I somehow fend them off, fighting my way upstairs to my rooms, suddenly remembering Giles Hamilton's imminent arrival for drinks after Prep. He's normally fairly punctual, added to which he's following the BBC serialization of Sartre's *L'Age de Raison* being broadcast over the recent Friday evenings and due to start in five minutes. I just hope he won't go on asking me more questions about Sartre and the Existentialist movement. J-P S was never on my degree course syllabus (wrongly) and I frankly don't know all that much about it all. I wouldn't tell him that, wouldn't tell anyone else here for that matter, but I suppose I'm going to have to do something about it sooner rather than later and certainly before I find myself having to teach his work as set texts. Dirty Paws, for example, *Les Mains Sales*.

A breathless Hamilton arrives almost immediately, out of breath because he's been fighting his way through again trying to get up here. He has to pass the Head of House's study and since the latter doesn't like him being here (because he's not in Turner) he'll push him around a bit to show he's unwelcome. All part of the tribal instinct implicit in the House system which I recognise only too well from my own not-so-distant schooldays. Anyway, Giles H. has nothing to worry about. He's a feisty little fighter and well able to look after himself. He's now beginning to make himself at home *chez moi* and doesn't hesitate going over to turn on the television before choosing his chair for the best view. "The usual?" I ask. "Yeah…. please." For most the usual is beer.

Not so for Giles, who's much more inclined to the wines and will be very happy with the chardonnay I usually have in stock. I shouldn't be surprised if he doesn't turn out to be a bit of a *bon viveur* in later life. He tells me that his father, is, like myself, a graduate of Trinity College, Dublin, so he, too, might be a man drawn to *la bonne chère et les bons vins*. TCD graduates I know rarely fight shy of the good things in life. "Hey, I didn't know you were TCD, too. I'll get them to invite you down one day. My father would like that. You could talk TCD. And we're in Amesbury, you know. It's not far. How about a Sunday lunch in the spring when the weather's better. You could then drive us over in your snazzy car – with the hood down!" Again that cheeky little smile which speaks volumes. "Sounds good," I reply somewhat noncommittally while he turns his attention to the screen, glass in hand. He's a fun kid all right even if, as a colleague told me only the other day, he tends to fall foul of his Housemaster's good books rather too often. Minor disciplinary matters, doubtless, but I must ask him one day all the same. I only half follow the Sartre and, seeing Giles is fairly well immersed into it, I turn to the desk and shuffle some of the papers around. Bills to pay, exams to set, reports to be written, meetings to attend, invitations to end-of-term Christmas parties to accept or decline. These things really need seeing to now, since there's going to be another similar load of bumph awaiting me in CR first thing tomorrow morning. *Ouf!* I need another glass of wine. So does Giles. "I do like this Chardonnay. Where exactly does it originate from?" "*C'est un vin de Bourgogne.* Burgundy. Or to be more precise it's from the Haut-Maconnais where you get the village of Chardonnay." "But now you find it everywhere, don't you?" "Well, not exactly everywhere, Giles, although it is a *cépage* which travels well. Found in twenty to thirty countries or so, I suppose. But France still produces among the best – I would say that, wouldn't I? Along with countries like Australia, South Africa, Chile. Canada, too, surprisingly, often does pretty well in the tastings."

Giles returns to the screen and I to my desk and papers. Thank God tomorrow is Saturday, even if there are still five periods to get through in the morning. And then suddenly the inevitable from out of the blue: "You know, there's something I still don't quite understand about this whole Existentialist thing...." Oh, Lord, I say to myself, well join the club then. What on earth am I going to be asked now? As I gather my wits for the next existentialist onslaught and before the question has had time to come out there's a timid knock at the door and who should creep in but a somewhat dejected creature, already in dressing gown and pyjamas, by the name of Molesworth. Yes, for our sins the boy is in Turner, so access to me is all too easy. What on earth does he want at this hour, I wonder. "Please, sir, I've come to apologise." "Oh, for what, may I ask?" "For putting Ben's shoe down the loo, sir." "Oh – well why did you do that then?" "Don't know, sir." "Bit silly, wasn't it?" "Yes, sir". I can see the eyes are moistening. "Hadn't you better apologize to Ben?" "I have, sir." "And what did he have to say?" "He accepted the apology, sir." "Good. Then don't you think that in future you ought to stop and think a bit before doing silly things like that?"

A tear falls and rolls down his left cheek. "Yes, sir." I must remember he's only thirteen years old. "I mean really, Jim, you do do and say some pretty silly things. What about all that smut and sleaze in class this evening? Bit over the top, wasn't it?" "Yes, sir." Silence, except for Dirty Paws instalment now drawing to a close, *Dieu merci*. "Well, thank you for coming to apologize anyway. You'd better go off to bed now, hadn't you?" "Yes, sir" "OK. Good night then." "*Bon nuit, Monsieur*;" "No, Jim, *bonne nuit* actually – it's feminine, Jim." "Oh yes, sir, I knew that. It's just that I'm not very good at genders, sir." (Neither am I, thinks I to myself.) "*Bonne nuit, Monsieur*."

Giles has turned the TV off, has plonked himself down in his chair again and is showing no sign of moving yet, in spite of the fact that it's already well past 10.30, the time when he has to be back in House. "Hey, Giles, it's past *couvre-feu*, you know?" "What's *couvre-feu*?" "Curfew. See? So don't say English has never taken from French." "Yes, but French has taken much more from English than English from French – what about *le weekend*? There're tons like that." "Yes, of course there're tons like that. But there're HUNDREDS of tons of English words which come straight from Norman French." "Norman? Why Norman?" "1066, stupid!"

Here we go again. I'm getting to know Giles well enough to guess his game. He reckons he might just squeeze a third glass of vino out of me if he can get me to rabbit on about something he knows interests me. Crafty thinking. He's deserved his third glass – me too.

"Well, where are the examples then?" "Yes, Giles, OK, but hold it. Hadn't you better be getting back to House? It's already 10.45, you know." "Yes, I know. That's OK. I got the Captain on duty to sign me in so I'm covered. I can get in by climbing up the rose-trellis round the back, so it's OK".

Hardly surprising that he's not exactly on slap-bottom terms with his Housemaster. "Ah, so that's why they say you don't exactly see eye to eye with your Housemaster, is it? What with monkey tricks like that." Another impish smile combined with a wink this time. Oh dear, I shouldn't be conniving with this maybe, but he's still not going to budge and, full glass in hand, is clearly expecting an answer to his question.

"Give me some examples." "Well, there are just thousands of examples, mostly words to do with government, war, religion, food, law, literature and so on – you know, the things that the Normans brought with them." "Yes, and the examples?" Lordee, these Marlburians certainly want their pound of flesh. Was I ever so demanding as a sixteen-year-old Cranleighan, I wonder? I think not. Didn't dare say boo to a goose.

"OK. Since you ask and since you're in the CCF, how about a few military examples? What about 'bayonet', 'manoeuvre', 'pistol, ' 'tower', 'enemy', 'army', 'fanfare', 'saboteur', 'epaulette', 'chief', 'platoon'? I could go on for ever. Then what about the ranks? 'Commandant', 'sergeant', 'corporal', 'general', 'captain', 'troops'– they are nearly all of French derivation. Not to say there aren't quite a number of military words coming straight from the Latin, too. Like 'bellicose', 'belligerent', 'equestrian', 'marine', 'annihilate', and so on." Giles pushes up his hand as if in class. "Hold on! 'Bellum', 'equus', 'mare', 'nihil'." Wow! Quite a little classical scholar, aren't we?" "No, not really. I just started at eight like everyone else and had to keep going till 'O' level when I dropped it like a hot potato." "What on earth do you mean 'like everyone else'? You don't fondly imagine that all eight-year-olds all over the country are doing their 'amo, amas, amats', do you? Or parsing and translating 'The sailors went into the city to buy girls' into Latin?" "Well YOU did, didn't you?" "Yes, Giles, I did – just like you. But there're not too many like us around now, what with all those grammar schools being slowly but surely relegated to the rubbish dump. We're in a minority here, you know. Most would say a privileged minority. A Latin and Greek speaking elite, if you like."

I really mustn't get on to the class issue now or we'll be here till Christmas. It's quite fun to do though, just to see which way these little rich boys are going to jump. "Hey, do you realise it's now 11.00? You really ought to be getting back, you know." "Yes, I know, but don't tell me that everyone in England suddenly had to start talking French in 1066 – what a nightmare!" "I didn't tell you that. After the Conquest the vast majority of the Anglo-Saxons continued to speak Anglo-Saxon, the Church and their monastic schools stuck with their Latin and the Normans brought their Norman French, which in itself had developed mostly from Latin. Don't you see, that's why English is such an incredibly rich language – it's got those three major strands, apart from a whole number of minor ones. So, if you like, the Normans are the toffs of the day, the Marlburians, ha!, and the Anglo-Saxons the plebs. And the divide is still reflected in the English you and I use today. Examples? Well 'Dead' coming from the common Anglo-Saxon, 'Deceased' and 'Defunct' coming from the more sophisticated Norman French and Latin roots. Or 'kingly', 'royal' and 'regal'. Exactly the same with 'house' and 'mansion', 'wood' and 'forest', 'yearly' and 'annual', 'room' and 'chamber', and so on. The common words we use are mostly from Anglo- Saxon roots, our more sophisticated language from Norman French and Latin origins. In fact, of the 1,000 most common words used in English today about 80% of them are from Anglo-Saxon roots. It's the same with verbs, too. 'Make' and 'fabricate, ' 'sleep' and 'hibernate', 'drink' and 'imbibe'. The same with adjectives. 'Good' and 'beneficial'. You must neither get 'drunk' like a Saxon nor 'inebriated' like the Norman French or Romans. Got it? And while we're at it, think about the vocabulary of Gastronomy. Here the French has won out over the Anglo-Saxon. 'Sheep' is a perfectly good word from the Saxon, yet we don't eat it. We eat 'mutton', French *mouton*. So too 'cow', but we eat 'beef', French *boeuf*, 'pig' and we eat 'pork', French *porc*. And then how about all those Norman names and places? Montagu of *Beau Lieu*. Bewley, if you insist. Beauchamp, *Beau Champ,* Beecham to you and me. Beaumont, *Beau Mont.* Not to mention all those who have the French *particule,* De Vere, de Montmorency, de Courcy, de Burgh, like Chris de Burgh – Old Marlburian, no? And your family name, too – Hamilton is Scottish, I know, but also very probably descended from Norman French. My name, Wilkinson, is very definitely Anglo-Saxon."

Giles now puts down his glass, empty again, I note, and proceeds with a round of silent applause. He can see I'm amused and gets up, fetches the remains of the chardonnay, takes my glass, also empty, from the side-table and raises it above me. "Hey, that was interesting. In fact, Mr Wilkinson, I would say that it was SO interesting that you deserve the remains of this cheeky little chardonnay!" He starts to pour in the studied manner of a Mayfair sommelier, both of us fully aware that there are at least two glasses left in the bottle. Having filled the glass he then presents it to me theatrically, holding it delicately by the stem as befits a glass of chilled white wine. "Fully deserved, might I say," he adds cheerily, as would a teacher to his pupil, and all done with such grace and a questioning smile, too, as if to say 'well, what are we going to do with the rest of this bottle, then?

Our eyes meet. I send back the same question in my smile. He breaks into a broad grin, standing there over me, bottle still raised. Waiting, waiting for just that slightest sign of assent. We both wait as if frozen by the camera, bound together by the spell of a mere second. Then the nod. "Go on then". I watch him now as he proudly fills his fourth glass, eyes sparkling and cheeks already slightly flushed.

"*Oh Monsieur! Je te remercie…je te remercie beaucoup! Santé!* "
"Giles, do you realise that not only have you forced me into giving a lesson on English etymology, as if I haven't done enough teaching today without that, but you're now also addressing me as your best mate by saying '*Je TE remercie*' rather than '*Je VOUS remercie, Monsieur le Professeur.*' *Un peu de respect pour le Prof, s'il te plaît, Monsieur Hamilton,*" I add a shade facetiously. He shares the joke. "Come on! You don't have to be the teacher up here. Anyway, you can't be much more than ten years older than me. In fact you could easily be my elder brother, couldn't you?"

"Yes, I could, but that would only be asking for more trouble than I already have by sending you off in the middle of the night with half a bottle of Chardonnay in your little belly. And what on earth would David Hamilton say if he knew?" I add in a tone of mock shock-horror. "Oh, sir!" in exact imitation of my tone, "You DON'T think I would tell my dad, do you? Anyway you've forgotten he's a TCD man. So he likes his drink- like you! No?" "Like ME? What a cheeky little idea from such a cheeky little pupil!"

"Giles, the wild student days are over. I've now become the serious young beak at the start of a brilliant teaching career." Said deadpan and without expression to see what he makes of that. Not sure, judging from the quizzical look in his eye. A pause, broken this time by the sudden ringing of the phone. It's the internal phone, which means a call from a colleague. *Merde!* Could it be one irate Housemaster trying to locate one missing Giles Hamilton?

"Hello, John Wilkinson.... Yes... yes...OK.... sounds fine.... What time? OK, look forward to it and thanks a lot. Good night." Phew! Ouf!" Panic over, Hamilton, that was my Housemaster, not yours." "Oh, Hugh Weldon. What did he want?" "To invite me to lunch tomorrow to meet a parent." "Bad luck. That can't be much fun. You'll have to talk shop all the time." "No, I don't somehow think we will, not with H de WW and this particular parent." "Who is it then?" "Christian Marriott's mother." "What's so special about her?" "Well, her name is Lois Maxwell." "And?" "And she's best known as Miss Moneypenny – yes, none other than 007's Private and Personal Secretary." "Wow! That could be fun. And I must say you're lucky having H de WW as your HM." "Oh? Why lucky?" "Well, he sounds quite a cool dude." "A cool dude, Giles? I hardly think THAT fits the image!" "Maybe not, but you know what I mean. And do you know what Toby told me in supper?" (Toby is Giles's great friend and partner in crime, I believe.) "He said that in Anthropology this morning Weldon spent the whole period talking about what the female baboon does when threatened!" "Oh, and what does she do when threatened?" "She presents the male with her rear quarters – her arse!"

He dissolves into a fit of laughter. Sounds fairly typical H de WW, I think to myself. "And do you know Weldon's theory as to why she does this?" Another fit of laughter. "No, I don't, Giles. But what I do know is that if we're going to discuss all the outrageous things Hugh Weldon is reported to have ever said we'll be here till five in the morning." I pull him out of his comfortable armchair and steer him purposefully towards the door. He's still chuckling about the wayward ways of the female baboon as I show him out onto the corridor. "I thought I'd bring Toby up here sometime. Will you be in tomorrow evening?" "No, tomorrow's no good. I'm on Vice Squad and after that I MUST get on with my End of Term reports. So I'll see you next week sometime when the pressure's off a bit. OK? Bye then –and for God's sake don't make a noise going past those dormitories, will you?" "No, I won't…. (in a whisper) and I'll tell you more about baboons next time! Bye…. and thanks." That impish smile again as he turns to feel his way down the darkened corridor and stairs to the front door. I hear it close gently behind him. Is that also the Housemaster's door I faintly hear opening? Or closing? Strange at this late hour. I'm aware too of noises from the bedsits above as I close my door and make for bed. I can't be bothered to go up there now and see what's going on. Too tired. An early start tomorrow. Shell French books to correct before Period 1. Must remember. Must remember. At least poor Ben's shoe has been sorted. Bed.

Chapter Three

The Weekend: Saturday Morning

7.45 Saturday morning. It's still raining and there's now a strong wind too, as I leave Turner House bound for breakfast in Common Room. Not much traffic at this hour of the morning so I cross the A4 opposite the Hole in the Wall and take the short cut through B House and into Court. Not much sign of life here either, just a few miserable-looking, shivering boys in games kit and on Blue Chits (punishment) reporting to a prefect at the Porter's Lodge prior to being told to leg it up to Wedgwood and back – and in double quick time if they didn't want to repeat the whole ghastly exercise the following morning. Wedgwood is the most remote of the games fields, uphill and on a crest of the downs – not a place to be before breakfast on a cold, dark November day with the rain lashing down and the wind biting through your house swipe. ('Swipe' – a Marlborough word for a striped rugger jersey, with the House determining the colour of the stripe.)

I cross Court, plunge down into the depths of C. House and come out into the Common Room Bin Room. This little room is the nerve centre, the power house of Common Room. In a State School it would be called the Staff Room, but no, not here. I'm a member of Common Room and definitely not a member of the staff. I must

23

remember too that I'm a schoolmaster and not a teacher. How nicely the independent sector differentiates itself from the state sector, even down to the language it uses and how subtly these little nuances all contribute to shore up the class distinctions with which the country is still so rottenly riddled. At least Marlborough has attempted to break down class barriers by pioneering a broader entry scheme which is what has come to be known as the Swindon Experiment – twenty-one boys from grammar and secondary schools in Swindon are awarded bursaries and have become boarders for two years in the VI form. Other less broad-minded independent educational establishments haven't bothered. Bravo to Marlborough!

Nevertheless bin rooms and staff rooms serve the same purpose – bins (pigeon-holes) for beaks and notice boards displaying all manner of information, there to be inwardly digested by all and sundry and particularly by new beaks like myself anxious not to miss the obligations, duties and deadlines sandwiched somewhere in the middle of it all. Boards for games, timetables, exams, careers, events and the like. And there, dead centre, the Masters' Board, telling of appointments, rustications, expulsions, college council meetings, exhortations of all sorts and other such weighty matters. I glance over all this, distribute the various papers I have for colleagues, make a beeline for my own bin and discover there the usual rich mix of mail, messages and notes. The secret is to off-load as much as one can immediately. For example notes from the Head of the Mod. Lang. Dept. Some will be for general consumption and will be headed WJL – IRP – PV – JCQR – KK – AC – R de CC – JDW (me) – EJN. These round-robins have information we should digest. They merely need a tick against the initials and can then be sent winging their way round the Department. On no account should one sit on them. One would simply clog up the whole system, so frequently are they dispatched by the various HODs (Heads of Departments) eager to be seen by all to be running an efficient ship. (Don't let's forget that like HMs (Housemasters), the HODs are on the promotion ladder, in with a chance of headmasterships and the like.)

So I shuffle around as much paper as I can before leaving for CR dining room, conveniently situated just round the corner. Here all is peace and quiet. The seductive sweet odours of freshly ground coffee assail me as I take *The Times* from a selection of the five or six dailies available. I'm the first in, so I have the pick of the newspapers.

Dear old Joe, CR Steward and a refugee from war-time Poland, is on duty with his customary warm welcome. "Good morning, Mr Wilkie. All right, then?" "Morning, Joe. Fine, thanks."

I don't really mind his 'Mr Wilkie' line. With the pupils it's either that or 'Wilks' or 'Wilko', 'Silky Wilkie', too, sometimes. In fact I think I've got off really rather lightly when you think of some of the other nicknames they've dreamt up. Dr Wright is generally known as Harpic. "Oh, why?" I ask. "Sir, didn't you know he's clean round the bend?" comes the reply. Then there's 'Monkey' Murray, 'Flossie' Barber, 'Pop' Venters, 'Lats' Latham, 'Olly Golly' Goldsmith, 'Bopper' Keighley, 'Badger' Heath, 'Gertie' Woods, 'Hippy' Hardman, 'Prune' Preston and so on. Origins are sometimes somewhat difficult to determine but once formulated these names tend to stick and are passed down naturally from one generation to the next. OM fathers up and down the country will be fondly asking their offspring, "How's that young Flossie Barber then?" "YOUNG, Dad? Come on, he's old enough to be your grandfather!"

Whatever the day ahead may bring, dangers or disasters, delights or distractions, one can at least be sure of one thing – that CR breakfast is going to get it all off to a thumping great start. I hesitate over the choice of juices. Then the cornflakes – will it be Shredded Wheat or Muesli? Weetabix or Puffed Wheat? Or indeed porridge? Moving on to the full cooked English breakfast: eggs scrambled or fried, bacon, tomatoes, mushrooms, baked beans, black pudding sometimes. Or will it be a fish morning? Kippers, fishcakes and kedgeree, why not? Polish off with toast and choice of marmalades, all washed down with a gallon or so of coffee or tea. Linger a little over *The Times* and try to forget the pile of the day's mail in front of me and more often than not tomato-egg-marmalade-coffee-stained by the time I've mopped the plates up clean. Not much disturbance down here. Just the faint playing of a radio squeezing its way in from the further recesses of the kitchens.

My bachelor colleagues quietly beginning to take their places around me. "Morning." "Morning." That's all. The boisterous ones too had better be quiet at the breakfast table if they don't want to be snapped at by one of the senior men. Gentle rustling of newspapers, soft clinking of china and cutlery. Must be a bit like White's and Boodles – that is, without the worry of four hours in the classroom to follow. Through the wide glass-plate windows the first of the married colleagues making for the bin room and its daily dose of *paperasses*. Woe betide any of them should they then dare set foot in the sanctity of the bachelor breakfast. To intrude and talk shop is very definitely not cricket, as many a one has learnt to his cost.

A distant bell ringing tells me time is up and battle must shortly be joined. Head straight across Court towards my classroom. Late-rising boys dash by in a bid to get to Norwood Hall and breakfast before the bell stops and the prefect on duty bars the passage. No breakfast for late-comers. Most of them probably wouldn't bother if they thought they could snatch an extra half-hour in bed. Difficult for them most times when House Tutors like me are busily and unceremoniously turfing them out of House and into the hurly-burly of the school day at an hour they clearly consider ungodly. I've only recently begun to understand the strength of feeling generated by compulsory early-rising when realising how lax this generation of parents has seemingly become, allowing their little treasures to wallow between the sheets and under the duvets until all hours of the morning in holiday time. Imagine my parents allowing my brother and me to sleep through breakfast. Out of the question. Very definitely not a movable feast in our household, which goes to show how quickly the times they are a' changing. So, even if, as young Giles Hamilton correctly points out, I am less than ten years older than most of the kids here, I clearly shouldn't assume that my *Weltanschauung* or *Optique du Monde*, if you prefer, is necessarily going to chime in with theirs. And also, in fact, since we're talking about them, I never even saw a duvet at home, to come to think of it, let alone sleep under one. Stiffly laundered sheets in my day, damn it, and none of those fancy, girly colours either, if you don't mind. White. Like cricket flannels, don't you know.

I reach the relative peace of the classroom with half an hour to go before the first onslaught. There'll be the Chapel bell at 8.50 and then again at 8.55 for the start of Morning Prayer and, since it's Saturday, Congregational Practice. I'll have to give this a miss for today. Which means there's just about enough time to finish correcting the Shell French books, then it'll be the 9.05 bell, signalling five minutes before the start of Period One. And from then on likewise throughout the morning. Five-minute warning bells, lesson time bells. Break time bell in the middle of it all. Then more bells, on and on till finally the lunch bell. *Ouf! On arrive.* No wonder Betjeman was spooked by these relentless bells dictating his every movement from sparrow-fart onwards, day by day, week after week, a full five years of it. I shouldn't be surprised if I have a lifetime of nightmares brought on by the sound of the Marlborough Bell. That's if I survive my spell, however long that is to be. Bells signifying Time Up – why haven't you finished? Five Minutes To Go – you're going to be late. Warning bells, pushing you on and down, unforgiving, punishing. Oh but, sir, I didn't hear the bell, sir. *Tant pis, mon petit, tu es en retard, donc tu es dans la merde. Compris?* Bloody bells. And not only the Porters Lodge bell. The Chapel bell, too, has its tinny word to say most days to add to the general merriment 'Hurry up! Hurry up! One minute to go before I cease to sound and you are punished for being ten seconds late for Divine Service. Quick! Get in! Get to your place and kneel, boy! Pray! Now get up! Sing! Worship!'

> *...The schoolboy sense of an impending doom*
> *Which goes with rows of desks and clanging bells.*
> *It filters down from God, to Master's Lodge,*
> *Through housemasters and prefects to the fags.*
> *Doom! Shivering doom! Inexorable bells*
> *To early school, to chapel, school again.*

Clearly schoolboy Betjeman and new beak Wilkinson think alike, except unlike him I don't have to suffer the added hell of 'early' school – pre-breakfast, pre-chapel school – just imagine...But here it starts now, the five-minute warning bell and Shell French Set 6 begins to trickle in, snail-like, creeping unwillingly to school. The pace quickens as the minutes tick away and what with the sound of running from outside and the stragglers tumbling into class, breathless, I can tell that it must be very close to 9.10. The bell rings. At the final stroke I look up from the last of my marking to a full class, twenty-three of them, all present, if not correct. Well not quite all present. Still no sign of Humpf and Notty, both of them presumably still sleeping it off in some royal palace or other.

"Come on, tuck your shirt in, you, And you, pull your tie up. Mallinson, when did your hair last see a comb?" The hour of the morning precludes retorts, so I proceed without further ado to hand back the exercise books. Hand back, no. Throw them back frisbee-style and aiming just below the chin – I'm getting quite accurate at it – so that the game is to catch them cleanly, à la cricket fielder or wicket-keeper. Easy to spot the ball game whiz-kids – both hands extended and then gracefully guiding the flying missile safely into the chest. The latter-day Betjemans in the class ('And greatest dread of all, the dread of games!'), however, awkwardly snatch, fumble, cower. It's a game and boys wake up for games. Plaudits for the graceful, nought for the clumsy. Applause and groans. Their game, my game. All now awake – even the slothful Ponsonby – so let's start. The message is clear and simple. The test results were poor – with the exception of Ben's 25/30 – corrections to be written in with a last chance to learn it before Monday's re-test. No re-test for Ben. They're knuckling down, hands are up, questions are asked – stupid ones from Digby-Jones, it doesn't matter – work is being done. Even the dreaded Molesworth is applying himself. Ben looks as if he's in a world of his own. Dream on. Let him be. Time flies. Bell goes. They're off.

Molesworth, anxious to build bridges, I suppose, lingers. "I'm still not too sure about genders, sir. I muddle up masculine and feminine." "So do I, Molesworth", I answer before I realise what I'd said. Bisexuality unguardedly raises its head, but luckily for me and unusually for him, he's failed to pick up on this my clumsy allusion. Just as well. If ever one is going to get into *that* sort of conversation with the kids, God forbid, it's not going to be with the likes of oafs like him, I wouldn't think.

Scarcely has the Shell scarpered (leaving me fairly upbeat) than the next packet tumbles in. No, not tumbles in. After all this is Lower Sixth French Set 2, which means that they've somehow or other popped through the 'O' level hoops to the general satisfaction of all and now find themselves members of the Upper School and at the start of a two-year dawdle/trot/canter (depending on the boy and perhaps – we like to think – the Beak, too) *en route* towards the dizzy heights of the 'A' level hurdles. No, very definitely, an Upper School boy doesn't want to give the impression of 'tumbling' anywhere. At around 16 years old he has lost, or at least is concealing as best he can, any remnants of his Lower School puppy dog persona. Besides which he's discarded his standard Lower School Lovett jacket and now has the privilege of wearing the jacket of his own choice. Nothing too flashy, of course – the HM would soon jump on him and it as being too ostentatious. But it's at least a start and he can at last think, subconsciously albeit, about the image he wants to project.

Personally I don't go big on 'image projection', particularly in little 16-year-old rich boys, when it can all begin to get out of hand. The 'just-look-at-me' syndrome. If they've got something to snort about, then fair enough. But this lot at any rate is hardly going to set the Thames alight with their linguistic talents. After all they're only Set 2 and the best linguists, the bilingual boys, the high fliers, have been carefully creamed off and poured into the rarefied atmosphere of the Top Set. *La crème de la crème.* Unapologetic streaming here and none of your trendy 'egalitarian' comprehensive school mixed-ability classes, thank God. Still, Set 2 suits me fine. Maybe next year it'll be Set 3, or – horrors! – even Set 4, the rump. I've noticed that EJN (HOD, Mod. Lang. Dept.) hasn't given me any top sets for my first year. Neither have I got an Upper Sixth set. All that's for next year, if I make it. Quite a relief really.

Today is a subjunctive-bashing day and not the first one when I found myself totally bogged down in preliminaries. Such as "Why do the French have to have subjunctives anyway, sir? *We* don't."

"Yes, we do." And having to explain 'may' and 'might'. And the difference between 'Almighty God, unto whom all hearts *be* open' and the wrongly translated 'modern' version, 'Almighty God, to whom all hearts *are* open', which is very patently not the case. God saves The Queen? Britannia rules the waves? No, boys, those are Indicatives denoting fact. God save The Queen – not an Imperative command but a subjunctive denoting a wish. *May* God save The Queen. And so on.

Forty minutes later and they're off, only to be replaced by Sixth Form 'A' level History students (Medievalists) who will need to offer a French translation paper if they are to attempt the Oxbridge entrance exam in the term following the 'A' levels. These are bright kids who need to look at texts with an historical bent and with a view to extending their vocabulary range. Since my own vocabulary range is fairly OK, or so I like to think, these tend to be fairly stress-free lessons. Although the Head of the History department, Peter Carter, did approach me the other day to ask whether I was up to taking them through *La Chanson de Roland*, whereupon I very nearly choked on my coffee and biscuits. Asking me to do that, as he fully well knows, is like asking an English beak to deliver a course on Chaucerian English. It's a totally different linguistic ball game – late 11[th] century Norman French in the case of the *Chanson* – and would require a whole lot more preparation. The first line goes 'Carles li reis, nostre emper[er]e magnes', which is easy enough, but it gets a lot more tricky than that and frankly I'm just not going to have the time. Not that it isn't a ripping good yarn. Roland, Charlemagne's nephew, is killed in the year 778 at the battle of Roncevaux (Pyrenees) while fighting a Frankish rearguard action against the Basques (historically) who became Muslim Saracens (legendary) when the events were eventually to receive their final form in the Epic poem we now know. It is said too that an earlier version (a 'song about Roland') was sung to the Norman troops before they joined battle at Hastings.

Then a song of Roland was begun, so that the man's warlike example would arouse the fighters. Calling on God for aid, they joined battle.

Taillefer, who sang very well, rode on a swift horse before the Duke singing of Charlemagne and Roland and Olivier and the knights who died at Roncevaux.

Choking fit over, I had to admit that I hadn't specialised in Medieval French at Trinity College, Dublin (TCD), which is strictly true, although what I didn't say was that even we, the non-medievalist linguists, had had to study a few of the better known medieval texts, *La Chanson de Roland* being one of them...deceitful? Well, maybe, but at least it got me off what could have been a most uncomfortable hook. We young beaks tend to give senior Beaks like Dr Carter a fairly wide berth. He's a formidable academic with an Oxford Ph.D, he will lecture his students rather than teach them and is known invariably to tear up his lecture notes at the end of each academic year, so as better to deliver a fresh approach to his pupils the following year. *Mon Dieu!* I really can't believe that I'll ever be rising to such heights of perfection myself. In fact I'm probably more likely to be numbered among those who – like some of my teachers at Cranleigh (no names no pack-drill) – live off the same old notes, sepia-brown in colour and curling at the edges with age, year after year, decade after decade and without which they would almost certainly be unable to continue to function. Lordee, save us, we beseech Thee, from such a fate as that! Not that, please. So people like Doc. Carter we, the young ones, call 'the Heavies', a term conveying a blend of awe, respect and fear, all three more or less equally balanced, at any rate, in *my* mind.

Today I have a text by Alexis de Tocqueville (1805-1859) – *juriste et penseur politique français* – which seems to keep them happy and which we complete just as the bell summons us to the mid-morning break.

Break, and the rain has now at last stopped. Great. A full twenty-minute respite. Buns for boys, biscuits for beaks. The former to the Norwood Hall, the latter to the Adderley, home to the largest canvas Gainsborough ever painted, a portrait of the Byam family, smug (oh, ever-so-pleased-with-ourselves-we-are) and in classic 18th century pose. Their smugness I had explained to me by a colleague. The Byams had 'interests' in the West Indies – I think we all know what *that* means…. There is also a fine Steinway grand here used for chamber music concerts held frequently in this equally fine 18th century room.

Yes, a twenty-minute break is, on paper at least, a thoroughly welcome release. However, once one is initiated into the ways of the MC world (I like to think that I'm already now at least partially *au fait* with some of the more idiosyncratic aspects of life here in this little pool), one realises that break can be a mixed blessing. Indeed, sometimes a veritable elephant-trap into which all but the most wary can easily fall. And believe you me I've already fallen into it more than once during the course of this my first term. By this I mean that colleagues, while downing their coffee or tea and biscuits, will at the same time be seeking out other colleagues with whom they need to discuss business. Yes, this is ideal 'talking shop' time, all the more so since the vast majority of CR will be here. So one can hardly blame a colleague when, list in hand, he bears down on one with the opening words "Oh, John, may I have a quick word with you?" He's merely making best use of time, rushing around like a bluebottle in a jam jar trying to 'get' as many 'hits' as possible. Those who wish to show themselves as the busiest of the bluebottles in the jar will be brandishing a list as long as your arm and will spend the full twenty minutes on the go.

Sometimes life is not as easy for them as might at first appear. For example they themselves will be on someone else's hit-list, hence blown off their own trajectory, at least temporarily. Then they might find themselves in a queue, particularly if they want 'a quick word' with a 'Heavy', or indeed with the Master himself. And so too they must reasonably expect their prospective prey to take evasive action as a measure of self-protection. I am myself now beginning to learn as how best to do this. Firstly one should avoid associating oneself with any one part of the room. Some prefer to be firmly anchored.

For example, Hugh Weldon can always be found in front of the fireplace, cup of coffee perched on the mantelpiece. *Never* will *he* be found running around with the bluebottle brigade. Gertrude Enoch of the Music Department, however, will always roost by the door, or behind it one should perhaps say, since it is usually wide open throughout the proceedings and Gertrude, being small of stature, is mostly hidden from view most of the time. Pretty good evasion tactics, I call it, even if she hasn't much to worry about and won't be appearing on too many of those dreaded hit-lists. (Gertrude is a woman, therefore a rarity in Common Room. But then she's 'only' a music teacher and therefore doesn't have full Common Room status – because she's a woman.) Others have their favourite perching places in the panelled window embrasures which line this fine room on the south side and look out onto the old duelling lawn of bygone days. But those who both want their cup of coffee *and* a little peace and quiet adopt the best strategy of all. They simply remove themselves into the room next door (Common Room Smoking Room), make a beeline for the comfortable leather chairs, sink in deep and camouflage themselves behind one of the daily broadsheets, there to remain undisturbed, they hope, till the ringing of the bell summoning for Period Four. Even here they don't always manage to escape the beady eyes of the 'hunters', as I know to my own cost.

Today feels good in there and I don't feel threatened, although I do keep a weather eye open for Giles Hamilton's HM, whom I see at the far end of the room with a dangerous-looking list in his hand. Just imagine the jotting: 'JDW re G. Hamilton. Back in House after midnight. Smelling of drink. Broken rose-trellis.' Heart thumps at the thought of it when a sudden tap on the shoulder at once kills off the uncomfortable train of thought. "John, a boy at the door for you." Oh, yes, here's another common distraction from uninterrupted coffee-drinking. Boys told or needing to see beaks will line up outside the Gainsborough-end door and ask for the beak in question. Who this could possibly be for me I've no idea. Horrors! It's Cornish, prefect and head of Giles's House. Heart re-thumps. So it's he who will be giving me the bollocking for last night. But no, I'm spared. He is merely here to arrange where and when we meet for this evening's Proctorial Round (Known by all and sundry as Vice Squad) Rendezvous arranged and I turn on my heel only to walk straight into none other than Giles himself. "Oh, hello, Giles. And how are we this merry morning? By the way, [in a whisper] did you get back OK last night?" The reply was a silent one. Thumbs up and a Giles wink.

The end-of-break bell rings and Adderley is emptying. I catch up Hugh Weldon also crossing Court and bound for his classroom. He cuts a solitary figure, alone on the central lawn on which other lesser mortals may not tread. (Rule Book: Only school prefects may walk on the grass in Court.) Seemingly impervious to the swarm of boys on all sides circumnavigating the hallowed turf, he ploughs on steadily, head down, gown draped over arm, Ovid's *Metamorphosis* in hand.

"And, pray, who is that child you were addressing so intimately at the door?" he asks provocatively as I catch up and walk at his side.

"Oh, that's Giles Hamilton. Just someone I know."

"Mm...most come-hither, if I may say so."

"Well...he's a nice kid, yes. Er...thanks for the lunch invitation. Shall I come round immediately after school?"

"Yes, that would be just splendid. And by the by, *did* the youth 'get back OK' last night?"

Our ways part and I hear him give a hint of a wicked chortle as he sails on towards Ovid and his myths of the Gods. Well, well, he must have overheard us, I suppose. I can't yet quite work this one out. How much does he know? In House opinion is divided. There are those who think he knows everything that goes on, others who think he's on another planet. Time will doubtless show. At least I'm beginning to see why his closer friends, mostly retired now, have nicknamed him 'The Cat' for his secretive manner.

Period Four and, would you believe it, a small group of Upper School scientists for a lesson in English Literature. *English* literature? I said in blank astonishment when told that I was one period 'light' on my timetable and that the Head of English could 'use' me to fill up one of his gaps. I was duly marched off to see Ian Davie – another

'Heavy' – who informed me that he'd already ordered the books I was to use, namely one volume of Keats and another of Robert Graves. Talk about being dropped in *une grande merde*, or in the deep end if you prefer, and that at the very start of term allowing me no time whatsoever to prepare for this major task ahead.

In fact things have turned out far better than I dared hope. The first principle to adopt is that *they* do the work, not I. Which means I send them away after each session with research to do. It's been Keats this term simply because, unlike Graves, I'm ashamed to say, I've actually read Keats. Keats on Nightingales, Urns and Melancholy. Keats On First Looking into Chapman's Homer. 'Much have I travelled in the realms of gold…' one of my favourite poems of all time. So some will prepare a biography, others his works, others his place within the Romantic Movement, and so on. Much depends on the composition of the group as regards the nature of the debate. Here it's been quick and lively, simply due to the fact that two out of the eight are 'characters', never at a loss for words, always ready to contribute, quick to adopt a contrary stance on ideas thrown out into the arena. These two kids are worth their weight in gold to me. In fact, such is my appreciation I'm actually showing it today by bringing in some French poetry of the same period and about which *I* will do the talking for a change. Alphonse de Lamartine's *Le Lac*:

'*O temps, suspends ton vol! et vous, heures propices,*
Suspendez votre cours!
Laissez-nous savourer les rapides délices
Des plus beaux de nos jours!

Sentiments which will surely resonate within the breasts of *la jeunesse dorée marlburienne*.

Another forty minutes swallowed up and the next and final batch of the morning are at the door. All smiles, too, they are, at the thought of a weekend ahead and bringing in with them now rays of welcome sunshine through the open door. This is Shell German and they are beginners. They've opted for German as second foreign language

35

and have been accepted, since their French is sufficiently good. We're steaming through the course book at a rate of knots and they hoover up all I set before them with alacrity. Today I'm going to feed them Johann Wolfgang von Goethe's ballad 'The Earl King' for a change.

Wer reitet so spät durch Nacht und Wind?
Es ist der Vater mit seinem Kind;
Er hat den Knaben wohl in dem Arm,
Er fasst ihn sicher, er hält ihn warm.

It's easy and they'll like the drama of the tale, the rhythmic beat of the lines recalling the galloping horse plunging through the night, heading straight for death and disaster. They'll maybe even like the spectacular Schubert setting, equally exhilarating rhythmically speaking and which I'll play them at the end.

Time! – and they're up, off and out with both bell and Schubert, I hope, ringing in their ears. I quickly gather up my books and make a beeline for Turner House and my rooms. Once there a quick wash and brush-up, particularly to remove the chalk from my jacket cuffs, which I've got into the bad habit of using as a board-rubber when the latter has been flung to some far corner of the classroom (to awaken the likes of the idle Ponsonby) and not retrieved. Once refreshed I'm off down the corridor to the other end of the building, as usual feeling somewhat apprehensive (Oh, God, will I be able to cope with Miss Moneypenny?) Outside the Housemaster's study I hitch up my tie a notch (Oh, God, this *must* be the timid schoolboy in me – *still* there) and knock. The familiar "trez!" and I'm in. It's another world in here. Plush carpeting, heavy brocaded curtains, rich damask wallpapering in dark red, one wall book-lined from top to toe, low lighting, the whole creating the impression of a soft and comfortable cocoon, infused today by a bright shaft of sunlight which falls obliquely onto the Housemaster's paper-strewn desk set at the window. A small study entirely dominated by four huge high-backed armchairs grouped around the fireplace and ensconced in two of which were the Housemaster and his lunch guest, the both of them, glass in hand, already engaged in animated conversation.

"Ah, yes, good. Mrs Marriott, do allow me to introduce you to my new Resident House Tutor, Mr Wilkinson. He's been with us since the start of term and has come from St John's College, Cambridge and Trinity College, Dublin" "Ah, TCD – how interesting." She stands, extends a welcoming hand and imparts a radiant smile. "Then you probably know…" And off she goes on a list of her Irish friends. Meanwhile the Housemaster has disappeared to fetch me an *apéritif*. No need for him to ask, it's always a gin and tonic.

Luckily there's a name on her list I recognise and an easy dialogue develops. So I'm talking to 007's secretary, Miss Moneypenny, and she's being simply charming, so I really needn't have worried. In her forties, I would imagine, still highly attractive, a soft Canadian note in her tone of voice and very definitely the flirtatious secretary I'd just recently seen in *Thunderball* and *Goldfinger*.

My glass arrives. A large and heavy cut-glass tumbler, as always, containing a large double gin, also as usual, heavy with ice-cubes and lemon *rondelles*. A second glass follows for Miss Moneypenny – gin and French, I notice – but the Housemaster abstains. This too I've noticed about him. While on the one hand he is a most generous host both at drinks and at table, on the other hand he is almost invariably most abstemious himself. Does he, like Proust, eat and drink beforehand to have more time for his guests? Time for his guests he has in abundance. Not only a fine conversationalist (that's the Irish in him – the Blarney Stone – which I recognise all too easily from my Dublin days) but a good listener too. I can sit back and relax while the two of them bat it back and forth in the manner of an exciting and prolonged Wimbledon rally. Exciting, yes, especially when Weldon gets into his stride, as he is doing now, and starts coming out with his thinly veiled indiscretions, calculated to titillate the amused listener. Or when he indulges in flights of self-parody, or best of all when he starts "I'm sorry but…" and follows either with a piece of sheer fantasy or outrageous exaggeration ("Thrash the lot of them, I say, those damnable youths, and to within an inch of their lives") or with a passionate and sincere outburst of some deeply held conviction. ("I'm sorry but schools exist for the benefit of the children and *not* to provide a living for Common Room.")

The amusing thing about his "I'm sorry but…" sentences is that one has no idea whether they'll turn out flippant or sincere. And sometimes, on their completion, I'm not even then quite sure which of the two it is, so thin does the dividing line between them sometimes seem. I'm beginning to think that Weldon at times lives in a pure fantasy world of his own creation into which one could so easily be tempted to go. After all I have to admit that it's an attractive world, if a little strange to a conventionally brought-up vicarage boy like myself. Is that what twenty-four years at MC as a bachelor beak does for you? Turn you into an eccentric? *Mon Dieu, il faut que je fasse attention.*

A head pops round the door to the dining room. It's Elizabeth Smith, the living-in housekeeper and cook. "Lunch is served, Mr Weldon." The dining room is of a similar *décor* but this time in dark green. Heavy gilt-framed family portraits on all sides look down impassively onto the large central dining table of the finest walnut, heaving under a plenitude of Georgian Irish silver. On it good food and fine wines. Around it the conversation, energetic, original, refreshing, continues to flow with the wine. Weldon at his best. I'm thinking to myself and wondering how on earth he gets his reputation as a misogynist. Perhaps because he doesn't much go for the woman who merely flutters her eyelashes and has nothing to *say*.

Moneypenny has pots to say. Talk about Canada, her country of origin, her studies at RADA with Roger Moore, filming and dancing with a young actor called Ronald Reagan, starring with David Niven. And then onto the Bond films with talk of both Sean Connery and Roger Moore again. Unfortunately for young Hamilton, nothing indiscreet, nothing salacious. Lunch draws to its close with coffee and Kummel and I am the first to ask to be allowed to leave. "Some pressing matter, I don't doubt, Mr Wilkinson?" asks my host with a glint in his eye.

"Yes, Housemaster, reports to write before 6pm on Monday."

"Ah! Well, that should at least keep you out of trouble and at best enhance your skills as a schoolmaster, shouldn't it?"

The same glint in the eye. Is he being serious or merely joking, I wonder, as I head back towards my rooms. A bit of both, perhaps?

Chapter Four

Saturday Afternoon and Evening

After a mere five minutes at the desk, my head drops and I know I'm going to lose the wine-induced battle against sleep. So a quick siesta or perhaps, better, a brisk walk upfield to clear the head and catch the tail end of the First XV rugger match against Sherborne. I decide on the latter, since the sun is still shining and taking a little of the cold out of that cruel Wiltshire November air. I can hear the cheers and groans of victory and defeat before even reaching the cricket XI and walking on up further, and I can now see the large crowd of spectators coming into view and baying for blood as the game enters its final fifteen minutes. The school watches from the far side, jumping up and down with excitement. Beaks and admiring parents (one or two also jumping up and down) from the near side.

My presence here is going to be a discreet one. Firstly I don't want to be collared by a parent and have to chew the cud over a boy's progress, or lack of it, as the case may be. Neither do I feel dressed for the occasion. Parents in their Barbours, peaked caps, green wellies and sporting shooting-sticks and/or brightly-coloured umbrellas, with the regulation Labrador straining at the leash to get to his little master, who's running all over the field in front of him and who he's not seen for weeks, poor animal. And the colleagues are similarly attired. No, very definitely, this is not my scene, although I do like to watch a good rugger tussle. Especially a closely fought one like this one today. It reminds me of my own mediocre schoolboy attempts at the game and I respect and admire these seventeen and eighteen-year-olds who have learnt to play it to such a high standard. No wonder the Oxbridge colleges couldn't resist giving them places on the strength of their prowess on the games fields – in the old days. But even now the public schools have still not entirely got over their love affair with games. Still more kudos to be gained from representing your school at the highest level in sport than in anything else, in spite of Betjeman and his Aesthetes. ('And, greatest dread of all, the dread of games.') In fact one might even ask whether anything has changed much in this respect at all since Betjeman's MC 1920s version.

> Great were the ranks and privileges there:
> Four captains ruled, selected for their brawn
> And skill at games; and how we reverenced them!

A huge cry goes up and Watson, the Captain, has scored in front of the posts, putting Marlborough in the lead with four minutes to go. An easy conversion followed by four minutes of fearsome 'play' as Sherborne desperately fight to regain the upper hand. To no avail. The final whistle blows and the plaudits resound from all around. The victorious team is first off and forms the 'tunnel' through which the defeated, heads hung low, must pass. All of them, victors and vanquished alike, though now battle-weary, are the finest specimens of young manhood. No wonder the crowd surges round to applaud these young Apollos. We're all pressing around them – a proud Master purring, doting parents cooing, admiring beaks sublimating, worshipping Shell boys fantasizing and slobbering Labradors salivating. All as happy as Larry, except perhaps for me when I suddenly realise that I shouldn't really be here at all, that I've still around ninety reports to write and that most of this evening will be taken up with Vice Squad. *Merde! Mille fois merde!* I mutter to myself as I make tracks back to Turner House. People spilling down towards College all around me. "John, coming for a cup of tea in Common Room?" "No, sorry I can't. Reports to write." "Oh, I've done mine." Then "Hello sir." Oh, no. It's the insufferable Digby-Jones from Shell French Set 6. The snobby one with an Etonian father, member of Pop. Remember?

"What did you think of the match, sir? Just as well we won 'cos it would've been a disgrace to lose against a school like Sherborne. You know, sir, they're totally dyed in the wool down there. In fact, my father says that they haven't even yet heard that the Archduke has been assassinated. (Pause)Sir, have you written our reports yet?" "Yes, of course, Digby." Lie. I manage to shake him off and continue on down alone. Wasn't that just typical Digby-Jones, I hear you say. Well, you're right, but unfortunately that's what it's like here. They call it 'healthy inter-school rivalry'. And if it's not Sherborne it's Wellington criticized for keeping on their best rugger players the extra year by which time they've become nineteen-year-old fifteen-stone bulldozers. Or it's Radley boys ("Ra! Ra! Radley!" we chant mockingly), the MC traditional No. 1 enemies, who are cordially detested for not only being snobs but for being Eton rejects, supposedly, and therefore socially inferior second-class snobs, *les derniers des derniers, quoi*. Downside for being Catholics or 'dirty, filthy, rotten, papist bastards' if you want it verbatim, excuse my French! Stowe – another bunch of second-class snobs. And so it goes on. On what these preconceptions and prejudices are based and where they come from, God only knows. They've certainly been around for a time and are not exactly discouraged by the 'authorities', as far as I can see. (Imagine, for example, the XV's rugby coach giving his pre-match pep-talk: "Now chaps, I want you to be nice to those poor little Catholic boys…" No, *that* very definitely is not the tenor of his talk, but I'll leave it to your imagination.) What does it all amount to? A healthy little bit of rivalry? Naked and unadulterated tribalism, that's what I call it. I don't suppose it matters that much – unless, of course they're going to be landed with that sort of mentality ('Bash the Unions! Bash the Soviets! Bash the ANC! *Vive, MOI, le plus fort!*) for the rest of their days. That would indeed be somewhat unfortunate, to put it mildly, particularly in those who will doubtless be reaching positions of influence and authority.

Putting these somewhat gloomy thoughts behind me, I once again find myself at the desk. The few reports I've already written – around twenty – I've not found all that easy. Nobody has given any advice, (except that 'they'd better not be late in or else…') and I've never had to do anything quite like this before. I did have a peep at some, however, which I found hanging out over an HM's bin. The few I managed to read while momentarily alone in the bin room left me somewhat aghast. Not only were they all highly articulate, carefully argued and beautifully polished linguistically speaking, they were also clearly directed towards an individual whose individual strengths and weaknesses were manifestly extremely well known to the Beak in question. The script, too, written in ink, was most attractive and fully filled the whole of the report form. Signed: P. N. C., initials I immediately recognised as those of Dr Peter Carter, Head of History, he who had earlier in the term frightened the wits out of me by casually suggesting that I might like to teach medieval French to his Upper Sixth history scholars. With a pit in my stomach I'd gone back to my rooms, torn up the twenty reports I'd already written and started again. This was clearly going to be a slow and painful operation, and the thought of the magnitude of the task ahead filled me with dread.

I decide to start at the bottom – Shell French Set 6. Not able to start, of course, until I've added up the total marks of the individual Fortnightly Orders to produce a term total from which I could then produce the final Term Order which had then to appear at the top of the report together with details of Shell Form and Set. Twenty minutes later I've finished doing all this and have still not written a single report. Knock at the door. "Please, sir, may we have permission to go to the film?" "Who's that?" "Ford and Eckersley." "OK. Put your names in the book." "Thank you, sir."

I'm going to have a lot more of these requests to be out of House in the next half-hour or so. Unwelcome distractions…. Bottom of the class, 25 out of 25: Clive Ponsonby – the idle boy who gets the brunt of the board rubber for falling asleep in class. I've a good mind to write 'For Clive, school in general (the French lesson in particular) is the snooze button on the clock-radio of life', or 'As with George Foreman Clive might later in life say 'I think sleeping was my problem in school." Or 'Is it conceivable Clive might possibly do better in French if he weren't sleeping his way through my classes?' But no, this is no good and, of course, I'm thinking of Doc Carter and his enviable powers of perception and analysis. Mind you he's been at it for donkey's years now so things could well get a bit easier for me next time round. 24 out of 25: Patrick Digby-Jones, and the upper-class twit thinks he's done well enough to go up a set, I ask you. I momentarily wonder if his Etonian father would appreciate Oscar Wilde's view of education in England. 'It produces no effect whatsoever. If it did it would prove a serious danger to the upper-classes, and would lead to acts of violence in Grosvenor Square.' 23 out of 25...and so on.

Further knocks on the door and further permissions to give. Until 2 out of 25: Christian Baveystock. Good, I'll try and get him pushed up a set and Howard, his father, will be pleased. And finally 1 out of 25– by a whisker – Ben Trimble. Well done Ben! Richly deserved, I say to myself, while realising that if I ask for promotion for Christian it's sadly going to have to be the same for Ben too. The sweetest-natured boy in the class and I'm certainly going to miss him. *Eh bien, rien n'est parfait.* By the time I've written the twenty-five Shell French Reports I realise I've been more or less saying the same thing of all of them – namely that they're all pretty hopeless and are getting nowhere fast. Ezra Pound suddenly springs to mind. '*Real* education must ultimately be limited to those who insist on knowing – the rest is mere sheep-herding.' Oh! OK. So I've been sheep-herding all term. Oh, well.

This time a more authoritative knock at the door and it's Cornish here to haul me out into the cold night air for the dubious pleasures of Vice Squad. He probably likes it no more than I do, but that's the system. The duty-week prefect and the beak (in rotating order) roam around, both on-campus and off-campus, on a Saturday evening rooting out miscreants when and wherever they are to be found. The latter tend to avoid the more obvious locations, such as the Upper School loos, which permanently reek of tobacco and are well known as a favourite smoker's haunt. Favourite because they're so conveniently placed just behind Court and it's easy to nip out of House or studies or libraries for a 'quick one'.

It's now 7.30 and time to be in House, unless you've had permission to be out, in which case you should be where you're supposed to be and not wandering around the place aimlessly. Wanderers are more likely than not to be challenged and, if found wanting, told to return to House and report to their HMs.

We decide to start operations on-campus and the first visit is to the Memorial Hall, where the film being shown will have just started. Or, to be more accurate, *should* have just started since sometimes things 'go wrong' in the lighting-box, probably due to a combination of outdated equipment and boy technicians. The result can be delays which, if protracted, can turn into rowdyism among the four hundred or so Lower School boys who usually attend these events.

What on earth are a beak and a prefect supposed to do with a pack of four hundred rowdy youths, I ask myself as we enter the darkened hall. Luckily I won't know the answer to that this evening. The film is underway and all is quiet on the western front. From here we decide to move on to the Mound, known to archaeologists as being around 4,500 years old and to Marlburians as another fairly safe smoking haven. It's some 20 metres high, about 100 metres in diameter and by far the oldest landmark in the College grounds. Certainly smaller than its sister mound further west down the Bath road at Silbury, but nevertheless impressive. Zealous Vice Squads take it happily in their stride, sprint up to the top and flush out whatever they find up there. I'm not too keen (neither is Cornish, thankfully), all the more so since a few weeks back during a similar flushing-out operation a boy, attempting to escape arrest, fell some 10 meters ending up smack against a tree trunk with a broken ankle.

So we skirt round and head down towards CR garden, where the little garden house has recently become a centre for various nefarious activities, or so the gardeners have said. Admittedly it's well set up for partying – deckchairs to sit in, sturdy wooden croquet set boxes on which to place booze and there you have it, all by kind courtesy of Common Room.

Cornish shines his torch on the ground, points to several butt ends scattered around and, Poirot-like, announces that they are fresh ones. His shrewd deductions are confirmed when with another sweep of the torch beam he comes upon a heap of empty beer bottles on the floor behind the deckchairs, then, sweeping further, picks out two more bottles standing proudly on a croquet box and only half-drunk. The two birds have clearly just flown and have probably legged it down to the bottom of the garden towards the trees standing on the banks of the river Kennet. Once there they would have worked their way along the river bank and got back to College via the parade ground. So says Cornish – poacher turned gamekeeper, for all I know – so who am I to say?

We next decide to attack the town. The betting shop has long since closed for the weekend, so we'll be concentrating on the pubs, which suits Cornish fine – me too. Sometimes a prefect will get on Vice Squad stuck with a non-pub beak, or a beak who will want to check a pub but will not have the imagination to have a pint at the same time. Tonight Cornish has struck gold, because not only am I thirsty but also I haven't eaten since lunch time. So we leave College grounds by the Master's Lodge and head up the broad central High Street as far as the Town Hall, then turn right down into the Parade and into the Lamb which, they say, serves the best pint of Wadworth's 6X in town and is also a place known to be frequented by College boys.

We plunge in to a full smoke-filled bar, with thick and strong Wiltshire accents ricocheting off all four walls. In amongst it all there eventually emerge three non-Wiltshire faces, College kids who all turn out to be prefects with every right to be there, or perhaps not, depending on their age. A slight hiatus here, surely, with one of the MC prefects' privileges being the right to go to the pub on Saturday evenings and the law of the land saying that under-age drinking in pubs is prohibited. The problem being that there's certainly more than one College prefect under the age of eighteen who should therefore technically not be here. The persons least likely to worry about this nonsense are the publicans themselves, some of whom have the reputation of wanting to pack in as many under-age drinkers as possible, be they town or gown. And for that reason the publicans in town generally resent the appearance of Vice Squad on their premises, asking what authority the College has to disrupt their trade, legal or illegal. I'd feel distinctly uneasy entering a premises, carrying out my inspection then walking straight out again without a by your leave. The least one can do is stop and have a drink.

Cornish agrees, unsurprisingly. So we have a drink, a pork pie and pickles and then join the three prefects, one of who smells strongly of tobacco. Not much to do about that, I guess, and as if to confirm my thoughts the boy in question offers me another drink. Churlish to refuse, I think to myself, all the while noting how at ease socially he is in this potentially tricky situation and recognising how I, at his age, was never in any way his match. Such amazing self-assurance coming from them all in conversation. And the talk is as if among equals. I don't go much for the affected superiority of a twit like Digby-Jones, but this here and now is a different ball game. A whiff of superiority, yes, maybe, but unconfrontational, unaffected and totally without malice. Just lucky boys fortunate enough to have been raised and educated in a milieu which can offer them the best without spoiling them, and without them perhaps even being aware of the fact that it is indeed the best that they're being offered.

I'm beginning to relax and enjoy this, but then I suddenly go and surprise myself by refusing yet another offered pint, muttering darkly about reports and saying we still had further proctorial visits to make, even though without being sure we had. Cornish decided we had and suggested we visit the Green Dragon on the way back down the High Street. Another favourite haunt, he said.

Had his choice not been the Green Dragon it could have been one of any number of public houses in the vicinity of the High Street, all of them a legacy of the days in the 18th century and early 19th century when Marlborough was an important staging-post on the road from London to Bath, with hostelries in town providing ostlers, fresh horses for the carriages and sustenance for those in transit. I'm quite happy to go to the Green Dragon for a last pint since it's on the way back to College and quite clearly marks the end of a wholly unproductive roundup. Added to which I thought I might just ask Cornish about Giles Hamilton and why it was that his relationship with his HM was apparently so strained. The answer was that Giles lived pretty much in the fast lane and that, while he was smart enough to get away with blue murder most of the time, he had recently been found in possession of live ammunition rounds in his study and the police had had to be called in. The rounds had clearly been signed out from the Armoury but had apparently never been signed back, either used or unused, as they should have been. Added to which (did I know?) he had supposedly brought back a motorbike (strictly forbidden) which he had hidden in the garden shed of Dave Jones the plumber.

Cornish is getting into his stride and his story (and his pint), and is basically telling me that Giles is at the same time a good bloke and a bit of a rogue. I listen politely and make sure not to let on that although I like the idea of the amiable rogue, ammunition rounds and police and motorbikes leave me feeling a bit queasy.

It's now 9:30 and I'm just about to suggest we call it a day when he suddenly announces that he'd forgotten to tell me something. "I forgot to say that the Second Master has a special request." "Oh, yes, and what's that then?" "He wants us to look in at the Oddies, where it seems a lot of the Preshute House kids have been seen recently."

"The Oddfellows? You must be joking. You mean we've now got to go all the way out to Manton and it's already 9.30?" I say, somewhat miffed at the thought of having to spend probably another hour at this pointless game. Preshute House is stuck out right on the western boundaries of College land and Manton is the next village just a quarter of a mile down the road from there with its two pubs the Oddies and the Up The Garden Path, a permanent temptation and particularly to the lads from Preshute.

I have a brainwave and we're now off, sharply bound for Turner and my car. That'll cut the time down. Within five minutes we draw up outside the Oddies with me having decided it's going to be a quick half-pint then immediately back to Turner and reports. But before even entering the premises I have already spotted the kids inside. Through the window. They too have seen me and are now clearly in full flight. After the few seconds taken to lift the latch and enter the place, we find ourselves in a deserted room. Four full pint-glasses stand on the bar, stools overturned and lying on the floor, no sign of a barman and then suddenly out of the corner of my eye the fleeting sight of a shirt-tail fast disappearing round a corner at the other end of the room. I give chase, Cornish at my heels, and find myself in a narrow corridor leading to a dimly lit flight of stairs. I take them at a run and emerge onto the landing upstairs. A door to the left, another to the right. An instant's hesitation and Cornish behind me "Sir, do you think we should be up here?" "Leave it to me, Cornish." Whereupon I lunge at the door on the left, which buckles on impact and reveals a dingy loo within.

"Sir, I don't think they're here, sir."

"No, Cornish, they're not," says I turning sharply to the right. I fling open the opposite door and find myself in a large double bedroom, lit dimly by a street light from without. Silence. Cornish: "Sir? Do you think...?" "Shut up, Cornish!"

We both shut up and then, in the silence, I hear the faintest of a sound from the huge wardrobe on the right. The tinkle of metal coat-hangers. I take one step to the right and.... bingo! A boy sandwiched in amongst the jackets and trousers, pale-faced and shaken. "Well, come on, get out of there, will you? And where are the others?" I needn't have asked, as I suddenly spot a foot and a shoe protruding from the end of the king-size double bed which takes up most of the rest of the room. Pulling one out from under the bed produces two other stowaways who, sardine-like, have also managed to squeeze in under.

"Right you four, get down those stairs fast and out of the building. Wait for me outside. Follow me, Cornish." And with that, a motley crew, we all six of us beat a retreat down the stairs, across the bar, four pints still standing flatly at the ready, out through the front door and into the street outside. I'm about to close the door behind me when a piercing yell rings out from within. "Oi! Oi! You there! What the hell do you think you're doing in here? Who the hell are you to go running up into my bedrooms like this? Well? Who are you?"

"I... I...I'm from the..." "Yes, I know," he interrupts, coming out from behind the bar and showing his great bulk as he menacingly moves in on me. "I know, you're from that bloody College. Don't worry, they're going to know all about this tomorrow morning. Trespassing, that's what it is, got it? And if you lot think you can come barging in here at all time of day and night you've got another thought coming, got it? So kindly get the hell out of it! Got it? Get out!" Whereupon he swivels me round and physically ejects me from the premises, slamming then locking the door behind me.

Feeling more than a little ruffled at this more than undignified throwing-out, I momentarily take my bearings and then falteringly cross the road towards the car, behind which five somewhat bedraggled specimens are attempting to take shelter from a gentle drizzle which has started to fall – four of them in a tight cluster, the fifth standing at a safe distance.

"Cornish, take their names, Will you?"

"Have already done so, sir. They're all in Preshute."

"Right, you lot get back to House this instant and report yourselves to your Housemaster. Cornish, you come with me."

We get in the car and I glance at his list. "Oh, another Cornish I see."

"Yes, sir, it's my brother."

Cornish is clearly not amused and we drive back in stony silence. He's probably already thinking of the bridge-building that's now going to have to be done in the Cornish household over the course of the holidays. The boys risk 'gating' for the rest of term if not worse. I mutter a 'well-it's-not-your-fault' and let him out opposite the gates.

"You won't say anything about Hamilton's motorbike, will you, sir?"

"No, I won't." I return to Turner and to my rooms, not in the best frame of mind. If the burly landlord is true to his word, the Master will hear about all this and I shall doubtless be summoned to explain. Trespassing on private property, undue zeal, the College's reputation at stake and now in tatters thanks to my blundering incompetence, and so on. I can see it coming. He'll throw the book at me. I shall hear him out while then and there secretly vowing to myself total inertia if and when next asked to repeat the whole ghastly operation.

I'm now in no mood whatsoever to settle down to more report writing, the more so since the four walls are resonating to sounds of over-amplified rock music drifting down from the bed-sit studies directly above me . If there's one thing I can't stand it's pounding, pulsating rock-screaming. It brings back the worst memories of my own schooldays, except then it was Elvis the King booming through-out the building. Hardly better. Up on the corridor above are the House Captains and Upper Sixth boys, each with his own bed-sitter. Technically they can keep the noise on till 11 o'clock when they have to be in their own rooms and quiet. This is only 10.30. Too bad – I'm still going up to tell them to turn the damn stuff down.

I get up there and find the usual weekend chaos. Three or four of them are in the 'brew area' cooking up beans on toast. "Oh, hello, sir, I thought you were on Vice."

"I was."

"Who did you bust, sir?"

"None of your business."

"Oh, sir, You wouldn't bust anyone, would you?"

"I might – if provoked".

I move further down the corridor and locate the devastating din. Unsurprisingly there's no response to my knock, so I move in to find a solitary youth rocking away all on his own and very clearly in a world of his own. "The volume!" I yell to make myself heard. "Oh, the volume? OK, sir" with a broad grin.

Two doors down I look in to see the ferret sitting on the back of an armchair and waiting while Nick prepares something for it to eat. "What's on the menu tonight then, Nick?"

"Oh, nothing much. Just bread and milk. The usual." Nick is the Master of the MC Beagle pack and is a country boy to his fingertips.

"A coffee, sir? There's one just here if you'd like it."

"Oh, thanks, Nick. That's just what I could do with right now." I collapse into the slightly dilapidated armchair, sharing it with the ferret, and more or less launch straight into the Oddies saga. Nick listens, the ferret nuzzles me behind the ears until its supper arrives and I begin to relax. Nick, now stretched out on his bed, is clearly enjoying the story. "You know, I wouldn't worry too much about the landlord if I were you 'cos he's already in trouble with the police for having under-age drinkers at his place, so he's hardly likely to be going to the Master tomorrow to give it away that he's *still* having them in. Is he?"

"No, Nick, you're probably right now you mention it. He isn't." That's plain common sense coming from a seventeen-year-old who in many other respects has already got his feet very firmly on the ground. Being Master of the Beagles means he has more than his fair share of responsibilities for someone of his age. The pack comprises some thirty to forty hounds which have to be fed and watered, exercised, seen by a vet when necessary and cleaned out – all on a regular basis. Births and deaths, too, are part of the seasonal routine. Food comes from the College kitchens and has to be wheeled up daily to kennels in a great war-horse of a swill-bin. Flesh, when they can get it, comes from friendly local farmers, over whose land the Master will have been granted permission to hunt. Then the hunting itself has to be organised. Dates fixed, again with the cooperation of neighbouring farmers, transport arranged both for the pack as well as for hunt followers who together with the whippers-in and a small band of lower school enthusiasts will often go to make up a field of twenty or so, sometimes more, sometimes less, depending on the day and the weather. Hunting twice a week during the season. Puppy walkers to find out of season with the Puppy Show over the Prize Day Weekend at the end of the school year. And in the holidays? The whole lot back with the Master for him to look after at home until the following term. And the responsibility for all this laid fairly and squarely on the slender shoulders of a seventeen-year-old, unlike at Eton, Stowe and Ampleforth where they have the services of a professional Kennel Huntsman to take the pressure off. Now you see why I admire people like young Nick.

As I look at him now chatting away happily with his ferret already curled up asleep on his stomach, I can't help thinking of what Weldon told me about the father. A strict disciplinarian, it appears, who doesn't shrink from taking a cane to his children when he considers it warranted. How could such a sweet-natured youth ever deserve such cruel treatment at the hands of his own father? The mere thought of it makes me want to weep. "Can I get you another coffee?" "*Non, merci,* Nicko, it's already 11.15 and I'd better be going. By the way, what happened to the rabbit you had up here earlier in the term?" "Oh, yes, I'm afraid to say it keeled over one day." "Really? Why?" "I think it mistook the carpet for grass which didn't do much for its gastric juices". He judges my reaction, amusement, then gives a little chuckle. "Anyway, it wouldn't have lasted long with the ferret, would it?"

I leave him with his furry friend, head back down the corridor ("Come on, turn that music off! And you, Dom, get back to your study, will you?") and down the stairs into my rooms. A pile of blank report forms on the desk eyes me reproachfully. No, I can't cope with them now. It's too late, I'm too tired and still not in the mood. I head for bed and set the alarm – 7.45 again – and mutter to myself 'Reports... reports...'

Chapter Five

Sunday morning

I wake up early after a good night's sleep and am at the desk by 6.00. Pitch black from outside and not a squeak from upstairs. No distractions, no excuses, so I plough on doggedly till 8.30. Progress has been encouraging and with a similar session I'll almost certainly have cracked the nut. So I down tools and skip over to CR Dining Room for a quick spot of breakfast before choir practice.

Chris, who also sings with the Chapel Choir is already there and buried deep in the *Sunday Times* travel section. "Morning, Wilky. Voice on good form then? Top notes OK?" He's a tenor, so he knows all about top notes early on a Sunday morning.

I pop my head through the door to the kitchen. "Morning, Joe." "Morning, Mr Wilky." "Two soft boiled, please Joe." "Very good, Mr Wilky." On Sundays there's only a skeleton staff in the kitchens so no choice of cooked breakfast, which suits me fine.

Chris and I reach the chapel for the pre-matins choir practice just as the Director of Music has started to attack the hymns. Late-comers – tenors and basses, altos and trebles alike – are scurrying in and hoping not to be noticed. By the time we get to the psalm of the day a full choir of sixty boys and five beaks has assembled and the cobwebs are at last beginning to be removed from the larynxes.

We eventually find our full collective voice for the anthem 'O Thou The Central Orb' which requires a great full *fortissimo* from all on the opening chords. A mighty sound with full organ backing which resounds down the whole length of the building and high into the vaulted barrel roofing. By now the school is beginning to drift in and we, the choir, have a ten-minute breather while the chapel bell coaxes us all slowly but surely towards the 10.00 deadline. Sometimes there's just time for a quick cup of coffee in CR, sometimes not. By the last stroke of 10.00, nigh on a thousand souls are assembled under the same roof. The boys, all in their dark suits, sit in their allocated places by houses in the pews which, à la Oxbridge colleges, are inward-looking. The beaks, in hoods and gowns, occupy the more comfortable back row pews and the Master and Second Master both look down the full length of the central nave towards the high altar from their exalted pews at the west end of the building. The length is truly impressive and the Head of Biology referred to it when addressing the school at a Monday morning assembly earlier in the term. He was trying to give an idea of the massive size of *Amphicoelias fragillimus,* one of the longest and largest of the dinosaurs. "Imagine, it sitting in the chapel with its snout resting on the high altar and its tail extending down the chapel steps beyond the west door," he said. "There you have an animal measuring fifty-eight meters in length and weighing one hundred and sixteen tons. Think about it when you're next in chapel."

The head of English thought about it too and now refers to the building as 'that Pre-Raphaelite dinosaur', thus aptly describing both the twelve large biblical scenes on the walls painted by Spencer-Stanhope, one of the foremost of the Pre-Raphaelite painters of his day and the soaring dimensions of both length and height. This chapel was completed in 1886, designed by the well-known firm of Bodley and Garner, and it replaced an earlier building out-grown by rising numbers; I wonder how many here today find in it the meaning Betjeman did all those years ago.

For safe in G. F. Bodley's greens and browns,
Safe in the surge of undogmatic hymns,

The Chapel was the centre of my life –
The only place where I could be alone.

Safety, doubtless, from the attacks, both physical and verbal, of the House bullies so much to be feared in the MC of the 1920s. The budding poet left alone at least temporarily to pursue the world of his inner thoughts and poetic imagination. Today's Marlburian faces fewer bullies, even if unkind, wounding words are surely still traded. But he too, Betjeman-like, will be drifting in and out of a world of private thoughts and fantasies as the OM Bishop drones on through his sermon.

I cast my gaze down the nave. Serried ranks of dark-suited youth as far as the eye can see, boys huddled, nestling closely and squashed tight up against each other in the lengthy and unforgiving wooden pews. A penny for their thoughts? Some, the older ones, heads hung low, would appear to be asleep. Some, more restless, are establishing eye-contact with friends in the pews opposite and wordless messages are being passed. Some, hands cupped over their mouths, are whispering to neighbours on either side, taking good care that the HM sitting opposite is otherwise occupied. Others are gazing out into open space. Or are they perhaps transfixed by the names of eminent OMs looking down on them from the boards which encircle the whole building? Names, famous some of them, inscribed in gold-leaf on the Bodley brown. I myself have a William Morris window opposite to keep me company. That's if my attention doesn't stray to the Spencer-Stanhope painting underneath it depicting Abraham on the point of sacrificing his son, Isaac. The vicious old man towers above his son, arm raised high, and with hand clasping the gleaming knife soon to plunge into the warm flesh of the sacrificial victim. Isaac, the son to be sacrificed, a beautiful Adonis – yes, very beautiful I've decided – naked but for the loin-cloth and bound tight by ropes and cords, awaits his fate meekly. Sexual sado-masochistic imagery is here in abundance for those who care to see it, I think to myself, with bondage thrown in for good measure. No telling the numbers of those in successive congregations who have been fascinated or indeed troubled by their contemplation of this brutal scene.

My gaze drops down to those in the choir sitting opposite on the cantoris side then further down to the first row, the treble-line. And yes, it's none other than Ben Trimble looking straight across at me. I get a broad and lingering smile. He gets one back. What a sweet kid with a great voice, too. Do I really have to recommend that he move up to a higher Shell French set? I'm definitely going to miss him.

"In the name of the Father, the Son and the Holy Ghost, Amen. "The sermon has at last ground to a halt and there's a muted muttering and shuffling as the chaplain announces the final hymn. The choir is generally first up on its toes and into the first verse by the time the rest of the congregation has finally dragged itself to its feet. There's palpably an element present that will at most tolerate sitting in silence but will clearly not appreciate being asked to stand and will outright refuse to participate in any singing. Reasons vary from 'singing's not cool' to 'you can force me to be present but you can't force me to worship.' All a great shame, I say, thinking back to my own school days and the inspiration to be had by all when raising the chapel roof off with the volume of the sound in the singing of some of the better-known Anglican hymns. Or ask a Welsh miner when he sings his heart out accompanied by the colliery band. Or those in the Albert Hall giving vent to their emotions at the last night of the Proms. Or indeed an inspired football crowd. There's nothing quite like community singing for uplifting the spirits, but it seems that this young generation by and large begs to differ. And I've already learnt to my cost that there's no point in introducing them to the delights of contemporary French song, *la belle chanson française.* The likes of Brel, Brassens, Léo Ferry and Barbara leave them totally unmoved and indifferent in spite of the fine poetry of so many of the texts. You've only to wander down the study corridors to realise that here and now it's all Beatles, Rolling Stones or worse (as far as I'm concerned). In my day it was Elvis Presley being pounded out day and night (and how I cordially detested it) so perhaps not all that much has changed after all. At least one can be thankful that schools like Cranleigh (that *minor* public school as the dreadful Digby-Jones was so keen to point out) and Marlborough have sufficient numbers of talented classical musicians to ensure choirs and orchestras of good quality.

The final hymn gives way to the final prayers. Some are refusing to kneel ('you can force me to be here but you can't force me to pray' again, I suppose) and just staring sullenly in front of them, some with heads bowed and eyes shut tight (through force of habit?), others peeping between the fingers of hands loosely cupped over hidden faces, doubtless curious to know just who is doing just what. And then a minute of silence before the organ crashes in to send us out into the world supposedly spiritually cleansed and morally uplifted, or not as the case may be. I suspect Betjeman's predicament all those years ago is much like the one felt by some of us here today:

> *The centre and the mainspring of your lives,*
> *The inspiration for your work and sport,*
> *The corporate life of this great public school*
> *Spring from its glorious chapel. Day by day*
> *You come to worship in its noble walls,*
> *Hallowed by half a century of prayer."*
> *The Old Marlburian bishop thundered on*
> *When all I worshiped were the athletes, ranged*
> *In the pews opposite. "Be pure," he cried,*
> *And, for a moment, stilled the sea of coughs.*
> *"Do nothing that would make your mother blush*
> *If she could see you. When the Tempter comes*
> *Spurn him and God will lift you from the mire."*
> *Oh, who is God? O tell me, who is God?*
> *Perhaps he hides behind the reredos...*
> *Give me a God whom I can touch and see.*

We're all swept out on a gust of organ voluntary – a movement from one of Louis Vierne's Six Symphonies for Organ, a fine example of another strong tradition in the world of French music and every bit as rich as that of the *chanson*, namely the wide 19th and early 20th century repertoire of music written for organ. I really must try and spread the message and promote France, the French and their culture for all I'm worth – part of the job, surely. How about a strong little nucleus of Francophiles as a healthy antidote to the prevailing Establishment thinking bred within these hallowed English walls? Yes, that's it – get them hooked on Gauloises and Pernod…

"What did you think of the Vierne voluntary then, Mr Molesworth?"

"The what, sir?

"The organ music as we were coming out."

"Oh, that. Cool. A bit loud though. Have you written our reports, sir?"

"Yes, I have." True.

"Where did I come in final order, sir?"

"I'll tell you tomorrow."

The sun is bravely trying to peep through and with colleagues and their wives I'm milling around outside the little chapel side door. Gossip is what we're mostly after and this is precisely what I get.

"Oh, John – you should never have done it!" (This is the housemaster of Preshute's wife bearing down on me; she's clearly not amused.)

"Done what?"

"Gone and busted four of our captains last night. (Oh God, she's on about my visit to the Oddies on Vice last night.) They're all perfectly respectable boys and were only having a quick pint on a Saturday evening, you know?"

"Yes, Ann, I know, but…"

"Oh, hello, Dotty, (Another HMs wife approaches while I struggle to justify myself.) I'm just telling this young John Wilkinson that he's ruined the Captains lunch today. He's reported over half our captains to Mike who's had to gate them for the rest of term. And all just because they were having a quick pint in the Oddies. Can you imagine the atmosphere around the lunch table there'll be?

"Yes, but hold it, Ann.…"

"Oh, but, John, (Dotty now teasingly joins in the attack) what a spoil-sport you are! You really must learn to turn a blind eye at times, you know.

"Yes, but Dotty they were breaking the school rules and...."

"Yes, well you'll doubtless learn there are rules and rules, you know. (Turning to Ann) Oh, Ann, you poor thing; I'm sure you'll be all right. You and Mike do these things so beautifully. We've got our house Christmas supper tonight – A full three-course supper, turkey AND trimmings, for sixty-five. I just don't know how Sarah manages it all on her own, poor thing. And you know she won't let me go anywhere near the kitchens. We'll be having our captains in for drinks beforehand. And I do think Brian's right to insist that they wear their Sunday suits - the house as well as the captains. Don't you agree? I know Bob allows his boys to come in T-shirts and jeans, but I just don't think it's right. Do you, my dear?"

I rapidly decide not to participate in what is clearly going to be another of these tedious and predictable conversations on pupil dress etiquette. Besides I'm furious at the criticism levelled at me by these two women, in jest or otherwise, so I turn on my heel and head out of Court and back to Turner House. And anyway just who do they think they are, these meddling housemasters' wives? Reporting boys out of bounds and drinking in pubs is exactly what Vice Squad is all about and had I merely turned a blind eye you can be sure the Second Master (i/c discipline) would have somehow heard about it and I would have certainly been hauled over the coals for not having done my job. My thoughts turn back to hounds and hares. Seemingly hunting with the hounds is not necessarily going to get one all the plaudits in the little world of MC. OK. Well then in that case let's try running with the hare for a while and see where that gets me. Should certainly be much more fun apart from anything else. More dangerous too, doubtless. By the time I reach Turner I've cooled down a bit. Besides I'm now beginning to appreciate better the role the HMs wives are called to play within the power structure of the place. Just as we're told that every Third Reich German general had a Brünnhilde behind him, so too the ambitious, career-minded young schoolmaster knows that support from his wife, who is sometimes every bit as ambitious as her husband, is indeed a valuable asset to be carefully cultivated, particularly if he aspires to climb the traditional ladder from schoolmaster to housemaster to headmaster.

Since it is the master who appoints new HMs, it is imperative that the aspiring couple know what stance the former is likely to take on the matter. Will he be looking for a conservative or a liberal, for example? Is policy that a retiring right-wing HM (a strict disciplinarian who abides by the rule-book and a fervent believer in house 'spirit' particularly as exemplified on the games fields) be followed by someone showing more liberal tendencies in the education of young adolescents (a man who, for example, will support and value the contributions of the musician or the boffin every bit as much as those of the rugby player and who will 'bend' the rules to suit the occasion)? The present Master is known generally for his liberal tendencies ('virile liberalism' is the catch-phrase, I'm told) but that hasn't prevented him from appointing some arch-conservatives to housemasterships, much to the chagrin of the boys who will have to endure them. Yes, the average Marlburian much prefers the liberal HM *in loco parentis* – the ride will almost certainly be a gentler one. So, for those looking for promotion it's all a bit of a lottery and no wonder there's scheming afoot whenever a housemastership becomes available. Hugh Weldon, earlier in the term, told me the story of the wife of a contender for a recent vacancy being so upset at the thought of her husband being passed over for the post that she rushed down to the Master's Lodge, demanded an appointment there and then, flew at the Master, eventually seized up in a near apoplectic fit and ended up on the floor screaming like a banshee, kicking her little legs in the air then breaking out into uncontrollable fits of sobbing while the startled Master very sensibly rang through for his eminently capable secretary, who was eventually able to calm down the poor woman and lead her gently out of the study. Whether or not this fervent 'application' was successful, history doesn't relate. Or rather Hugh Weldon didn't relate, in spite of my pestering him for the identity of this fearsome woman.

Hugh really does like to tease one in the telling of his salacious and more often than not larger-than-life-size stories. He'll delight to lay it on with a trowel and then, just when he's aroused the interest of the listener, will choose not to deliver the punch line – in this case the identity of the main protagonist. He will draw the line at indiscretion. I've not yet heard Hugh tell a cruel story told at the expense of another. His anecdotes are often highly witty and amusing although one would be unwise to take them at face value given the embroidery and embellishment which goes into the telling of them. I sometimes wonder whether his real world is his fantasy world. There certainly appears to be a lot of mixing up of the two somewhere along the line.

With these thoughts in mind, I reach Turner House surrounded by a gaggle of boys also returning from Chapel. They look pretty fed up, heads down, slouching, hands in pockets. The body language speaks volumes.

"Sir, why do we have to go to Chapel?"

"Because it's Sunday, Malcolm. Why else do you think? It's the Lord's day and that's how we celebrate it. Besides, this is an Anglican school founded principally for the sons of the clergy. Isn't that right? Look at all those bishops, deans and archdeacons on the Council if you don't believe me. Who's the Visitor, James?"

"The what, sir?"

"The Visitor."

"Never heard of it, sir."

"It's the Archbishop of Canterbury, James. Heard of *him*? He has the last word in theory even if in practice it's the Council who formulate college policy. So at MC you've got the C of E breathing down your neck whether you like it or not. Tough luck, Malcolm, and it also means we've got to get out of our nice, warm beds on a cold Sunday morning which we don't much like either, do we, Malcolm?"

"No, sir, we definitely don't. But what happens if you aren't a believer? It's OK if you're a Christian, but if you don't believe in God it's crazy to have to go and pray to someone who doesn't even exist, isn't it? And anyway, I've got a friend at Bedales and I don't think they even have a chapel there. And other friends too at places where they at least have a choice, so chapel is not compulsory like it is here but if you choose not to go then you have to go to a talk or something like that. Why can't we do that here, sir?"

"Don't know, Malcolm. You'll have to ask the Chaplain. He'll doubtless tell you."

It's not the first time I've been dragged into a dismal conversation like this. They've got a point, OK? As long as they have to attend RE classes where they study the Bible and discuss related matters, I don't really see why they should be forced to worship in chapel too. They're right. Of course it should be a matter of choice. I refrain from telling them they're more than lucky not to be in my shoes when this time next week I will have already been to church twice with the prospect of Evensong to follow. That's the penalty of having an Anglican priest as a father and a mother whose duty it rightly is to get us to 'support dad', which in this case means us all (mum, brother and I) getting up at the unearthly hour of 7.30 on most Sunday mornings of the holidays to leg it down the hill and get to the church in time for the 8.30 Holy Communion. If *we* didn't go there'd probably only be the Tylers (from the 'big' house) together with a clutch of old biddies roosting somewhere in the relative safety of the back pews. (Yes, this is one of those churches which still more or less reserve the front pews for the village big-wigs. No brass plates, admittedly, but very definitely front left for the vicars family, front right for the Tylers. A tangible example of the 'rich man in his castle/poor man at his gate' mentality which the Anglican hierarchy has so successfully carried around in its baggage over the centuries.)

We're now back at House, so I thankfully leave Malcolm (mumbling something about 'it's just not fair') and his cronies to their brooding and head off to my rooms to fetch my clarinet. Yes, you've guessed, it's another rehearsal coming up. Let no one be deluded into thinking that weekends here are time off. Very definitely not. Having already swallowed a choir practice and then matins I'm now confronted by an hour's rehearsal with 'Brasser', the college brass band, which is there to give regular concerts and provide marching music for the CCF (Combined Cadet Force). This is going to be a dress rehearsal with a concert to be given on Friday evening, the last night of term. Both rehearsal and concert are as usual to take place in the Mem. (Memorial) Hall. Together with the chapel and the dining hall this is the only college building able to contain the whole school and Common Room. Seating for around a thousand.

The Mem Hall, with its fine Ionic pillars on the north side and built in the form of an amphitheatre, was finally completed in 1925 and stands in memory of the 742 OMs who had died in the First World War. To their names, chiselled into the stone of the hemi circular back wall of the hall, have been added those of the further 415 Marlburian dead of the Second World War. And together with them are recorded the names of those fallen in earlier conflicts, the names of boys who had entered the school in the 1840s, its very earliest years, and had left to fight and be killed in the 1850s in India. Following generations were lost at later stages in Afghanistan, Sudan and South Africa. It's a sobering thought to be here and contemplate the enormity of the sacrifice made by just one school.

Earlier in the term I came in alone to look at these names more closely. Nearly all of them were lost in the flower of their youth, all of them young officers. I counted no fewer than 13 Victoria Crosses, each with a citation telling of untold acts of valour. As an example and taken at random, the story of Captain John Niel Randle VC, who was attacking Japanese positions at Kohima, in Assam on 4th May, 1944: 'Although already severely wounded in the knee by grenade splinters and with utter disregard to the obvious danger to himself, Captain Randle charged the Japanese machine gun post, the destruction of which was imperative if the operation was to succeed, single-handed with rifle and bayonet. Although bleeding in the face and mortally wounded by numerous bursts of machine-gun fire, he reached the bunker and silenced the gun with a grenade thrown through the bunker slit. He then flung his body across the slit so that the aperture should be completely sealed. The bravery shown by this officer could not have been surpassed and by sacrificing himself he saved the lives of many of his men and enabled not only his Company but the whole Battalion to gain its objective and win decisive victory over the enemy.' (*London Gazette*, 12 December, 1944.)

The other 12 Marlburian VC holders, also recorded in the London Gazette, tell similar stories of acts of horrendous bravery and every bit as astounding as that of Captain Randle. Even the names of some of these great heroes are the very stuff of chivalry and distinction. Captain The Hon. Raymond Hervey Lodge Joseph de Montmorency VC, Maj. General Llewelyn Alberic Emilius Price-Davies VC, CB, CMG, DSO. How many schools in the country, I wonder, can hold records as proud as these? Not many, if any, I would think.

Today, however, the Hall has shed its sombre memories and its walls echo the squeaks, poops and all manner of other sounds associated with a band warming up. Cacophony eventually brought to order by Bob Peel, our enthusiastic and friendly Bandmaster. A man of imposing stature, standing high on his conductor's podium, his arms spread wide with baton at the ready, he envelopes and launches us into immediate battle with colossal verve and often at the tempo of a horse *au triple galop*. We cling on like grim death and eventually arrive at the finishing line (more or less at the same time) exhausted but triumphant. Yes, Brasser is a great 'blow' and good fun is had by all.

Chapter Six

Sunday Afternoon

Midday, and I've intentionally no plans for lunch. Often on a Sunday I'm invited to Hugh Weldon's for one of Elizabeth's succulent roasts and normally late afternoon and early evening are spent sleeping it off gently dozing in my armchair in front of the box. But today Hugh has been invited out by one of his 'county set' friends, Esmé Kenyon-Jones, in fact, whom I've already met earlier in the term at one of Hugh's drinks parties. She is indeed a *grande dame formidable* who will talk most volubly and knowledgeably about Emperor Haile Selassie and his family – "all very good friends of mine, John, don't you know" – and about her villa in Addis where she spends a lot of her time dispensing largesse seemingly to all and sundry. When in the UK she weekends in her delightful Queen Anne mansion outside Marlborough where she presides over the entertainment of her county friends in a manner to which they are surely accustomed. So I'm going to scratch together a snack lunch in my flat and then attack the last set of reports.

My flat (or rooms) isn't very much to write home about, although I'm not complaining after seeing the accommodation of a young colleague of mine the other day. He, like me, is a bachelor beak and resident house tutor and has the use of four rooms, all of them individually dotted around in various parts of the building. So, if, for example, he wants to get from his study/sitting room to his bedroom he must walk down a flight of stairs to the ground floor, turn right, follow the corridor to the end of the building and then walk back upstairs again – two flights this time. Having rapidly got fed up with this arrangement he soon discovered a short cut which involves walking through the junior boys' dormitory and now regularly uses it at all times of day or night, initially much to the consternation of the boys, who in various stages of undress, sleeping and wakening were understandably concerned by this unsolicited invasion of their privacy by the 'authorities'. Time has once again worked its magic and the principal of dorm-cum-tutor's- corridor is now tacitly accepted by all as a fact of life. He also has a bathroom at one end of the building and a loo at the opposite end.

My circumstances in Turner House are greatly preferable in that I have a front door which opens on to a small kitchen with a bedroom beyond and a reasonable-sized study/sitting room leading off to the right. However, in order to wash or have a bath I have to leave the flat and cross over to the other side of the corridor. The loo too is on the corridor but still further down and opposite one of the dormitories. It's supposed to be my private loo, but being the closest to their dorm it is used by the boys when they think I'm safely out of the way. I wouldn't object too much but for the fact that half of them appear still not to be house-trained and the place is constantly awash with boy pee – and sometimes worse, vomit, for example. We otherwise share the *parties communes* amicably enough. They've got used to the sight of me darting semi-clad across to my bathroom and vice versa, except that some of them are less than semi-clad and are a cause for comment when they unexpectedly run up against prospective parents being shown round the house.

There was one such occasion earlier in the term involving one of the house captains, hotfooting it back to his bedsit after a shower, and a set of parents (belonging to the head of house) with whom he collided on turning a blind corner at speed. Still wet and bedraggled from his shower he skidded to a halt at their feet, lost both his balance and, more importantly, the towel which had been loosely wrapped around his waist. Doubtless aware by now that the father was wearing uniform (Captain of the Royal Navy) his instinctive reaction, being the son of a military officer himself, was to pick himself up, stand aside and to attention, hands at the side, all the while omitting to retrieve his towel. The Captain RN, visibly amused, pulled himself up to his full height and in a mock-military tone issued his orders. "Stand – at ease!" The boy stood promptly at ease, hands clasped behind his back. "Stand – easy! Now retrieve towel and carry on!" Much relief all round, especially from Madame, who had clearly been much surprised agreeably or otherwise at having been unexpectedly confronted by this fine specimen of Marlburian manhood in all its glory.

The snack lunch in my rooms turns out to be a pretty sorry affair. I've neither bread, butter nor milk, just one egg, a can of baked beans and a half-packet of stale digestive biscuits. And not even a glass of wine, the last bottle having been well and truly polished off by Giles and myself on Friday evening. The milk I can 'borrow' from the Sanatorium next door (time spent chatting up the three resident nurses has paid off) but I draw the line at going all the way across to Common Room cellar to sign out for more booze. An alcohol-free Sunday lunch for a change won't do any harm, I mutter to myself, eyeing the remaining twenty blank report forms still to be filled in.

A poor lunch ends on an upbeat note – a good strong cup of Arabica coffee which propels me back to the desk. No sooner is the pen raised (no biros, please) then there's a thundering knock at the door and in bursts an excited Savory.

"Sir, you haven't forgotten, have you?"

"Forgotten what, Malcolm?"

"The play rehearsal, sir."

"The play rehearsal. Ah, yes. Actually it's not a rehearsal – just a preliminary read through. No, Malcolm, of course I've not forgotten (lie). Just remind me what time we said."

"Four o'clock in the house library, sir."

"And have people been told?"

"Yes, sir, everyone'll be there. Are the girls coming, sir?"

"Yes, Malcolm, the girls are most certainly coming and you just make sure that you keep your nasty little hands off them, OK?"

"Oh, sir! Sir!"

Malcolm is a highly attractive seventeen-year-old showing every sign that he's already well on the road to becoming a serial lady killer in later life. That's one of the reasons why I've cast him in the main role to play against the leading female part. I gather that normally in House plays the female parts are taken by the younger boys dressed up in their blouses and skirts, maquillage applied liberally. The overall effect can be hilarious and it's a brave kid who will take on this daunting challenge, not that he'll always have much choice in the matter ("Hey, let's get Pye-Smith for Cecily. He's vaguely girly. He'll do. Hey, Smith, you're doing Cecily. Don't argue! Where's your house spirit, young man?")

Earlier in the term I attended one such House play to get some idea as to what was required. The leading boy/girl playing heroine in an obscure Greek tragedy had for some reason been endowed with a buxom bosom of wondrous proportions, which from the start he was clearly having difficulties in controlling. The serious nature of the play was equally clearly being lost on an audience which, both by now equally absorbed and amused by the poor boy's evident inability to cope with his protuberant bust, was increasingly being taken over by fits of laughter. If at first stifled, by the end of Act One it was well on the way to bringing the whole performance down to the level of a Feydeau farce. The props department had been remiss in its attention to detail, and while the idea of a bra containing two blown-up balloons was in itself not a bad one, it would have better had both balloons been airtight. As things were, they weren't and from almost the start the boy was losing significant quantities of air from the left-hand balloon. Added to which the whole ghastly contraption was gradually slipping off the wearer's slender chest and, in spite of valiant attempts by him at retrieval, by the end of the act it wound up around his waist, to the intense amusement of all and sundry, as can be imagined. There was thunderous applause as the curtain came down from both parents and boys in the audience, the latter relishing the evident discomfort of one of their own.

And that was not all. There was more to follow for their further entertainment in the following act. There was renewed applause for our 'heroine', who had undergone a lightning mastectomy and now looked much more appealing. However, the attention switched from 'her' to an inert corpse which was wheeled on and remained centre stage for the rest of the act. This passive part was played by none other than the Head of House, thought to be ideal in this role, since by no means was he considered to be of the literary sort and nobody was going to force him into learning some pansy lines from Ancient Greece, certainly not someone a year beneath him in House who clearly considered himself a rising literary star and had been asked by the HM to produce the play since the House Tutor (who would normally undertake such things) had for some reason been unable to do so. In normal circumstances there was surely no risk to the Head of House in his taking this entirely passive role in the play.

Hard to think how his carefully cultivated amour-propre could possibly be dented in any way when all he was required to do was to lie inert and horizontal on a slab with a white shroud – one of the sheets from off his own bed doubtless – draped over him. However, as I was beginning to become aware, amateur dramatics contain many a pitfall for the unsuspecting amateur – actor and producer alike. The saga of the deflated boob was now to turn rapidly into the saga of the not-so-inert corpse. Audience attention switched instantly to the latter on a direct reference having been made to it by our now boobless, grieving 'heroine' (the corpse had been her lover). And there, rather than the state of total inertness required by the part, we were witnessing distinct movement. Yes, palpable stirrings, gentle at first but swelling considerably by the minute, permeating from the body's centre to the extent that what had started the act as a loosely draped shroud ended it as a tautly stretched tent propped up by a colossal central tent-pole. Certainly the part had been well-cast if this had been the intended 'special effect', but since the hapless producer clearly had no inkling that his prestigious corpse would suddenly be overcome by a fit of erotic fantasizing (about what, we ask?) he could hardly be blamed for not having insisted that he wear a tight rugby jockstrap rather than the flimsy boxer shorts which were painfully and woefully unequal to the task of containing such fierce masculine ardour. Audience reaction was yet again entirely predictable. Muffled sniggers crescendoing to gales of uncontrolled mirth levelled at an equally uncontrolled Head-of-House-cum-corpse. The audience, mostly members of the House whose play was being performed and most of who had against their will been dragooned into attending (house spirit) what they had supposed to be some dreary Greek classic, left the theatre well pleased with the evening's unexpected entertainment. I, too, left highly amused but at the same time now fully aware of the risk I was running by having agreed to play at being producer when I knew nothing about it, having never even acted in a play let alone directed one.

"What's the time then, Malcolm?" "Two fifteen, sir." Good. An hour and a half in which to kill off this last set of reports. The unmentionable Shell French Set 6. "Good. Well, look, Malcolm. I've got these reports I must finish this afternoon, so I'll see you all in the library at four as agreed. OK?" "Yes, sir, but what about the girls?" "What about the girls?" "Well, sir, I mean they won't know where to go, will they?" "Yes, they will, Malcolm. I shall be showing them where to go. OK? Now if you don't mind..."

My thwarted principal actor leaves the room doubtless cursing me under his breath, and yet again I poise the pen. My mind, how-ever, is on girls, and particularly on the two who I've asked to meet me at three fifty-five in front of House, Julie Boys and Rosie Hedges, both of whom I found at St John's Grammar School at the top of the hill and overlooking the town. I had already chosen a play – Jean Anouilh's *Eurydice* or *Point of Departure* in translation – which I already knew and thought suitable, and I had then demanded to see the Head of English at St John's to ask whether she could find me the two budding actresses I was looking for. Given the poor state of play existing between the College and the Grammar school ("You sissy toffs, you!" "You oafish oiks, you!") I wasn't exactly expecting a rapturous reception and was agreeably surprised when a dozen or so girls studying 'A' level English came forward wanting to audition for the parts. The auditions, rudimentary, took place there and then. I needed first to hear the sound of their voices (the strong Wiltshire accents had to be eliminated immediately, I'm ashamed to say) and then I concentrated on finding the two who best 'looked' the parts. Eurydice, the tragic and mysterious *femme fatale* seeking out her lonely path to Truth and Destiny, was here and now destined to have the lovely Orpheus alias Malcolm swooning at her feet, if nothing else. Eurydice's mother was the counterfoil, the mundane mother living out a meaningless life of compromise, insincerity, vulgarity and promiscuity. For the former I picked Julie – long, straight jet-black hair, of a sallow complexion, slender in figure and with a distinct Juliette Greco look. And for the latter, Rosie – altogether a plumper proposition, chubby and ruddy faced, well suited too, I thought, to blurt out the comical platitudes with which her lines are heavily peppered.

Audition over, I announced the 'winners' to the evident amusement of all present. General merriment all round, their teacher included, doubtless occasioned by the ticklish thought of two of their number having landed the prize, none other than the right of entry to the 'ivory tower' – that male bastion of class and privilege sat solidly at the end of the High Street: the College.

The pen hits the report form. One hour later and I'm already on the last one. 'Name: Ben Trimble. Comment: An active member of the set and a willing participator in class proceedings. He has scored consistently well in tests throughout the term and if his end of term exam results are true to form I shall happily (lie – unhappily) recommend that he move up a set. John Wilkinson.'

Pen down and a sigh of relief. Just time to run over to Common Room with this last batch and distribute into the form masters' bins. A glance at my own bin reveals an unmistakable sheaf of reports with accompanying note reading: 'JDW/ Please correct the spelling mistakes & return to me before Mon. AFE. (NB Latin: Translatus)' Oh God! Please no... I go hot all over at the thought and then sight of my underlined-in-red misdemeanour jumping out at me from off the paper – 'TRANSALATION' – not only once but repeated again and again on each of the slips returned. I'm temporarily glued to the spot, horror-struck. Of course, you idiot, it's a Latin prefix, you fool! What's more, AFE is none other than Alan Elliott, powerful Housemaster and revered member of the Classics department (1st class degree from New Coll Oxon in Classical Mods and Literature). I'm just imagining what he's thinking and doubtless saying. "Look at this! These new appointments aren't even educated. Can't even spell. Who do these young puppy-dogs think they are? Sack 'em all, I say." These gloomy thoughts leave me head bowed, staring down at the offending word. Shame at the incompetence. I'm ashamed of myself. Not up to the mark. Not good enough. What now?

After a moment or two of hurtful introspective brooding, the door suddenly bursts open and in bounces Chris, the ever busy and bustling hyper-efficient Head of Geography. "What-ho, Wilky! All OK then?"

"Yes, fine thanks, Chris. Just offloading the last of the reports. Quite a relief really."

"Yes, but you just wait till they make you a form master, when you have to sort all the blasted things into the report folders. You haven't seen anything yet. That's when the fun starts."

Chris is fishing for the Common Room wine cellar key and I find myself following him through. A bottle of wine to have handy after the play read-through. Yes, that's a good idea.

I trudge back to house clasping bottle and rejected reports and feeling somewhat deflated and empty, even a little sick, and certainly not in the mood for tussling with Monsieur Jean Anouilh and his prissy Eurydice. Too late, I realise, as I spot the two girls standing waiting for me at the front door as instructed. Standing - no, more like cowering - and it's not hard to see why. A host of little noses pressed hard up to the window panes from within from where a dozen or so boys observe this sight all too rare – girls in front of Turner House. Whatever next they must be thinking. I sweep them away with an irate gesture from the arm and they scatter. Two much relieved demoiselles submissively follow me up to my rooms. Luckily, it being a Sunday afternoon, there are not many people in the corridors so it's hardly a question of them having to run the gauntlet. Nevertheless they both walk close by my side rather as young chicks would with the mother hen. Security is the name of the game, I suppose. Bottle straight to the fridge, reports slammed back on the desk from whence they so recently came and I'm ready to face the next hurdle.

"Girls, you don't need to worry about the lads, you know. They'll be all right. They might perhaps get a little giggly but you can probably put that down to nerves. In fact they're probably going to be more nervous than you are." And possibly the most nervous of all is going to be me, I think to myself as I sweep up the texts from the table and lead my two little apprehensive chicks back down the corridor again and on to the library – the lion's den. Stage whispers of 'They're coming! They're coming!' herald our arrival. I immediately see that they've arranged the chairs in a circle, which seems sensible enough.

"Good. OK. Well, sit down everyone and, Malcolm, can you distribute the texts, please? First allow me to welcome and intro-duce Julie and Rosie from St John's. They're both busy people with 'A' levels coming up in the summer, just like some of you, so I've assured them that this isn't to be a time-wasting operation and that punctuality and full cooperation are the key words." As I then go on to give a brief synopsis of the play I'm not at all sure whether anyone at all is listening. I still have my two fledglings sitting one on either side, and I notice that Malcolm is quick to snatch the place on Julie's other side. As for the rest of them, they merely gawp open-mouthed at the two creatures from another planet. Cowed into momentary silence – unusual for some of them – they let me have my say, and before long we're launched into the preliminary read-through.

Things go smoothly enough even if they're not all fluent readers, some of them certainly aren't in the habit of reading out loud in public. Out of their comfort zone, too, in present company, I think to myself. Some are stumbling over their words (not the girls), others are missing their cues (not the girls), and yet others making precious little sense out of what they say. Julian has a prolonged attack of the hiccups, which causes a certain amount of amusement all round, and Michael, a bit of a buffoon at the best of times, swinging on the back legs of his chair while delivering his lines, finally tips over backwards, crashing to the ground and banging his head on the ra-diator. *Quel idiot!* Otherwise I let the proceedings take their course and we finish reading just before six.

"Well, that's it, ladies and gentlemen. So now you know what it's all about. All parts to be learnt over the holidays ready for the beginning of next term. Performance last weekend in February." Whereupon the session closes, and I gather up my charges and leave the room. Smiles from both girls (so they're OK at least, I think to myself) as we make our way down to my car.

I find none other than Giles Hamilton at the other end of the landing, sitting warming himself on the radiator and clearly waiting for me to be free. The complicity already between us ensures that he realises that he has only to wait a few minutes more while I whisk the girls back to their homes on the other side of town. He leaves it till we reach the bottom of the stairs before letting out an ear-splitting wolf whistle, which of course brings the noses back pressed against the window panes. "Cheeky little devil," I say, half to myself half out loud. Just you wait till I get back. The girls turn to me, only to see that I'm not exactly being serious. Wide grins all round.

Once back I find Giles still sitting on the radiator.

"Giles, have you time for a glass of vino before supper?" Yes, please. And who were those girls then?"

I explain the girls away and square up for the next question. How some of these young kids with their inquisitive minds love to chew the cud. "And shall I tell you what Toby's just told me?" I remember that Toby is one of Giles's inner circle and is in Preshute.

"Yes, go on? Tell me what he's just told you."

"Well, you know that you busted that Preshute lot in the Oddies on Vice Squad last night?"

"Yes, I know."

"They've got a new nickname for you."

"Oh, yes. And what may that be?"

"Janus."

"Janus?"

"Yes, Janus."

"What? You mean…"

"Yes. Two-faced."

Giles is now looking closely for a reaction from me. I don't show any. I'm just thinking they've got both the intellect to know their Roman deities and the perspicacity to choose the name of one of the less appealing among them as a suitable name for me. Janus, guardian of doorways and gates and protector of the state in time of war. Usually represented with two faces, so that he looks both forwards and backwards. Two-faced indeed.

"Giles, look, you'd better drink up. It's 6.30 and time for your supper. Besides, I've got work for tomorrow. Why don't you look up again sometime during the week before the holidays?"

"Yes, OK. How about Friday the day before we break up? For the last episode of the Sartre?"

"Fine, we'll celebrate the end of my first term – if I make it that far. 'They' might want to come and cut off one of my two faces in which case we'll raise a glass to the end of my first and last term."

"No, come on. The first term of a 40-year brilliant teaching career during which you'll rise to the summits.... Headmaster of Eton?" Another of those winning smiles, a tip of the head as he downs the last of the wine – and he's gone.

I instinctively drain my glass – *faire cul sec* – reach for a refill and turn to the desk, where I sullenly rewrite the mis-spelt reports. 'Translate', of course, you idiot. Transfer, transform, transgress, transport, and transmogrify (whatever that bloody means). Bloody languages. Pen down and I look up and out through the window. Pitch black outside and a gentle drizzle falling steadily. Sounds of ferocious activity from the squash courts from across the way. The crack of the ball, the skid of the gym shoe, the squeals of delight and horror from eager participants as they crash around expending all that youthful energy and ardour. I momentarily wonder whether to put in an appearance there. (On appointment I was informed not only that I would be a Resident House Tutor but also Master i/c Squash. Me? Squash? I play the game, but hardly well enough to start telling others how to do so.) On second thoughts, no. I've had enough for today. I'm not even sure I feel like knocking on the HM's door. Hugh would certainly offer me a drink and probably supper too, but right now I really feel like 'getting away from it all'. The trouble is, where to go? Out of College, yes, but even after twelve weeks in harness here I don't know anyone in town well enough to be able to knock on the door unannounced.

The faint ringing of the Porter's Lodge bell tells me it is almost time for Prep. So too the less distant sound of feet on the stairs outside making for the bedsits up above me. Good. All normally quiet in five minutes when I decide to slip out unseen, unheard and down to the local, The Sun Inn, for a quick pint of 6X and the usual steak and egg sandwich.

An empty bar with just John Jones, *le patron*, anchored firmly behind it. I take the settle beside a roaring log fire and, now hungry, soon demolish what he sets before me. I'm already thinking of going when over he comes with a second glass ("One on the house, sir. After all you are quite a good client, you know!") and sits himself down beside me. Cheery, genial, *sympa* – yes, these are the words to describe John. Before long he's chatting away happily, puffing contentedly on his briarwood pipe and perfectly prepared to accept a drink 'on me'. Conversation turns towards the College. "How does it feel then at the end of your first term? Are you fitting in OK? Do you reckon you'll be staying there long?"

I field a battery of questions as best I can, finding it difficult to answer some with any degree of confidence. Then comes what he really wants to say, to the point and without warning. "You know, John, you want to think carefully before staying there too long. You'll get dragged in and get stuck like some of your colleagues. And look what it's done to them. Some of them hardly even step out of the place from one term to the next. Do you know what one of the bachelor Housemasters once said to me? He said, "Do you know, Jones old boy, the only reason why I have to leave College grounds from time to time is to purchase postage stamps at the post office." I mean to say, he's not exactly seen much of the world, has he? Trouble is that you're all too comfortable in there. Waited on hand and foot, fed and watered, next to no expenses."

As I listen to all this I realise he's being serious. "Yes, OK, John, I can see what you're getting at. But maybe I'll stick around here for a couple of years or so and then get myself a job somewhere less cloistered. Don't forget Marlborough is a good first appointment and a good stepping-stone. Maybe, for example, I could go on to teach at a day school in London. What about St Paul's?"

"Ah, yes, that's what you say, but the longer you stay here the more comfortable you'll feel and the less likely you'll be to want to uproot. St Paul's and London, great! But you'll then have to find and pay for your own accommodation, and who's going to clean your shoes, make your bed, clean the sheets, clean the flat, cook for you through the day, fix the plumbing and electricity and so on and so on? All of this you get given free at the moment and the longer you leave it the harder you'll find it to break out of this false paradise."

Les Paradis Artificiels, Charles Baudelaire, I muse to myself as John gets into his stride. But the poet was on about drugs and drink, I seem to remember, and not about a life made easy surrounded by beautiful buildings and intelligent boys. As for the cleaning of shoes, John's right. I'm already well into the habit of having this sort of thing done for me. Ever since the tender age of eight, in fact, when at prep school Old Varney spent his whole working day either stoking boilers or cleaning one hundred and twenty pairs of little boy's shoes. Being a 'fag' at public school came as a bit of a shock when you were having to do the shoe cleaning for the prefects yourself. But the world again eventually found its true colours and little Peter Boardman used to clean my shoes beautifully during my last year at Cranleigh. So too did Mick, my 'skip' at Trinity College, Dublin.

I'm awoken and brought back from my wandering thoughts by a sharp tug on the sleeve. "And anyway, John, answer me this. Marlborough, St Paul's and the like are all very well, but why do you have to go to a 'posh' school? All those hoity-toity people. Why can't you go to an ordinary school, a secondary modern for example, where most teachers go? Answer me that if you can!"

He's looking at me straight in the eye, probing. Good question, I'm thinking to myself and wondering whether to attempt a serious or a flippant answer. "Um, well, yes, good question. I...I..." There's a sudden rattle at the door and in walks Michael Gray, one of the regulars from the town. John looks up, acknowledges Michael, then, still tugging at my sleeve, looks back at me and again straight in the eye. "Well, Johnny Wilkinson, I reckon you should be thinking about these things. Yes, I really do." A friendly pat on the shoulder for me and he's off back behind his bar to cope with a thirsty Michael Gray.

I sit alone for a moment, wondering whether to stay and carry on the conversation. No, on balance. With Michael here too it's going to be two against one and I haven't at the moment got the stomach for that. It's either that or Michael will buttonhole me with his favourite topic of conversation: Where can we get hold of some girls in Marlborough? I don't quite feel up to that either, so I make a discreet exit.

All quiet on the Turner House front as I get back just before the end of prep. The BBC nine o'clock news is about all I'm fit for as well as anything that might come on after. I finish the wine and since there are thankfully no knockings at the door decide to lock up and go for an early night.

Sleep comes, but not easily and not before my mind has exhausted itself on worries in general and then on worries more specific. Tonight, namely, Spelling, Janus and Posh Schools.

Chapter Seven

The Last Week of Term

"You may start now." And one hour later, "Stop writing." Yes, it's the season for exams, not public exams you'll understand (most of those follow in the summer) but merely internal ones, the results of which are of use for re-setting and forecasting in reports to parents.

This means that a lot of us are on reduced timetables during this last week of term, but I realise now that the welcome reduction in classes is more than compensated for by the extra demands these exams are going to make on one – setting exams, invigilating exams, marking exams, recording exam results. This is unfamiliar country for the new beak and I can see immediately I'm going to have to keep my wits about me if I'm going to avoid new pitfalls. Luckily no one has asked me to do any of the setting of the papers – considered beyond the capabilities of the 'new boy' perhaps? – but there seems to be plenty of invigilation and marking for me to do. CR Bin Room becomes a maze of information and it's not always easy to unearth what is relevant to oneself. Where exactly am I invigilating? Who with? Which sets are involved? Do I have to collect the exam papers beforehand? From where? What do I then do with the answer sheets? Send them to the beak(s) who will be correcting them? Which beak(s)? And then what am I correcting?

When will I get the scripts? When do they have to be marked by? Is there a marking scheme? If so, what is it? Where do I have to send the marked scripts? And the results? It's easy to see that one faulty cog in the wheel is more than likely to bring the whole machine to a juddering halt – catastrophic when time is so short. One small slip-up and one could be held responsible for a major cock-up. With these uncomfortable thoughts preying on my mind I manage to negotiate my way through Monday, Tuesday and Wednesday and come through more or less unscathed. Phew!

Tuesday evening finds me with a huge pile of marking spilling out of my bin – quite a depressing sight, frankly. However there's no point in hanging around and I've calculated it's going to mean all Tuesday evening and Wednesday morning at the desk if I'm going to get through it all by the given deadline. Tuesday evening means simply closing the door to all-comers, Giles included. As for Wednesday morning, I'm lucky in not having been given invigilation and I've also seen to it that the two 'A' level classes I should nor-mally be teaching take a 'study period' (i. e. they go back to their studies and study! – rather than come to class and be taught). These should technically be given only to Upper School pupils and when a beak feels that they need the extra time for study before further meaningful progress can be made on the teaching front. Well, that's the theory at any rate, even if the reality is somewhat different. Most times a pupil with a 'stud' will simply go back to his study for another cup of coffee and a chat with whoever's around. ("Bloggs! What are you doing wandering around in the middle of periods?" "Oh, sir, we've just been given a 'stud' by Mr X and I'm going back to house." "Well get a move on then, will you!")

More often than not, I've noticed, 'studs' are given purely for the convenience of the beak concerned. No more, no less. And that's just what I'm going to do to ensure that my scripts are corrected on time, in other words by Wednesday midday. I've also noticed it's best not to let it be known that you're giving these 'studs'. One or two of my colleagues (no names, no pack drill, but we all know who they are!) have got themselves reputations for sending classes away for weeks on end, much to the annoyance of Housemasters who don't relish the idea of 'their' boys permanently padding around the houses when they should be in school being taught. Inevitably someone (The Master?) is eventually going to have to tighten up if the system continues to be abused.

It's a relief to offload the exam marking on time, and I head for lunch in Norwood Hall with a spring in my step. No one had told me that it's the Christmas lunch today – turkey and trimmings with orange juice instead of water on the tables – and there's a merry mood in evidence as I sit down at the head of one of the two Turner House tables. I can see that H de WW has already taken his place at the far end of my table and is engaged in animated conversation with the Head of House sitting to his left. One can never know who will be sitting next to one, since places alternate daily, the idea being that all members of House will have the dubious pleasure of conversing with both Housemaster and House tutor at least three or four times a term. Some cordially detest the idea and conversation can be laboured, to put it mildly. Others take to it like a duck to water and lunch becomes a running commentary on everything and anything. Sometimes I leave the table shell-shocked and wondering at the self-assuredness and *savoir faire* of even some of the little fourteen-year-olds. I think of myself at that age – gauche and bashful, particularly in the presence of adults. To have to sit next to my Housemaster (Major Oswald Francis Tucker, Black Watch, known as Effie) at lunch was nothing less than torture, the more so (as I now realise) in that he was every bit as socially awkward as the shyest of the fifty or so boys in his charge. His 'treat' to his house captains was to take them out to a slap-up cooked Sunday breakfast. Luckily this turned out to be less daunting than one might have presupposed – he simply dished out the Sunday newspapers to all present and not a word was uttered throughout. Musings on the Cranleigh of the past suddenly give way to dealing with Marlborough of the present as the senior prefect sitting at high table on the dais now stands to ring the dining hall bell and deliver his speech of thanks to the steward, the cooks and dining hall staff for their special Yule tide efforts. Speech over and Grace said ("For what we have received may the good Lord make us truly thankful. Amen.") the school files out, table by table, into yet another freezing cold winter afternoon and onward into the various activities aimed at keeping us all busy till afternoon school.

For me it's to be an extra choir practice for Friday's end of term carol service followed by a game of junior house rugby with me supposedly refereeing. I say 'supposedly' because I'm hardly the greatest authority on the rules of the game. Luckily for me I'm sent the 'left-overs' – those not good enough to have been selected for their house teams – and they know even less than I do about the rules of the game. The blind leading the blind, you might say, even though I like to think that I give a pretty good impression of decisiveness on the pitch blowing the whistle with authority. To be honest nobody worries in the slightest whether I blow the wretched thing or not and there's never been anyone actually ask me *why* they've suddenly been whistled up. Just as well. The main thing is, I'm told, that they run around getting exercise for an hour or so and even if they hate it (it's starting to rain again and the wind is sweeping across from the downs above) it's going to be oh! so good for their little bodies and souls.

"Please, sir, can't we stop. It's raining." "Stop bleating, Nikpour, and get stuck into that scum!" Doubly difficult for the likes of Freydown Nikpour being made to thrash around aimlessly in the mud, rain and wind when you come from the balmy southern climes of Teheran. "Come on, whites! Tackle! Tackle that man! And low – not round the neck, Lim, you maniac!" Lim's from Kuala Lumpur, so goodness knows what he makes of it all. As usual the blues are winning – 75 to 3 – and this simply because they have a big fatty twice the size and weight of the others, whose first reactions are to get out of his way fast as he lumbers on unchallenged to score yet again. I do my best to control the Bulldozer with the whistle and by the end more or less resort to blowing it whenever the ball looks like going his way. Accidental off-side! Forward pass! High tackle! Ball in not straight! Handling in the scrum! Knocked forward!" It doesn't matter what – as long as the ball is kept from the Bulldozer. In spite of the rude elements (in spite of myself too) I keep them at it for the full hour.

The one good thing about bad weather is it doesn't encourage spectators on the touchline. Last Wednesday was different and I was all too conscious of a housemaster watching. Just before half-time I'd called for a five-yard scrum. "John, don't you realise that yards are out? It's metres now. We've gone metric since you left school." Shortly after that players from the First XV pass on their way down from practice. Calls of "Sir, aren't you playing the no advantage rule?" and other such remarks calculated to yet further destabilize an already wobbly referee.

The final whistle and they're off dashing down the hill to the showers and afternoon school. I'm following in hot pursuit, but to Turner and a quick bath before CR tea and yes, then back to the classroom for the two afternoon periods.

The first in are the small group of Upper School scientists for their twice-weekly dose of non-specialist English. This is the last session of the term and we're supposedly 'finishing off' Keats with 'Keats and the Romantic Generation' – a prepared talk to be given by Mark Jefferies. These prepared talks have been going much better than I'd dared to expect. People are really coming up to the mark when put on the spot. Mark's contribution turns out to be well up to standard, as I thought it would. He's not only highly articulate but has also clearly done some research on the topic – certainly more than I have and enough to keep us going for the full forty-five minutes. Bless him!

My feelings of gratitude are short-lived, however, and turn to anxiety when I'm asked for next term's syllabus: Robert Graves. "Oh!" says Jefferies chirpily. "Robert Graves. Poetry or prose? Wasn't he great friends with Siegfried Sassoon, sir? You know Sassoon was here at school? I read somewhere that Graves helped save Sassoon from court-martial in the Second World War. True?"

Johnson joins in. "Oh, sir, we were in Majorca in the summer and went to see the house where he lives. Just past where Chopin stayed in the monastery." I'm quick to answer only the first question, Poetry or Prose? "Well, gentlemen, I think we'll do the bird's eye thing on him, don't you? Dip into a bit of everything, you know, if that's OK by you. "OK by them or not, it's far more OK by *me* than having to concentrate exclusively on the poetry, as I've been specifically asked to do. Imagine having to talk on Graves' poetry *for a whole term* when I know nothing about him or it. The very thought frightens me rigid. Impossible. There must be some fiction to help pad things out a bit. If not, the impending Christmas holidays are a foregone washout. And as regards Sassoon and the court-martial, God only knows. The Graves house on Majorca? Again God only knows. These boys really do put one on one's mettle. At least I can preserve some sense of self-esteem knowing, as I do, all about Chopin and the Majorcan monastery. He was holed up there with that saucy George Sand in the winter of 1841 while she was penning her *Un Hiver à Majorque* and wrote his Prelude No. 6 (The Raindrop) while listening to the sound of the falling raindrops mingling with the chanting of the monks floating out from the nearby chapel. If Graves lives nearby he could do worse, I imagine.

Bells ring, big boys leave ("Happy Christmas hols, sir.") Small ones arrive. Yes, it's hello to Shell French Set 6 again, also for the last time this term, *Gott sei Dank!* In they tumble, pushing and shoving, chattering away like monkeys.

"Sir, as this is the last French lesson can we play hangman's noose?" "Sir, have you got our exam papers? Can we have them back?" "Sir, for question 3 Notty wrote the same as me and he's got more marks than me. Not fair, sir." "Sir, how important are the exam results? If we've done well, do we go up a set, sir?" And on and on and on...

Luckily they (like me) are soon tired and chatter subsides of its own accord as I plough on through the exam paper. Protests over marking are thankfully few and half-hearted. I grind to a halt five minutes before time and momentarily wonder what to do with the remaining minutes. A mantle of silence, not imposed by me, has gently descended over us all. It is as if a truce had been called. For these last few minutes at least let's leave each other alone, it seemed to say. As I shuffle my papers I cast an eye over my sleepy charges. What a mixed bunch they are, I can say now that I'm beginning to know them. Our Hon. Friends Humph and Notty at the top of the pile, their Lordships-in-Waiting and already keenly aware of their elevated status (*bottom* of the pile linguistically speaking – are you aware of this, my Lords? *Un*aware and unconcerned, perhaps, for all I know.). The idle Ponsonby snoozing gently as usual. The smug Digby-Jones preening himself, every bit the cat's whiskers, so he thinks. That great slouching lump Molesworth simultaneously picking his fat, turned-up nose and scratching between his legs – disgusting boy. The beautifully brought-up Baveystock, fingertips of both hands delicately placed on the edge of the table, his books neatly piled in front of him. And, yes, Ben Trimble, centre front, curling his long, blond hair with his pencil and just looking dreamy.

"And before you go, your Final Term Order." A gentle stir as I begin to read. "Twenty-third out of twenty-three, Ponsonby." A ripple of titters. "Twenty-second: Molesworth...fifteenth: Digby-Jones ("Oh, sir, I'm sure I did better than that." "Shut up, Digby! *Ferme ta gueule!*" ...fourth: Baveystock...and finally first: Trimble. Well done, Ben." A few muffled boos from the back row and from Molesworth, of course, principally. I let it pass. Bells, and with a 'Happy Christmas, sir' they're off.

Ben lingers. "Ben, you're going up to set 5 next term. OK?"

"Oh, well, yes, sir, but I'd be quite happy to stay down."

"I know, and I'd be more than happy to keep you here. But on balance it's better you move up. It will stretch you more, you see. You need to be stretched, Ben."

"Stretched, sir? I don't think I like the idea of that!" And breaking into a smile, "Why? Do you think I need to be taller? (He pulls himself up to his full height and stands on tiptoe.)

"No, silly, metaphorically speaking. Stretched academically. Besides, you're going to get taller anyway next year whether you *need* to or not and irrespective as to whether you move up a French set or not. And anyway, looking at you now, I don't think putting on an inch or two is that much going to detract from the essential Ben, do you?" Smile turns into laughter. "But I *am* worried about the length of your flowing golden locks. Much longer and you'll be tying a pony-tail and someone is going to say something."

"Someone already has – my Housemaster! Got to get it cut tomorrow!"

"Good!" ('Pity' is what I nearly said. What a pity! What a crying shame to inflict the pudding-bowl short back and sides on such impressive golden locks! A wanton crime against all the laws of aesthetics.) "Good. Just what you need. A short back and sides. The thought stems the laughter. "Oh, sniff, sniff, you sound just like my father now."

I let him go, but only after hearing what I wanted to hear. ("Perhaps I'll have you for French again in the Removes or the Hundreds. Hope so, 'cos I like your teaching.") Funny, I think to myself as he happily trots off and temporarily out of my life, how some teachers can maintain that they never have favourites. Can that be possible? *Never* have a favourite pupil? Unimaginable. I've already got one in every single set I teach and I'm still not at the end of my first term in teaching. Never *show* favouritism, perhaps, but even that seems a bit of a tall order. And anyway aren't the pupils sharp enough to know to a nicety who are the teachers' pets no matter how great the efforts at concealment? Doesn't Shell French set 6 know exactly who the teacher's pet is? Can they not read me like an open book? Yes, of course they can.

It is with such disquieting thoughts in mind that I set back to Turner House and to the Captains' Dinner. These, I gather, take place in all houses during the last week of term when the Housemaster invites the House Tutor (me), the Head of House and House Captains to a formal dinner by way of thanking them for duties done and services rendered through the term. I'm not sure I'm exactly going to enjoy this. The Captains will be clearly on their best behaviour. Dark suits will be worn. I fear most being put on the spot, by whom and in what way I have no idea, but just an unnerving feeling that the new, green and as yet untested House Tutor will be made to 'perform'. Sing for his supper, if you like. Made to squirm, put through his paces. Tested. Found wanting. Not up to the mark...Here I go again, cutting the stick with which to beat my own back... Why, oh why these constant gloomy thoughts revolving around inadequacy and being exposed to ridicule or worse? Stop! Snap out of it, Wilkinson! Get changed and head down to Weldon's well before the others for a couple of his stiff gins and all will be well. Dutch courage – that'll do the trick.

This is precisely what I do, only on approaching the HM's study door I'm met with a sudden, violent burst of laughter rippling out from within telling me that Weldon is already entertaining. The nature of the laughter – more of a shrill, strident shriek than a laugh – identifies the visitor without doubt. It's the highly infectious laughter of the School Librarian, Gerald Murray ('Monkey' Murray to the boys). My entry is greeted by another ringing peel of mirth which has him rocking to and fro in the high-backed chair in which he is sprawled legs kicking up and down in front, arms flailing wildly as another of his hilarious anecdotes is clearly reaching its climax. Weldon (known to Murray and the rest of the 'Old Guard' as The Cat) characteristically retains his composure, allowing himself only the faintest hint of a smile as he secretly savours and relishes the rich flavour of the moment.

On sight of me Murray immediately flings himself out of his chair, the force of his thrust propelling him across the length of the room. "The Lord Wilkinson himself, for the love of Jesus! Splendid!" Half-bowing, half-curtsying, he eventually grasps me with both hands in a dramatic and theatrical show of welcome. "Well, what brings you here, you old bugger? Drink, I suppose!" Followed by another gale of laughter which sees him collapse back into the recesses of his chair, as Weldon, motioning me to sit, places a large gin by my side. "You're all the same these days, you Trinity Dublin men – all of you drunk as lords. In my day we went there to study. You know, books and things. Reading, they call it." Then, peering forward at me, a conspiratorial note of mock-concern in the tone of his voice the loaded question follows. "You *can* read, I presume, can you, my Lord?" A further bout of infectious laughter in which I too am now happy to engage having taken a couple of good pulls at my glass.

Weldon, enigmatic and all-knowing and still the smile. Am I already 'on the spot'? My literacy in question? From Murray this is pure buffoonery. From Weldon, I'm not sure. He keeps his cards so close to his chest. Inscrutable. Sphinx-like. God knows what he thinks of me. Maybe that I don't carry the academic weight? He's a member of the Classical Department – traditionally a snooty lot. To them other disciplines, including Modern Languages, are lesser ones to be looked down upon. A school of the stature of Marlborough is to be judged solely on the number of classical scholarships gained every year to Oxbridge – and to Balliol, preferably – so they think. Until not all that long ago, so I'm told, the College would employ only Oxbridge graduates as beaks. Other universities, including my own alma mater, Trinity Dublin, were considered distinctly under par. Although this is thankfully no longer the case, these conservative instincts still live on in the minds of the likes of Weldon and Murray to mention but two of common room's long-serving charismatic 'characters'.

Gerald Walter Murray arrived at Marlborough from Mill Hill in 1946 to run the PE department, but he's so much more than a PE teacher. Born in Dublin of an Anglo-Irish family, he was sent to TCD/Trinity College Dublin (like me – which is probably why he seems to have taken me under his wing), but had to leave early owing to the family's straitened financial circumstances, thus forgoing the chance to become a doctor. Instead he taught and became a leader in the movement which transformed PT (Physical Training) to PE (Physical Education). After his war service in the RAF he finally gained his degree – in English. The early years at MC were largely devoted to pioneering work on circuit-training and remedial gymnastics and saw the publication of his book *Physical Education and Health*. Then with age came more time in the classroom teaching English and spreading his infectious love for MacNeice, Sorley, Sassoon (all three Marlburians) and Richard Jeffries far and wide. Now in old age he's chiefly to be seen presiding over the Literary Society and running the college library, but is still active enough to indulge his passion for horticulture and can be counted on to pop up from the midst of some herbaceous border or other when least expected, secateurs and wicker basket in hand and dressed in a full-length 'gardening' mac (ie old, torn and dirty), a beaten-up tattered and battered trilby plonked on his head.

One would have taken him for the under-gardener were he not

continually accosting passing boys he knew in those loud and rich tones so redolent of the Anglo-Irish protestant haute bourgeoisie I had known in my Dublin student days. "Ah! Splendid, my dear! And how is my Lord Archbishop on this very merry morning? In the rudest of health, I trust. And top of the morning to you, my Lord!" And this to some grubby, insignificant little boy crawling to school who would then immediately rise to ten feet in stature basking in the glory of the unexpected salutation. His day had been made and he strode out now with the best of them. Why 'Archbishop'? you may ask. Simply because the boy's father happened to be a vicar. Others would receive similarly generous military greetings for similar reasons. "Ah! The Field Marshall, I presume! And I once heard "And may the Good Lord bless Your Holiness!" to the accompaniment of much bobbing of the knee and signs of the cross. And this to one of the few Catholic pupils whose path he had somehow crossed.

Conversation flows, rich and varied. I listen. Glasses are recharged (Murray another La Ina sherry, Weldon's glass, also La Ina, remains largely untouched). I'm feeling much more relaxed. The gin is pumping fast around the system. I hear the faint tones of the first bell for prep (7.25) ringing in the distance. We have but five minutes before the arrival of the Head of House and his six Captains who will almost certainly arrive on the dot of 7.30.

"Well, Cat, I must be leaving you to the delights of your dinner and your splendid young guests. They won't be wanting a withered old orange like me around when they arrive, will they now? I will leave them to the tender attentions of this your lusty young House Tutor (theatrical wink) who will doubtless rise to the challenge of tussling with them over the mahogany. And in true TCD style, I trust, my Lord!"

We all three rise and I help him on with his heavy winter overcoat (high quality), hand him leather gloves, woollen scarf, walking-stick and trilby (not the gardening one!) and hold open the door for his exit. Of course he isn't going to leave without a final *bon mot*. "Well, sir, what is it they say in the Bible?" he asks me impishly jabbing at me in the chest with extended index finger. "I don't know, Gerald, you tell me. What is it they say?" "Ha! Ha! (more jabbing).

They say better be a doorkeeper in the House of the Lord than dwell in the tents of the ungodly. Yes? Yes? You know your Bible, yes?" "Yes, Gerald, but we're not exactly in the House of the Lord here, are we?" "Precisely, dear boy, precisely. So just you think that one out! Ha!" And with a final jab and a flourish he rounds on his heel and has turned the corner. I have only time to close the door, sit down again, take another hard swig at the gin, when further gales of laughter ripple back towards us from the end of the corridor where he has clearly just run into the approaching dinner guests.

Weldon slowly turns his eyes heavenwards and lets out a gentle sigh. "Oh, well, he'll now simply get them all over-excited, but let us fret not. Let me get you another glass." He's right. There are sounds of much merriment arriving from the end of the corridor and I'm suddenly hit by a fit of the giggles. This is pure vaudeville, I think to myself, and I can't help laughing at the thought of Monkey Murray 'entertaining' these startled boys who, once his act started, cannot help but warm to his antics, his wit and humour, his charisma. I try to imagine the body language which is accompanying doubtless yet another of his amusing anecdotes. The waving of hands and walking-stick, the bowing and scraping, the raising and flourishing of the trilby, the nifty footwork, the sparkle in those pale blue Irish eyes. What a character!

The soft knock at the door is on cue. "'trez!" (the HM's highly individualistic form of 'come in!'). and there they are, Turner house's *crème de la crème*, dressed in their Sunday bests and radiating Murray bonhomie from faces flushed by laughter. The evening is clearly getting off to a good start with Weldon dispensing sherry all round and smells of roast lamb emanating from without. "Sir? Is it true that you once beat a boy for drinking a bottle of South African sherry and told him afterwards that you only beat him because the bottle was of poor quality and that had he drunk a quality bottle you wouldn't have minded?"

Weldon purrs. He likes this. These boys sure know how to 'play' their Housemaster. I suppose if they didn't they wouldn't be the Captains now.

At eight o'clock Elizabeth pops her head round the door to announce dinner is served. Weldon motions us to the dining room where a fine spread awaits. "Well, gentlemen, let us not stand on ceremony. Pray take your seats where you will. We shall ask the House Tutor to take his place at the end of the table." I notice that the Head of House immediately takes his seat on the Housemaster's right. Very proper. I find myself with Malcolm Savory (Orpheus – so we can always talk about the play) on the one side and Chris Gillson (a modern linguist – that should be OK) on the other side. Candles flicker gently from their fine Irish Georgian silver candelabras, and gilt-framed family portraits look down from the shadows onto a cornucopia of good food and fine wines. All is mellowness and invites the loosening of tongues.

Weldon gets off to a flying start on one of his pet subjects – girls! It appears that earlier in the term the Master had ended a House-master's meeting with the words "Well, Gentlemen, how about girls for Marlborough? Think about it." This had clearly come as a bit of a bombshell, particularly to the likes of Weldon, and has since inevitably become a matter of intense interest and speculation among the boys. "Sir, is it true that Marlborough is going to get girls?" "Wenches? Wenches at Marlborough? Tosh! All tosh, I tell you. Rubbish! All stuff and nonsense if you ask me."

This gets him going on his anthropological high horse and the talk from the other end of the table is suddenly all about the Yoruba and Ibo tribes of Nigeria and West Africa and how such primitive tribes never countenanced the bringing together of the opposite sexes in their young unless it were for purposes of marriage. "Wenches at Marlborough? Whatever next? It would be like taunting the lions in their cages with meat on the other side of the bars and saying 'Here you are – smell but don't touch!' Really! I've never heard such piffle and bunkum in all my life!"

Hot talk of lions, cages and meat gets the conversation moving up a gear (so does the effect of the wines!) and I find Malcolm at my side dragging me into it too. "Sir, didn't you teach girls in your year out in France?" And before I know it I'm telling him all about Claudine, who was not only a pupil of mine but ended the year as my girlfriend. ("Wow, sir! You mean you were allowed to…?) I have to point out to him that the school in question was an Ecole Normale d'Instituteurs for post-baccalaureat students aged nineteen and above – therefore not exactly 'in statu pupillari' – who, apart from attending lectures at the school, led otherwise totally 'normal' lives living in and sharing flats in town – Nancy in Lorraine – as I did.

"Not like living in the Tutor's flat in Turner then?" "No, not exactly." "Well, who was that girl you were in chapel with last Sunday?" "Sarah John. Ever heard of Augustus John the artist? His grand-daughter." I have the feeling that for as long as we go on talking about girls the conversation will continue to flow freely. Funny, I don't remember ever being that interested in the private lives of my teachers at school. Maybe the times are a' changing? Certainly this generation seems more relaxed with its teachers than I ever was with mine. Teachers, especially the younger ones, now more often seem to be treated more like friends, especially by the older boys. Malcolm here would be a great friend. Handsome, intelligent and articulate. Six years younger than I am. So what? Anyway Giles is already well on the road to being a friend. There doesn't seem to be much harm in that. So far. It's just a bit difficult to know where to draw the lines. Ah well, perhaps with experience…

"Sir, could you please pass the port?" I'm dragged from my thoughts and back into the conversation. Weldon is proposing a toast to me. I manage to make some sort of an impromptu reply on behalf of the guests and before we know where we are, the clocks are striking eleven and the evening is gradually drawing to its close.

Thursday and Friday classes come and go, presenting no great problems. Further exam 'hand-backs', a succession of 'last' periods with no further preps to set, no further marking piling up in the in-tray. Things are gradually winding down after thirteen weeks of pretty solid grind. At last. A couple of choir practices thrown in for good measure to prepare for the carol services on Saturday (for parents and town) and Sunday (for the school). Traditional carol services, of course, livened up with one or two jaunty little numbers by the likes of John Rutter.

Friday evening sees me returning to Turner House after a somewhat extended session in the Sun Inn. (I really am beginning to get a taste for the Wadworth's 6X.) The 7.30 prep bell is ringing as I enter the house. In front of me and blocking my path are two boys sitting side by side on the bottom step of the staircase, the elder of the two with his arm around the shoulder of the younger one. The latter I recognise immediately as Nick Fawkes. He's in the Shell (1st year) and is in Turner. The former is totally unknown to me. Making no attempt to move, he looks at me straight in the eye and somewhat disrespectfully. (Or am I imagining this? What's he doing with Nick anyway?)

"What are you doing here?" "Just talking, sir." (A hint of the impertinent in his voice?)

"Yes, I can see that, but why are you here when you should be in your house for prep?"

"There's no prep tonight, sir. It's quiet time and I've got permission to be out."

(He's quite right about quiet time but this is direct confrontation and the Wadworth's in me doesn't like it.)

"I don't care if you've got permission to be out or not, you've not got permission to be here so kindly get out of my way and remove yourself from the premises, whoever you are." He bridles and I get the look of daggers thrown at me. But still no sign of movement.

"Move!" (I'm shouting now.) "And get the hell out of here before I call the Housemaster!" He now moves but with visible reluctance and still looking me directly in the eye with insolence writ large over his face as he whispers to a somewhat shaken Nick "See you later, Nick".

I now see red. "See him later?" I yell. "You most certainly won't! And I don't want to see you in here ever again either. Got It? OUT!!"

I earn myself another thunderous look and he's gone. I find myself shaking. (Totally out of control – this is not good, I'm thinking.) Nick is still rooted to the spot, pale and wide-eyed, with a few others now lined up behind him doubtless drawn by the general kerfuffle.

"Well, Nick? Who on earth was that?" (I'm fast calming down.)

"Oh, that was Lovell, sir. Toby Lovell from Preshute."

"Ah. A friend of yours?"

He blushes. "Well, sort of, sir." Then the penny suddenly drops and I remember the name. Toby Lovell, oh dear, that's Giles' great friend. The one who told him about Weldon and the baboons in anthropology. The one he now wants me to meet because we'd get on so well.... *merde!* I've gone and put my foot in it now. Just wait till Giles hears about this mega-barney between the two of us.

I'm going to have some explaining to do, and suddenly realise that I won't have long to wait. The last episode of the Sartre is on in half an hour and Giles will almost certainly be up to see it to its conclusion. Nothing for it but to wait and face the guns.

He arrives on cue but thankfully not carrying guns. He seems subdued and I can tell immediately that he knows. Toby has already told all, and in all probability in highly-coloured terms. Giles now clearly prefers not to discuss the matter. Shall I then try and bring it up? Am I then now going to try and excuse the inexcusable? No point. I was over the top and had wildly over-reacted. And anyhow, on what basis am I ejecting some from the house while accepting others? Not good. Two-faced. Janus. So I hold my tongue, feeling somewhat bruised, and we watch the film in more or less total silence. At least it means that for once I'm not being bombarded with questions on existentialism, which allows me some relief.

It's a relief too, frankly, when the titles finally appear and Giles gets up to go. He declines a second glass of wine (unusual). "I've got to get back before House Assembly otherwise they'll know I've been out without permission." Toby gets permission and Giles doesn't. That doesn't bear thinking about much either. Then with mutual mutterings of 'happy holidays' and 'see you next term' he's suddenly gone. I instinctively lock the door, fill the glass, flop back into my chair and half-watch some third-rate stand-up comedian before calling it a day and falling into bed for a largely sleepless night. Janus. Janus.

Saturday and Sunday fly by in a flash. A lot of 'tying up of ends' and administrative chores. Hundreds arriving for the two evening carol services. Trunks appearing in houses and being filled in preparation for a brisk departure on Monday at noon – that is if parents can be persuaded to arrive on time.

Monday morning. Lists for the whole school in the Memorial Hall. This turns out to be a formal address by the Master. I half expect him to talk about the 'wenches', but no, he contents himself with handing out a few prizes (the bulk of these will come at the end of the school year on Prize Day) and making some general announcements. Followed by Chapel for the whole school (a couple of hymns, a reading and a few prayers), followed by forms to Form Masters (admin. matters); the Court is already filling up with parental Volvos and a plethora of dogs of all shapes and sizes (although Labradors still seem to be the flavour of the month), all of which are going berserk at the sight of their little masters whom they had clearly fondly believed lost forever. I cross Court, head for Gates to cross the A4 then to return to house, pack and make a speedy departure myself. A departing green Volvo causes me to pause on the kerb. It is none other than David Hamilton, Giles sitting by his side, older brother in the back. Waves from all three. A broad smile from Giles. I return the wave with a flourish. Good. So perhaps all is still well between us after all. Perhaps I've been forgiven for Friday evening's brutal attack on Toby Lovell. Perhaps? I already realise the doubts over this will now lie on my mind over the next four-week holiday. Doubts about all sorts of things related to this my first term in teaching. Where's it all going to lead to, I ask myself? Some serious soul-searching and perhaps a New Year's resolution or two would seem to be called for. Where do I go from here?

Chapter Eight

A Boy in Kent and Cornwall

Question: What have the following names in common?

William MORRIS *Artist, Craftsman and Socialist*

Field Marshal Sir Evelyn WOOD *VC in Army; later recommended for VC in the R.N.*

The 2nd Lord TENNYSON PC *Governor General of Australia 1902-03*

Allan G. STEEL *Played for England at cricket; inventor of leg break bowling*

The Rt. Rev. WINNINGTON-INGRAM PC KCVO *Bishop of London 1901-39*

Sir Anthony Hopoe HAWKINS *Author of Plays and Novels ("Prisoner of Zenda" etc)*

E. F. BENSON MBE *Novelist, Traveller and Archaeologist*

C. A. ALINGTON *Headmaster of Eton College 1916-33*

Sir Nigel GRESLEY *Designer of locomotive holding the world steam speed record*

Sir Arthur HILL FRS *Director of the Royal Botanic Gardens, Kew 1922-41*

Lord GODDARD of Aldbourne *Lord Chief Justice of England 1946-58*

Reggie H. SPOONER *Played for England at both Rugby and Cricket*

Earl JOWITT of Stevenage *Lord High Chancellor of G.B. 1945-51*

Sir Charles DARWIN MC FRS *Director of National Physical Laboratory*

Lord FISHER of Lambeth GCVO *Archbishop of Canterbury*

Siegfried SASSOON MC CBE *Author and War Poet*

Henry WAKELAM *1ˢᵗ BBC Sports Commentator on both Radio and T. V.*

Charles SORLEY *World War I War Poet*

Sir Edward FELLOWES *Clerk to the House of Commons 1954-61*

Air Marshal Sir Aubrey ELLWOOD DSc OC *Bomber and Transport Commands*

R. J. YEATMAN *Co-Author of "1066 And All That"*

Beverley NICHOLS *Artist and Dramatist*

Sir Francis CHICHESTER KBE *First lone sailor to circumnavigate the Globe*

Lord BROOKE of Cumnor PC CH *Home Secretary*

Lord BUTLER of Saffron Walden CH KG *Foreign Secretary*

Wilfred HYDE WHITE *Film Actor*

Sir George ABELL *Priv Sec to The Viceroy of India 1945*

Sir Ellis WATERHOUSE *Art Historian; Slade Professor of Fine Art at U. of Oxford.*

Professor F. E. CAMPS *Expert on Forensic Medicine*

Sir John BETJEMAN *Poet Laureate*

Gordon WELCHMAN OBE *2 i/c at Bletchley Park in WWII breaking German codes.*

Anthony BLUNT *Art Historian, Russian Spy, Keeper of H. M. The Queen's pictures.*

James Robertson JUSTICE *Film Actor*

Louis MACNEICE *Poet, Author and Radio Producer*

James MASON *Film Star*

Marshal of the RAF, The LORD ELWORTHY *Chief of Defence Staff*

Professor Sir Edmund LEACH *Provost of King's College, Cambridge.*

Lord HUNT of Llanfairwaterdine DSO *Leader of 1st successful Everest Expedition*

Sir Peter MEDAWAR OM CH CBE FRS *Awarded Nobel Prize for Medicine in 1960*

Norman DEL MAR CBE *Author and Conductor*

Sir Alex MOULTON *Designed Moulton Bicycle & hydrolastic car suspension*

The Rt. Rev. J. A. T. ROBINSON DD *Bishop of Woolwich, Theologian and Author*

Sir Peter DAUBENY *Director of the Royal Shakespeare Company 1966-75*

Lord WRIGHT of Richmond GCMG *Head of the Diplomatic Service 1986- 91*

Lord BROOKE of Sutton Mandeville *Secretary of State for Northern Ireland*

Sir Nicholas GOODISON *Chairman of the London Stock Exchange*

Sir Mark TULLY OBE *BBC Correspondent on India*

Bruce CHATWIN *Traveller, Author and Photographer*

Christopher DAVISON (aka Chris de BURGH) *Pop Musician*

Nick DRAKE *Cult Pop Guitarist and Composer*

Answer: They all went to school at Marlborough College.

I found this list in my bin, which I'd gone to clear on the last morning of term before leaving for a well-earned Christmas holiday. Who put it there I've no idea. Maybe that old wag 'Monkey' Murray, the Librarian, who will doubtless find it appropriate that young men like me know a little about the history of the prestigious establishment they are joining. He himself, I'm told, is steeped in it. ("What, you old bugger? Am I to understand you don't even know Chatwin is an Old Marlburian? Darling Bruce, we used to call him. Splendid fellow. Great friend of the Cat, he was.")

It's a list that's going to impress my mother and father, I think to myself, as I leap into the car, swing out of Turner House drive and onto the Old Bath Road en route for South Devon and home.

It's quite an exhilarating moment in spite of the grey skies and the thin rain which has clearly set in for the afternoon. Both map and list are by my side, the former to show me the way back (I'll take the same road I used to come up on at the start of term – Salisbury, Blandford Forum, Exeter) and the latter I'll glance at from time to time and try and work out perhaps what it is that all these men may have in common apart from, that is, having attended the same school. Are there characteristics, qualities and virtues which bind these people together? Do they all show the MC 'stamp'? Are they all 'staunch and stalwart-hearted', the qualities extolled in the School Song? What is it that allows one school to produce a 'top' list of alumni like this and another not? Good teaching? The ethos? High quality intake? A bit of all three and more perhaps? But what strikes me most is the varied fields in which these former pupils have excelled. It's all there. The state, church, law, diplomatic, military and the world of literature all amply represented apart from much else. I shudder to put up Cranleigh for comparison. No comparison to be made. Marlborough – prestigious. Cranleigh – a mediocre school turning out mostly mediocre products.

Not to say that I blame my parents for the choice of schools they made for me. They clearly believed they had acted in my best interests, I suppose, added to which they had personal connections with both my prep school and Cranleigh. My prep school, Carn Brea in Bromley, Kent, had been billeted to Cranleigh during the war and my father, the Chaplain and a Housemaster there at the time, had got to know H.J.O. Marshall, the Carn Brea Headmaster. He and his school duly returned to Bromley, Kent at the end of the war and it was there I was sent to start my formal education at the tender age of eight. A late start, you may think. Correct. My father having suffered a serious mental breakdown was forced to resign from Cranleigh (my mother has never forgiven the Headmaster, The Reverend DG Loveday, for his harsh treatment of a man who was sick through no fault of his own) and was found a quiet parish 'away from it all' in which to recover his health. The parish in question was the island of Tresco, Isles of Scilly, whose local school was not considered suitable for the likes of my brother and me. We were therefore accordingly educated privately and tutored individually in the vicarage at the top of the hill by both our parents, my father maths and scripture and my mother more or less everything else. I remember very little about these lessons and a lot more about running wild all over the island playing and exploring during the full extent of our two year stay there. Cromwellian castles, deserted beaches, dark coastal caves lashed by the fierce Atlantic seas, exotic plants in the sub-tropical gardens of the Abbey, home to the island's owner Major Arthur Dorrien-Smith (known to all as 'The Major'). This was our playground, extended frequently by visits to other neighbouring islands. Birthday picnics on Samson, rabbit shoots on the Eastern Isles, fishing for pollack in the choppy waters off Round Island, the rock on which stood the lighthouse, whose gloomy foghorn punctured our lives during the winter months when mist swirled and curled around us and our island for sometimes weeks at a time.

A launch would gingerly take us out to this rocky and danger-ous outcrop once a month when my father administered the Holy Sacrament to the three plucky lighthouse men who manned their post day and night three hundred and sixty-five days of the year. Talk about devotion to duty. Another favourite outing was to row father across the narrow strait that separates Tresco from Bryher, also part of the parish and where he was required to say Evensong from time to time. Brother Mark and I would take an oar apiece and thrash our way across the shallow waters, erratic, at times wildly off course, rowlocks and sometimes oars sent flying, crabs caught, with father clinging on in the prow, issuing prayerful instructions to his chaotic crew, fending off approaching sandbanks as best he could, a commanding figure of a captain but dressed in black from head to foot, cassock and cloak with a Breton beret to top it all and with only the white of his tabs fluttering in the gentle breeze to stand out in stark contrast.

There would be times when we ran aground, or were pulled completely off course by unexpected currents, or were practically blown back from whence we came by strong winds. At such times the tinkling little Bryher church bell would continue to ring, to en-courage, while the tiny congregation (most of them called Jenkins) would stand at the end of the jetty waiting and watching to see if the vicar was going to make it or not this time. Most times we did, even if there was sometimes much amusement caused at our expense. We were to learn later that soon islanders were bringing binoculars with them to Evensong so as better to be able to appreciate the antics of their vicar and his two young boys in midstream. Possibly with a view to sending out a rescue boat if need be?

These were veritable Robinson Crusoe days filled with the Boy's Own experiences any child would relish. And relish them we did. The white sands of Pentle and Appletree bays, deserted but for two little boys scampering and splashing around in the rock pools. The beauty and variety of the sea shells. The early daffodils, a sea of yellow swaying in the spring breezes. The early morning walk to the farm to fetch the milk, little tin milk can swinging at my side. Scrambling up the hill to watch the *Mauretania* sail by for a last time, ("Look, John there she goes, that four-funnelled leviathan, on her way to the breaker's yard. Don't forget her, will you?" "No, dad, I won't"), sitting on an oak beer barrel at the end of the jetty having my hair cut by Willie Howard, the Major's boatman. These are the memories, strong ones even to this day, of a happy seven-year-old full of the joys of life and living. Idyllic.

But the idyll was not to last. Do they ever? My father had a serious relapse and was told he would have to get treatment on the mainland. He didn't like the idea and became violent. Memories of his shouting and my mother's crying cast a dreadful and dark cloud over this episode of my life. Eventually Willy Howard and three strong fishermen were called to the vicarage to take him away by force, leaving a tearful mother to explain the meaning of the word 'sectioned' to her two bewildered little children. He was being compulsorily committed to the psychiatric hospital in Bodmin, Cornwall in accordance with a section of the Mental Health Act.

It is only quite recently that I learned from my mother why he had been so reluctant to leave for psychiatric help. It was because he knew he would again have to endure the horrendous electric shock treatment which at the time was the standard medical 'care' issued to patients with mental health problems. He was away for months and for a time that seemed longer than months to me, while my courageous mother soldiered on as best she could educating and providing for her two children, waiting and praying for the day of his return.

The next departure from the family and island – and no less traumatic – was to be mine. It was my father, now returned and restored to health again, who took me aside one day and explained that now that I was fast growing up to be a big boy it was time for me to go off to school to be properly educated. Enter Carn Brea School and that monster headmaster H. J. O. Marshall into my life. My mother was definitely not keen on the idea that her first born was suddenly to be whisked away from her and family for months on end at what she considered to be a ridiculously young age.

I should at this stage perhaps explain that my mother is Dutch and therefore has sensible ideas on how best to bring up a family.

These certainly do not include the sending away of young children to boarding schools for periods of up to ten years, thus effectively driving an artificial wedge between parents and their children during the most formative period of children's lives. In Holland everyone goes to local day schools. It's more 'natural', she would always say. Unfortunately for her local day schools were few and far between, stuck out on an island in the middle of the Atlantic as we were. So my father prevailed. "That's how *we* do it in England, Ponnie." There was not much my mother could do about it. Preparations for my departure were already being made weeks ahead of the day itself.

Mother muttered darkly on discovering that the school uniform –obligatory – could only be bought from Harrods and at great expense. Hours and hours she spent over the weeks sewing Cash's nametapes – name and school number – onto every conceivable item of clothing. A trunk was produced from the attic – my father's old trunk from his days at Oundle and Peterhouse, Cambridge –and it was gradually filled with the required kit, my mother meticulously ticking off the items on the Clothing List provided by matron. The trunk was sent a full two weeks before I was to be sent myself (PLA– passenger luggage in advance).

The fatal day arrived in early September 1950. Passenger – me – was due to depart. It meant an early rising. It meant a final rehearsal of travel instructions which had already been much rehearsed. Two things strike me as strange now that I look back on these times seventeen years later. Firstly, that an eight-year-old can be sent off virtually on his own to make a journey from the Isles of Scilly to Kent. Secondly, that nobody thought to say "Don't speak to strangers, John dear." Nobody said that, so I was perfectly happy to speak to the few strangers I met on this first lone journey of mine out into the big wide world.

Scarcely had dawn arrived when the Major's gig arrived, Willie Howard with reins in hand. The gig or trap – a light two-wheeled one-horse carriage – was the only form of transport on the island. The motor-combustion engine was unknown. Stiff upper lip farewells were exchanged (Father a firm handshake, Mother a kiss), and

I climbed up beside Howard clasping my overnight case close to my bosom. 'Giddy-up' and off we went, bound for the Major's private jetty where his little motorised yacht was ready to skim me across the waters to St. Mary's, the main island, where I took my leave of Howard. "Good luck, Master John. Come back again soon."

There awaiting me by the harbour side was the taxi ordered by my father, in which I was whisked up to the airfield – field it was, with one solitary Nissen hut – where the nine-seater short-haul de Havilland was already preparing for take-off, propellers turning and whirring. I was swiftly identified, and being the only child passenger I was unceremoniously bundled into the single back seat and told to keep an eye on the luggage the other passengers had brought with them and which they now deposited in a great pile by my side before hauling themselves up into their seats at the front.

Within minutes we were wobbling our way to the far end of the field, where we turned about and now with full throttle prepared to charge at full speed the cliffs at the very end of the airfield. Full speed has never felt so slow, and I was terrified. We eventually left the ground however within feet of the cliff edge, and there suddenly below threatened the angry and heavy swell of the Atlantic Ocean beating mercilessly on the jagged rocks of an unforgiving coastline. We were beaten and buffeted by the winds above the seas below and clearly made some sort of forward movement before we could eventually make out the land ahead of us – the equally frightening (as far as I was concerned) cliffs of Land's End, towards which we hurtled crazily and managed to clear with only a few feet to spare before bumping down and jolting along to a sudden and juddering halt. Phew!

I left the contraption feeling more than a little drained by my first flight and more or less fell straight into the arms of my next challenge of the day – my Universal Aunt No1. The Universal Aunt phenomenon had been carefully explained to me by my parents. These were kindly little old ladies who volunteered to escort young children on journeys when their parents were otherwise occupied. Such was my case, and I was to be extremely polite to these pub-lic-spirited old biddies, who asked not a penny for their troubles.

Off to Penzance Station, where the Paddington train was wheezing and awaiting the green flag. Little old Auntie U. did a great job guiding me to the right carriage, right compartment and right seat, where she helped to install me and my overnight case on the luggage rack above, too high for me to reach. She then introduced herself and me to the only other occupant of the compartment, a little old man sitting by the window reading a book, telling him that I was travelling alone and was to be met at Paddington by Auntie U. No. 2 and would he kindly keep an eye on me and my case. Lots of smiles and nods and another departure embrace for me from the kindly old biddy, who smelt horribly of rotten old mothballs.

The train, having got up steam, pulled out of Penzance station, whistles blowing and steam billowing from the funnel. We were on our way to London town and further fields afresh. *What larks!* I thought to myself, remembering Pip and the Dickens my father had been recently reading me and now beginning to feel a little more at ease ensconced in the comfort of a first-class carriage. The journey was for the most part uneventful. The Devon coastline was beautiful. Exeter St. David's came and went. People got on and got off. The little old man briefly broke off his reading to offer me two blocks from his bar of chocolate which I graciously accepted, never having been told not to take sweeties from strangers. He later helped me retrieve my case from the luggage rack; in it were the chicken sandwiches, apple and two biscuits prepared for me by my mother.

It was early evening by the time the train panted into Paddington. I found myself, name card – Master J. D. Wilkinson – hung around my neck, on a platform seething with humanity. Never in my short life had I seen such a concourse. I was swept along to the platform gates and, bewildered, stood there rooted to the spot, as instructed, waiting for the next onslaught of mothball. It wasn't long in coming. She swept down on me, propelled me towards a waiting taxi, and before I knew where I was, we'd reached Charing Cross and I was on the next train to Bromley. I dozed off to a fitful sleep.

Darkness had fallen by the time I stepped out onto the platform. I spotted the under matron before she saw me, her stiffly starched blue and white uniform standing out clearly against a dimly-lit station platform. Within ten minutes I was not only at the school but also being shown to my bed in a darkened dormitory where the other seven occupants were either already sleeping or were trying to do so. As I climbed into bed, curled up into a tight ball and prepared to spend my first night ever away from home and parents, I thought I heard a suppressed whimper.

Next day brought with it more matrons, breakfast and a dollop of extract of malt after breakfast, followed by assembly for the whole school. One hundred and twenty boys aged between eight and twelve trooped into the gym to hear a welcoming address from the Headmaster, H. J. O. Marshall. So this is my father's friend 'Pud', I thought to myself as he strode in to take his place in front of the assembled congregation. 'Pud' for pudding. At least that much was now clear, I mused, as I observed the vast girth of the man. Thick, heavy tortoise-shell glasses, a booming voice and intimidating with the volume raised. First the school prayer ('Forgive us, O father, for the wrong things we have thought, spoken or done this day...' I can recite it even today by heart), followed by a welcome to each of the twelve new boys. My name, beginning with a 'W', I was the last to be introduced. "And last but not least – Wilkinson. Stand up, Wilkinson. Wilkinson comes from the Scilly Islands." (Sniggers all round. Oh, yes – 'Silly' Islands, of course. He should have said Isles of Scilly, even I knew that.) "And he's going to need your help, because where he comes from they don't know about cars." Further sniggers and the blood rises to my cheeks. "So when you see him near a road I want you to give him a hand across. Is that fully understood?" A murmur rises from the serried benches. "Sit down now, Wilkinson."

Such was the unpromising start of my first day at school. Being made to feel different, to feel a fool. Life in the classroom was to follow much in the same pattern with my end of term reports not offering much in the way of promise. If I was a pupil who showed little promise, all I can now say in my defence is that here was a school that failed miserably to instil any spark of enthusiasm in me for anything, be it in the classroom or on games fields. I sat through my lessons uninterested and unconcerned. The games I took part in, but only half-heartedly. In boxing I managed more or less to hold my own, but that was merely the instinct for survival. Hit out hard or be hit, a simple enough philosophy to adopt until the day I was drawn to box against my best friend, Silbiger, in the house competitions. Even at this early age I was becoming aware of the tribal nature of so much of what passes under the name of sport. Give all, fight to the death for the house, the team, the club, the country. Kill the enemy, even if he is your friend. So I was forced to fight Silbiger and was jeered from the ropes by teachers and pupils alike for not going in 'hard'.

In the classroom things got worse in the third year when I first came up against 'Pud' for Latin. His reputation went before him and I knew this was going to be no doddle. Each lesson of his started with recitations of the 'Fives', the five verbs he had selected the previous lesson to be learnt by heart, all parts included (present, past and future tenses, passive, present and past participles, gerunds and gerundives – it was endless). Woe betide the boy who was unable to recite these verbs faultlessly if asked. The fear in the room was palpable, the wrath ferocious.

I had already twice personally experienced the wrath of Pud, but in a different context. One day I was in the lavatories having a pee and standing next to Frampton who happened to be there too when for some unaccountable reason I suddenly grabbed his fountain pen from out of his top breast pocket and ran round into the nearest cubicle, where I proceeded to fling it in and flush it down the loo. Frampton was understandably not best pleased by this totally unprovoked attack on his property – for all I know this was an expensive and treasured birthday present I had so uncouthly wrested from him –and ran off tearfully to 'sneak' on me to none other than the Headmaster, into whose presence I was immediately and summarily delivered.

I hadn't even time to be frightened before the great ogre grabbed me by the collar, forced me down over the arm of the nearest chair, ripped down my trousers and pants and thrashed me on the bare buttocks – six of the best – with his well-worn leather slipper. And all this to the accompaniment of growls from the perpetrator – "This had better teach you a lesson, you vile boy" – and high-pitched yelps of pain from the victim. Fear prior to the assault was never really allowed the time to set in. Shock, however, utter shock at what had just happened to me, set in instantly as the study door was slammed on me and I was left a trembling wreck to consider the implications of the first savage physical attack I had ever experienced. No home to run to, no mother's arms to enfold one. Just a snivelling little ten-year old crouching alone in the corner of an empty classroom. Corporal punishment must work. I've never since flushed anyone's pen down a loo.

My second unfortunate brush with Pud occurred the following summer when the South of England was experiencing a rare and extended heat wave. It was impossible to sleep at night, such were the temperatures. Damp sheets stuck to perspiring, tossing and turning little ten-year-old bodies. My bed happened to be the one nearest the door, where fifteen little dressing-gowns were neatly hanging on their hooks. My idea was a simple one. I firstly removed the cords from their dressing-gowns, tied them end to end, then attached one end of the rope – quite long it was – to the bed-head above me before taking it down to the bedstead at the foot of the bed, wrapping it around and thence back up to the bed-head again. This, completed several times, produced a rope frame over which I then threw my top sheet, leaving me lying under a tent-like construction and free from contact with a damp and unpleasant sheet which had seriously prevented sleep.

I had just the time to congratulate myself and was already looking forward to the prospect of a better night when suddenly the door was flung open and the lights brutally switched on. I immediately sensed Pud. Not that I could actually see anything – my tent flaps were down. However my worst suspicions were confirmed when I smelt the whisky and heard the heavy breathing. (The poor man had to make it up three steep flights of stairs if and when he wanted to check his upper dormitories and his weight saw to it that he was always badly out of breath by the time he had made it.)

"Well, boy, what's this going on here then, may I ask?" he

boomed, in tones calculated to awaken the dead, let alone those in the dorm who had been sleeping or trying to sleep.

"Well, boy?" (volume up and sheet now pulled off violently from above me revealing one terrified child squinting up at the Monster and the glaring lights behind him.) "What's the meaning of all this then, Wilkinson? Come on, explain yourself, boy!"

Whatever the explanation ("Sir... the heat... I couldn't get to sleep... the sheet...") it was offered heavily interspersed by sobs and snivels while all the time, grunting and growling, Pud tore at my oh-so-cleverly conceived structure and eventually dismantled the whole contraption. He then gathered up the cords, reduced them to an intertwined and knotted whip, grabbed me by the scruff of my neck and threw me over the bottom bedstead. And after another "This had better teach you a lesson, you vile boy" I was soundly thrashed – six of the best again – with the fifteen dressing-gown cords I myself had so carefully knotted together, little suspecting the use to which they were to be put. Same scenario. No home to run to. No mother's arms to enfold one. Just a little ten year-old boy lying in bed, foetal position, crying himself to sleep. Corporal punishment must work. I've never since knotted dressing-gown cords to create myself a tent over my bed. Never!

Thoughts and memories of my Carn Brea past fade as I give closer attention to the road ahead and heavy Christmas traffic. I've been making good progress and there's not much on the roads. However I'm now approaching Tidworth and have hit the tail end of some sort of military convoy – lorries and armoured vehicles probably returning from exercise on Salisbury Plain. South of Tidworth I'll be joining the A303 and from then it's a straight run down to Exeter and home beyond. No further need of the map by my side. I give my list of Old Marlburians a quick glance and the name Fisher catches my eye. A former Archbishop of Canterbury. That should impress the vicar, my father.

Once through Tidworth the road is again straight and empty. and my thoughts turn back again down through the years. It would be wrong of me to suggest that my prep school days were nothing other than doom and gloom. The happy memories I connect with free time and the weekends. In the summer we were allowed off into the bushes and woods surrounding the playing fields and it is here that we would build 'camps' – African straw hut style – out of branches and the long grass. This done we would then canter off to a nearby pit where we would gather up as much sticky clay as possible to take back to camp. There we would fashion the clay into golf ball-size-and-shape clumps and stockpile huge quantities to be used as missiles to be hurled at the end of swishy sticks, or used as grenades when attacking 'enemy' camps. Camps were trashed, little tempers flared, cuts, bruises and torn clothes were the norm in spite of matron's repeated protestations (were we unwittingly preparing the scenario for *Lord of the Flies?*) These were indeed fun times and firm bonds of friendship were forged in the heat of the moment and the stout defence of one's territory.

It was one day during such a foraging expedition to the clay pit that I stumbled on five or six of the older boys standing in a group near the edge of the wood bordering on the Sundridge Park golf course and on the very extremity of the school grounds. They were standing in a semi-circle with their attention clearly held, so I remained unnoticed by them as I crawled up closer in the long grass to get a better look. You can imagine my surprise when I realised that the object of the rapt attention of the assembly was none other than Rice-Oxley, who, standing in front of his audience, had boldly pulled his trousers down and was happily engaged in 'massaging' his pert little penis, to the apparent utter bemusement of those viewing the spectacle. (I say 'massaging' because I was still a year away from knowing the meaning of the word masturbation and was blissfully unaware of what the purpose of his 'massage' was.) Had Rice-Oxley been allowed to complete his exhibitionist task I would have doubtless learnt a lot there and then and my sex education would have been well and truly on the launching-pad. But it was not to be. Just as Rice-Oxley was hotting up, a missile in the form of a golf ball came winging its way through the air and struck ground just in front of a doubly bewildered Rice-Oxley. Self-preservation took precedence over self-pleasure and he ran for the shelter of the trees, hitching up his trousers as best he could as he went and followed by an audience which was doubtless disappointed through having had the performance artificially cut short. From my vantage point I was able to witness two golfers from the Sundridge Park golf club vainly thrash around looking for the lost ball. I could have told them exactly where it was but didn't.

The Rice-Oxley incident got me thinking. I was intrigued, even if I wasn't making much sense of it all. Not that seeing naked boys was a big deal. Games were always followed by romping and splashing around in a great communal bath taking ten or so at a time. But there were boys – two in particular – towards whom I felt being drawn. Nothing overtly sexual, but certainly a physical attraction. Hodder-Williams, who ended up being senior prefect and winning a major scholarship to a major public school. Clearly others thought he had qualities too. And Brett Jones, who shone on the games fields and was generally rated by all and sundry for that reason. Not by me. I rated him solely on his good looks and was totally indifferent to his prowess on the cricket field or wherever, even if I was learning at this early age and to my chagrin that gamesmanship is, at least during one's schooldays, a sure passport to success and admiration. (Poor Betjeman, Blunt and the Aesthetes at pre-war Marlborough College. How they must have suffered at the hands of the cocksure rugby elite.)

Confirmation of this simple fact of life was there for all to see at the annual prize-giving on Sports Day. Most of the prizes, most years, were won by Newsome. "Oh! Isn't he wonderful," Pud's wife would coo in the ears of the proud, preening parents. "Just wonderful! We've never had a boy like him. And how mature he is for his age. Do you know, I do believe he reminds me of James Mason to look at. What a handsome young man he will surely be!" Such gush. Stupid woman. Of course he was mature, of course he won all the races and charged through the defences on whatever games pitch you put him. He was simply twice as big, twice as heavy as anyone else around. It was a doddle. Pig-shit thick to boot and he walks off – again! – with the prize of all prizes, not only the Victor Ludorum Trophy but all the adulation that goes with it – and all that without so much as lifting a finger. Unfair! I protest to myself and unheard.

We lesser mortals are beginning to learn some of the harsh truths of life as we struggle to prepare ourselves for the yet harsher realities of life at our next school. Maybe there, however, even the Newsomes of this world will have to climb down and start on another long haul up. There would at least be some justice in that.

Happy moments, too, I associate with the musical life of the school even if, as I now realise, it was fairly restricted. I made a bamboo pipe and joined a pipe band. I had piano lessons from Mrs Halstead and got on reasonably well – well enough to be asked to play the hymn at the service of Compline held on Sunday evenings. This was a mixed blessing. I would sit at the keyboard in front of the whole school waiting for my moment to strike up with 'Abide with me' or some such suitable evening hymn. But I was terrified both of this unaccustomed exposure to playing in public (would I hit fistfuls of wrong notes and then grind to an ignominious halt in the middle of it all?) and also of Pud standing right behind me breathing whisky fumes down my neck while growling his way through the prayers. "Brethren, be sober (hypocrite!), be vigilant because your adversary the devil, as a roaring lion, walketh about, seeking whom he may devour..." The end of Compline would invariably find me in a right old state, nervous exhaustion brought on by stage fright and terrifying thoughts of drunken headmasters, devils and roaring lions in my mind.

The best musical times, however, were those when the whole school assembled to sing through a vast repertory of community songs, everything from *The Vicar Of Bray* to *My Bonnie Is Over The Ocean* and from *The British Grenadiers* to *Oh No John*. From *Londonderry Air* to *Bound For The Rio Grande*. And then, of course, to end it all off and as a grand finale, *Jerusalem* and *Auld Lang Syne*. One hundred and twenty boys packed tight sitting on the wide sweeping staircase which led up from the hallway in the main house – Pud's quarters – with the teachers sitting in the stair-well and Mr Hallward bashing out the tunes with embellishments aplenty. And oh! the singing! It had to be heard to be believed. Every little lung singing and stretched to bursting; inspirational it was. Well, to me at any rate. I loved it. And more than anything else that school had to offer, which wasn't much. No, very definitely I was not inspired by Carn Brea School, Nr. Bromley, Kent. Very definitely, not a prestigious school.

Chapter Nine

Cranleigh

Enter Cranleigh School, near Guildford, Surrey – a minor (so I had been recently reminded by that pompous twat Digby-Jones of Shell French set 6) Public School taking in between five and six hundred teenage boys. Not for me the big hitters like Eton, Winchester or Marlborough. Prestigious schools like these took only the best of the Common Entrance candidates, in whose ranks I was clearly not to be found. The person chosen to replace Pud in my life was to be Major Oswald Francis Tucker, my housemaster and formerly of the Black Watch. If Pud had not exactly been the sort of man a young boy would naturally want to snuggle up to, neither was 'Effie' Tucker. However let's remember that he wasn't chosen as someone to be snuggled up to, but because he (as with Pud) had been friends with my parents when my father had been Chaplain and a Housemaster at the school.

As a housemaster, Effie was always going to be a fairly distant figure in the life of the boys under his 'care'. Firstly because the house was effectively run by the Head of House – a school prefect – and a clutch of house captains, and secondly because Effie was excruciatingly shy and naturally enough avoided contact wherever and whenever possible. A confirmed bachelor, he was particularly ill at ease in the company of the opposite sex. He positively squirmed, blinking owlishly behind his thick horn-rimmed glasses, twitching and fidgeting nervously as a more than stilted attempt at conversation was made. Even at the best of times he was gruff in speech and monosyllabic. He taught Greek and Latin. Badly. Altogether he was a somewhat frightening figure to all and sundry, and even to Jill, his timid Welsh collie dog who would silently and nervously pad around after him at all times of day and night.

The only one who seemed undaunted by him was his beloved Lucy, a sturdy hunter and clearly an animal with a mind of her own. We boys would witness a battle of wills when once a year the local Hunt met in front of the school and Effie, in the saddle and fully kitted up, had the greatest difficulty keeping his place and dignity while a boisterous animal beneath him, bucking, snorting and pawing the ground, was clearly determined to show who was master. Much sherry was slopped in the process before the Hunt eventually moved off with Tucker bobbing up and down like a sack of potatoes on the back of his unruly mount. We loved it.

Starting life at a new boarding school at the tender age of thirteen is not unlike starting aged eight, except that it is worse. Far worse. The thirteen-year-old is thrust under the same roof as the eighteen-year-old, who is both physically fully mature and, in the eyes of the thirteen-year-old at least, a creature of a weight and authority as yet unknown to him. Clearly a creature to be feared.

The Head of House, always a Prefect, exerted power over the entire school, the Captains within the confines of the house only. Both power and privileges were far-ranging. Prefects and Captains alike chose their 'fags' from the most recent intake of new boys. 'Fagging' for your Prefect meant making his bed, cleaning his shoes, running errands, making the coffee and, worst of all, cleaning his CCF (Combined Cadet Force) kit before the weekly parades, buffing the boots and blancoing the belt and ankle webbings to the high standard required. Fall short of that standard and you were certainly in for the high jump and possibly for one of a range of punishments those in authority could and would wield at the slightest provocation.

Most feared of these was a beating from the Head of House.

These beatings had to be carried out in the presence of a witness whose job it was to see that the bamboo cane was not raised above shoulder-level before it came crashing down onto the buttocks of the miserable offender. Punishments worse than these were beatings by either Housemaster or Headmaster and the final punishment and the greatest indignity of all: expulsion. For the more minor indiscretions a range of lesser punishments was available, for example having to learn by heart and recite a poem or one of the Psalms. Having to get up early and being made to sweep the house classroom, to clean the brass of the hinges and knobs of the lockers – or indeed the urinal and shower-room brass – such were the common day-to-day punishments dreamt up by those in authority and dished out liberally to deserving and undeserving juniors alike. To object, protest, complain – unthinkable. To grin and bear it was the only possible way through.

Dodging one's way through the strict discipline and a maze of punishments was one thing, keeping the peace with one's teachers in the classroom was another matter not to be taken lightly either. Not that classroom standards were set particularly high. I soon found that with the minimum effort it was possible to 'get by', and one had to be really very stupid or idle to incur the wrath of the teacher and extra work. Here again, as at Carn Brea, I failed to be ignited either by my teachers or by the subjects they taught. I merely drifted and dreamed my way through literally hundreds of hours of lessons and tuition, becoming only marginally concerned at the approach of public exams, when the teachers would darkly predict failure and ignominy for those failing to take their work more seriously.

The only lessons I now remember are those in which we had fun. Mr Craik's French lessons when we'd keep tally on the number of times we had made him say "don't annoy me, boy!" The Rev. Desmond ('Dai') Evans' Scripture lessons when this fiery little Welshman would literally explode with fury when wound up by pupils bored with the Acts of the Apostles and looking for a bit of light relief. Mr Pat 'Muggsy' Maguire's English lesson on the day when some wag decided to 'doctor' his desk set up high on a dais at the front of the classroom. This fine and heavy piece of furniture, on which were displayed dictionaries, works of reference, inkwells, blotters and a host of other articles, had four sturdy legs with swivelling castors set in four cupped wooden blocks to prevent them rolling. 'Doctoring' the desk simply meant removing the wooden blocks from under the castors so that they were free to roll. Since the perpetrator of the joke knew – we all knew – that Muggsy was frequently in the habit of swinging on the back legs of his chair then propelling himself forwards, hands outstretched to meet the front of the desk with the full weight of his body behind them, he correctly calculated the dramatic consequences that the removal of the blocks would almost certainly have.

The stage is set, Muggsy enters and the class follows his every movement with rapt attention. He spends the first five minutes cruising up and down the aisles between the desks. He then takes up position by the windows for a further five minutes. He then gravitates towards the dais, which he finally mounts fifteen minutes into the lesson. The tension rises. Will he now sit down at the desk? No. He continues to stand, talking. He's then turning to the blackboard – writing. He turns back round with a flourish and a billowing of his gown. He's now up against the desk, his thighs surely applying the pressure needed. Tension up another notch. But the castors, poised a mere quarter inch from the edge, refuse to roll. At last he takes to his chair. His lecture is over and he's now taking questions. He's clearly in a good mood, the class is unusually well-behaved and attentive. Up to us now to ask the question that will have him rocking in his chair. Eventually it comes and, yes, he's rocking. Another amusing question and he's really rocking now, in full swing. Tension at breaking point with only four minutes of the lesson remaining. One knockout question now and he'll be propelling himself forward to the inevitable climax to the last forty minutes. It happens just as the bell rings. Pandemonium as desk, Muggsy and all come crashing down into the front row, books flung far and wide, papers strewn to the four winds, ink bespattering the boys nearest to the scene of the disaster. By the time Muggsy extricates himself from it all, the class has scarpered. Guffaws ring down the corridors and through the courts as we relish this most memorable of all English lessons.

No such fun to be had in Lovell ('Shovel') Garrett's History lessons, during which we spent most of our time and energy trying to avoid his own highly individualistic form of chastisement. This involved selecting a victim – usually a comely boy – grabbing him with the one hand by the scruff of his neck, forcing the head down into his crutch and locking it in between two strong thighs, then with the other hand walloping him on the bottom as many times as he saw fit.

Close physical contact with one's teachers– too close for comfort – could also be a hazard to be faced during music lessons. Being shut in a room alone with a teacher known for liking to 'get close' to his pupil could be tricky. My own piano teacher, Warren ('Bunny') Green was a case in point. He would snuggle up close on the shared piano stool, stretch out one hand in front of me pointing to the music while with the other hand support himself on the back of the stool and just where, of course, my buttocks were supporting me...I would shuffle forward and the wandering hand would follow. Most times I would end up perching on the very edge of the front of the stool in my attempts to escape the unwanted contact, but the hand was never very far behind and my attention was continually being diverted more than a little from the music I was supposed to be studying. ('Bunny' probably had an easier time with the rugby fifteen – he somehow managed to get himself appointed team masseur!)

Not that *all* physical contact was unwanted. Far from it. Mr Comberlege's Latin classes, for example, took place in a room where we sat squeezed up on long benches at long tables and many were the happy, little hands that 'wandered' beneath the table while Mr C. droned his way through Ovid's Metamorphosis.

Such are some of the memories of my lessons at school, I am almost ashamed to say. Memories of school life *outside* the classroom are hardly less shameful. When not engaged in trying to avoid the more unpleasant aspects of life – compulsory games, Combined Cadet Force parades, bullying, punishments and the wrath of housemasters, teachers and prefects alike – our thoughts were more often than not dwelling on the thorny issue which both fascinates and frightens adolescents the world over – sex. For my own part I arrived at Cranleigh totally uninitiated in a subject which I rapidly became aware was a major preoccupation of all and sundry, big boys and small alike.

It all started almost immediately. New boys on arrival were selected by the prefects as fags on their looks – the pretty boys were inevitably the first to be snapped up. Dormitory talk revolved around little other than the Facts of Life. How much did the new boys know? Did we realise there was to be a new boys test on them? Ridicule to be poured on those unable to answer the questions. Dark mutterings about the new boys' flannel parade to be held at the end of term. We understood that we, the new boys, would be stripped of all our clothes and told to run naked round and round the dormitory while the others taunted us and flicked at us with wet flannels and towels. The most unpopular among us, of course, would be dealt the harshest punishment. That the flannel parade never in fact actually materialized was no comfort to us at the time. The threat of it was sufficient to keep us cowering in fear at the prospect of such unpleasant treatment destined to be meted out to us at the end of our first term – if ever we made it that far.

Fear is a great educator, and inevitably it wasn't long before we had all been all pretty well initiated into the mysteries of the murky world of sex – both the theory and, for some of us, the practice. The delights of masturbation were gradually explained and in some cases demonstrated. Masturbation, both solitary and mutual, sooner or later became the norm for all of us. Those who fell to practising the latter, myself included, found no particular difficulty in finding the partner or partners with whom to indulge in what we considered a highly satisfactory, if forbidden, form of sexual activity. Satisfactory if only because other forms of such activity – oral sex and penetration – had at that stage not yet entered our vocabulary. All sex was forbidden and even if nothing about it was written in the School Rules we were acutely aware of the serious consequences awaiting if ever our 'sins' were to come to light.

Come to light indeed they did in my case, and early on in my second year. To be summoned to see the housemaster was always a cause for concern. What does he want? What have I done now? Sometimes we knew what to expect – an obligation to account for a bad set of reports, to recite the Creed and General Confession prior to Confirmation – other times the call came out of the blue and one had no idea what one was to face.

My call came one winter evening during evening prep time. Fifty boys in the house classroom, fifty heads bowed over work to be done for the morrow. Silence reigns. House prefect in charge. Suddenly the door is thrown open. Enter MacDermott, Head of House. The tap on the shoulder. "Wilkinson, the Housemaster wants to see you. In his study. Now. Jump to it!" Immediately? What does he want? What have I done now? Growing anxiety as I negotiate the long corridor through the Connaught block, turn right opposite the Dining Hall and up the stairs towards Effie's study on the first floor. His gruff 'Come!' responds to my timid knock. "Sir, you sent for me, sir." Never a person for small talk, the man turns to face me, pipe in hand, Welsh sheepdog cowering in the background, and comes straight to the point. "You've been messing around with Moss. Have you?" With those curt words my fate is sealed. I am about to be given six of the best with the cane. Standard procedure. My reply is more a quivering bleat than an answer. "Yes, sir." "Go to your dormitory. Now. Wait for me there." "Yes, sir."

The walk to the dormitory – the scaffold – is a longer walk still. Plenty of time for the anxiety level to rise several notches to sheer panic. The pit at the bottom of the stomach I had already experienced, having been slippered and whipped by Pud. But this is worse, far worse – a caning from a man with a well-founded reputation as a fearsome beater. You only had to look at the thickness of his wrists to know that here was a man capable of inflicting serious damage on one's tenderest parts. I'm feeling positively sick by the time my quaking legs have somehow pulled me up to the second-floor junior dormitory which is mine. I wait immobilized through abject fear and in total silence and darkness for what appears like an eternity. All part of the punishment. And then through the deafening silence I hear a distant footfall climbing the stairs. The squelching sound is unmistakable – Effie's a hush puppy man – and I brace myself as eventually the door latch is lifted.

"Well, turn the lights on then, boy!" I fumble for the switch and he blinks his owlish blink as his pale eyes adjust to the sudden glare of light with difficulty. The cane is now produced from behind his back. "Take your trousers down and bend down over there!" He points with the dreaded instrument of torture to a spot in the middle of the room, a spot calculated to give him the widest sweep possible when administering his six carefully judged blows.

"Further down! So you touch your toes!" Hands and legs shaking, buttocks and teeth clenched, I wait. More squelching as he retreats so as to get the run-up to give the added force to the blow and, swish! The first one is landed. "Ow!"

"Bend down again! Right down!" Squelch, squelch, and swish! And again and again and all unswervingly on target. My 'Ows!' become 'Aarghs!' and they become more piercing and throttled as the pain level increases. When number six finally lands I'm a gibbering wreck, but somehow I manage to find the presence of mind to do what I somehow know is now expected of me, namely pull up my trousers, stand up straight to face my tormentor, take and shake the hand he now extends to me – a sign that all is now again fine between us – and say in as steady a voice as the circumstances allow "Thank you, sir." I somehow manage to croak the words as the tears begin to flow.

"You can wait here till you're ready to get back into prep. All right?" Another stifled croak. "And by the way", he adds on departing and as an afterthought, "your parents won't hear about this."

The mention of my parents causes the floodgates to open and I'm left standing – sitting is not an option – weeping bitterly and profusely for the considerable time it takes me to regain my composure. Pain, fear, guilt, loneliness all churning around within me. Severely reprimanded, shaken, chastened and humiliated I eventually return to prep, red-eyed but with no one the wiser about my chastisement. The show must go on.

Go on it did, and I certainly mustn't paint a picture of the poor little boy locked into a life of permanent and utter misery. Others had it far worse than I did and, besides, here again as at Carn Brea, the musical life of the school once more came to my rescue. On arrival I'd been awarded a Music Exhibition – not a Scholarship, which was more highly prized and reserved for musicians more competent than I – on the strength of having sung a song or two and played the piano at someone who presumably thought I was worth encouraging. As an Exhibitioner and in return for a small reduction in the fees – which pleased my parents – I was expected to play a full part in the musical life of the school, which meant singing in choirs – principally the chapel choir and the choral society – and playing in orchestras, bands and chamber music groups. All this musical activity operated not only on a school level but also within the confines of the individual houses when annual inter-house music competitions, both vocal and instrumental, were held.

For people like myself, hopeless at games, here was a chance to counter the serious charge of having no house 'spirit', even if one had to admit to oneself that there was not all that much credit to be gained by simply blowing down a clarinet to help carry off the Instrumental Cup for the house. Proper house 'spirit' was to be found on the rugger field, where I least liked to be. It was to be found in the middle of a sweaty, muddy scrum or maul, your head firmly wedged between someone's smelly buttocks, on a filthy, blustery, rainy dark December afternoon shoving and pushing a fiery opposition back those last five yards onto their own line and going over to score the winning points of the final with one last heroic combined heave from our heroes in the dying seconds of the game. That was where proper glory was to be found with the whole house cheering you on from the touchlines – and woe to the boy who was found not to have been on that touchline to cheer his team to victory. Or the glory to be had in the summer by busting a gut running faster than anyone else and winning the mile together with a fistful of points for the house. Lots of credit to be had there too. Less for me singing the treble line of a Thomas Morley four-part song even if we did win the Madrigal Cup for the house.

However the pleasure was not in the competition but rather in the participation in these musical activities. The Choral Society was a case in point. It gave its one annual concert towards the end of each school year and much time was spent rehearsing for the great day. It would all start fairly low-key – weekly sectional rehearsals spent learning the notes. Then full rehearsals with trebles, altos, tenors and basses all together. Then, nearer the time, rehearsals taking in serried ranks of sopranos and altos from our sister school, St. Katherine's Bramley, to boost the top lines, together with members of the Cranleigh Village Choral Society. All of this to produce a choir of hundreds and a lot of noise. But the greatest moments of all were yet to come. Up to this point all rehearsals had been to the accompaniment of a piano and a pianist playing from a reduced score. But on the day of the concert, all this changed. I arrived at the afternoon dress rehearsal in the Speech Hall to find to my astonishment that a vast symphonic orchestra had assembled, ready to join forces with the combined choirs and the four professional soloists in a performance of the Verdi Requiem. The joining of these forces made an immediate impact on me and by the time we had reached the mighty, terrifying Dies Irae with the full brass section going full belt I was totally bowled over, not merely by the dramatic intensity of the music per se, but chiefly by the emotional response I felt towards it from deep within me. Right the way through that performance I was on an emotional roller-coaster, likewise in the following years when other great choral works – Handel, Bach, Elgar – were performed.

Similar emotional reactions were triggered within me regularly in the chapel when, on Sundays, the chapel choir would be called upon to lead the worship musically, both at Matins and at Evensong. It was there that my eyes began to be opened to the vast repertoire of liturgical music– not only Anglican – available. We were singing everything from Purcell to Stanford, from Bach to Britten. Over the five years the settings of the Hymns and Psalms became ever more familiar, so too those of the Magnificat and Nunc Dimittis, sung at choral evensongs. The Hymns in particular used to get us going. Sometimes we'd adapt the words – While Shepherds Washed Their Socks By Night – sometimes we'd sing them with the clipped, military precision of a Prussian officer – Onward, Christian Soldiers (later banned by the chaplain). Sometimes we'd ask for a favourite to be played (mine was Dear Lord And Father Of Mankind No. 383 – never forget a number. My school number was 247). Sometimes the words were an acute embarrassment to one of our number, for example the hymn Turn Back Oh Man, Forswear Thy Foolish Ways. There happened to be a boy in the school called Mann, generally considered to be the most comely of his year, the most 'lush' or 'luscious' (these were the words we used) of his year. Just imagine him having to sing this line in a full chapel with a barrage of lascivious eyes turned on him – puce red was the colour he turned, understandably. The irony, and sadness to some, was that he had no known foolish ways to forswear. Pure as the driven snow was the general consensus, and what a pity too.

But Sunday wasn't only the day for singing and praying in Chapel. It was also a day for fighting and brawling in the dormitories. On weekday mornings this just wasn't possible – breakfast was followed by bed-making (hospital corners, and woe betide if they weren't at exactly 45°) was followed by chapel, was followed by lesson one. No time there for larking about in the dorms. Sunday, however, was different. Getting-up time was later, breakfast more leisurely, bed-making too since there was all the time in the world until the call to Sunday morning chapel – compulsory, of course.

One of two things would generally happen as we trooped back to the dorm to make our beds. The first was that on arrival we would be faced by a scene of utter destruction and desolation. The dorm had been 'raided' by members of 1 North (their dormitory was directly below ours) who had craftily left breakfast earlier so as to execute their dastardly deed in our absence. Mattresses, sheets and blankets ('rasers' we called them) had all been thrown to the four winds, the iron bedsteads had been dismantled into their component parts and the lockers upended, their contents strewn far and wide, left right and centre, making it a nightmare trying to identify, then retrieve, one's own personal effects.

Our initial reaction was immediate. The ring-leaders among us –not me! – shouted 'At 'em lads!' or some such rallying cry, which prompted a headlong rush to the narrow spiral staircase (there for fire precaution purposes) which connected the two dormitories. Armed with pillows and charging down the stairs, we soon met the opposing forces blocking our path at the bottom. Much punching and pushing, shoving and shouting would ensue. There were times when their line held fast, other times when we (I say 'we' but to be honest I was generally hanging around at the back hoping not to get too close to the action for comfort) managed a breakthrough and gained access to the enemy territory. Once there we laid into them with our pillows, and a few punches were landed, a few noses bloodied. But generally there was little we could do to exact a fitting revenge. They were there to a man each one defending his bed, his locker, his all as if his life depended on it. The 'attack' would normally peter out after five minutes or so, when we would somewhat ignominiously retreat back up the staircase whence we had come to face the mammoth task of putting both the dormitory and our property back together again. Much swearing, cussing and bad temper all around as we discussed the revenge attack for the following Sunday.

Understandably, therefore, Sunday morning was not one of my favourite times and it was always with a certain trepidation that I climbed those dormitory stairs not knowing quite what to expect. A 1 North 'raid', or worse? And by worse, I mean bullying. As with the 'raids', both the time and the place for a little bit of bullying were ideal. The dorm bullies could get their hands on any victim of their choice with impunity. There was never any sign of prefects – their beds, of course, were made by their 'fags' (the story goes that some prefects also required the 'fag' to sleep in the prefect's bed before he arrived at night to ensure it was warm) – and both Housemaster and house Tutor, who had bedrooms close by, could be relied upon to be tucking into a hearty cooked English breakfast in Common Room, well out of the range of the sound of iron bedsteads being flung around or the cries of victims suffering at the hands of their tormentors.

The bullying could take various forms. One was the simple 'pushing around' of a junior considered by the bully boys to be too bumptious. This in itself would generally suffice; the junior would get the message and, if he were sensible, he would step back into line smartly. If he didn't, he could expect worse to follow. (The dormitories were not the only domain in which bullies liked to operate. They favoured too the dark and secluded Fives Courts. To be told to report to the Fives Courts at night after prep could mean trouble ahead.) But sometimes the attacks of the strong on the weak would take a nastier turn.

One victim had a particularly bad time of it. Tall, gangly, uncoordinated and clumsy in movement, he was a sitting duck and an obvious target. Once the signal was given he would be set upon by a bully together with two or three of his henchmen, held down spread-eagled on his bed and have his trousers and underpants ripped from him. Then one of the nastier boys in the dormitory, a boy small in stature, unprepossessing and bespectacled, cackling wildly and clearly in a state of great excitement, would push his way through the crowd of expectant onlookers wielding a large pair of scissors, with which he proceeded, cackling throughout, to cut his way through the luxuriant crop of pubic hair sported by the unfortunate victim. The latter, in no way the sort of person to offer any resistance, merely took his punishment in silence, his large, open and frightened eyes staring fixedly at the girders above him. Once the deed was done, the onlooking crowd, complicit in every way – and, yes, I was a part of it too – merely turned its callous back on the scene and drifted off on its way, leaving the shorn victim to 'clear up' as best he could before dormitory inspection. Shame on us all. Shame on me.

Similar treatments were meted out on others too. One was a friend of mine and in the same year. He was a talented violinist and a music scholar. In his case the Achilles heel was that he didn't quite speak 'proper'- not the standard RP English – added to which it was reported that his father either ran a taxi business or, worse still, drove a taxi himself. Whichever it was it didn't really matter. Either way it wasn't considered quite 'proper', so another poor boy was singled out for harsh treatment. I arrived back up at the dormitory one Sunday morning to find he'd been stripped totally naked, had been smeared with black boot polish from head to foot and was being required to circuit the dormitory to the taunts and further boot polish smears of yet another complicit crowd. Yes, and I was there too, his friend… shame on me. Shame on us all. An hour later found us both standing side by side in Chapel in cassocks and surplices singing the morning service. The show must go on.

Taking up learning the clarinet brought further musical commitments – the orchestra and the CCF band. Of the two I instinctively preferred the time spent playing with the former. After all there's a limit to the number of Souza marches one can play without getting serious indigestion. Not to say that the band didn't have its uses. Being a member of the band meant that one could avoid one's platoon inspections at the beginning of the weekly CCF parades. For some reason the band was not generally inspected, goodness knows why not. Perhaps it was thought they were otherwise occupied gearing up for performance while the contingent was being inspected. Anyhow, after having played for the march past members of the band were supposed to join their platoons for the remainder of the afternoon's activity – learning the parts of the rifle or how to clean the wretched thing or whatever. Several of us, however, failed to do this on a regular basis and managed to remain undetected. Simply because, I suppose, the platoon commander forgot that there was a band member in his platoon, never having seen him at inspection. Instead we'd make a beeline for the music rooms to return our instruments and there we would listen to records, play around on the pianos and otherwise have a jolly old merry time socialising for the remainder of the afternoon. This suited my purposes particularly well, since I could spend valuable time with my 'special' friend Nick Graham, who was also in the band and played the oboe (better than I did the clarinet). The time was valuable in so far as Nick was in a different house and two years my junior, which meant there were only limited times during the week when our paths would naturally cross. Not that very much happened between us – just the usual 'romping about' or 'horsing around', as Salinger calls it in *Catcher In The Rye* – it was just that I felt myself drawn to him. Sexually, yes, of course, but in other respects too – and in a way I'd not felt before. Something within me wanted to put him on a pedestal. Something else very definitely did not. All very confusing, I thought to myself. Is this falling in love? I asked myself, having no one else to ask.

Routine was broken when the school fell prey to a 'flu epidemic one term and more and more dormitories had to be requisitioned as sick bays as every minute of the day more and more boys were falling like flies and were being packed into every available spare bed in these converted dormitories. When I too eventually succumbed to the plague and was bundled off to the appointed dormitory-cum-sick bay, I was more than agreeably surprised to find that the boy to have been admitted immediately prior to me was none other than Nick Graham. I was ordered by a grumpy, overworked matron to take the bed next to his. Little did she realise that never was an order executed with greater pleasure, even if sick bays aren't exactly the ideal locations for carrying on an amorous relationship, the more so since both Nick and I were in the grip of high temperatures and not exactly in the mood for 'horsing around'.

But Nick needn't have worried, and perhaps he didn't. For the first days I just was feeling too groggy and was sleeping deeply through the nights, and when eventually strength began to seep back and the sap began to rise, so too did moral qualms begin to raise their heads. So I would simply turn and, before sleep and by the glow of the night-light, gaze and gaze into the face of this oh-so-attractive sleeping apparition by my side. So close, this forbidden fruit and oh! so tempting. But I resisted (fool!) and thereby forfeited all the pleasure that would have resulted, I imagined, from the physical consummation of such a pure and beautiful relationship.

On the eve of my discharge I was asked to read from the Acts of the Apostles for prayers before lights-out. Just my luck, it was a passage from one of St. Paul's epistles in which the peevish old man brings down fire and brimstone on all who commit acts of lasciviousness. For me the word meant sex and here was that nasty St. Paul ganging up with that nasty 'Effie' Tucker to prevent the likes of Nick and me from indulging in what was perfectly natural sexual activity. (I omitted to ask myself, of course, whether Nick would have considered same-sex sexual activity 'natural'.) So no comfort for me from the scriptures and I continued for many a week and month to chastise myself with the thought of a golden opportunity missed. Doubtless missed for ever, and all down to my feebleness.

It was a recording of Britten's Nocturne – a setting of a collection of English poems the themes of which relate to sleep and darkness – which meant much to me during these days of mixed emotions. Scored for tenor voice (very obviously written for Peter Pears), seven obbligato instruments and strings, each song is accompanied by an obbligato instrument and the one to which I related most closely was the setting of a poem by Coleridge, 'The Wanderings Of Cain', with the harp as the chosen obbligato instrument.

> *Encinctured with a twine of leaves,*
> *That leafy twine his only dress!*
> *A lovely Boy was plucking fruits,*
> *By moonlight, in a wilderness.*
> *The moon was bright, the air was free,*
> *And fruits and flowers together grew*
> *On many a shrub and many a tree:*
> *And all put on a gentle hue,*
> *Hanging in the shadowy air*
> *Like a picture rich and rare.*
> *It was a climate where, they say,*
> *The night is more belov'd than day.*
> *But who that beauteous Boy beguil'd,*
> *That beauteous Boy to linger here?*
> *Alone, by night, a little child,*
> *In place so silent and so wild...*
> *Has he no friend, no loving mother near?*

The poem, of course, much moved me and the setting to music doubly so. Not that I was unfamiliar with the Britten idiom. As a choir we'd already sung in performances of Noye's Fludde and Saint Nicholas and there was more in the offing. Doubtless part of the attraction for me lay in the fact that my parents didn't go big on this 'modern music'. 'No tunes', my mother would say dismissively, which made me all the keener to defend the cause against unenlightened parental authority. Added to which I'd learnt that Britten was 'queer' – the word we used – not that this could have ever been a bone of contention between me and my mother and father, let alone even a subject of conversation. The topic of sex was simply taboo in the household.

So in my mind Nick became that lovely Boy.... by moonlight, alone, by night. I imagined he was without friends (of course he had plenty), without a loving mother (of course he had one) and that I was to be his one and only real friend. Of course it never happened like that. What did happen, however, was that we found ourselves playing clarinet and oboe in my last concert with the school orchestra. In the programme was Schubert's Symphony No. 8 – The Unfinished. The beautiful slow movement is built around a charming dialogue between clarinet and oboe with the two instruments calling out to each other in plaintive tones. This is music which, together with its emotional associations, will be with me for the rest of my life, of that much at least I am quite certain.

It was immediately after this concert that my housemaster – a man called Sandy Steede ('Schmoo'), who had succeeded Effie The Galloping Major – sent for me to say that he'd decided not to appoint me to be Head of House for the following term (my last term). This came as a bit of a blow, as I was the next in line and had considered my appointment a *fait accompli.* But no, he had decided otherwise, claiming that I would be too taken up with my Oxbridge exams and that Martin Shaw from the year below me would altogether be the better choice. I reeled out of the room feeling let down, unappreciated and rejected. Was I so obviously lacking in leadership qualities? Could I not be expected to hold down a position of responsibility? It was hurtful to have been bypassed, even if in my more lucid moments I had to admit to myself that Shaw better fitted the bill than I did. He played a good game of rugby, had an impressive physical presence and wasn't permanently skiving and 'horsing around' as I was. He hunted with the hounds, whereas I wanted both to hunt with the hounds and run with the hare. The impression of being a square peg in a round hole was reinforced, and I realised that I was simply not playing the game according to the rules. Besides, the deterrent effects of the caning I had received had long since worn off – my new housemaster was not the frightening force that Effie Tucker had once been – and I was back to 'messing around' again, both with Moss and more or less any others who wanted to join the fun.

If anyone thought I would return to school for my last term – the Oxbridge term – a reformed character, a model student determined to give his all to gain admission to Peterhouse, my father's college at Cambridge, they were in for a disappointment. I continued to drift along, hoovering up increasing numbers of French and German plays, poems and novels without much enthusiasm and fearing the failure which I already suspected was coming straight my way. The two days spent at Cambridge confirmed my worst suspicions. The written papers were beyond me and in interview things turned out no better. The interviewer chose to grill me on the string quartet (seeing I was interested in music). I chose to give the little I knew on Beethoven. "And the Haydn string quartets?" he chipped in "Oh! Nothing to compare with Beethoven" I replied dismissively, before suddenly waking up to the fact that I'd never actually knowingly heard a Haydn string quartet. It wasn't long before my inquisitor picked up on my predicament and proceeded to give a brilliant ex-posé on the many virtues of the Haydn string quartet. I could only listen, and eventually I left the room with my tail very much between my legs. Haydn, I now agree, wrote fabulous string quartets.

The last day of the last term at school found me feeling empty and deflated. Goodbyes all round from me, although no sign of Nick. 'See-you-next-terms' all round from my younger brother, Mark.

The car was loaded to the gunwales. One silent 18-year-old and a chirpy, chatty 16-year-old were squashed into the back. Mother read the situation at once. "Now, Mark, just be quiet for a moment, can you? You can see that John wants quiet. You know it's a turning point for him, leaving school for the last time. It's an important moment, you know." A turning point, OK. But a turning point to where? That's what I wanted to know. Not for Cambridge, that was for sure, although my parents weren't to know that till the results came through just before Christmas. It would be a disappointment to them. To me, too, but five years at Cranleigh had at least taught me that coping with disappointments is part of the fabric of life. Disappointment in love, in work, in self. But what scope for love and for emotional development in a single-sex boarding school for thirteen to eighteen year olds? What scope for good work from classrooms that were largely devoid of inspiration? What scope for the self, having failed in these former spheres? Where would the confidence now spring from? Or had it already been severely dented? What about self-esteem? These were the gloomy thoughts accompanying me as the four of us hurtled down the A303 en route for Broadhempston Vicarage, Near Totnes, Devon (telephone: Ipplepen 232) and the traditional family Christmas at home.

My father, from Yorkshire, and my mother, from Holland, on their wedding day.

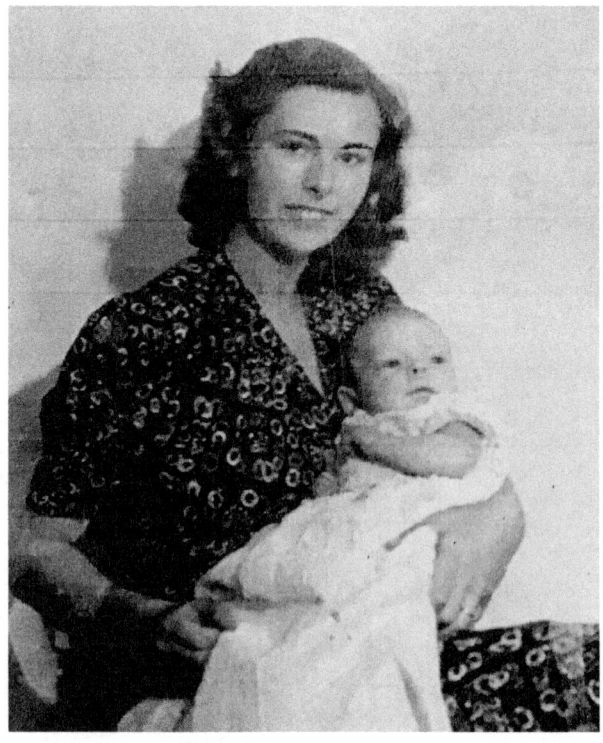

My earliest days.

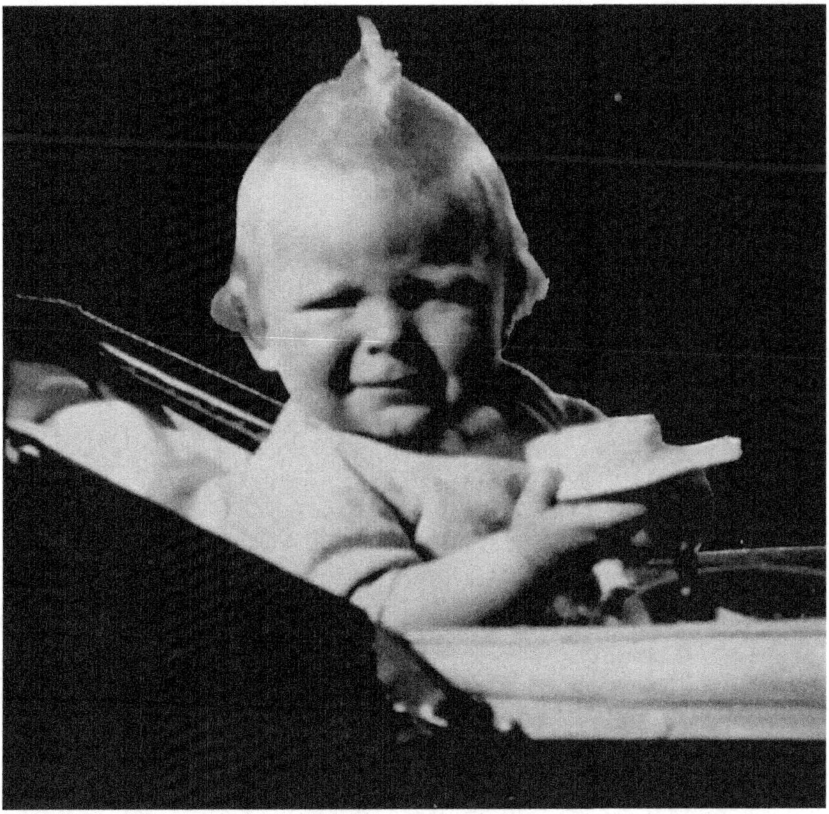

Me – pre-dating the fashionable Mohican hairstyle by decades.

Family walk from Tresco to Bryher, Isles of Scilly, at low tide.

The happiest of pre-school days for brother Mark and me.

The vicarage.

View from the vicarage.

WILLIE

Willie Howard, Major Arthur Dorrien Smith's boatman.

Brother Mark and I kitted out for Carn Brea Preparatory School – courtesy of Harrods.

Carn Brea, with Headmaster H.J.O. Marshall ('Pud') in central position.

2 North House, Cranleigh School. I am third row back from the front, third from the left. Photo presided over by Sandy ('Schmoo') Steede, my second housemaster, and Warren ('Bunny') Green, house tutor and my piano teacher.

Major O.F. ('Effie') Tucker, my first housemaster, off to hunt with Lucy, his fiery steed.

The vicarage, Broadhempston, South Devon.

Vicarage orchards (cider apples) and outbuildings.

The walled vegetable garden – too vast to keep up.

Trinity College, Dublin Front Square. with the Campanile, whose mournful bell
summoned us to our Finals.

Michael de Larrabeiti ('Larras') – a
formidable formative influence on me.

Carl-Hendric Bonaventura Harald Bontoft
('Bon'), Vicomte de Saint Quentin –
another formidable formative influence.

Dublin docks. Me with my two 'wives' – William, the wild Irishman, Michael, the
thoughtful Scot. Someone is going somewhere on a ferry.

Heather, my girlfriend, and I at a Trinity Week ball.

A SERENADE CONCERT

IN THE EXAMINATION HALL
TRINITY COLLEGE

By permission of the Senior Dean

THE COLLEGE SINGERS
& D.U. MUSIC SOCIETY

Conductor: John Wilkinson

Friday May 22nd 1964 at 8 o'clock

Admission by Programme 3 / -

A College Singers concert – one per term and they kept me on my toes.

The cast of *Trial By Jury*, Gilbert and Sullivan, in the dining hall.

Trial By Jury; the conductor (me) and the two pianists.

Captain Alexander Henry - walking history.

Rathescar, Captain Henry's country house. My job was to mow the extensive lawns.

A portrait of me by my mother, after I had graduated from TCD.
I don't like sitting for portraits.

Chapter Ten

The Vicarage

Being driven down the A303 as a schoolboy from Cranleigh School, Surrey to Broadhempston Vicarage, Near Totnes, South Devon was not unlike taking the same road some seven years later, but this time as a qualified schoolmaster having somehow managed to complete the first term in my first job. Differences there clearly were. I was no longer being driven but was driving myself in my first car, a light blue drop-head Hillman Minx (the pride and joy of my life). The road itself had changed too, and the various new bypasses made the run a faster and easier one. But had I myself changed over those seven years? The closer I drew to home and my parents the more I thought not, as I began to detect that slight build-up of apprehension at the prospect of returning home again after a period of prolonged absence. It was merely a question of adjustment, and I somehow imagined I wasn't very good at it. Yes, it was probably largely rooted in the imagination, for example the idea of there being underlying tensions between myself and my father, always a somewhat distant figure, I found. With my mother it was the reverse. A demonstratively loving mother, she gave of her love unstintingly and this too made me tense and uncomfortable. Adolescent growing pains, I explain to myself as I turn off the Newton Abbott-Totnes road and plunge into the steep-banked Devon lanes. What? Adolescent growing pains? And here I am now at the age of twenty-five and still with destructive feelings gnawing at me.

Home previous to the Vicarage had been a very different affair. After his two-year stint on the Isles of Scilly my father, cured of his illness, had been appointed Minor Canon at Worcester Cathedral, where we lived in a close opposite the cathedral, in a Georgian town house hardly big enough for the four of us. My brother and I shared a bedroom – fine as pre-teenagers but less appealing when I was rising sixteen and Mark, my brother, fourteen. It was then that the move to the Vicarage in a country parish in Devon was made, and very satisfactory it was too. From a cramped town house set in the very centre of a busy, noisy city – no garden – to a sprawling Queen Ann stone-built house set at the top of the hill in its own grounds with views looking down over the village and church at the bottom of the hill. The grounds included two large orchards of mainly cider apple trees; the apples were picked up by Mark, me and Ron Hannaford-Hill, the gardener, and sent off in sacks to the Landscove cider factory a few miles down the road. The paddock was used by a local farmer for grazing his sheep from time to time and the huge, high-walled vegetable garden was only partly used by us – it was just far too big, Ron was with us only two days a week and my father had no ideas of turning himself into a part-time market gardener. His self-appointed job in the garden was to mow the lawns with a fiery, petrol-fuelled old mower he christened Boanerges, The Sons Of Thunder, the nickname applied by Jesus, we were told, to the brothers James and John to reflect their impetuosity. Added to all this was a series of outbuildings all of which would have had their uses in earlier days gone by – stabling for two horses, provision for the 'trap' – the two-wheeled carriage the vicars of a bygone age would have used for visiting – pigsties, coal-house, rooms for storing and preserving fruit and vegetables and more besides.

From the start my mother was sure this was the home for us. At first sight she immediately fell in love with the honeysuckle cascading down over the front porch, and from then on the move was more or less a foregone conclusion, my father tending to rely heavily on my mother for the big decisions. For him this was indeed a big decision, moving from a cloistered cathedral existence to the rough and tumble of a rural parish. Would he identify with the Devonian farmers who formed the bulk of the parish? Would he find them forming the bulk of his church congregation too? The answer to the latter question turned out to be no, although they did turn out for the big occasions. (They also came and rang the church bells, but they always slipped out fast before any service looked like getting underway.)

The regular congregation consisted of local little old spinsters and the non-locals who had bought property, usually the bigger houses, either for retirement purposes or because they preferred to live a village life commuting to work even as far as to towns like Torquay on the coast. These were the people who were to become not only my father's churchgoers but also our friends. The 'Sherry Party Brigade' I called them, and very definitely not the *real* villagers, the farming folk, who never so much as got a sniff of a glass of sherry and who were anyway far too busy devoting themselves to the back-breaking work handed down to them through the generations. The Harrisons, the Hewetts, the Fords, little old Katherine Parker and above all the Tylers – these were the people in whose drawing-rooms sherry would be fairly regularly sloshed out to those considered to be members of the 'Brigade'. We too at the vicarage did our fair share and my father produced a lethal Cup – champagne cider, brandy, Cointreau and goodness knows what else – which produced the required effect. Prior to these occasions I'd be fretting for fear that everything might not be ready for the arrival of the guests at 7.30. "Mum, look the sausage-rolls aren't anything like cooked and they're coming in ten minutes" or "Mum, hadn't you better go and get changed? It's already 7.15."

"Now darling, don't *worry!* Everything's going to be all right. You really are a *worrier*, aren't you?" Yes, I was.

My social skills at the age of sixteen were also not great and it was usually a question of the shy adolescent being unwillingly dragged along to these parish drinks parties by his parents with a "Come on, darling, you know you'll like it when you get there."

When I got there I normally *didn't* like it. Being shunted from one group of strangers to another and thrown into their midst with a "Oh! I *do* want you to meet our new vicar's eldest son. John, isn't it?" wasn't exactly my idea of bliss. The situation improved, of course, as I got to know people, and by the time I'd left school my brother and I had both made good friends with the Tyler family – Tom, Paul, Kate and John were all of them, like us, of school and university age and many were the outings we made with them both at home and abroad.

My first post-school holidays were always going to be stressful as I was waiting for the day when the postman would deliver the results of my three university applications – Peterhouse, Cambridge, Trinity College, Dublin and Edinburgh. Christmas – the usual family affair, with three nights of village carol singing in bitter, freezing conditions thrown in for good measure – came and went. Still no results. It was only towards the middle of January that the first of those envelopes popped through the letter-box. Just my luck it was the Cambridge rejection. No surprise to me, but almost certainly a disappointment to my parents, my father particularly, even if they attempted to put a brave face on it. Gloom hung heavily, if not in the vicarage, then in my mind, the more so since Paul Tyler had been accepted by Exeter College, Oxford.

Luckily the wait for the two remaining results was not a protracted one. Acceptances from both Dublin and Edinburgh gave a welcome boost to my self-confidence, but then promptly put me in a quandary as to which of the two to take. I knew no one in either university or city. In fact I couldn't even be sure of ever having met an Irishman or a Scot in all my life – talk about a sheltered existence. So it ended up with the two names being written on paper, the two pieces of paper being screwed up into a ball then thrown into the hat together with a dozen or so other blank screwed up balls of paper. The first to be drawn out was the one. Suspense, but not much, since the very first ball I drew out had inscribed on it the three letters TCD – Trinity College Dublin. I can't say I leapt for joy, knowing absolutely nothing about the institution, except that my Housemaster at Cranleigh, Sandy 'Schmoo' Steede, had studied there as an undergraduate and had recommended that I apply.

It fairly rapidly dawned upon me that ten months stretched ahead of me for which I had made absolutely no plans. Living that length of time at home would be a novel experience, as since the age of seven I'd spent only a third of my life sharing a home with my parents. No wonder I found the prospect somewhat daunting. But what were the alternatives? A trip round the world? Yes, but who was going to fund it? ("Darling, we're not wealthy, you know – just comfortably off.") Hitch-hiking round Europe? Well, frankly I lacked the spirit of adventure. Instead I ended up accepting a job from Bill Harrison – one of the Sherry Party Brigade – who was the owner of a hand-made paper mill in the little village of Tuckenhay which nestled in a secluded riverside creek about a forty-five-minute drive from Broadhempston. The mill had been in the family for some time and in earlier days had had an important production line going with barges and tall-masted ships coming up to the quays that lay alongside the riverbank. It was producing the finest quality paper for artists, also for banknotes and Royal Proclamations. Rows of worker's cottages still bear witness to the size of the enterprise. However, those were the glory days and the scale of operations was now much reduced, so too the number of skilled papermakers, who were all approaching retirement age with no younger replacements in view.

The whole process of handmade paper making – Tuckenhay was one of the last three such mills left in the country – starts with huge bales of rags which have to be sorted and prepared and then treated in water causing a dilute suspension of fibres. The fibres are then again suspended in water in large vats to form a slurry. The slurry is then scooped out of the vats with a mould – a wire screen in a wooden frame – and sloshed around in the mould until it forms a uniform coating (this is the job of the papermaker – not an easy one to get it right). The fibres then settle and the water drains. They are then turned out onto a felt sheet by the papermaker, who starts the whole process again for the next sheet – and again and again. Layers of paper and felt are thus built up into a pile (my job) with a weight placed on top to press out excess water and keep the paper fibres flat and tight. After all this, the paper is hung out in drying rooms.

When I wasn't in the thick of it with the papermakers (a pretty surly breed with hands gnarled and deformed through decades of grasping tight and manoeuvring only with great effort their heavy moulds), I was sent off to give a hand in the rag depot. Just as the papermaker's emporium set right at the heart of this rickety Dickensian mill was strictly all-male, so the rag depot at the south end of the building was very much the preserve of the women. And what a formidable bunch of women they were – fifteen to twenty of them most days, middle-aged or older, Devonian to their fingertips and endowed with a more than rich use of the vernacular, which they used to great effect to try to shock, embarrass or amuse the sensitive nineteen-year-old public school boy who had so suddenly and unexpectedly been foisted upon them. I was clearly every bit as much as a phenomenon to them as they were to me, and some of them were clearly out to have a bit of fun at my expense whilst they could.

Banter and good-humoured teasing was the norm and I did my best to return it. More than not it was flavoured with a good dollop of sexual innuendo which tended to fluster me – and they knew it. Some of the bolder ones, aided and abetted by their colleagues, would stealthily creep up behind me as I was sorting and try and steal a kiss off me before I'd realised what was happening. Much cackling would ensue and I would blush like a child, wondering how best to cope with this unruly bunch of gorgons.

Things came to a head when a concerted attempt was made to remove my trousers. At a given signal three or four of the fittest charged at me, got me down on the huge pile of rags I was attempting to sort and proceeded to tug at my jeans, which luckily, being tight-fitting and anchored by a strong leather belt, refused to budge. There was a lot of rolling and fumbling around on the rag pile as I attempted to retain my sartorial integrity. The romp came to a sudden and unexpected end when the door at the end of the room opened and in walked Bill Harrison. He stopped in his tracks, observed the unseemly sight on the rag pile with every sign of disapproval etched on his face, turned on his heels and exited, slamming the door behind him. The women immediately all scuttled back to their posts, where they remained rooted till it was time to go, and that was the end of the fun and the sexual harassment of the student part-timer. The good-natured banter of course continued, but the limits had now been set. The boss had disapproved and the rag depot women had quickly got the message.

For the first month Bill Harrison and I drove in to work and back again together. All he had to do was stop for me outside the vicarage gates on his way past, most convenient for me and at no inconvenience to himself. One day when driving in, however, he informed me that the mill driver had fallen sick and a replacement was rapidly needed to ferry people in and out of work. Would I be interested? I said yes without really knowing what exactly was required, and later that day I found myself in possession of one beaten-up old van which for the foreseeable future was to be not only my means of transport but also that of the ten or so women – yes, the rag depot women – who lived outside the village and had no other form of transport available to them. My job was simply to collect them from their homes, deposit them at the mill, then return them home again when we'd all finished work. I then drove myself home, parked the van at the bottom of the back orchard on a slope to make sure that the next morning I could roll down Vicarage Hill with it and have the engine spring into life before I'd reached the bottom. The starter motor refused to cooperate in the early morning, I'd been warned.

My first run back home from the mill brought with it an agreeable surprise. The motley bunch of the rag depot brigade had already piled in behind and I was revving up on the point of departure when one of the women calls out "Wait, John. Wait for Jane."

"Who's Jane?" I reply, but I needn't have bothered. An attractive young girl was already crossing the yard and making straight for the van and the front passenger door, which she opened before easing herself gracefully onto the front bench seat beside me. I had already had a glimpse or two of her from afar, but only now realised that this was Jane Williams, secretary to Bill Harrison, who was a local-born girl and lived at home with her parents and family in the village of Blackawton, which meant she was the last person to be dropped off.

I duly left her opposite her front door and watched as she crossed the road, a shy smile and a little wave to me as she did so. 'Wow! Yes, ' said I to myself, 'Not a bad looker...not bad at all.' Day by day her prettiness grew on me, her shyness evaporated (mine too) and it seemed to me that we both equally valued the ten minutes or so we had together in the front of the van at the end of the day. Not that we were going to find topics of mutual interest to discuss. They probably didn't exist, and anyway even an attempt to find one would merely draw attention to the wide differences between our backgrounds. No, this was a physical attraction, and for me was none the worse for being so.

Into the second week of ferrying I decided some sort of action was required, and one day I summoned up the courage to lean over and give her a peck on the cheek as she was getting out of the van. Since this bold manoeuvre was gracefully accepted – I got the same smile and wave as she crossed the road – I immediately decided that further, bolder action should be undertaken the very next day. The blood was heating in the veins that evening as I plotted and planned my ploy, which turned out to be neither bold nor original. I decided that I'd simply stop the van, saying I thought we'd a back tyre puncture, get out to inspect the tyre, get in again (with the good news that the suspect tyre was in fact OK) and promptly move over on the bench seat and towards her, to see if I could then do better than a mere peck on the cheek. I was to be happily surprised when the plan was put into operation the next day and worked without a hitch. From that day forth it became standard practice that I should stop the van and that we should both indulge in a little sex-play. Given that I was almost totally inexperienced in the matter as far as girls were concerned, I was pretty pleased with the way things went, and over the weeks they went further step by step until we'd reached the stage of 'heavy petting', or so I imagined, having heard the term used fairly graphically at school by friends who had gone that far with girls in the holidays.

It was at this stage that the shutters suddenly came down and I found myself facing a totally unexpected 'No! Stop!' I of course tried to negotiate myself around this untimely barrier, but to no avail. So much for my first intimate encounter with the opposite sex – not an unmitigated disaster, but nevertheless somewhat frustrating.

It wasn't too long before the mill driver was back from his sick leave, so I lost both the van and the opportunities it had brought with it. Determined not to lose contact altogether, I took to pen and paper and tried my hand at a few saucy letters. Replies were forthcoming in a similarly saucy vein and a lengthy correspondence might well have developed but for the fact that I stupidly left one of her letters lying around in my bedroom and the inevitable happened. Yes, my mother came upon it, read it and, shocked at the lewd content, took it straight to my father, who having also read it, summoned me to his study and demanded an explanation.

Furious and in no mood for dreaming up explanations, I demanded to know by what right my mother had entered my bedroom and read a private letter addressed to me without my consent. My father snapped back at me and immediately launched into a stern, moral lecture about women and the dangers they represented. The theme of his lecture: Once a woman decides she wants something there is nothing she will not do to get it. Bemused I stood and listened as the tirade continued, momentarily wondering whether I was facing my father, the vicar or my housemaster – the line became increasingly blurred.

I eventually left the room without offering an explanation and with the firm knowledge that my parents imagined that a girl called Jane, the temptress, was intent on leading me, the tempted one, down the paths of sin to a state of utter depravity and debauchery. All quite untrue, I convinced myself, and anyway what business is it of theirs? I prepared for a few days of frostiness at the vicarage.

Meanwhile the summer was passing by, my job at the mill came to an end and September saw me preparing to set out on my first trip to the Republic of Ireland a little better prepared to face the wider world now thanks to the rag depot women and the sweet Miss Jane Williams.

The journey from the Vicarage, Broadhempston to Trinity College, Dublin could have been tricky but for the fact that Exeter Airport provided regular direct flights to Dublin, flights which over the course of the following four years I was to get to know well. But as time went by the distance between the Vicarage and TCD seemed to grow as my horizons broadened. Tuckenhay Mill, the rag depot women and Jane Williams had set in motion a process that was to accelerate from the very first day that I set foot in Ireland when I realised that on leaving the Vicarage I was in fact leaving behind an entirely English and somewhat Victorian view of the world.

The taxi driver who first drove me into central Dublin from the airport realised this instinctively. "I suppose the young gentleman will be wanting to be taken to Trinity, to be sure I'm right," he said after cursorily looking me up and down. He had determined my Englishness without my even having opened my mouth.

"Yes, that's right. Trinity College, please."

"We call it TCD here. Not to be confused with UCD, don't you know."

"What's UCD then?" I asked tentatively.

"UCD? University College? That's for the Catholics. That's for us. *You* wouldn't want to be going there then, would you, sir?"

"Me? No, I don't suppose I would. I'm not Catholic."

"Of course you're not a Catholic, sir. If you were a Catholic you wouldn't be going to TCD, would you, sir? You wouldn't be *allowed* to go to TCD."

"*Allowed*? Allowed by whom?"

"Well, by the Archbishop for one, of course. Who else? John Charles McQuaid, Archbishop of Dublin and Primate of Ireland since 1940. Now you don't want to be arguing with your man, do you, sir, when he's a Prince of the Church. If he says you don't go to TCD if you're a Catholic, you don't go, do you?"

"I suppose not. But why not?"

"Why not? Well, what a question. Why not? You don't seem to realise that TCD is Protestant. Yes, Protestant, sir, strange though it may seem set in the middle of a Catholic country. Do you not know it's an English institution? Founded by your Queen Elizabeth I. It's for the English. It's for people like you. It's not for us, the Irish. We have to make do with UCD, the second best. Very much the second best, if I may be so bold as to say so."

My driver chortled to himself as he swerved to avoid an oncoming horse-drawn dray stacked high with barrels of Guinness. We were now approaching central Dublin and the horse-drawn traffic was increasing. I was sitting quietly in the back with thoughts of Catholicism and Protestantism much in mind, nursing my English, Anglican sensibilities.

"Anyway I'm not a Protestant. I'm an Anglican."

"Anglican. Huh! Anglican, Protestant, Methodist, Presbyterian, Quaker – they're all the same to us. They're all anti-Catholic. Dangerous the lot of them. You'll find them all in TCD, and that's why we don't want any Catholics going there to be corrupted. And if you don't believe me, go and listen to the Archbishop in the Pro-cathedral when he next delivers his Lenten Pastoral. He'll tell you what happens to Catholics who enter the portals of TCD. They won't be seeing St. Peter before those pearly gates, that's for sure."

"Why do you call it a *Pro*-cathedral?"

"Because it's a temporary arrangement, sir. And why is it temporary, you'll doubtless be asking me now. Simply because the two Dublin cathedrals have been taken over by the Church of Ireland. Stolen by the Protestants, I call it. Both cathedrals –St Patrick's and Christchurch – stolen by the Prots. Greedy, I call it. Once again we, the Catholics of a Catholic country, are made to make do with the second best – a Pro-cathedral, I ask you. No wonder we've been at each other's throats over the centuries, the Protestants and the Catholics of this Emerald Isle. No wonder with the injustices of it all."

Leaving the Vicarage to spend four years living in the centre of the city of Dublin was clearly going to be a steep learning curve for me if my first-day conversation with the airport taxi cab driver was anything to go by. And so it turned out to be.

Chapter Eleven

Trinity College Dublin– The Beginning

The taxi driver persisted with his lesson on Ireland and the Irish and I had little choice but to listen, even if his strong Dublin brogue had me struggling at times to follow exactly what he was saying. My ears were simply not attuned to the dialect, intonation and accent, since never in my whole sheltered life had I met an Irishman, let alone heard one speak. Listen I did, however, judging his tone of voice to be neither aggressive nor condescending. I guessed he was rather having a leg-pull at the expense of this somewhat naïve young Englishman who was in his country for the first time and was clearly out of his comfort zone.

We sped on through the suburbs and on towards central Dublin and the evening rush hour. Dusk was now falling, the finest of drizzle too, and street lighting awakened to cast a yellowish glow over dampening streets. Much like any other European city so far, I thought to myself before we suddenly braked to avoid a gang of young ragamuffins – genuine Dickensian street urchins these were, some of them shoeless, I noticed. "Jesus!" cursed the driver, who then immediately swung left and into a fine, broad avenue busy with the bustle of crowds and the roar of traffic.

"Yes", he volunteered. "O'Connell Street and one of the widest thoroughfares in all Europe, I tell you. Sackville Street when you Brits were here, but we changed all that, to be sure we did. Daniel O'Connell, the great nineteenth century campaigner for Catholic emancipation in Ireland. Now you will have heard of him, won't you?"

I hadn't. No idea.

"And who's that standing on top of that pillar then?" I ventured.

"That? That's your Admiral Nelson for you. Your English Admiral Nelson, I tell you, and a crying shame it is too. Shame on us all having *him* up there of all people. Topple him, I say, and the sooner the better."

"Then who would you put up there – O'Connell?"

"O'Connell? Well to be sure, why not? Or the Mother of God, The Virgin Mary, either would be better than that one-eyed, one-armed English bandit of yours."

Wiser in the circumstances, I thought to myself, not to spring to the defence of one of our greatest national treasures, although I was severely tempted and Trafalgar hung fiercely on my lips– lips only too anxious to give voice to English honour when and where it was surely due. Goodness me, he'll be wading into the Monarchy next and then what will I do – speak out boldly or continue to hold my tongue? We shall never know, since the history lesson moved on as we inched our way down this impressive avenue.

"And on the right you have the General Post Office, a building more than sacred in our history."

It was indeed an impressive building – stone built, pillared and in a pure classical design – but I failed to see how a post office could ever be considered sacred.

"Sacred, yes, indeed, sir. Is that building not the very symbol of the 1916 Easter Monday Rising by the Irish Citizen Army? The rising against the British. Did you not know it was here they had their HQ? That the Proclamation of the Irish Republic was read from those very steps by none other than Patrick Pearse himself? Did you not know this? Have you not heard talk of your man Patrick Pearse, the great Patrick Pearse and his brother William – may God bless them both – two of the greatest of our national martyrs. Court-martialled, both of them with tens of others on that glorious day. Court-martialled after the British Army had shelled and destroyed the General Post Office, reducing it to a pile of rubble. Closed trials they got before three British officers. No jury. The defendants had no lawyers. No witnesses allowed to be called. All found guilty and condemned to death, may God save their souls. Shot, they were, the poor men. And that's justice for you. That's *British* justice for you."

There was emotion in his voice, and I felt we were now entering upon slippery ground. Discretion seemed the better part of valour, so I remained stonily silent. Besides there was nothing I could do to protect British military honour, knowing absolutely nothing about the wider circumstances of the atrocities of the killing of these men.

More statues lining the central alley as we proceeded down towards the bottom of the street and over a fine bridge straddling a wide river.

"And there you have the River Liffey come straight from the Wicklow mountains. 'Tis from the river just over there your British gunboat fired upon the General Post Office. Deadly fire it was too."

At least I'd heard about British gunboat diplomacy from my history lessons at Cranleigh. So this was it? 'Diplomacy'?

Within minutes we were there, drawn to a halt opposite the south front of Trinity College, to be my home for the next four years, my Alma Mater. A fine 18c building sitting safely behind its tall and solid iron railings which marched off proudly left and right meeting upon the north side to enclose the whole forty-seven acre site in a close embrace.

"Front Gate, Trinity, sir. You'll be safe in there, to be sure you will. And good luck to you, sir."

I stood momentarily glued to the pavement, my two suitcases by my side, drizzled upon and washed over by streams of Dubliners making their way homewards after work. A sea of bustle and umbrellas. But Trinity in front beckoned, and I took my first hesitant steps. Past the outer railings behind which lay manicured lawns and on which stood two fine pedestalled statues on either side of the gate – Oliver Goldsmith and Edmund Burke, both presumably previous alumni and both of whom I had heard, which was of some comfort to me, having had my ignorance so conclusively proven by my garrulous taxi-driver. Through the proud portals of Front Gate and left into the Porter's Lodge to discover the details of my accommodation. So far, so good – this was just like an Oxbridge college, and I was beginning to feel more at home.

Armed with key, staircase number – No.15 Botany Bay – together with the knowledge that I was to be sharing the rooms with two other 'young gentlemen' due to arrive on the following day, I made my way through the dark and silent squares to my allocated quarters. Top floor, large living room, two bedrooms and a kitchenette, with a sink which was clearly meant to double up for one's personal ablutions. No sign of a loo, which I eventually found on venturing out again to be a communal one tucked under the stairs on the ground floor. Not ideal for us on the third floor and no more so than the fact that there seemed to be no sign of hot water anywhere. Never mind, these were minor matters and I was more than relieved to have negotiated the trip from Devon to Dublin without major mishap.

It didn't take me long to decide to occupy the single bedroom, unpack and slip between the sheets. Sleep came shortly, but not before some of the more memorable images of the day had flicked through my mind – Archbishop McQuaid's Lenten Pastorals, Pro-Cathedrals, Greedy Prots, Daniel O'Connell, Irish Proclamations, the Pearse brothers, post offices and British gunboats on the Liffey…all became increasingly jumbled up as I gradually dozed off into a deep sleep.

I woke up to a gentle autumnal sun peeping in through my bedroom window and to the sound of someone moving around in the living room. Jumping out of bed, I donned a dressing-gown and made for the bedroom door to investigate.

"And the top of the morning to you, Mr Wilkinson, sir. My name's Mick and I'm your skip. I hope I didn't awaken you. I've heated some water for you for when you'll want to be washing and breakfasting."

In front of me stood a middle-aged man of smallish stature, peaked cap perched on his head, white shirt, collar and tie with a long, dark blue apron tied securely around his waist. Skip? Yes, of course. My father had on occasions referred to his 'gyp' (college manservant) at Cambridge, friends at Oxford talked about their 'scouts'. So 'skip' was the Trinity compromise. I liked it.

"Will you be wanting to light a fire this evening, sir? (I hadn't even noticed the open fireplace.) I'll be bringing up the coal and peat later in the morning when I come to wash and tidy up your breakfast. Be sure to leave your shoes out for me if you've any that need a quick shine. You'll feel right dandy this lovely morning stepping out in shoes with a fine shine on them, that's for sure. Is there anything more I can do for you just now, sir?"

"No thanks, Mick, that will be all for now. Oh, by the way, where can I get a shower and a bath?"

"No showers in college, sir, but baths aplenty. If you look out of the window there you'll see the bathhouse on the other side of the square. The best bath you'll get in the country, sir."

Sure enough dressing-gown clad figures were making their way across the square in that very direction, and I decided to join them. Strange at first to be wandering around outside in one's pyjamas, I thought, bath towel slung over one's shoulder, sponge-bag in hand. Strange clearly too to the group of American tourists who raised cameras in my direction when I was half way to the bath house. The building itself bore the name of Guinness – at least I'd heard of *that* – who had seemingly contributed to the construction of the place. Once inside, I was in another world. Two long rows of cubicles from out of which there issued steam, sounds of splashing water, humming, whistling, singing and all manner of other noises, all of them seemingly denoting contentment and relaxation. I found an empty cubicle and was faced with a cast iron bath the size of which I'd never seen before. Huge. So too the gleaming brass taps through which flowed the water, both piping hot and cold, in vast quantities. It almost felt like stepping into a swimming pool. I luxuriated, just as others were doing all around me. Taking one's ease, relaxing in comfort – if this was university life, it was going to be all right. And what with Mick the Skip shining my shoes – a luxury I'd not known since prep school days when Old Varney spent his whole time shining one hundred and twenty pairs of shoes when he was not stoking the boilers, which was his other job. (Oh, and let's not forget my fag at Cranleigh, young Boardman, who had had to clean my shoes daily when I'd become a House Prefect.) And the thought of a peat fire in the grate in the evenings. And having somebody to clear up after me for the next four years…no wonderI found myself joining in the happy chorus of humming, whistling and singing issuing from all around me. Bathing in the Trinity Guinness bath house was to become a protracted affair. A good, lovely, long soak.

I emerged forty-five minutes later, rejuvenated, skipped back to No.15 whistling all the way, to find Mick had cleared the breakfast, laid a fire and polished a pair of shoes which looked as if they were about to go on parade for inspection by the commanding officer.

"The Lady Housekeeper tells me you are to be expecting the arrival of your wives later in the day, sir. Late afternoon, early evening, so she told me just now."

"Wives? What? What wives, Mick?"

He smiled, a glint in the eye. "Yes, your wives, sir. That's what we call them here in Trinity, the students who you share rooms with. You're a lucky one, sir – you're to have two of them. A Mr Young and a Mr Hope, I believe. So you can relax, sir, we have no girls living in college and the wives are all male. Simpler like that – perhaps you'll agree, sir?"

"Yes, perhaps, Mick." I had no idea. But he was right – I could relax. Living in an all-male community was already known territory to me. To have had to live cheek by jowl with two members of the fair sex would have been another matter entirely. I dismissed the idea instantly, slung my camera over my shoulder and set out to see what Trinity had to offer. I was not alone and the squares were filling up with the Junior Freshers (first-year students) who were arriving now a week before the start of term and lectures in order to partake in Freshers' Week, when all the college clubs and societies displayed their wares and activities, hoping to excite the interest of the new entrants. I traced my way back to Front Gate, which was now a hive of activity. Porters, looking distinguished in their dark blue coachmen's uniforms, were busy directing both students looking for their rooms and tourists wanting to take a peep into what was clearly a major city landmark.

A start to any visit was surely Front Square. And an impressive start it made too. Sir William Chambers had been the principal 18th century architect and had built in Portland stone. Fine typically 18th century buildings variously adorned with Ionic, Doric and Corinthian columns, enriched pediments, handsome porticos and rich cornices. Front Square contained not only student rooms but also the Chapel and opposite it, built in symmetrical style, the Examination Hall, with its huge and richly decorated interior and a ceiling of fine and delicate plasterwork. On the back wall was a gallery of carved wood on which stood an ancient and highly decorated Spanish chamber organ – said to have been captured from the Spanish Armada floundering off the coast of Ireland – and on the side walls two rows of full-length portraits of the great and the good associated with the college through its long history. First and foremost the founder of the college herself, Queen Elizabeth the First of England. On either side of her Bishops and Archbishops, Dean Jonathan Swift too, Lords and Ladies galore. Among them Archbishop James Ussher (1581-1656), whom I later discovered had been the Primate of All Ireland (Archbishop of Armagh) as well as Professor of Theology, Vice-Provost and Vice-Chancellor of TCD. But his greatest claim to fame is for having carefully (mis)calculated the date of creation as the night preceding Sunday 23rd of October, 4004 BC.

Moving on from Front Square I face full on the massive Campanile dominating all from its central position and housing the great bell which would toll lugubriously and summon students to their Final Examinations. No need for me to worry about that day of reckoning just quite yet, I thought to myself, passing under its great arch and onto the well-tended lawns of Library Square. Even at first sight one suspected the library was something special, and indeed so it turned out to be – one of four 'legal deposit' libraries entitled to a copy of every book published in Great Britain and Ireland and housing over four and a half million books. The main room – the

Long Room, running almost the whole length of the building – was breathtaking. The largest and longest chamber library in the world, it contains in its solid original oak bookcases two hundred thousand of its oldest texts including the Book of Kells – known to the students as Kelly's Book – a 9th century illuminated edition of the gospels, written and illustrated by Irish monks initially in Iona then later in the monastery at Kells. It is arguably the most famous book on earth and on display in pride of position in the centre of this vast room.

Outside in the sun again I passed by the Rubrics, the oldest standing building in the college, built of red brick in the 1700s and later topped with its attractive Dutch gables. Then on through to yet another square – New Square – where I glimpsed the pretty little stone-built Printing House to my left before skirting by the Museum Building, a later addition constructed in the mid-nineteenth century with Byzantine, Lombardesque and Moorish influences evident both inside and out and which took up the whole side of a square otherwise devoted largely to student accommodation. And beyond this I came upon acres of green grass – yes, in central Dublin – largely given over to a rugby ground and a fine cricket pitch surrounded by mature trees wearing their autumnal colours which followed the outer railings along towards the pavilion behind which I discovered the way to the back gate – Lincoln Gate – from which I timidly emerged, leaving the peace and calm of the campus for the noise and bustle of the Dublin streets. I didn't get far. Just next to the Lincoln Gate stood a pub –the Lincoln Inn, not surprisingly.

It was by now lunchtime, and I could think of nothing better than a round of sandwiches washed down with my first-ever pint of Guinness. Nothing better than spending the first pennies of my generous Devon County grant on a bite to eat and a drink. I found myself in a crowded bar with much talk and laughter from all corners. I immediately detected the Dublin accent I had first encountered in my taxi-driver. An attractive lilt it had about it, and I instinctively realised I was going to have to take some note of it over the next weeks, months and years if I was not to stick out like a sore thumb in a crowd whenever I opened my mouth. So I made my order as brief and inconspicuous as possible ("Guinness. Round of beef, please.") and then concentrated solely on what was placed before me. Such was the start of the loving relationship which rapidly developed between me and the black Liffey water with its delicious rich, creamy head. If I ever had any doubts about the wisdom of my attending Trinity, Dublin for a full four years of my life, they were fast disappearing as I left the Lincoln and strode off confidently into the city. Up Kildare Street with its fine Georgian facades and doors, on through St. Stephen's Green and after a brief snooze on a park bench, back towards college down Grafton Street.

Half way down Grafton Street my nostrils caught the distinct aroma of coffee beans being freshly ground. Too weak to resist this unsolicited temptation and attack on my senses, I at once wheeled left and straight into Bewley's coffee house. It was only later I was to be told what a well-known institution Bewley's had become over the years since its opening in 1927. The Bewley family were originally Quakers from France but emigrated to Ireland, setting up a tea and coffee trade in Dublin. Several cafés were already in operation before 1927 when the Grafton Street café first opened its doors, rapidly becoming the most famous of them all. From a plaque on the wall I discovered that this had once been the site of Whyte's Academy, whose pupils had included the Duke of Wellington. The Duke, formerly The Hon. Arthur Wellesley, was the third son of the first Earl of Mornington, who I later found out had been educated at TCD and in 1764 was elected its first Professor of Music.

It was nearly five o'clock by the time I emerged from Bewley's fortified by their excellent coffee. An afternoon well spent, I thought to myself, as I wended my way through the start of the rush hour crowds. The now familiar Trinity railings soon came into sight, as did the splendid 18th century stone-built town house – the Provost's House – standing proudly behind its high stone walls. And then, a mere stone's throw further down, the welcoming sight of the Front Gate with its happy prospect of immediate escape from the crowd and its promise of peace and quiet in its hallowed precincts within.

The lights of the rooms on the top floor of No.15 Botany Bay were on. So, I now braced myself to meet a wife – or two. The door was opened by a neatly dressed young man of medium height – Mr

Michael Edmund Hope, it transpired – who had a good peep at me through the glasses he was wearing before allowing me access.

"Ah! Hello, I'm John Wilkinson and you must be one of my wives."

He at once gave me another closer look, clearly perturbed at the words he'd just heard.

"Me? One of your wives? I don't understand. Kindly explain."

If ever there's any truth in the saying that first impressions are the best, then here is a case in point. The underlying seriousness of the man was evident in those very first words we exchanged. Here was a man – a wife, too – who was on a serious mission to learn. The acquisition of knowledge was to be the primary consideration for Michael during his university days. (Quite right too, most would say.) Knowledge of his subjects certainly, but also knowledge in other spheres too, principally religion and music. There was much scope for religious debate at Trinity – the Catholic-Protestant divide in the country saw to that. Discussion groups abounded, along with one-to-one encounters with the Church of Ireland Chaplain (No place for a Roman Catholic chaplain in college, thanks to the dreaded Archbishop McQuaid) as well as with earnest Divinity School students from Northern Ireland, were commonplace, and Michael Hope was to enter into the great maelstrom of it all with a vengeance. Serious matters to be treated seriously, and the time to be filled meaningfully. Wasting time was sinful.

These too were the guiding principles of his music-making. His oboe was there to be practised on. Practice, more practice, regular practice. (Quite right too, most would say.) The actual enjoyment of the music came further down on his list of priorities. Rigorous discipline was all-important, pleasure suspect.

However, once the ice was broken we were clearly going to be able to get along together happily enough. He was a person one could hardly take exception to, mild-mannered, courteous and with a sense of humour. What's more, our backgrounds were broadly similar, both of us coming from an upper-middle-class milieu, both of us educated in the independent sector. Our differences lay, or so I thought, in the fact that he was Edinburgh born and bred and

I was a southerner. He had been brought up with a grey Scottish, Presbyterian work ethic, I with a more happy-go-lucky and 'sunnier' view. He was morally principled while I was lax in my outlook on people, events and life in general. He was 'respectable', I was less so.

He too was doubtless gathering his first impressions of me as we both sat there, cups of coffee in hand, in front of a warm, slow-burning peat fire. The peace was soon disturbed by a noise from the stairs outside – the clomp of heavy boots approaching. With no other warning the door was flung open wide and in strode J. William ffoliat Young, followed by a porter weighed down by suitcases and bags of various sizes and description.

"Ha ha!" he announced himself. And then for good measure "Ha ha!" again, followed by a protracted palaver while he frantically searched through pockets – jacket, waistcoat and trousers – to find the money with which to tip an exhausted porter.

"Ah! Yes! It's coming! Money! Money! Fear not, ye of little faith, 'tis here!" he chortled as he sought out pennies from the various pockets all over his person. A further song and dance while he theatrically counted out his worldly wealth into the extended palm and then bid the porter an extravagant farewell with a dramatic flourish of the hand worthy of a West End theatrical production.

"Thank you, my good man. Thank you for your timely labours. May God go wi' 'ee! Ha ha!" he cried out before slumping down on to the sofa in an uncoordinated great heap.

Here, too, first impressions turned out to be not far off the mark. William, my second wife, was clearly going to be another kettle of fish entirely. His dress alone spoke volumes. Heavy brown brogue shoes, thick corduroys, a brightly coloured waistcoat with brass buttons, a tweed jacket with a multicoloured handkerchief hanging floppily out of its breast pocket. All this might have denoted the attire of the typical country gentleman. However, this was only the exterior, and apart from the unruly shock of long, curly hair, it gave little indication of the character beneath. William may well have come from the squirearchy, but there was more to him than that. On his very first entrance into our lives he had shown a flamboyance and theatricality which overrode distinctions of class and background. Indeed, as time passed one detected his inbuilt irreverence for all things politically correct. It was often as if he wanted to shock while never appearing to take himself seriously. He would be at once frivolous, childish and sometimes just plain silly. Annoying, fickle too. At other times he was provocative and funny with it. There was a louche and disreputable side to him too of which one gradually became aware over time. In this he was at his most far removed from the values with which he had been brought up in Northern Ireland. His father, a Trinity graduate, had become a priest in the Church of Ireland and was a fervent member of the Orange Lodge, an organisation the significance of which had yet to be explained to me.

So there we were, the three of us – an Englishman, a Scot and a Northern Irishman destined to share rooms and rub shoulders for four years. I, already on this first evening, had cast myself in the role of the middleman and had decided that if any of us were to put the cat among the pigeons it would be Mr J. William ffoliat Young.

The following morning saw us set off towards the Examination Hall and the Freshers' Week stalls, around which thronged hundreds of junior Freshers eager to see what was on offer. I soon lost sight of both Michael and William, the former, I imagined, having made a beeline for the God squad stalls which were much in evidence. William on the other hand, I supposed, might well have gravitated in the direction of the DU Players – the college theatre group – or perhaps the Historical Society, the debating society. As for me, I soon found myself signed up for both orchestra and choral society and put my name down for an audition for a place in the DU College Singers, a select group of some twenty or so singers who sang a wide repertoire of music written for the chamber choir.

To the rugby, rowing and countless other sports clubs represented I gave a wide berth, happy in the thought that games were no longer compulsory, even if it wasn't long before I realised that it was those who excelled on the games field who were generally considered to be *la crème de la crème* – as had been the case at Cranleigh – and were the most highly esteemed of all. To have been elected a Knight of the Campanile and awarded one's 'Pink' (an Oxbridge 'Blue') was about as high as one could expect to go. As at Cranleigh, I continued to seethe silently at the idea of it all. Why *these* people? What about the top scholars, the first-rate musicians, actors and debaters, for example? Should they too not be held in similar esteem by the general consensus? What was so infinitely superior about the ability to hoof an oval-shaped ball around a rugby pitch, for heaven's sake? This was clearly to be part of a status quo I was never going to understand, let alone accept. Let it be, whispered the voice of reason within me.

The next few days were busy ones: registering here and there for this and that, buying the statutory Junior Freshman's gown – the short one, the 'bum-freezer' – working out one's timetable for the following week – the Honours Degree Course in French and German, in my case – arranging a time to meet one's personal tutor, and so on. Almost one full day was taken up with the finding, choosing, buying and transporting of a beaten-up second-hand upright piano. We found an old storage depot down on the Quays stuffed full of them. Choosing one and haggling fiercely over the price took most of the morning, but it was the transporting of said piano from the Quays on the north side of the Liffey to 15, Botany Bay, Trinity College which was to prove the greater headache. It took us another several hours to track down a none too sturdy four-wheeled handcart which we thought might just be up to the job. 'Just' turned out to be the operative word. Six of us it took to load this heavy, metal-framed piano onto our creaking cart. Six of us it took to wheel the wobbly wagon through the busy streets of central Dublin, avoiding all manner of dangers set around us in doing so, but attracting the unwanted gaze of the traffic police who somehow decided to allow us on our way without let or hindrance, although they might easily have charged us for being a public danger to both pedestrian and motorist alike. Phew! And so eventually into the safety of Front Gate, where we came to a stop and took a well-earned breather, realising that the worst was still to come. Negotiating the cobbles of Front Square was a nightmare with our precious cargo bouncing around, up and down, left to right, with every step we took. How the staircase, let alone the piano, survived the final leg of the journey will never be known. Suffice it to say, with a lot of shoving, pulling and pushing, puffing and panting we finally made it to the third floor with only minor damage to report – a few scratches and scrapes to the plasterwork on the way up and one of the ornamental brass candlesticks on the front of the piano broken off. The former nobody would notice – Mick, the Skip, perhaps? The latter we would repair ourselves.

And so Fresher's Week was happily spent settling in and pottering around here, there and everywhere. One could almost be excused thinking that one had walked into a high-class holiday camp, so few were the restrictions of that first week. One was required merely to eat on either First or Second 'Commons', the formal evening meals which were taken in the fine panelled dining room hung throughout with impressive full-length portraits. This was a formal occasion. Gowns were worn and the College Latin graces before and after meat – long ones – were recited by heart by a scholar from a raised oak pulpit set at one end of the High Table where the Dons also took their meals before retiring to their Common Room where coffee and port was served them in the best of the Oxbridge traditions.

We undergraduates had to make do with jugs of Guinness – 'porter' we called it – set at intervals down the full length of the oak tables at which we sat. The secret, we soon discovered, was to sit at a table around which were gathered a gaggle of divinity students, the theory being that they were serious-minded teetotallers and would pass all the jugs down our way. When this was the case the result was fairly predictable – the lucky imbibers staggered unsteadily out of the hall having downed several pints with their meal. It usually meant that the rest of the evening was a write-off, so why not head straight for Front Gate and start the evening pub crawl?

One then somehow had to remember to be back in college by ten o'clock – curfew time – when the Junior Dean, Dr Robert Brendan McDowell, accompanied by a porter carrying a lantern, would take roll-call in the Front Square. The role of the porter we were later to learn was to ensure by the light of his lantern that the JD, as this most charismatic don in charge of discipline was fondly known, didn't come to any harm on his nocturnal rounds. It appears that some of the undergraduates of a previous generation had wanted, for reasons best known to themselves, to obstruct the Junior Dean of his day on his rounds and had dug a hole or a trench into which the poor man had fallen head first. A student prank taken a little too far, the authorities had clearly thought. Hence the lantern.

Shades of other matters on the horizon arrived on the Thursday in the form of a letter sent to me through the internal post. It was signed by a Dr Owen Lancelot Sheehy-Skeffington, the don who had been asked to be my tutor, requesting that we meet the following afternoon in his rooms. I suddenly and instinctively found myself being transported back to school all over again. Summoned by the housemaster. What had I done wrong? What was the punishment to be this time? Or summoned by my father to his study. Same thing. What now?

I needn't have worried. The interview was fine. Dr Skeffington – 'Skeff' as he was known by all and sundry, a lecturer in the French Department – had simply wanted to discuss the course I had chosen with me. With evident charm and a ready smile he soon put me at ease and conversation flowed naturally into matters of wider interest. He gave me the immediate impression of a man of wide experience in life.

And so it came as no surprise to me when I discovered that 'Skeff' was indeed a man of many parts. As well as lecturing in French at Trinity, he bore the letters TD after his name, denoting that he had been elected to a seat in the Irish Senate. I soon discovered he was very much a public figure, known throughout the country for carrying the flame of individual conscience and humanitarianism during his entire life. He came from a strong socialist-republican background. His father, a well-known pacifist during the 1916 uprising, had been murdered by the British when 'Skeff' was only six years old – shot without trial by a British officer who was later declared mentally unstable. The officer was found guilty of murder but insane and therefore incarcerated in Broadmoor Criminal Asylum. It was with this background that 'Skeff' had dedicated himself to the defence of liberal values and causes in education, law, politics and religious and social affairs. I counted myself indeed fortunate to have a man of such high calibre as my academic tutor.

The story of the murder of his father at the hands of a British officer saddened me. It merely confirmed in my mind what my airport taxi-driver had been implying all along – that the British in Ireland had a lot to answer for.

Chapter Twelve

TCD – the Middle

Lectures started with a vengeance on the Monday morning. One could hardly complain at the number of these we were expected to attend – twelve per week averaging out at two a day of three or four hours between Monday and Friday. We did however object to those scheduled for 9 am, even if these would usually occur only once or twice a week at most, considering it unreasonable to expect the average student to be anything approaching compos mentis at such an unreasonably early hour. In my case these early starts usually meant leaping out of bed at 8.50, flinging on the nearest clothes at hand, grabbing a quick cup of coffee and legging it round the corner to Number 35 New Square, home to the Modern Languages Department. Depending on who was giving the lecture and its subject, I would either gently doze through the hour or lend a sleepy ear to the proceedings.

Some lecturers were clearly more engaging than others. Some were plain boring. Also the topics under discussion varied enormously. What I hadn't initially realised was that those of us studying Double Honours in French and German were expected to have a working knowledge of the history of the development of both languages from their earliest roots. In German this meant delving back as far as

Indo-European, through Indo-Germanic and on to Old High German (c. 600-1050), Middle High German (c. 1050-1350) and finally to New High German, which reassuringly was at last beginning to resemble the German I'd learnt at school. All this involved grappling with alarming monsters like Grimm's Law and Verner's Law, which seemingly explained such things as first and second sound-shiftings (*die erste und zweite Lautverschiebungen*). Lots of time and effort was devoted to the development of the consonants – voiceless stops, voiced stops, aspirated voiceless stops, aspirated voiced stops, voiceless spirants, voiced spirants, nasals, liquids, sonants as consonants. Whole lectures were devoted to labials, dentals, palatals, pure velars and labialised velars. And on and on.

I would leave these lectures dazed and bewildered by it all and wondering what use this was ever going to be to me. Clearly I was not an academic at heart. The development of the verbs too was every bit as much of a mystery to me and to many another, thankfully. At least I wasn't the only one being slowly drowned in a toxic bath of philology, etymology, linguistics and phonetics. And the whole process was repeated when it came to the history of the French language, how modern French had developed from Latin through Vulgar Latin and Old French to the modern-day language, which didn't really begin to emerge until the 17th century.

Luckily we weren't restricted to the study of language. The literature of both languages was also central to our diet, and this turned out to be much more to my liking, even if it meant studying texts from the 12th century and before in both Middle High German and Old French, languages which bear little relation to their modern counterparts. In German lectures we waded through a whole mass of medieval poets, of which one of my favourites was Hartman von Aue, who wrote mainly courtly love-songs and crusading lyrics. His long poem *Der Arme Heinrich*, which describes the life of a 12th century noble knight whom he named Hartman, we studied in great depth.

Ein ritter so geleret was
daz er an den buochen las
swaz er dar an geschriben vant;

der was Hartman genant
dienstman was er ze Ouwe.

The language of these texts is clearly Germanic, but we still sweated over them as we plodded on page after page. Another favourite of mine was Walther von der Vogelweide. He spoke lyrically about the spring and the beauties of nature:

Do der sumer komen was
und die bloumen durch das gras
wunnelich eensprungen,
alda die vogele sungen,
do kom ich gegangen
an einen anger langen,
da ein luter brunne entspranc;
vor dem walde was sin ganc,
da diu nahtegale sanc.

Then there are the even longer epic poems, and still we ploughed on: Wolfram von Eschenbach's *Parzival*, Gottfried von Strassburg's *Tristan* and the protracted, seemingly never-ending *Das Nibelungen-lied*, whose author not even my lecturer, Herr Lösel, knew. All these texts were later to exert a profound influence on Richard Wagner in his search for the soul and identity of the Germanic peoples.

And the same went for the French lectures. Here we plunged straight into one of the greatest of 11th century French texts, *La Chanson de Roland*, an epic poem (oh, dear! long again!) and chanson de geste (lat. gesta – an adventurous action), the remaining copies of which exist in Anglo-Norman (Bodleian Library, Oxford) and Old French. It was this latter version we had dished out to us for close inspection.

Carles li reis, nostre emperer magnes
Set anz tuz pleins ad estet en Espaigne.
Tresqu'en la mer cunquisit la tere altaigne.
N'i ad castel ki devant lui remaigne;

Mur ne citet n'i est remes a freindre,
Fors Sarraguce, ki est en une muntaigne.
Li reis Marsilie la tient, ki Deu nen aimet;
Mahumet sert e Apollin recleimet :
Nes poet guarden que mals ne l'i ateignet.

At least here was a thumping great action-packed story, and even if it was a struggle to get to the heart of it, the effort was gradually paying dividends. One could imagine the story being sung by itinerant troubadours to show the threat represented by the Saracens (Arabs) in Spain and already knocking at the doors of France. A song sung too to encourage the building of Christian armies to fight the Crusades against the Infidels (Arabs). The tale told is one of both history and legend, and is only partly historically valid. It is partly myth, not unlike our own Arthurian legends and the myths surrounding the great Irish High Kings, Brian Boru among others. Nevertheless it is a fine story of soul-stirring and emotive events told with verve and vigour. I loved it.

Starting with these early, challenging texts we were then bounced along through the centuries, swooping down on the major literary figures each had to offer. Essayists, dramatists, novelists, poets, short story writers, polemicists, philosophers, both French and German – you name it and we had to know about them. The reading lists were colossal and I now wonder how it was that so few of us crumpled under the weight of it all. Maybe it was because, being young, we were quite happy cruising along with the flow, reading a play here a novel there, more or less keeping pace, or not, as the case may be, but certainly not in those halcyon early days hoisting in the fact that at the end of it all there was to be a day of reckoning, a day when all would be examined and tested. For the first-year student – the junior freshman – that day was an eternity away. Nearly four years. Let it wait. Let us now play and amuse ourselves as best we can. *Carpe diem.* Such was the thinking in those carefree first years, and so it was that one had the time and space to discover more than books and libraries, time to discover life, others – and oneself.

The secluded existence of home and the vicarage hadn't exactly prepared me well for the bigger life beyond. Closeted schooldays had told me a certain amount about myself by awakening emotions within me which would later prove impossible to shake off. But now other very different calls were about to be made on my thoughts and emotions. Girls. Young women. The fair sex had up to this point played almost no part in my life, if one were to exclude the brief flirtation with Jane of the Tuckenhay paper-making factory, a few clumsy kisses stolen at holiday dances and awkward groping in either cars or shrubberies – depending on the weather – after them. It was a different matter being sandwiched between blondes and brunettes on the long benches of the lecture rooms of the Modern Languages Department. Not much wriggle room there, and one was forced into close contact, both physically and metaphorically. Social interaction with the opposite sex was now clearly inevitable and the shy, inexperienced ex-public schoolboy was going to have to rapidly develop new skills in communication and relationships which he did not yet know he possessed. As with so many things in life it turned out to be a question of time, trial and error.

Over the following weeks and months, like others in the same boat, as I imagined, I came up against all manner of young girls – girls I very much liked, girls I quite liked, girls I lusted after and those in whom I could summon up not the slightest interest. They were a mixed bag of sweeties designed to keep the testosterone-fuelled male on the hop and, in some cases, on heat. The beautiful, soft and gentle Gillian – oh! To have her squeeze up against you on the benches, what bliss and rapture unconfined! And oh Fiona, with your beautiful figure, who could not but turn his head, swivel his eyes and ogle you as you made your stately way across Front Square? And you, Daphne of the Buttery Bar, who hour by hour served up the cakes and coffee with your radiant smile and lips to die for! Was it surprising that one day I jumped the counter (figuratively speaking, I'm no athlete!) and whisked you out to Howth Head on that fine summer afternoon to taste those lips for myself? The sun kissing us, the blue sea of Dublin Bay set below. And the nameless beauty from the café on O'Connell Street –you never noticed that lonesome young English Trinity student beside the juke box sitting and gazing, gazing and yearning for you. (No, no counter-jumping here – too shy). And you, Judith from Birmingham – the first of your sex to reveal all to me, not that I ever let on to you. And Jill and Diana and Melissa and Frances and all the other girls from the Elizabethan Society who at one time or another invited me to sherry parties, tea parties, garden parties and dances. Thanks be to God for you, for all of you. You who all did your best to bring the boy on and out, crossing the gender-barrier into the man.

One day someone told me that Frances 'fancied' me and that she was losing sleep over it. This somewhat puzzled me, as I had only met the girl two or three times and scarcely knew her. It was also quite flattering, since she was a pretty girl by any standards. So at the next opportunity I told my friend Mike, who I knew would give me his mind on the matter. He did, in his own inimitable manner: "Well, what are you waiting for, mate? Wimp! Get right on with it! Wang it right up there!"

Mike's language was always colourful, to say the least. At first he was way outside my comfort zone, to use the modern idiom, but he too was a linguist, so over the weeks and months I got to know him and we became friends. He was all but ten years older than the rest of us – a mature student – and already, compared to us, he had vast experience under his belt. Michael de Larrabeiti, son of a philandering Basque émigré and a long-suffering woman from Battersea, had done it all, seen it all (especially when it came to women) and from the start he made sure we others all knew it.

He had been brought up in poverty on the rough-and-tumble streets of pre-war Battersea. An education wasn't an option, and by his early teens he had already left the elementary school for work in local shops and a library. An elder brother eventually lifted him out of a treadmill existence by teaching him about photography, which he put to good effect in the mid-1950s when he was selected to be the official photographer to the Oxford University Expedition to Afghanistan. Overland London-Afghanistan on the back of a motorbike – Mike's stories of the trip and time spent in that almost totally undeveloped country were hair-raising. However, the irrepressible adventurous streak within him had already showed itself long before then when at the age of only fifteen he announced to his waitressing mother that he was off to Paris to visit – on his own, on his bike. This is precisely what he did, taking all day to cycle the 60 miles from London to Newhaven, where he took the night boat to Dieppe and then on to the excitement of the days and nights discovering Paris.

So started Mike's lifelong love affair with France.

'…for I love France so well that I will not part with a village of it; I will have it all mine…' (Henry V: Act V, scene II)

By the time he eventually arrived at TCD, Mike had criss-crossed France innumerable times. He had collected experiences as broad as his backpack, learnt to speak the language fluently and made a host of friends and acquaintances from all walks of life up and down the country. Those he treasured the most were the shepherds of Cogolin in Provence, with whom he would stay for months on end and especially during the season of the *transhumance* when he would help them move their flocks from Grimaud to La Colle St Michel – a trek of about 150 miles on foot – from the burnt-out grass of summer and up to the fresh mountain pastures of the Basses Alpes. Moving flocks of up to 3,000 sheep, not to mention half a dozen spare mules and thirty goats, was hard work, but Mike didn't shrink from it. He later relished telling these stories from his 'golden days' and was clearly proud of that close affinity which he had established and developed with the simple, friendly and hard-working folk who had adopted him and made him one of them.

Who could not but admire the zest and enthusiasm of this colourful, charismatic character? By his late twenties, when he entered Trinity, he already had so much to say about and for himself. We felt admiration too for the determined way in which he straddled the only remaining barrier which still stood between him and a university education by learning enough Latin in six months to pass the 'O' Level exam – an entrance requirement – at the first attempt. Impressive, I thought to myself, mulling over the fact that my privileged education had allowed me the luxury of no less than seven years study to achieve the same objective.

"Well, come on, Wilko, what's up with this young Frances, then? Where've you got to? I'm coming up for a coffee and you'd better tell me all."

Much as I appreciated Mike's concern over my love-life – or rather lack of one – I just didn't find the fire within me to make things happen, and the lovely Frances was soon to be seen looking elsewhere, having given up her hopes of stirring Wilko into some form of action.

Most of us, I suspected, – and certainly this was the case with my two 'wives', William and Michael – simply weren't too bothered by the idea of a regular, steady girlfriend. The odd 'encounter' here and there, the occasional 'ship in the night', was all that was required. And in a very real sense girls were anyway only appendages – they were after all banned from the campus after 10pm, and woe betide those of us rash enough to attempt to smuggle one in after that hour. He ran the risk of having to run the gauntlet with the Junior Dean (the JD in charge of discipline), who was frequently to be seen prowling around in Front Square before and after the nightly roll-call, rattling his bunch of keys, muttering volubly to himself in his piercing and unmistakable Belfast accent. Battered pork pie hat pushed well down onto the top of his heavy horn-rimmed glasses, glinting owl-like eyes peering through them, heavy woollen scarf flailing, equally heavy overcoat (whatever the season of the year) trailing – here was a character known to and beloved of generations of students, the eccentric professor *par excellence*.

The prestigious Historical Society (founded in the mid-18th century with Edmund Burke as one of the founder members) forbade women membership, considering the gentle sex unequal to the challenge of fierce debate, so we men were left to hold the fort while the girls would nightly disappear through the portals of the campus, leaving us to our own devices until the following morning. Groups would naturally form and bond. The Boat Club and Rugby Club boys would come together to talk tactics and down the pints. The Knights of the Campanile would mutually 'peacock' and preen their feathers. The students of the Divinity School would go into corners and huddles to chew over dogma. The DU Players would seek each other out to enthuse about and bask in the glories of literary Dublin. The musicians, me included, would form coteries around pianos to sing over Bach cantatas or Schubert songs and marvel at the operas of Wagner. Yes, life went on happily enough in the absence of the girls. Then there was always the pub-crawl that beckoned from beyond Front Gate, a serious all-male activity if ever there was one.

It was not until my third year that life took a new turn and I found myself with a proper girlfriend. ("At last, Wilko. Now go for it like the clappers, boy!")

I'd been singing on the bass line with the DU Singers for two years when simultaneously I was elected conductor and Heather, still only in her first year, joined the sopranos. From the start it was fairly clear that we were going to become friends. Eventually good friends. I suddenly had both hands full and was at first more than a little unsettled – flattered too, I must admit – at the prospect of facing up to these two new, uncalled-for responsibilities, which would most certainly test me, both musically and emotionally. Having to stand up in front of a chamber choir of twenty or so talented singers, every bit as experienced as I was, having to choose the repertoire and then rehearse it to the high standard expected, all this was calculated to draw me out of my protective shell. It did. Fast. Deep-seated in-stincts of self-survival came rapidly to the surface and to the rescue. Confidence was much boosted as time went by. Concerts in College, written up favourably in the next day's *Irish Times* by chief music critic Charles Acton, a visit to St. Columba's school and then to the summer Edinburgh Festival Fringe, the winning of the mixed voice choir section of the Feis Ceoil (Dublin's music festival) – all this and more kept me busy and buoyant. Not to mention a performance of Gilbert and Sullivan's *Trial by Jury* which I conducted in front of an audience which packed the Dining Hall.

Heather, too, kept me both busy and buoyant. It was a voyage of discovery for both of us, and although it didn't ever quite take us the whole distance ("Get a move on, Wilko!") it was nevertheless instructive. Both Michael and William, my 'wives', had to live with the fact that Heather and I were an 'item', also with the sight of us snuggling up close – very close – on the sofa throughout the long winter afternoons in front of a glowing peat fire. Michael would shuffle in and out, embarrassed. William would barge in and chortle.

Even if I can't admit to 'losing sleep' over her – this was not a case of the forlorn, love-smitten Romantic – she did in fact occupy my thoughts for much of the time and as such kept me on the straight and narrow, more or less. Besides, as well as finding her attractive physically and sexually, I was somewhat in awe of her. Her grandfather had been a bishop in the Church of Ireland, she was clearly from a well-to-do family with a nice house in Rathgar (a 'nice' and up-market district of Dublin) and she was a much better pianist than I was. I was staggered to watch her give an assured performance of Beethoven's piano sonata opus 110 – not easy – for a midday chamber music concert in the Department of Music.

Had Michael de Larrabeiti been the sole influence on my emotional life, matters might well have continued to proceed predictably enough and along the same lines. A steady-ish girlfriend with a little extra 'on the side' from time to time – what more could one possibly want? Nothing more – for as long as that was all that was on offer. It was only when Carl made his dramatic entrance into my life that I realised that I was seeing only half the picture. Seen through *his* eyes the world was a very different place from the one de Larrabeiti was showing me and one which appeared equally attractive, if not more so.

Carl Henrik Bonaventura Harald Bontoft, Vicomte de Saint Quentin – known simply as 'Bon' to his friends – was as extravagant a person as his name would suggest. Son of a Church of England country clergyman, he was of Swedish extraction and was two years in advance of me and in his final Senior Sophister year when we first met. He was both extrovert and charismatic in the extreme, and I had heard about him by repute some time before we first met. So too had most of the Trinity of his time, owing to the fact that he was the only one to openly declare himself to be a homosexual ('gay', not a word in use at the time). To use the modern expression, he had 'come out' at a time when it was definitely not the 'thing to do'. He attracted enormous attention to himself by flamboyantly flaunting his sexuality to all and sundry both within and without the college precincts.

"Hello! John Wilkinson, I presume? Here, have a look at this." Our first meeting was in Front Square when he bounded up to me and thrust into my hands a hand-written music manuscript. "I've just written it. Take it away with you, look at it and tell me what you think." In my hands I was holding a short mass – a Missa Brevis – written by Bon in memory of Pope John XXIII, a man whom he much admired and who had just died. I realised at once that he was hoping for it to have its first performance from the Singers – which it did. So started a friendship – no more than that – which was to outlast our Trinity days.

Just as Michael de Larrabeiti had opened my eyes (well, half-opened them perhaps) to the delights of the world of girls and women, so now Bon took me in hand to show me the wider world of Dublin and his friends beyond the confines of Trinity. He had a wide spread of these in both musical and gay circles. Quite frequently the two circles coincided. Often his musical friends were gay too. If not they were almost certainly gay-friendly. For a young undergraduate to mix in these circles and with people of all ages was heady stuff. John Beckett and John O'Sullivan, fine harpsichordists both of them, David Lee, former organ scholar of Peterhouse, Cambridge – all three lions of the Dublin musical world. The world of Tibor Paul and Janos Furst, conductor and leader of the Radio Eireann Symphony Orchestra suddenly opened up in front of me. I took a walk-on part as a toreador in Bizet's opera Carmen at the Gaiety theatre. I was rubbing shoulders with the Grand Old Man of Irish music, George Henry Phillips Hewson, BA, Mus. D, Hon FRCO, first appointed as organist of St. Patrick's Cathedral in 1920, where he remained for decades, then as Professor of Music at TCD in 1935, where he remained till 1962. He had first entered Trinity as a boy chorister in the 1890s – here was walking history indeed. The DU Choral Society had sung his great anthem 'Let us now praise famous men' on the occasion of the bicentenary of the founding of the Chair of Music – a fine piece of Victorian writing.

I crossed paths too with another well-known pillar of the pre-war

Dublin musical scene. Captain Alexander John Dawson Henry, an amateur musician and pianist, had given public recitals in those far-off days when live classical music was heard only rarely in Ireland, in the same way that Professor Hewson had regaled the Dublin public in the 1930s with his adaptations for organ of the Wagner overtures at a time when orchestral concerts were scarce. Captain Henry, Alex to his friends, was a delightful eccentric to say the least. Our paths first crossed outside the porter's lodge, Front Gate, where he had been asking after me just as I happened to be passing through.

"Well now, sir, you're in luck. There's Mr Wilkinson passing by right there in front of you."

A distinguished-looking elderly gentleman turned to face me, squinted at me through tortoise shell rimmed glasses and extended a hand.

"Good morning to you, Mr Wilkinson. My name is Henry, Alex Henry, and I've come to invite you out to lunch at my club. Will you do me the pleasure of joining me there for lunch? One o'clock at the RAC club, Dawson Street."

Having acknowledged my acquiescence in the matter before I'd hardly had time to realise I'd even given it, he turned briskly on his heel and was hurrying off back through Front Gate and into the crowded streets beyond. Surprised at myself and how easily I'd accepted a lunch invitation from a total stranger (what would mum say!) I turned to the porter.

"Ah! To be sure, sir, that's Captain Henry for you. A quaint old cove, that one. Always down here on the look-out for helpful young undergraduates he is. Quite harmless too, sir. If I were you I'd go down to the Club for a nice spot of lunch. He'll make you most welcome, that I can assure you, and it'll make a change from the Buttery Bar now won't it, sir?"

I wasn't going to disagree. Yes, it would certainly make a nice change. The RAC club was housed in a very fine classical Georgian town house, and if the interior was anything like as impressive as the exterior we were clearly going to be lunching in some style. It remained for me to wonder in what way I was going to be 'helpful' to a gentleman old enough to be my grandfather.

Brushing aside last-minute doubts, I found myself boldly marching out of gates and arriving at the club just as the old Irish grandfather clock in the spacious entrance hall was striking the hour. Through a door leading on to the bar I could see and hear the Captain talking animatedly to the young barman, who was clearly amused by what he was hearing.

I stopped momentarily in my tracks to observe the scene, unobserved. I judged the old chap to be at least in his eighties, in spite of his animated conversation and the still sprightly gait he showed. He betrayed a slight stoop, but in all other respects he seemed to have retained an agility of both mind and body fairly remarkable for someone of his advanced age. Beautifully turned out, too, wearing a well-cut check sporting jacket complete with velvet collar, a canary-yellow pullover with socks to match, cavalry twill trousers and a brand new pair of spongy suede shoes upon which he appeared almost to dance as he engaged the enchanted young barman in rich conversation, gesticulating all the while. And to add to that, beautifully groomed he was as well. His sparse white hair was brushed back firmly to the rear of his head, accentuating a weasel-like face with a pointed nose. A military-style moustache, white and clipped close completed a picture of elegance and distinction.

The porter was dead right and Alex Henry made me most welcome. We had an excellent lunch washed down with a fine bottle of claret in sumptuous surroundings. That in itself would have been enough, but I hadn't bargained for the mesmerising conversational skills and anecdotes with which the old man regaled me throughout the meal. The stories in themselves were riveting, but so too the manner in which they were told. The Irish have the gift of the gab, so they say. They can speak eloquently and profusely. They've kissed the Blarney Stone. But it's more than that. To listen to old Henry telling his stories was to listen to a poet. The Irish know instinctively how to use the language deliciously and as a vehicle for poetry. He had that gift in abundance and I could happily have listened to him for hours on end, just as he would have equally happily continued to entertain and amuse me for hours on end.

I was right and his story began in 1886. Among his early memories was welcoming Queen Victoria, the little old lady on her last official visit abroad, when she arrived in great state at Kingstown (now Dun Laoghaire) harbour in 1900 on her way to Dublin. He described in detail the crowds wild with joy and an atmosphere charged with emotion and how he too was swept up by it all. Listening to him recount his early days was indeed history at first hand, and I was fascinated. Stories about his family, the Henrys, a well-known and well-heeled Protestant ascendancy family, and about their losses during the Troubles in 1916 and thereafter, about his Trinity days at the dawn of the 20th century and the role he had subsequently played during the First World War. All of this pure history. Fascinating.

The hours slipped by and we slowly moved to present times. He'd been given my name by my friend from Broadhempston, Tom Tyler, whom he had met when visiting Selwyn College, Cambridge. Tom must have told him I was a helpful sort of chap, because here he was now inviting me for weekends at his stately mansion in County Louth.

"For you see, John (we were on Christian name terms by the time coffee and brandy arrived), I have this large house, Rathescar in Dunleer, to run and at my advanced age it's becoming just a wee little difficult. And I was thinking to myself maybe you'd be liking a weekend in the country from time to time and give me a hand in the park and round and about in the grounds. That's only if you're not spending all your time in the libraries poring over your books, to be sure." he added, a mischievous glint in the eye.

And so it happened that I came to spend weekends – not all of them – at Rathescar, Dunleer, Co. Louth. Getting there involved taking the train to Dunleer from Westland Street Station on a Saturday afternoon. A slow old loco it was, too, stopping at any and every village station on the way irrespective of whether there was anyone wanting to get on or off. No one was in a hurry and timetables didn't seem to matter. This was a blessing indeed when on my first trip I was in urgent need of relieving myself (too much Guinness in the station bar before boarding) and only then realised that I was trapped in my carriage, the train being corridorless. No loos. Panic!

I wriggled, crossed and uncrossed my legs in increasing agony until mercifully the next station came into view. It took me a minute or so to work out that the door could only be opened from the outside and this could only be done by releasing the leather strap on the inside, which then caused the window to come crashing down, thus enabling one to operate the outside door handle. I then almost fell out into the arms of the station master, bladder on the point of bursting.

"Excuse me, but have you toilets here?"

"To be sure we have, sir."

"Have I time to use them?"

"To be sure you have, sir."

"I won't be long."

"You'll be as long as it takes, sir, and the train will too await you as long as it takes."

I made a dash for it and just made it. Sure enough the train waited and I hopped back on board much relieved.

This same scenario played itself out fairly frequently on subsequent journeys, and by the end I'd made quite a friend of the obliging station master to the point that I'd find him waiting for me on my return from the loo and ready to engage in sometimes lengthy conversation, seemingly oblivious of the patient driver peering down the platform at the two of us and waiting for the green flag to wave him on his way again.

Once the train arrived at Dunleer station –often late, probably on account of my incontinence – I would be met by the good Captain at the wheel of his ancient tank-like Volvo, and he would whisk me the mile or so to the fine Georgian country house that is Rathescar. It took me no time to realise why Henry should be permanently on the look-out for helpful young pairs of hands in his attempt to keep both house and grounds in some reasonable state of repair. The house was large and far too big for a single old bachelor rattling around it all alone. He was alone apart from the mad Peggy, the wild-eyed cook, who would pop up around meal times, serve at table and then scuttle off to goodness knows where – to one of the attic bedrooms, for all I knew, where the servants of happier days would have doubtless been lodged. Reception rooms and bedrooms alike seemed surprisingly well looked-after – a woman from the village, I understood, who from time to time came in to dust and clean. Flicking a duster in these rooms would have to be done with some care. Objets d'art were in evidence everywhere, with the finest bone china decorating the mantelpieces, antique glass displayed in many a wall cabinet and antique furniture scattered throughout the house bedrooms included. Life-sized statuary graced the impressive entrance hall – gods and nymphs from classical antiquity for the most part – but the *pièce de résistance* was without doubt a magnificent fresco set into the top frame of a highly decorated ironwork table, a fresco excavated from Pompeii and shipped back to Ireland by one of Henry's more perspicacious ancestors doubtless when doing his European Grand Tour. Its detail and the freshness of its colours were a marvel to behold.

"Yes, you're right, a remarkable piece of work", said Henry, showing me round the house shortly after my arrival. "But I have to careful about my statues. You know John, some people just don't like to see nudity, strange as that might seem. When the Church of Ireland bishops meet here for their annual convention I have to drape them all with bed sheets so their lordships can better concentrate on the spiritual. Or else they would accuse me of encouraging the sins of the flesh, to be sure they would, their lordships." A mischievous glint in the eyes and the hint of an amused smile as he pondered the matter.

The tour continued up to the observatory tower, through corridors and rooms clearly no longer in use and ended up in what was to be my bedroom. In both bedroom and bathroom time had stopped somewhere in the Victorian era. In the bedroom was an iron bedstead with brass knobs the size of which I'd never seen before, a floral-decorated washbowl and accessories, a fine mahogany clothes-horse and shoe-trees neatly tucked in between wardrobe and dresser, both monumental. In the bathroom, king-sized bath with fine brass taps and mahogany surrounds, loo with mahogany seat and a chain supporting a decorated porcelain handle, with loofahs and natural sponges in plenty. When I eventually took my first bath I was totally unprepared for the shaking, rumbling, clanging and gurgling that preceded the eventual arrival of the hot water. The antiquated system was clearly at its last gasp.

Saturdays was usually a fairly relaxed affair. Before supper there would perhaps be time for me to do a few odd jobs around the house, teetering at the top of a stepladder, for example, replacing bulbs in one or other of the vast cut-glass chandeliers. After supper we would repair to the drawing room, where I would be invited to play on the Steinway concert grand piano. If I pressed him Henry, too, would take to the keyboard – Liszt, often, *con brio* and with fistfuls of wrong notes.

Sundays, weather permitting, was devoted exclusively to work in the garden and grounds. Sitting behind a great powerful Ransome motor-mower and permanently in fear of it running away with me, clipping edges and hedges in the rose garden, replacing broken glass panes in the huge green houses in the equally huge walled garden, such were the tasks I was given. Needless to say I barely scratched the surface of what needed to be done and there was clearly work enough for two or three full-time gardeners. Nevertheless the old boy seemed happy enough with my labours and would happily regale me with further tales from the past over supper – talk of the Troubles leading up to 1916, stories from the war years, both First and Second World Wars. I would afterwards mull over it all in a steaming hot bath before an early night.

No sooner had I got into bed than there would often be a knock at the door and in he would come, to sit at the bottom of the bed and add to the anecdotes he had been recounting over the supper table. Not since my boyhood, when my mother would linger before saying goodnight and turning off the light, had I been regaled with such vivid bedtime stories from the past. Living history was laid before me.

The early morning Monday train saw me back in Trinity, usually in time for lectures. Not that to miss a lecture from time to time was a hanging offence. It wasn't, and by the time we were into our second year we knew to a nicety which of those definitely had to be attended and which could be skipped with impunity. By then we were well into the swing of things and besides, the social life of the campus was claiming more and more of our thoughts and time, often to the detriment of academic work and study. Social life ranged from the Trinity Week Ball to parties, pub crawls and endless coffee-drinking sessions in a string of sets of rooms, passing all manner of matters in review. Our rooms were no exception.

One such drinks party (bring a bird and a bottle) was given there on 22 November 1963. It was in full swing when the news filtered through of the assassination of President Kennedy. Things suddenly went very quiet and people began to melt away, some of them, I was told later, to say a prayer in the Chapel. The upside was that I and my 'wives', Michael and William, were left with a multitude of half-full bottles of wine to work our way through over the following days.

The three of us were managing more or less to live amicably together in spite of the high level of unpredictability William was to continue to show. At least Michael was learning to ignore him when he chose to be in the teasing mode. What's more, there were long periods of time when Michael and I hardly even saw him. Seemingly he would be trawling the streets of Dublin and coming up against all manner of strange encounters. Occasionally we would see a few of them in the rooms. Once I walked in when he was entertaining George Otto Simms, Church of Ireland Archbishop of Dublin. Another time Patrick Moore, the astronomer, who'd been speaking at the Hist. and then on one occasion a tramp he'd picked up from the Quays. With William you could never be sure what he'd be up to next.

Once he disappeared off the scene for a whole week. It turned out that he'd taken a flight to Edinburgh on a whim to buy gold and antiquarian books. While at it he'd invited himself to lunch at Michael's parent's house in Morningside (very respectable, and they weren't best pleased to have this uninvited, wild, uncouth and unkempt Irishman on their doorstep) before booking appointments with Ken Carey, Bishop of Edinburgh, and Dr Grier, Bishop of

Manchester. Michael thought he'd completely lost the plot. I did too. History doesn't relate what the two princes of the Church made of it all – perhaps just as well.

William's appearances at the Historical Society's debates were memorable, often outrageous. His performances either as a speaker or from the floor were often highly amusing, even if, more often than not, totally off the point. The Regius Professor of Divinity, however, was far from amused when, half way through his Sunday sermon, William boldly stood up in the middle of a packed Chapel and asked if he could ask questions. So much for political correctness.

Before we had really fully realised it, we were already approaching the end of our Senior Freshman year – the half way mark with two years still to follow as Junior and Senior Sophisters. The Englishman, the Scot and the Irishman had seemingly learnt to co-habit happily enough in spite of the wide differences of character and temperament. Long may it continue thus, we thought.

Chapter 13

TCD– Graduation

University terms – only six weeks long, they were – and vacations alike continued to slip by at an alarming speed. Not that we were that much alarmed. As Junior Sophisters (third year) we were able to take comfort in the thought of a fourth year and a buttress between us and the day of the final reckoning. Vacations saw us flung far and wide, especially during the long summer vacation when for two successive years I took off to Munich to find student work and improve on my far from fluent spoken German. One year I spent working in the *Hauptbahnhof* as a *Gepäckträger*, which meant loading and unloading the goods vans of the trains as they came in and out. Accommodation was provided in a railwayman's hostel where twenty or so of us were double-bunked and where I got no sleep owing to the prolonged nocturnal activities of the Bavarian sleeping above me who nightly brought back one of the wenches parading the streets below.

The following year we were accommodated in student university rooms, sleeping well but working hard in a kitchen in the bowels of an upmarket restaurant on Ludwigstrasse. Since I was surrounded throughout the day mostly by Greek and Turkish *Gastarbeiter* I was arguably learning more Greek and Turkish than German. Another summer was spent at the Edinburgh Festival conducting the Trinity Singers at a Fringe event, and yet another working for Clarkson's Travel Agency in France with Michael de Larrabeiti, who had got me the job. We were to meet day trippers from Luton (pensioners most of them and first trip abroad for a lot of them) at Beauvais Airport in the morning, whisk them into Paris for a six-hour sight-seeing tour and return them to Beauvais, on their last legs, that same evening for the flight back to Luton. Timing was of the essence. Not a minute to be lost.

Mike impressed on us that we, his guides, were in this to make money. Each of us on the drive into Paris was to impress on his coach load that there would be a unscheduled stop (unbeknown to Clarksons) at a world-renowned perfume shop (it wasn't) opposite Notre Dame, their only chance to buy the finest perfumes (they weren't) for their loved ones. Ten percent of the sales went straight into the pockets of the guides. Second (scheduled) stop for lunch. Third stop was not at a department store – no 10% scam available there – as advertised on the Clarkson brochure but instead a trip down the Seine on a *bateau mouche* (another 10% of ticket sales straight to the pocket of the guide). This last scam was sometimes difficult to sell and took the smooth talk of the serpent, especially on days when it was bucketing down with rain.

The third scam took place after a hectic, action-packed day on the coach returning to Beauvais. (Michael called it the *déclaration de guerre*). I was to impress on my charges that whereas I, the friendly guide, was not supposed to accept tips (sob! sob!), it was quite in order should they wish to show appreciation of our friendly driver who had done such a splendid job (hadn't he?) weaving us all so skilfully in and out of the nightmare of Parisian traffic. Besides he, the friendly driver, being Catholic, had eleven children (lie) to feed, clothe and educate (sob! sob!) and all on the meagre pay allowed to him by the nasty Clarkson man. If I delivered this sob speech convincingly enough I could be sure that not only would the driver reap a handsome reward but that I too would be well remunerated for my efforts. The total contributions were to be shared equally by guide and driver. All in all, a good day's work. Thank you, Michael de Larrabeiti.

These holiday escapades were all very well, but time was insidiously and relentlessly creeping on and before I knew it I'd become a Senior Sophister, yes, a student in my fourth and final year. Finals. Horrors! The nightmare of it all was at last beginning to dawn on even the most sanguine among us (I panicked and promptly gave up the conductorship of the College Singers). The final exams which were to test us on everything we'd supposedly learned and inwardly digested over the previous four years, exams which were to seal our fate for a lifetime. We were to be indefinitely branded. ("Oh John, you mean you only got a Third?") I was at least honest enough with myself to know that a First was out of the question, but the very thought of my coming down with only a Third sent shivers down my spine. The shame of it. (My father – both judge and castigator in my mind – had only just missed a First and that because the chemicals he was handling decided to explode causing much pandemonium and damage – a little of that only, luckily – in the laboratory where his chemistry Tripos was taking place.) I simply *had* to come up with a Second, preferably a Two Part One (as opposed to a Two Part Two) so as to at least stand equal with my father. There would be no shame in that, indeed it would be a much-needed boost to my self-confidence which, during those critical summer months of 1965, was beginning to show clear signs of collapsing under the strain.

To give credit where it's due Heather, now only in her second year, helped me not a little to take the strain of those final few months. I invited her to spend a week at the Vicarage over Easter and somewhat to my surprise, she accepted. Equally to my surprise (I don't know why) she had immediately formed a close rapport with both my father and, what's more, my mother, with whom she appeared to be permanently in cahoots over her week's stay, to the extent that I became worried lest it were thought there were wedding bells in the offing. (Perish the thought). Suffice it to say that by the end of the stay Heather had clearly been given the parental imprimatur as my girlfriend and was doubtless invited to 'look after' me during the testing months ahead.

Unlike Oxford and Cambridge, TCD holds its Finals in September, after the long summer break rather than before. The good thing is one can enjoy the May Trinity Week to the full – the College Races, the Elizabethan Garden Party, the Provost's Drinks Party and most of all, the Trinity Ball at the end of the week. And enjoy it we surely did. What a relief to have a girlfriend to invite to the Garden Party – a prized invitation indeed – and to the Ball. Dancing till daylight was followed by a leisurely walk in the Wicklow hills the next day – hills bathed in a gentle Irish spring sunlight, cuckoos calling, the long grass inviting. Yes, all was well with the world throughout that week of magical moments.

The downside of September Finals was all too evident once the May festivities were over. Three long, hot summer months closeted in libraries and reading rooms. The work and revising to be done was prodigious. Where to begin? Brecht on the *Verfremdungseffekt*? The sermons of Bossuet? Grillparzer, Hebbel, Schiller and 18th century German drama? Baudelaire's *Fleurs du Mal*? The *Minnesänger*? The *Essais* of Michel de Montaigne? Mallarmé, Verlaine, Rimbaud and the Symbolist poets? The list of 'things to be done' was endless. I panicked. I wasn't going to be able to cope. It was all too much.

I rang my mother, a witness to how bad things had got. She listened to my tale of woe and immediately proposed flying over to give me the moral support she clearly (and understandably) thought I was in need of. No sooner was the offer made than I found myself backtracking furiously. No, I was really perfectly OK and in no need of parental support, thank you very much. I surprised myself at the vehemence with which I fought the prospect of maternal interference into my affairs. The idea that my mother should supervise me and my studies was unthinkable, and quite enough for me at once to take a grip on myself and my predicament.

It was one thing being cooped up poring over texts all day (surrounded by the Northern Irish contingent who seemingly had spent a full four years at it – the protestant work ethic in full swing), another walking out onto the campus after a hard day's work only to find it had been taken over by cavorting, blonde, blue-eyed Swedish girls on summer language courses. What more could they have wanted than to be taken care of by handsome young graduates-to-be such as ourselves? Alas, it was not to be. Temptation was to be resisted, the work pattern to remain unmolested.

Not to say that there were not moments of relief from the tedium of it all. Such moments tended to centre around the weekends when libraries and reading rooms were closed. Saturday evening was the one and only pub visit I allowed myself of the week during those long, hot summer months of 1965. Over the years my 'local' had become Davy Byrne's, just off Grafton Street and a stone's throw from Trinity. (It gets a mention in Joyce's Ulysses when Leopold Bloom stops for a gorgonzola cheese sandwich and a glass of burgundy while on his wanderings through Dublin.) It was 'Bon', the extrovert Swedish count, who had first introduced me to this delightful hostelry and its interesting clientele (yes, largely gay and musical). It was he who there introduced me to his wide circle of friends, some of them, like us, Trinity undergraduates, others graduates, some Dubliners, others of an older generation. It was a rich mix and I adored it. It wasn't long before Bon's friends became my friends, and here was I continuing the Davy Byrne's tradition two years after 'Bon' had left the Dublin scene.

Our tightly knit group of like-minded individuals was led by two highly charismatic characters, David Lee and Peter Mellon (the latter nicknamed 'Katie Cantaloupe' by 'Bon'). They were the greatest of friends, and squabbled endlessly. David, in his mid-twenties and a former organ scholar from Peterhouse, Cambridge, was a hugely talented musician who turned his hand principally to the harpsichord and the organ but whose mind and interests encompassed the whole gamut of classical music, particularly church music. His wide knowledge of the latter he put to good use at St. Bartholomew's Church, Ballsbridge ('Testicles Viaduct' to Trinity students), where he was the resident organist. Peter, considerably older, was a flamboyant business man who lived and worked in Sligo but regularly drove down to Dublin to spend the weekends in his sumptuous flat in Fitzwilliam Square, one of Dublin's finest. And when not in his flat he was in the pub, Davy Byrne's, of course, with all of us, knocking back the lagers and Guinnesses as if there was no tomorrow. On his arrival on Saturday evenings he was always greeted with open arms by all and sundry. He usually brought with him lurid accounts of his drive down.

"J-John, I have to t-tell you," (he spoke with a pronounced stutter) "the young hitch-hiker I picked up outside Sligo, was the most b-beautiful young th-thing I've set eyes on in ages. He must have b-been your age. And most come-hither, t-too, if I m-may say so. (A wink and a twinkle in the eye.)

Or "J- John, you should have s-seen the one I picked up today. Just your t-type. A serious-minded student from Queen's (Belfast). Too serious for me. I prefer mine f-f-f-frivolous...."

And then there was young Tom behind the bar, pulling the pints with those strong arms of his. Oh, Tom! Oh, Tom! ("J-John, he knows you f-fancy him, of course he does. *Do* something about it. Invite him to your rooms and who knows w-what.") It was not to be. There was no 'w-what'. Courage failed me. I could only fantasize.

Meanwhile both drink and conversation flowed furiously with the twin threads of sex and music weaving their alluring ways through it all. Exhilarating it most definitely was.

"Time gentlemen, please!" David, Peter, David Ledbetter, Tom Pockley, Michael Hope (my 'wife') sometimes, Bill Fuge *et alia* and I, armed with crates of bottled stout, would then wend our wobbly way to the top flat of No. 43 Fitzwilliam Square, there to settle down to a serious night of further carousing to the accompaniment of lager-soaked LPs pushing out choral music from John's and King's (Cambridge), both college choirs coming under close and sozzled scrutiny as regards the quality of the sound of the treble voices. Some preferred the oboe-like sound from St. John's, others the mellifluous quality of the tone produced by King's. Plenty of scope for heated argument there. Down with the drink, up with the volume of general excitement and debate. The two went hand in hand right into the early hours of the morning.

Getting back to Trinity more than often more than slightly worse for wear was a hazardous affair and invariably took some considerable time. Staggering on through Dublin's deserted streets, weaving one's tortuous way back towards first those reassuring tall, green, iron railings – oh, so valuable in providing support and giving direction! – and then on towards Front Gate, there to be admitted by a bleary-eyed porter to the sanctuary within.

"Brendan, I've brought you a bothel of porter."

"Tanks, sir. Most kind of you to be sure. And just mind how you go, sir. Steady there, sir."

"I'm perfectly shteady, Brendan. Shteady and shober as a judge. You know me, Brendan."

"Yes, indeed, sir, I know you… steady, steady…. and now top of the morning to you, sir."

How on earth I managed to be up and about early on Sunday mornings and in time for choir practice and the following Sung Eucharist at St. Bart's will for ever remain a mystery to me. (Bart's was one of only two churches in Dublin that could properly be called High Anglican – smells and bells aplenty with the likes of Katie Cantaloupe mincing their way down the nave and then bobbing up and down like yo-yos in front of the high altar.)

"J-John, don't tell me you haven't n-noticed the new tenor sitting opposite you. G-gorgeous, simply g-gorgeous. You've n-noticed him, haven't you?

"No." (Lie.)

"Well, I got talking to him last Sunday and he was asking me all about you."

"About *me*?

"Yes, about *you*. W-what on earth are you w-waiting for?"

Valuable information indeed and I didn't w-wait. I acted on it with uncharacteristic speed and bravado. Suffice it to say that the following Sunday, Patrick was mine. He was a Dubliner born and bred, living out the last months of his teens and, yes, he was indeed g-gorgeous. And so it came to pass that I was to spend Sunday afternoons during those long summer months locked into the arms of my sweet, blond, tousle-haired Dublin lover-boy. Bliss and rapture unconfined. I had known nothing like it. Not for me now those hasty and ill-considered sexual encounters I had experienced in my schooldays. No longer the guilty fumblings of my younger days, no longer the secret, furtive assignations in the lavatories in the dark, no longer the constant fear of exposure and punishment and pain. Here was plain unbridled sex, unencumbered. Sex for sex's sake. Kissing and more galore. For hours and hours at a time, safe behind the locked door of Flat No. 43, Fitzwilliam Square. (Yes, dear Katie Cantaloupe had given me a key." J-John, you'll be doing the same when you're m-my age. Looking after the y-young men, standing them drinks, helping them on their w-way. You'll see you w-will.")

Once over it was back down to Trinity again. Back to the real world but with a difference. Here was now a new young man walking tall, head held high, happily humming to himself and to anyone who might care to listen in. And all the while playing back in his mind the words that had been said, the deeds that had been done. *Oh Patrick, you will never know the good you did me that summer. You will never know.* Funny, I thought to myself tripping down Grafton Street, that I was always leaving Patrick in such high spirits whereas on leaving Heather I more often than not found myself a prey to mixed feelings. Did she love me? Almost certainly not, otherwise she'd surely 'go the whole hog' with me, wouldn't she? (Larrabeiti: "Well, Wilko, wanged it up there yet, have you? What? *Still* not?")

What was wrong with me? Didn't I have the right technique? What more did she expect me to do? Should I somehow try harder? How? Or did I really care all that much? None of these doubts with young Patrick – it was all so much simpler with him, and destructive feelings of self-doubt just didn't come into it. I decided I had better try and keep the two of them on the go. After all Patrick seemed to manage OK without seemingly losing any sleep about it. (He had told me in detail about the steady girlfriend he had, too.)

Monday mornings found me up and about early, bright eyed and bushy-tailed eager to confront once again yet another full five days of solid study – morning, afternoon and, yes, evening too. If I stuck at it head down for those three full months (which I did) it was largely because those weekends provided the necessary light at the end of the tunnel. Weekdays working hard, weekends playing hard, I'd found the balance that was to see me through those testing times.

Not all weekends necessarily followed the same pattern, and

Saturday evenings often brought with them variations on the theme. For example if rumour was going around that Brendan Behan was in town, we'd forsake Davy Byrne's for the Old Bailey opposite where we knew he'd be holding court, dispensing pints of stout to all and sundry – that's if he wasn't already too drunk – and generally cultivating his reputation as one of the more rumbustious figures in the city's literary circles. Nobody knew for sure where he'd spent the major part of his life – was it in prisons or in pubs? Probably quite a close-run thing, we reckoned.

"J-John, next S-Saturday let's meet for a quick jar in Davy B's and then I'll stand you d-dinner at m-my club." Katie Cantaloupe was a member of the highly prestigious Royal Irish Yacht Club in Dun Laoghaire south of Dublin and was proud to show me the fine facilities of the club house which included a first-class restaurant. Founded in 1831, its first Commodore had been the redoubtable Marquis of Anglesey, who commanded the cavalry at the battle of Waterloo, and past members included the first Duke of Wellington. But I couldn't resist asking our distinguished-looking waiter why in a republic there was ever such a thing as a *Royal* Irish Yacht Club.

"And what now, sir, would ever prevent us from calling it the Royal Irish Republic should we ever wish so to do?" Touché.

The following Saturday I was again invited out to dinner, this time by David Lee (so as not to be outdone by Katie C?) and to undoubtedly Dublin's finest restaurant – Jammet's. In the party was John Beckett, the famous Dublin harpsichordist, dwarfing us all by his colossal presence and looking every bit like a larger version of Orson Welles. It came to the ordering of the *digestifs*.

Waiter: (superciliously) And what will you be taking this evening, Mr Beckett?

Beckett: Brandy. Bring me brandy, my good man.

Waiter: (same tone) *Which* brandy, Mr Beckett? (The list of brandies and Armagnacs was endless. Armagnacs from the Bas-Armagnac, Ténerèze and Haut-Armagnac regions, cognacs à gogo from Charente and Charente-Maritime)

Beckett: (with a withering look) The *largest* one, of course. What else?

And on yet another memorable Saturday evening we partied out at Malahide Castle, north of Dublin, the country seat of the Talbot family since early in the 9th century. Hugh Cobbe, whose party it was, had ordered horse-drawn cabs as the transport. Three loving-ly- polished horse-drawn cabs, each smartly painted (lilac, green, yellow) discreetly promoting three different Dublin hotels, waited in Front Square, doors open. Six young couples, all of us elegant in our evening wear, climbed in and clip-clopped away across the cobbles through a warm summer evening. Had we been in 18th century dress, this delightful scene would have been complete.

One day J. William ffolliat Young (my 'wayward' wife) issued both me and Michael Edmond Hope (my 'respectable' wife) with a surprise invitation – not that anything really ever came as that much of a surprise when it concerned William, so unpredictable did he continue to be. He invited us to spend the weekend at his parent's home in the North. Michael turned it down there and then without so much as giving it a thought – he had far too much work to do and, besides, his oboe was causing him concern (a hairline split had opened up in the wood) and, more important, he had nothing to learn from going to the North (his regard for the Trinity northerners was clearly no higher than mine.) To leave by train for Belfast on Saturday morning and return to Dublin on Monday afternoon, also by train, meant, of course, losing valuable revision time on the Monday, and also missing out on Patrick, who by this stage had become very much part of my staple weekend diet. But go, in the event, I decided I would. Finals were now only three weeks away and I felt that a last total break from Dublin for the two days would do me good. A chance to de-pressurize before the final run-in.

Nothing had really prepared me for Northern Ireland. I knew not what to expect that August Saturday afternoon when stepping into the home of the Reverend Francis Young, William's father and pastor and chaplain to the Orange Order. Suffice it to say that by the time of my departure on the Monday I felt I knew all I was ever going to need to know about Northern Ireland – that poor, benighted province – and its troubled history. In the telling of the history it became immediately clear to me that the twin strands of politics and religion had from the beginning been inextricably entwined – and clearly still were. The account of events from both William and his parents was very definitely a Protestant one. Their admiration of the conquest of Ireland by the English, starting with Henry VIII and the Tudors, was plain to see. Cromwell, a beacon for the Protestant cause, was, too, a big hero, although his bloody campaigns throughout Ireland saw the slaughter of hundreds of thousands of the innocent Catholic peasantry and made the way clear for the extensive confiscation of Catholic lands by English, Scottish and Welsh colonists culminating in the completion of the Plantation of Ulster begun in 1606.

But the biggest man of all, according to my hosts, was without doubt their beloved 'King Billy' – William III of the Protestant House of Orange – who finally and conclusively put pay to any hopes of a Catholic Ireland by trouncing his Catholic predecessor on the English throne, James II, at the Battle of the Boyne in 1690. Enter on stage the Orange Order, that Protestant organisation which ever since that victory has spearheaded the sectarian, supremacist triumphalism of the Protestant cause in the North, its anti-Catholicism, its anti-Irish nationalism.

To this and more I listened spellbound, surprised but also shocked at the strength of the feeling in the telling of these momentous events of long ago. It seemed to me that the spirit of anti-Catholicism, in this particular household at least, was still very much alive and kicking. It was only on the following day that I was made aware that what I was hearing was by no means an isolated example of sectarian hatred. My Sunday morning visit to nearby Londonderry would quickly disabuse me of any such thoughts. Religious bigotry throughout the North, I was to see for myself, was rife.

On the road to Derry, William gave me a potted history of the famous Siege – about which, of course, I knew nothing – the Siege of Derry on April 20th, 1689. It began when thirteen brave – Protestant, of course – apprentice boys managed just in time to slam shut the city gates in the face of James II's advancing Catholic armies. James responded by laying siege to the city, demanding that the trapped inhabitants should "surrender or die", whereupon came from within the famous retort "No surrender!", a slogan adopted by the Protestant faction ever since then to the present day to demonstrate fierce opposition to all things Catholic. The siege was to last one hundred and five days, causing the city population horrendous suffering and in many cases death through starvation. Rescue finally arrived in the form of King Billy – our great protestant King, our guardian angel and knight in shining armour – who relieved the city by fighting off the popish James, then going on to crush him for ever the following year on the Boyne.

No sooner had we arrived up on the old city walls looking down on the sprawl of modern Derry when I heard in the distance the faint sound of a band playing. It turned out to be several bands, both military and fife and drum – on the march pushing out martial music for the benefit of those who were walking with them. They were clearly getting closer.

"William, what on earth is all this going on?"

"Oh, that's just the apprentice boy's parade. They celebrate twice a year. Once in December, 'the Closing of the Gates', and once now in August, 'The Relief of Derry'. All good fun. Also to remind the Catholics who's boss round here, hee hee!"

All the while the noise was growing and we were soon able to appreciate the size of this 'demonstration'. There were literally thousands of marchers beneath us following the bands with singing, chanting, flag-waving (apprentice boy flags, Orange Order flags, Union Jacks, of course) and at times with loud drumming to add to the distinctly military tone of the parade. Paramilitary regalia were prominently on display for all to see – the apprentice boys with their crimson collarets slung over their shoulders, the Orange Lodge with its own regalia, bowler hats and white gloves. All marched purposely forward, heads held high, as if marching to war to the wild applause of the crowds which had turned out in vast numbers to witness this highly symbolic event.

I looked on in silence, aghast. Was this not the very same sectarian, supremacist triumphalism I had detected in the tone of the previous evening's conversation? The same fierce anti-Catholicism and anti-Irish nationalism only now played out in public before my very own eyes? I shifted my gaze from the parade winding its noisy way through the leafy suburbs below and turned towards my left to cast my eyes over a very different Derry stretched out beneath me. Here were no leafy boulevards, no parks and squares, just row after row of dilapidated miserable-looking tenement houses back to back set in dark and narrow streets.

"William, look down over here then. What's all this down here then?"

"Oh, that. It's the slum area. They call it the Bogside. It's where the Catholics live. The Bogside for the bog Irish, hee hee!"

"Do you mean to say they *choose* to live there?"

"No, of course not. But they have no choice. We don't want them living around us. Neither do they want us living around them. Fair enough, isn't it?"

"But they seem to be living in abject poverty down there."

"Yeah, well, they only get the grotty jobs, you see. Manual labour and the like. Bottom of the pile stuff."

"I can't imagine they much appreciate these anti-Catholic parades, do they? Outright provocation, if you ask me. Best not to go shouting Catholic insults in places like the Bogside, I would imagine."

"The parades will go where they've always gone. If Catholics get in the way too bad for them. They can like it or lump it."

On the way back to Dungiven, conversation turned to political representation. Clearly the Catholics had a raw deal here too. Derry was a prime example of Protestant 'gerrymandering' – the manipulation of the boundaries of the constituencies so as to give undue influence to the Protestant population of the city.

"You know, William, from what you've told me I can't imagine that the Catholic minority in Northern Ireland is going to continue to put up with such injustices for all that much longer."

"Well they can go back to the Republic for all I care. Good riddance, says I."

We drove on in a heavy silence with William muttering under his breath from time to time 'No surrender! Kick the Pope! The Scarlet Harlot!' I could hardly believe what I was hearing. The bigotry in it all was totally unacceptable. I boiled inwardly but remained silent. No room for dialogue here.

It was a relief to be back on the train Dublin-bound the following day. Good-bye to the dour, sad, sectarian North. Hello again to the friendly Republic! The Catholic Republic!

Tuesday morning in the Reading Room is enlivened by a kerfuffle at the desk. Harry Bovanizer is there on duty as usual when in comes my friend Michael de Larrabeiti staggering under the weight of a whole pile of books which he is returning to Harry, his best mate. A mutual friend of ours spots him, runs up to the desk and roundly accuses him (Michael) of asking for books, removing them from the Reading Room (illegal) and clinging on to them for weeks on end. Very naughty of him, I agree, especially since these are reference books which are crucial to revision for those of us reading French.

Michael is now a law unto himself. He's got Harry right under his thumb and plays havoc with the system. Being that much older than us – a mature student – he tends to consider us all as school kids to be twirled round his little finger and at his beck and call whenever needed. His saving grace is his charisma. He's definitely one of the 'characters' on the block. The reason we've seen so little of him this last year is because he's been living out (illegally) with the lovely Celia (illegally, too) in a rented cottage near Delgany, Co. Wicklow. He stumbled on the cottage in the middle of nowhere, derelict and with a corrugated roof, pays a peppercorn rent for it and spends days and weeks digging an outside loo when he should be at lectures in Trinity. He buys a Ford Prefect (1929) for a song and drives in to Trinity only when he feels like nicking another armful of library books. What a jammy b------ he is!

No sooner has Mike disentangled himself from the brouhaha at the desk than he is at my side and whispering in my ear.

"Wilko, how about if I were to crash out on your floor during the exams? I can't possibly come in all the way from Delgany, and you've got those lovely rooms in New Square. That would be just perfect now, wouldn't it?"

"Perfect for you, Larras, yes. But what about my wives?"

"Oh, forget the wives, Wilko. It's me, Larras, your best mate.

Besides, that William of yours has never done a day's work in his life, so *he* won't be revising. And the other one you say you never see in the rooms now anyway. Perhaps he's taken his mattress to the library. Come on, Wilko, be a sport."

"Oh, OK."

The only other interruption of the day occurs later in the afternoon when there is a resounding crash from somewhere high in the gallery. The JD (Junior Dean) who has been at the top of a ladder for the last half an hour, his nose deep in some learned historical tome and muttering furiously to himself all the time, has finally placed the book back in its shelf and forgetting that he's up a ladder promptly walked off into thin air... Thump! He has hit the ground. Harry thoughtfully rushes off to his side. No bones broken, luckily, just a rather shaken-up JD, who, having been helped to his feet by the ever-attentive Harry, simply brushes himself down, retrieves his battered old pork-pie hat and proceeds to totter out of the reading room as if nothing has happened.

The weeks and days of intensive revision have now ebbed away. It is Sunday (No St. Bart's, no Patrick today) and D-Day is tomorrow. Sure enough Larras is there on cue to take up his residence in New Square. He is right: William still shows no sign of revising and Michael is nowhere to be seen. We strike up a bargain. He will give me much-needed tuition in Old French if I will play him a Bach Prelude and Fugue every morning before breakfast. Deal done to our mutual satisfaction.

'Ask not for whom the bell tolls; it tolls for thee'. Never a truer word on that memorable Monday morning in early September when the great Campanile bell tolled for us, summoning us to the place of execution, or so it seemed. In a way it was a relief to be in the starting-blocks. The waiting had been stressful.

With my ever-solicitous mother's words ringing in my ears ("Darling, just do your best. That's all we expect of you.") I put my head down on that Monday morning and wrote and wrote over a period of two full weeks. Time flew. As I suspected, the paper which was to cause me the most difficulties was the Old French one. Larras had done his best, but I was still very unsure of myself.

I more or less managed to scrape together enough material to write on two of the twelve questions set. It now remained for me to choose one of the remaining ten questions to answer on. I was stumped. I knew virtually nothing about any of them. Eventually I reluctantly plumped for Question No. 5 ('Account for the loss of the Old French 'S") and that only because I knew that the Latin 'castellum' or 'castrum' (Eng: 'castle') eventually landed up as 'château' in modern French. So it was something to do with the suppression of the 'S' in favour of the circumflex accent. Other examples perhaps: Lat. 'foresta', 'festivus', 'tempestas' to Fr. 'forêt', 'fête', 'tempête' to Eng. 'forest', 'festival', 'tempest'. All fascinating, I'm sure, but how on earth to write a six-page essay on such slender evidence? Well-nigh impossible.

So I turned to my left to where Ruth was sitting. To my surprise she seemed to be sleeping, head down, eyes closed, pen down. Leaning over closer I was able to see (the desks were not as far apart as they should have been) that she too had chosen to attempt Question No. 5. She had written but one sentence – 'The loss of the Old French 'S' can be put down to reckless carelessness on the part of the Old French' – and had then clearly given up the ghost. There was certainly no hope to come from that quarter so, with half an hour to go, I proceeded to scribble away for as long as I could on a subject about which I knew virtually nothing.

Latin: 'castellum', 'castrum' to Old North French: 'castel', 'chastel' (?) to Modern French 'château.' God knows why. What about Castelsarrasin, Castelnau-Barbarens, Castelnaudary, etc. – don't they come into it somewhere? Modern English suffixes '-caster' '-chester' must have something to do with it. Surely? Lancaster. Manchester. And let's face it, not all English towns took their names from Latin/Old French roots. Some came from German roots. Ex: Old High German 'burg' as in Edinburgh and Marlborough. And so I wittered on and on, covering an impressive five sides with almost total drivel. Ruth woke up after her thirty-minute snooze just as the papers were being collected in.

"Yes, Wilko, I did Question No. 5 too. Only I gave them the short answer. No point in drivelling on like you did." Just a shame we shall never know which of us got the higher mark.

Then all of a sudden it was all over. The last paper done and dusted. Elation at the thought of having survived the whole ordeal? Not really. Rather a weary fatigue and a sense of anti-climax. I could think of nothing better to do than make for the Guinness bath house to wallow in deep water and self-pity, feeling somewhat bruised and battered. Others were doing likewise. The singing was muted and in a minor key.

The few remaining days are spent packing up and preparing for the final departure. On the last afternoon I sit on the Chapel steps with Heather, watching the world go by. A gentle Irish September sun. Unforgettable. And there goes Prof. Stanford (WB), the world authority on Ovid, serenely striding out towards the Front Gate. And who are those two excitable creatures locked in animated debate over by the Campanile? Of course, they are the two greatest wits, raconteurs and conversationalists in all of Ireland – The Junior Dean, gesticulating wildly, keys clattering at his side, and Eoin 'The Pope' O'Mahony, former barrister and genealogist, known as 'The Pope' since the day when, as a pupil at the Jesuit college in Clongowes Wood, he declared his ambition to become Pope. He was unmarried, but he still never became Pope. And to our right there goes that dreadful old tramp Judge Kelly loitering as usual around the toilets between Players (No. 4) and Front Gate with his baggy pants and bloodshot eyes. They say the rot set in when he once sentenced a student to death for riding a bicycle without lights.

For these last four golden years I've lived in two worlds, buffeted from one to the other. The world of Heather and the world of Patrick. (Perhaps I should be preparing for a lifetime of bisexuality – who knows?) The intimate and privileged world of the campus and the bustling world of the streets of the country's capital city, Baille Atha Cliath. And between those two worlds stands proudly Front Gate, both beckoning one in and showing one the way out. I now walk through it for the last time. Degree-bearing? I hope so. Educated? Partially. I think I feel as Rastignac (Balzac's hero from the *Comédie Humaine*) felt on leaving his home in the provinces bound for the bright lights of Paris. Hungry for life and eager to discover.

This taxi driver was less garrulous than the first one.

"Leaving Trinity are we, sir?"

"Yes, we are."

"You tink you've learnt a little about our dear old country?"

"Yes, I think so. I tink so."

And at the airport "May God go with you, sir."

"Thank you. Tank you. I think I'm going to miss you all."

Marlborough College, The Court.

Turner House with H de W W, the housemaster, presiding.

My rooms in Turner House.

Hugh Weldon and I Chez Maxim, Paris – a temple to fine dining.

Three great teachers: L-R Gerald 'Monkey' Murray, a giant among men; Dr Peter Carter, a doyen among history teachers; and Dr 'Tommy' Hunter MC, a no-nonsense college medical officer.

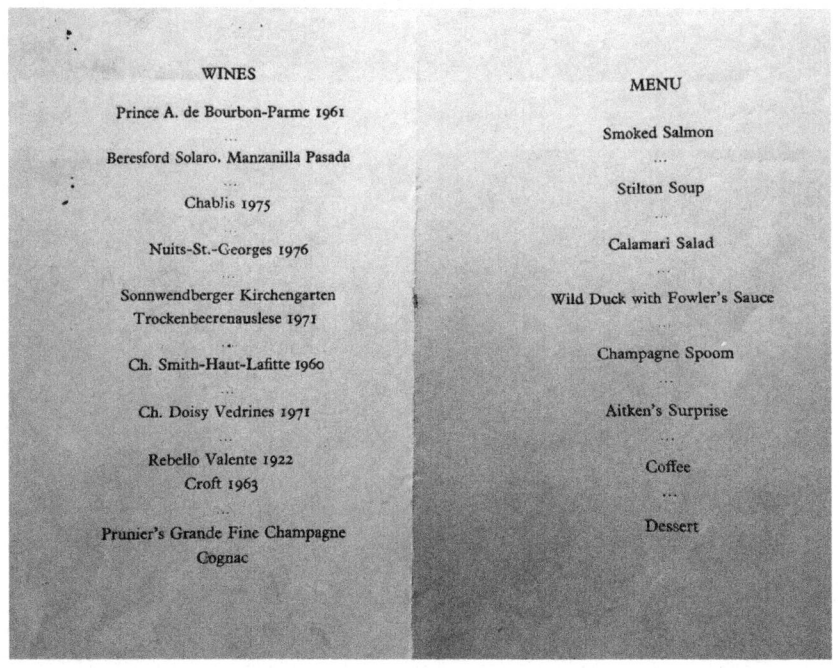

WINES	MENU
Prince A. de Bourbon-Parme 1961	
	Smoked Salmon
Beresford Solaro. Manzanilla Pasada	
	Stilton Soup
Chablis 1975	
	Calamari Salad
Nuits-St.-Georges 1976	
	Wild Duck with Fowler's Sauce
Sonnwendberger Kirchengarten Trockenbeerenauslese 1971	
	Champagne Spoom
Ch. Smith-Haut-Lafitte 1960	
	Aitken's Surprise
Ch. Doisy Vedrines 1971	
	Coffee
Rebello Valente 1922 Croft 1963	
	Dessert
Prunier's Grande Fine Champagne Cognac	

Hugh Weldon's annual birthday dinner – good food and fine wines in abundance.

Common Room smoking room.

Common Room dining room.

Common Room break. Coffee to be drunk but also colleagues to be seen and business to be discussed.

Shell (first year) French with me on the podium.

Shell French. A view from the podium.

Leavers dressed for a leaver's dinner. The finished product ready to be
launched into the wide world.

A social services group on Field Day. Muck-raking on the Kennet and Avon canal with a lunch break in the local pub.

A school trip. A morning race on Omaha beach, Normandy.

Lunch – recovering from the beach race.

School trip to Paris with supper in a bistro on the left bank. Hilarious, smutty songs from the guitarist appreciated by myself and M. Clément de l'Epine.

Martin Evans ('Farty Marty') and I ('Silky Wilky') in my flat.

Martin Evans squaring up to making an
after dinner speech.

My reply.

41 George Lane, Marlborough. The haven I created for myself having left living in Turner House.

41 George Lane again. The back garden with the brick wall I built myself – therapeutic and a good antidote to teaching.

Chez Sophie Wickham and her girls, Phoebe and Kate, outside Marlborough. Another haven from the rough and tumble of life on the campus.

The last farewell dinner. The guests have gone and I am the last to leave. Typical!

Chapter 14

Return to Marlborough

Leaving Broadhempston Vicarage to return to Marlborough for my second term was not unlike leaving the Isles of Scilly all those years ago to return to Carn Brea Preparatory school, Bromley, Kent. The fluttering of the heart, the pit in the stomach. Being packed off for my first term at Carn Brea had been no problem. I was walking into unknown territory and had no reason to be fearful. However, returning for a second time was entirely another matter. I now knew exactly what I was going into, and it was certainly no bed of roses. On arrival with my father and on being handed over to the detestable 'Pud', I promptly burst into tears and, much to the embarrassment of all, proceeded to scream like a banshee for the remainder of the interview. And here I was now, over fifteen years later, an adult but still plagued by those same feelings of fear, doubt and anxiety. Had nothing changed then? Well, yes, there were no tears and screaming now and I was careful to manage it so that my parents had no inkling of what I was feeling. (They probably did anyway, my mother especially.) The holidays had been stress-free and it was with a cheery smile that I bade them both goodbye before taking to the road –an icy January one – back to Wiltshire.

Getting firmly back into the saddle again was in itself, I reckoned, going to be difficult enough, but what I hadn't bargained for was the sense of impending doom while one waited for the arrival of the boys. Three days of waiting, of getting the books, worrying, preparing one's syllabuses, worrying, attending meetings, worrying. Yes, compulsory meetings, which over the years I began to find increasingly irksome. Committees ditto. The start of a term regularly brought at least two of these meetings with it, sometimes more. Firstly a full Common Room meeting presided over by the Master. Here the 'Heavies' would get on their hind legs to have their say – the Second Master, the Bursar, the Chaplain, the Librarian, the President of CR, for example. All would drone on over matters they considered important and would we all kindly take note. More interesting was the Master's summing up at the end. Were there to be unexpected strictures? New policies on discipline? Exhortations to all to be more vigilant over some matter or other – often disciplinary? (Policies relating to matters of dress code – uniform and the length (excessive) of the boys' hair could be calculated to raise the hackles of a good few, particularly the more reactionary of one's colleagues.) This meeting was expected to last two hours or more, winding up for a lunch break. Lunch was immediately followed by Departmental meetings, in my case the modern language department, gathering into one room teachers of French, German, Spanish, Russian, Chinese and, later, Italian and Arabic. A large meeting with lots of people with lots to say. I kept quiet.

Maybe my dislike of meetings of this nature has its roots in my post-TCD year at St. John's, Cambridge – yes, I did after all make it (much to my father's delight) to study for a Diploma of Education *and* with something more respectable (slightly) than a third-class degree. The one-year course I found tedious in the extreme. Lectures there were not exactly meetings, but there were certainly to my mind similarities in that the content of both tended to revolve around the theory of education and teaching methodology. The one redeeming feature of the one-year course was the term spent on teaching practice, in my case at St. Paul's School, Hammersmith, which I thoroughly enjoyed (apart from being ticked off by the Second Master for wearing a roll-top pullover in the school – tut

tut!) Otherwise the endless lectures on the History and Philosophy of education, with others on the principles involved in the teaching of languages, all of which bored me intensely. It was only later that it was brought to my attention that those who entered the world of education as lecturers, examiners, inspectors, were often those who earlier in their careers had failed in the classroom. I already knew that teaching in a classroom could at its best be inspiring.

I was now discovering that *talking* about teaching in a meeting could be far less so – a turn-off, as far as I was concerned. No amount of theory could help you become a good teacher. A lot of practice, however, certainly could, and at the end of the day you either had a gift for it or you didn't. Luckily for me Marlborough College Modern Language Department seemed to adopt a liberal policy as regards the content and presentation of one's lessons – sink or swim – which suited me fine. I was going to do my level best to swim in the classroom, whatever doubts I might have had with regard to other aspects of the job.

Meetings over and pupils having returned, the teaching could at last resume. It was almost a relief to plunge in again – this time no longer at the deep end. After all, I comforted myself, I now know the pupils, they now know me and we're already well into the year's syllabus. So why the apprehension? Do I draw the conclusion that I'm congenitally deficient in self-confidence? Or are all of us – the beginners – going through the same traumas of self-doubt, all of us doubt-ridden and doing our best not to show it? If they say animals can detect fear, so too can a pack of kids in a classroom. They've got to know that you are in charge, not only of them but of your subject and yourself. Show a chink in the armour and they'll find and exploit it.

I'm finding I spend too much of my time examining myself for the 'chinks'. One of them this term will show itself, I fear, in my non-specialist English classes. I've 'done' Keats with them and must now move on to Robert Graves. Perish the thought! In spite of spending holiday time propped up in front of a slim volume of collected poems, I still fail to see how I can be expected to teach them and convey a meaning on the slender acquaintance I have of them. It'll be a miracle if I get away with it. Otherwise a repeat of last term's performance should see me through the rest of my classes. (What a pity Ben Trimble is no longer in my Shell French set – he's been moved up a set and on my recommendation, drat it.) At least I have no public examinations to face at the end of the year. (The Head of Department is probably waiting to see if I make a pig's ear of what I've already got before letting me loose on 'O' and 'A' level classes – very sensible.) And at least I've not (so far) been landed with a Religious Education class, which would almost certainly cause me even more anxiety than does the poetry of Mr Graves. So things could be much worse. Phew! Let's just try and relax.

Relaxed certainly describes the atmosphere in Turner House, where now I'm looking forward to my second term as resident house tutor. Whatever may be said about the housemaster, Hugh de Weltden Weldon, he certainly doesn't over-impose himself on his charges, unlike some other housemasters we know. The unwritten mantra appears to be 'live and let live' as far as possible in the cir-cumstances, which accounts for the prevailing relaxed atmosphere. Not to say that Weldon is not treated with respect. He is, by 13 and 18-year-olds alike, the reason being, I'm beginning to suspect, that they don't really quite know what to make of him. What is he thinking? Which way is he going to jump? No wonder his friends refer to him as 'the Cat' – there's more than a hint of the enigmatic which trails around after him. Deliberately cultivated, I wonder? A cloak behind which to hide, perhaps? Maybe time will tell.

Meanwhile I just carry on with my house tutor's duties (hardly onerous) – dishing out pocket money to the little ones, having them up for coffee and biscuits from time to time (trying to be civil to that dreadful Molesworth), attending Captain's meetings, support-ing teams from the touchline and so on. Were that the sum total I would indeed be fortunate. But no, there's the house play looming over me with a performance scheduled for the end of February. My exhortations that they should learn the lines over the holidays have clearly for the most part fallen on deaf ears. The end of the first rehearsal sees my blood pressure beginning to rise. It's clear that the only ones to have made any attempt at learning their lines are the two girls – they seem more or less word perfect. The rest? Practically all of them are floundering around, unable to proceed without the text. Not even Act 1 have they bothered to learn.

"Well, sir, don't forget we've had a lot on" says Malcolm, in the lead role, as if to say I was being unreasonable in my expectations.

"What do you mean 'a lot on'?"

"Well, you know what it's like. Christmas, the New Year – lots of parties, dances and so on."

"Oh, for God's sake don't give me that, Malcolm. Parties, dances and so on? Well, what on earth were you all doing when you weren't partying and dancing then? Why weren't you learning your parts *then*? Like the girls. If they can do it, why can't *you*? (My feeble attempts to shame them in front of the fair sex – unfair?) Or are you now going to tell me girls don't party and dance?

"No, sir. But most of us have been skiing too – unlike the girls probably (girls both flush) and it doesn't leave much time for much else. What with the *après-ski*, you know what I mean, sir."

"*Après-ski*? Malcolm, yes, I know exactly what you mean – more parties, dancing, discos and a hell of a hangover the next morning, I bet."

"Oh no, sir. Alpine air is very good for hangovers. You should try it, sir" chips in the dreadful Molesworth, determined to have his ounce of flesh. (He was alluding to my drinking habits, wasn't he, the ghastly child? Better let it pass.)

Luckily I manage – just – to stop my blood boiling over. Note Malcolm's waspish swipe at the poor girls, the assumption being that they wouldn't be able to afford the sort of skiing holiday he's just returned from. Almost certainly not. Ten days staying at a five-star hotel in Klosters (or was it Méribel?) is beyond even *my* financial means. Malcolm and his like being rich is one thing. His flaunting his wealth in front of others less fortunate (myself included!) is entirely another matter. To me it's like a red rag to a bull. Enough said. Let's pass on.

"Well, ladies and gentlemen (irony), if you've not learnt your

227

lines – at least Act 1 – by the next rehearsal, God help you all. And I mean word perfect. Got it?

No answer. Sullen silence as I turn on my heel and leave the room, slamming the door behind me for added effect. I'm not sure about the added effect, hearing the stifled giggles from within as I stomp off down the corridor towards my rooms. Bloody kids!

But who's that sitting on the radiator at the end of the corridor? Is it Giles Hamilton? Yes it is. Good. (I was beginning to wonder if he'd forgotten me over the holidays, but no, here he is again as chirpy as ever and just when I need someone to calm me down.)

"Yes, but don't worry. It's always like that with plays. No one learns their part till the last moment, that's just how it is."

So here he is again happily ensconced in 'his' chair with a glass in hand.

"And anyway just remember that they're not going to want to look like fools on the stage in front of parents, friends and all, are they? I reckon you're really more worried about *you* looking the fool if they don't pull off a good performance, isn't that right?'

How right – *my* reputation at stake. And yes, of course, he's right – they'll pull themselves together. Eventually.

"But, Giles, supposing they *still* haven't learnt the lines by next week. What am I going to do then?

"Well, whatever you do don't lash out at them with punishments or whatever. Jason. Remember?

Remember? How will I ever forget?

"Thank you, how right you are. I just needed a bit of reassurance, that's all."

Bells ringing and off he goes to prep. And I? Shall I go into common room dinner? Or shall I scoot back down the corridor to see if Weldon is in? An *apéritif* or two perhaps? Followed by dinner maybe? I'm in luck – sounds of animated discussion from within as I knock on the door.

"'trez! Well, well, if it isn't the house tutor himself. Pray come and be seated and allow me to introduce you to Dr Hunter – or maybe you've already met?"

We hadn't, although I'd heard much talk of the man and knew

that he was a force to be reckoned with. Dr Thomas ('Tommy') Alexander Alfred Hunter – appointed college medical officer in 1947 (I was only five years old) and now one of the Grand Old Men of the community. I immediately bracket him in my mind with the other legend in his own time, Gerald W. 'Monkey' Murray, who had been appointed only the previous year and whom I had also first met over drinks at Weldon's. Both of them were Marlborough institutions and close friends of the 'Cat', whom they had both surely 'adopted' when he, Weldon, had arrived on the scene as a new boy later in 1952 (when I was 10 years old). These men were mighty oaks. while I was merely the tender shoot, there to grow, listen and learn. Added to which Tommy's pre-Marlborough life had been an impressive one – educated at Winchester and Pembroke, Cambridge followed by a 'good' war at the end of which he had been appointed Lt. Col. in the Royal Army Medical Corps, picking up a Military Cross on the way. Not bad, I thought to myself as I sized up the man in front of me ensconced in one of the study high-backed chairs.

"Ah, yes – hello. TCD, I gather. Damned good medical school there, what! Not as good as the London Hospital where *I* was, though." All with a twinkle in the eye. He raises a monocle to his eye so as to view me better. I view back. What he lacks in stature he makes up for in decibels – he doesn't talk, he positively *booms*. The exterior is certainly gruff, but inside I instinctively detect a kind man.

I soon nestle down, large gin in hand, and listen as they both pick up the threads of conversation. Under discussion is 'Little Windflower'. I gather that this is a 20-metre ketch which Tommy has cruised and raced from the south coast. Talk of Ireland ("Do you know of the Royal Irish Yacht Club, Wilkinson?" "Yes, I do, Dr Hunter. Been there to dinner.") Talk of Brittany ("Brittany, know it? "Yes, Dr Hunter, family holidays.") Talk of the Isles of Scilly ("Know them, do you?" "Yes, Dr Hunter; I've lived there.") He raises the monocle for another look. Perhaps I've passed muster? Hope so. Talk then turns to the famous Royal Ocean Racing Club Belle Isle Race when Tommy and *Little Windflower*, defying the worst of weather conditions, went on to win their class.

I'm thinking I just love hearing older people telling their stories (will I ever forget dear Alex Henry and his Irish yarns of days gone by?) In fact I'm thinking that I seem to get along much better with my elders and youngers than I do with those of my own age. Funny.

The doctor glances at his watch, then heaves himself up and out of his chair.

"Well, Cat, must be off. Pleased to have met you, Wilkinson."

He's doubtless off home to his supper and his American wife, fortified by two large whiskies. I attempt to get a look at his hands as he leaves. They say he lost a finger out shooting. Reputedly one of the worst shots in the county (his beaters are terrified of finding themselves suddenly in the firing line), he has somehow managed to shoot off one of his own fingers. He was able to retrieve the said 'lost' finger just as his dog (also a retriever) was on the point of snaffling it up. To no avail, since the medics were at the time unable to sew it on again.

Yes, I like the man, though I'm told the boys are terrified by his bark and gruff demeanour. He's well known to have no time for malingerers, and those feigning headaches, sickness or high temperatures in the hope of being put off games are invariably sent away with a flea in the ear (LMF– lack of moral fibre) and tend not to try it on again. (At Cranleigh in our attempts to avoid the weekly CCF parade we would surreptitiously place the thermometer on the nearest radiator when Matron's back was turned. It often worked.)

Giles tells me a story of a boy presenting himself to morning surgery with an arm problem.

Boy (in pain): "Sir, I can't raise my right arm above shoulder level."

Doctor (growling): Well, why on earth would you want to do that? Stop wasting my time, boy. Next!"

The poor boy wasn't even given the time to explain that he was the opening fast bowler of the cricket XI.

The Michaelmas and Lent terms have much in common, not least teaching afternoon classes in the dark and often playing games in filthy weather conditions. Of course rugger has given over to hockey and I now find myself thwacking a hockey ball around the pitch on two afternoons a week, still with the junior house non-performers. Just as well, since I know no more about the rules of hockey than I do those of rugger. The only other sport I'm involved in is squash – I've always quite liked a good knock-about in the squash courts. It's short, sharp and satisfying. In fact I have the dubious honour of being Master i/c Squash –an appointment made before I'd even set foot in the college, probably as a result of the fact that on my job application form under Other Interests I'd boldly written 'Playing squash'. (On the same application form I had stupidly written 'Cranleigh School Combined Cadet Force: Signals Corps (technically correct even if constant skiving meant I didn't ever even see – or rarely – a signals set let alone learn how to operate one) and it took me some fast talk at interview to deflect attempts to enrol me as Beak i/c Signals Section of the Marlborough College CCF. A narrow escape indeed.) So play squash I do, at least with the junior boys – the First 6 are far too good – arrange the match fixtures and generally try to appear interested. That is until the day I happen to pass by and see Michael Preston playing a fiercely contested game against James Grimke-Drayton. Michael, a colleague, is like me in his second term. James, Captain of Squash, is in his last year. Seeing this game makes it quite plain to me who should be the Beak i/c Squash and Michael is quite happy to take over from me. Quite a relief really.

If I'm happily thinking that I'm lightening my workload by offloading Squash, I'm shortly to be disabused of that nice thought. As if to compensate, within the week I find myself appointed to a committee set up to consider changes to the Book of Rules. More meetings. At least I'm learning fast that there are clearly powers behind the scenes who are briefed to see that we masters at all times have plenty enough on our plates to keep us busy. Similarly, at the beginning of the year I had naively thought that by cleverly dodging the CCF trap I had ensured for myself a free Wednesday afternoon. Not a bit of it. Those not performing on the Parade Ground are 'invited' to join either the Social Services group or the Works group. The former, among other things, involves College boys trooping off down into town visiting elderly and sometimes handicapped folk (known by the kids as 'granny-bashing'). What they actually do on arrival varies. Some will be there merely to provide company – if lucky they might find themselves being offered tea and cake. Others might be helping out with jobs in the garden and the like. Those opting for the latter, the Works group, find themselves facing a wide range of activities on and around the campus – brick-laying, painting, maintenance of the water meadows, building a stone foot-bridge, cataloguing library books, working at the beagle kennels and such like.

I'm in charge of the Kennet and Avon Canal group. Twelve or so of us pile into a minibus after lunch on Wednesdays and, with me at the wheel, charge off down to Pewsey wharf. It's here that the Kennet and Avon Canal Trust have a depot. Rakes and other muck-raking material are available to volunteers helping with the upkeep of the Pewsey stretch. We also have a boat at our disposal – a mini-version of the landing-crafts used during the Allied Normandy landings. This craft is endowed with a temperamental engine with a will of its own. Also a Heath Robinsonish contraption at the rear designed (aptly enough by a Captain Mansfield-Robinson, the local Trust bigwig) to trawl along the canal and dredge up the weed clogging up much of the waterway. The group seems to be a popular choice and it's always over-subscribed. I'm lucky in having two boys who happily rise to the challenge of cranking up a recalcitrant engine into spluttering life – mechanical engineers in the making, surely. Others seem happy enough just disappearing down the towpath armed with muck-rakes (and – I only discovered later – enough cigarettes to last them the two-hour session). All of us, I know, are pleased to be off the campus for the afternoon – it's liberating.

So far only one session has not met with general approval. That was at the end of last term when we were honoured by a visit from none other than the President of the Trust, General Sir Hugh Stockwell. Now retired but still every bit the military gentleman, the general turned up unannounced with Captain Mansfield-Robinson in tow just as we were packing up for the afternoon. He briskly assembled the 'troops' (a pretty bedraggled lot they looked – torn jeans, long hair) and proceeded to address them on the work of the Trust.

"And, of course, we rely almost entirely on volunteers like you young people. You've a big job on hand. We count on you all to get stuck in and give it your best. Understood? That's it, men. Dismiss."

Unused to being addressed by a general the 'troops' hesitated momentarily, clearly wondering whether they were supposed to salute (shoulder muck-rakes perhaps?) or not, decided not and slouched off to put their muck-rakes away. It was only on returning to college that I was told with whom I had been talking – none other than General Sir Hugh Charles Stockwell, GCB, KBE, DSO and Bar. Among many other things, he was Commander of the Allied Anglo-French forces during the Suez crisis and then Deputy Supreme Allied Commander Europe in NATO. On retirement he had settled in Wiltshire and had now taken on the challenge of the restoration of the canal.

He had recently been received by the Queen, who having done her homework enquired of him whether he was succeeding in tricky negotiations with British Waterways (owners of the canal). He replied somewhat tersely "I've lost one canal, Ma'am, and I'm buggered if I'm going to lose another." Some plain straight talking from a Marlburian of a much earlier generation – the 1917 intake.

Returning for a third term, the summer term, turns out to be less daunting, the waiting before stepping up to the mark less worrying. I'm pleased that I'd survived – somehow – the Graves poetry ordeal, also that the house play had gone well – my fears that the actors would let me down on the night were unfounded (Giles had been right).The only tricky moment had been when the Master had buttonholed me in the interval, asking where I placed Anouilh in the general scheme of French 20th century theatre. I was not only tongue-tied (I'm not good when put on the spot like that) but also at the same time worrying about a difficult scene-change taking place behind the scenes. Would they make a mess of it, as in the dress-rehearsal? Would they remember the props?

Summer brings with it the sound of bat on ball, smells of linseed oil and freshly mown grass. Mercifully I'm spared the time-wasting involved in the playing of cricket – a game invented by the English, so someone said, to give them an idea of eternity. Instead I'm put in charge of organising junior houses tennis – much preferable.

The sun and the warm weather put a different complexion on daily life. It's as if there's less dragging of the heels – beaks and boys alike stepping out purposely to both work and play. I'm finding myself rising early with the day and the sun, sometimes out of the house at 6.30am. Up the playing fields and out onto the Wiltshire Downs with the broad sweep of the downlands offering wide vistas to the left and the right, even as far as Hackpen Hill. It is here that Charles Hamilton Sorley came to seek respite from the relentless pressures of college life and inspiration from the natural beauty laid out at his feet. There's nobody much around at this time of day – just sheep, surprised to see me, and the odd mole coming to the surface. Hedgehogs too sometimes. On my return I sometimes run into gaggles of 'punishment' boys on an early morning run legging it up to the Wedgewood stone and back. I greet them with a cheery 'good morning, lads', but don't get much more in reply than a disgruntled snort – they would clearly prefer to be in bed.

Another favourite summer 'escape' of mine is walking in Savernake Forest. The 4,500-acre 'royal' forest lying just south of the town was first beloved by the Norman kings and became one of their favourite hunting grounds. Ownership has been in the hands of the family of the Earl of Cardigan for over thirty generations and not once has the estate been bought or sold in a thousand years. The place positively oozes history. Its noble beeches and centenarian oaks are a wonder to behold as one sets off down 'Capability' Brown's fine Grand Avenue, its main artery and the longest tree-lined avenue in the United Kingdom – nearly four miles long. My thoughts turn to Henry VIII, who also hunted the land here, invited by Sir John Seymour (the forest Warden at the time). whose home was Wulfhall, a manor house on the edge of the forest and whose daughter, Jane, was soon to capture the King's attention. Perhaps he first clapped eyes on her when out hunting and here where I'm now walking? Is it true that they were first introduced down the road in that fine

Tudor mansion, Littlecot Manor? Yes, history is peeping out at me from all sides.

Another welcome termly 'day out' from college is Field Day. The CCF – army, naval, air force sections and all – ups sticks for the day (sometimes night, too) on various military exercises (the Solent and Salisbury Plain are both at hand). The Social Services have a full day to perfect the art of 'granny bashing'. The Works Group, too, continue doing what they're normally doing, but for a whole day. My Michaelmas term and first Field Day had not been a success. I'd run into two boys smoking behind the Pewsey Wharf depot, reported them and had then been sent for by the Master, who made it clear that he thought I should not have taken any action over the matter.

"After all, John, think back to your own school days. Smoking on Field Days was fair game, wasn't it?"

I had to agree it was and not only smoking but drinking and generally promiscuous behaviour, too. (I wasn't going to tell him that.)

"You know, punishment is more often than not a question of judgement. Less a matter of the letter of the law, don't you see?"

Yes, I did see. So this was the Master's 'virile liberalism'. (A term he'd coined to replace the Arnoldian idea of 'muscular Christianity' as the guiding force behind the public school ethos.) So be it. Punishment a question of judgement – it just remains to be seen what my judgement will turn out to be like. I reckon it's about to be tested on a lovely warm summer field day down on the banks of the canal.

"Please, sir, can we go to the pub for lunch?"

"Well, I don't see why not (my judgement). Apart from the fact that half of you are probably under age."

"Oh, sir, that doesn't matter. We could go to the Ferryman's Arms. Nodge and I cycle down there most weekends. The publican knows we're under age and he doesn't mind. He's a mate."

"Fine by me. Just put in some good work between now and lunch and we'll go."

"That's great, sir. Stand you a pint!"

To give them their due they do do some good work and midday

sees us all piling into the minibus bound for the Ferryman's Arms a five-minute drive away. The publican does indeed know Nodge and Julian and welcomes them with open arms. They are clearly valued customers. I can well imagine them on bikes scooting down into the Pewsey Vale, tongues hanging out at the thought of the pints awaiting after the forty-five-minute ride. Less easy to imagine how on earth they hauled themselves and bikes up and back again their little bellies awash with innumerable pints of Wadworth's 6X.

The pints are poured, the packed lunches produced and all is well with the world. Pool is played, darts are thrown and the garden offers tables and chairs in the warm June sun. My glass, once emptied, is whisked away for a refill – who am I to object? – and by the time 'Last Orders' is called, we are all in the best of humours.

There's a right old sing-song in the bus as we wend our way back to the wharf. On arrival they surprisingly gather up their muck-rakes without a word of instruction from me and whistle their way down the towpath to the place where they left off before lunch. I wander down later to see how things are. All of them are fast asleep in the grass, dozing gently under a gentle summer sun. Hardly surprising. Let them be. They can smoke, too, for all I care (good judgement?), think I, as I wander back to the wharf and my book.

For all the apparent relaxation a summer term brings with it, one nevertheless gradually becomes aware of a growing, underlying and all-pervading tension which imbues both beaks and boys. The approach of the external exams – 'O' and 'A' levels – which will put us all on the spot, followed by the annual Prize Day weekend during which the college must endeavour to demonstrate to parents that their boys are indeed receiving a first-class education (worth every penny) and one which will go on to bear fine fruits in the future. Thankfully the external examinations don't concern me this year – I have neither 'O' nor 'A' level classes – but I still get roped in for invigilation. Boring. Prize Day weekend, however, is far from boring. Departmental exhibitions to be set up, high quality work to be exhibited, the language laboratory open for examination, first lessons in Russian and Chinese on offer.

The musicians, too, are on display with a sung Sunday morning service in Chapel, an open-air brass band performance to entertain those after the service and, this year, a small group singing close harmony barber-shop songs in the early evening. Further merry-making up at the cricket pavilion throughout the weekend – a fully licensed marquee competing with fully licensed parental cars disgorging Fortnum and Mason picnic hampers, Pimm's, magnums of champagne, tartan rugs and golden Labradors. Cricket for those who care to watch, tennis, too, on the other side of the campus.

The *pièce de résistance* of the weekend is, of course, the distribution of the prizes on the Saturday morning. A packed Memorial Hall sees the President of the Council, The Right Reverend Joseph Edward Fison, Bishop of Salisbury, launch the proceedings. On the stage beside him the Master and Members of the Council (more bishops, High Court judges, top brass military, etc.) and behind them the full Common Room in gowns and hoods. All in all, an impressive array. A key-note speech from the Master (yes, indeed, the first of the girls *are* due to arrive in September – a stir in the auditorium), followed by the distribution of prizes and cups (purring from proud parents), followed by drinks for all on the lawns of the Master's Lodge.

Drinks sound a good idea after having sat out and clapped one's way through two hours in a stiflingly hot hall. The Lodge garden looks inviting with its manicured lawns and a host of waiting waiters serving wines in glasses twinkling in the sunshine. But nobody had thought to tell me that this was to be a 'working' drinks party. We are immediately handed name tabs and told to proceed to our designated departmental totem poles to await the onslaught of parents anxious to hear all about their child's progress – or, as the case may be, lack of it. I soon find myself with a queue stretched out in front of me and the questions are raining down thick and fast. For the most part it appears to be the mothers leading the 'attack'. Fathers step back and shift from one foot to the other. Maybe 'attack' is not the right word, although I'm hyper-sensitive to any detrimental remark which could be interpreted as being levelled at my own performance.

"You know, Mr Wilkinson, Johnny *does* respond to a challenge.

But the challenge does have to be laid squarely before him. Otherwise he'll just merge into the background and merely coast along. He does need a little special attention, you know."

"Yes, Mrs Carruthers, I know what you mean. I'm sure you're right." (As right as most of the other mums in the queue who will surely also want their little Johnnies to have that extra little bit of special attention. The only problem being that the special attention has to be spread over a class of twenty-five little Johnnies, added to which some need more than others. I'm told state schools have up to *forty* in a class – how on earth would one manage?)

This turns out to be a gruelling session (parents want their pound of flesh, unsurprisingly), made worse by the fact that I'm glued to the spot and unable to get a much-needed recharge to my empty glass. Glancing down at the queue stretched out in front of me, I catch sight of a face I recognise. Who is he? Who on *earth* is he? I should know. The penny eventually drops just as he's on the point of introducing himself – yes, of course, it's Alec's father. Why my heart almost loses a beat I don't know. Panic. Do I manage to hide it?

"Good morning, Sir Geoffrey. Can I help you?

"Yes, indeed you can, Mr Wilkinson. A few words with you on Alec's French. How's he doing?" The Rt. Hon. Sir Geoffrey Howe QC MP is a softly-spoken and charming man. No need for panic here – phew!

Eventually hunger drives the remaining few off to the restaurants in town or their picnics up field. I make a dash for the bar and find I'm not alone – I join a gaggle of exhausted colleagues knocking back the glasses to fortify and restore themselves. That done, I'm my way out of the garden when I run into a somewhat agitated looking middle-aged woman pushing before her a very, very old gentleman in a wheelchair.

"Excuse me. Oh, I'm so sorry to bother you. You couldn't possibly show me to the nearest lavatories, could you?"

I could, the only problem being that they are some way off (the school not being exactly well endowed with ladies' lavatories) and I find myself offering to stand by the old boy while she trots off to find relief.

"Oh, how very kind of you! I don't suppose you could gently wheel him down the garden – he's asked to see the river. It's been such a long time, you know."

It had indeed been a long time. Lord Goddard, Lord Chief Justice of England and Wales 1946-1958, had been at Marlborough in the 1880s and was now in his nineties. His reputation went before him and he was known to all. Dubbed 'The Tiger' or 'Justice-in-a-Jiffy' or 'The Swinging Judge', he was a strong supporter of corporal and capital punishment. Flogging and the gallows were never far away for those who were sent before him. A brutal man, some say. Controversy dogged him and his judgements throughout the course of his tenure of office, none more so than when he sentenced Derek Bentley to death when trying the highly publicized Craig-Bentley case. (William Jowitt, 1st Earl Jowitt, Lord Chancellor 1945-1961, said of Goddard that he had amused his contemporaries at Marlborough by reciting, word for word, the form of the death sentence he would enact upon those whom he disliked.)

I do as I'm bidden and wheel Goddard down to the Kennet but, not knowing who he is, fail to tip him straight in, the dreadful old man.

The Sunday of the Prize Day weekend is much more to my liking. Once my choral and instrumental (clarinet) obligations over it's time to head back over the Bath Road to Turner House and to Weldon's drinks party for the Turner House parents. My fellow resident house tutors have already hinted more than once that they envy me my position in Turner House. The word has long since got out that I dine there in state with Weldon more or less when I feel like it, waited on hand and foot by Elizabeth, the resident cook, with the drink sloshed out liberally. They've also noticed that I'm to be seen less and less in Common Room dining room, where we bachelors take our evening meals. I shouldn't be surprised if some of them don't approve. Today, Prize Weekend Sunday, they know, too, full well that I'm off to a stylish drinks party – champagne is always served, I've been told – while they can look forward at most to a glass or two of white wine or, if less lucky, a glass of warm, sticky sweet sherry. Ugh!

Weldon doesn't disappoint. A Louis Roederer Cristal Brut Millé-simé is on offer – wow! That doesn't come cheap, I think to myself, accepting gratefully a glass proffered by the Head of House, who courteously introduces me to his parents. How self-assured are these young seventeen-year-olds –debonair, urbane and seemingly already totally at ease with themselves socially speaking and when in adult company. Myself at their age? A shrinking violet, tongue-tied, bash-ful, shy and uncommunicative.

We're in the old walled garden of the Hermitage (one of Marl-borough's oldest and prettiest houses, now inhabited by Dr Tommy and Mrs Hunter) behind Turner House. With the sun shining and the conversation and drink flowing, and Weldon at his most skittish and amusing (particularly with the mothers, I notice– how on earth did he ever earn his reputation for misogyny?) – all of us are clearly having a great party and all is well with the world.

Talking to the head of house and his parents turns out to be a pleasurable experience, and it is only when I'm in mid-flow that I no-tice from the father's name-tab that I'm talking to a fellow academic, albeit a somewhat more senior one – Professor Charles Wroth. Only later in the day did Weldon let on that the professor had worked at both Oxford and Cambridge and was a world pioneer in Geotech-nical Engineering and Soil Mechanics (he was later to be appointed Master of Emmanuel College, Cambridge). Had I known at the time that I was to converse with such a distinguished academic, I would have doubtless frozen to the spot, but what a friendly man and how lightly he wore his scholarship. (Over the years I was to meet other equally distinguished Turner House parents and not only from the world of academia. The Church produced The Rt. Rev. John Bickersteth, Suffragan Bishop of Warrington, later Bishop of Bath and Wells. From the judiciary there came Sir Henry Fisher QC, son of an Old Marlburian former Archbishop of Canterbury, later High Court Judge and President of Wolfson College, Oxford. From the Armed Services there was Capt. John Fieldhouse, later Commander of the Task Force to recover the Falklands, First Sea Lord, Admiral of the Fleet, Chief of the Defence Staff. All of them were able to put at his ease this young house tutor who was somewhat overawed suddenly to find himself in such elevated company.)

One o'clock has come and gone, yet the party is still in full swing – just a few people starting to make the move after having taken their leave of the housemaster.

"John, don't you go yet, will you?" It's Elizabeth (Weldon's cook-cum-housekeeper) who now teeteringly approaches me, glass in one hand, cigarette and holder in the other. (With her it's never either one or the other – both invariably go hand in hand. No half measures with her.)

"You know you're invited to stay on for lunch, do you?"

"Oh, really, Elizabeth? Are you sure?

"Yes, indeed. I've only just put the name-tabs on the table. You're sitting next to Mrs Wroth and I can't remember who."

She takes a swig at her glass and a long draw on her holder – not quite, but nearly, simultaneously.

"So come up and join the select few when these people start leaving – if ever they do!"

This time she manages a saucy wink with the swig and the puff – she really is quite a character, I think to myself, while accepting a refill from Richard, who tells me that he too has the invitation to stay on to lunch with his parents.

The select few turns out to be Weldon, the Wroths, me, Elizabeth, Elizabeth McGill (Turner House Dame – she oversees the sewing ladies and the laundry side) and finally the 'Old Guard', as Weldon refers to the colleagues who are also his friends. In other words Dr Tommy Hunter and wife, Gerald 'Monkey' Murray, Dr Peter Carter and wife, and Raymond Cook and wife. Raymond is recently retired and previously taught French, I'm told – badly. The story goes that he was appointed to the post by mistake. Of the two applicants to present themselves, one was called Cook and the other Cooke. The latter had been by far the better candidate, but the job had gone to the former due to an administrative slip. Raymond had apparently not exactly over-exerted himself during a long Marlborough teaching career, had been entrusted only with Lower School classes and had once been overheard to advise a young, new colleague to 'never let the boys put pen to paper, you know.' This advice he himself had apparently been allowed to follow with impunity, thus saving himself hundreds and hundreds of hours correcting piles upon piles of exercise books. Couldn't get away with that now – unfortunately, correcting hardly being the most exciting aspect of the job.

We settle down round a table groaning with summer salads and lobster. Yes, on my left is Mrs Wroth and on my right Dr Peter Carter, the inspirational head of the history department. (He was the one who at the start of the year had suggested that I might like to instruct his sixth form scholars in a little medieval French – horrors! – but luckily for me has never since mentioned the matter again.) With Mrs Wroth being more than fully taken up with Weldon – now firing on full cylinders – I'm mostly left to holding my own in deep conversation and waters with Carter, who is revealing his passion for medieval art. I struggle a bit, but it's OK – just.

Glancing down to the end of the table I notice Raymond Cook licking the mayonnaise and lobster off first his moustache then his fingers, one by one. Then I see his problem. He's let his serviette fall to the floor under the table and, being a man of some considerable girth, has been either unwilling or unable to retrieve it. The licking operation over, he then reaches out to one of the fine, heavy damask floor-length curtains and proceeds to dry his hands on it. Luckily all around are fully occupied in conversation and nobody notices this serious lapse in decorum – except for me. I think Weldon would be amused. I must remember to tell him later.

Elizabeth, with now a more pronounced teeter (will she trip over the carpet?) is bringing in the dessert. It's a Pavlova – meringue cake with clotted cream and fresh strawberries served with a very fine Château d'Yquem. Delicious. Not for nothing was Weldon briefly in the wine trade before entering teaching. Why on earth the English will insist on serving dessert before cheese I'll never understand. One explanation is that the custom comes from the London Gentlemen's Clubs – White's, Boodle's and the like. Coerced into holding ladies' guest nights from time to time, the gentlemen decided to bring on dessert as soon as possible during the proceedings so as to be rid of the women, who would then leave table to go off and powder their noses while they could continue the more serious business of consuming huge quantities of port and cheese while discussing matters pertaining to men and men alone. Seems plausible.

Term and end of academic year is rapidly running out. Just one more weekend before the huge vista of a two-month holiday dawns. That weekend is already taken – *il est déjà pris*. A phone call from Giles's father, David Hamilton (ex-TCD), brings with it an invitation to Amesbury: would I like to drive Giles and Richard (Giles's elder brother to Amesbury (home) and have Sunday lunch with the family? Yes, I would.

So the last Sunday of the school year sees me, Giles and Richard bowling along the Wiltshire country lanes on the short run south to Amesbury and lunch. A cloudless, warm early-July morning, hood down, the gentle breeze through one's hair, a favourite Bach Cantata issuing from the car radio – how much better can life get, I think to myself, *and* to think I'm being paid for it!

Lunch turns out to be a family affair with Giles's younger brother and sister around the table. Conversation is relaxed and with father Hamilton turns largely on memories and anecdotes from our Trinity College and Dublin days. I already have an inkling of how strong and beguiling these TCD memories will continue to be through the remainder of my days. They're clearly still glowing brightly within David as he fondly reminisces on his own far-off student days.

Lunch over, Giles guides me out to the garage, where he proceeds to introduce me to the love of his life – his motorbike. A powerful-looking beast indeed.

"Come on, I'll treat you to a gentle spin down the lane."

I unsuspectingly climb up onto the pillion seat behind him and off we go – at breakneck speed. Nothing to be done for it now but to cling on desperately like grim death as we career down the surrounding narrow lanes as if competing at Silverstone. Cutting corners and tilting dangerously, we hurtle past all and sundry – cars swerving, pedestrians diving into the hedges and safety – as if on some Ride of the Valkyries en route for Valhalla with Wotan in hot pursuit. My wild and piercing screeches of protestation fall on deaf ears as Giles continues to open up the throttle, clearly having the time of his life. Now *he* is in control and *I* am his subordinate. A reversal of roles, that is precisely what this is all about. The schoolboy flexing his young muscles for his teacher to take note. Take note I certainly do, while vowing never to allow myself on the back of such a monster ever again.

I'm eventually returned to base a nervous wreck, while at the same time mightily relieved to have survived the ordeal with my life intact. Never, never again – a promise I feel sure I will keep for the rest of my days. More or less returned to 'normal', I take leave of my hosts later in the afternoon and the three of us take to the road back to Marlborough – at a distinctly gentle pace. No, I at least have the sense not to want to compete and show them just what *I* can do at the controls.

There's a general air of *remue-ménage* on this, the last day of the school year. The Volvos and the Golden Labradors are again at the gates while the school gathers in Chapel to raise the roof with a staunch rendering of *Jerusalem* – a final one for the leavers, some of whom are clearly affected by the emotion of it all.

I'm packing my bags when there's a knock at the door. It's the Turner House leavers come to say a final good-bye. How kind.

"Sir, we've brought you a small present to thank you for all you've done for the house this year. We hope you'll be back again to continue the good work after a really good holiday. Good luck, sir."

How kind, and how much I appreciate those few encouraging words. More than they can imagine, I suspect. The small present turns out to be an LP in an all-white cover. The White Album. The Beatles. Oh dear, not quite my cup of tea, as they must well know having heard nothing but classical music emanating from my rooms throughout the year. Perhaps they think I need 'educating' into their popular culture of today. At least this kind gesture shows they've not yet entirely given up on me as a lost cause, which I fear I am.

While finishing the packing I play the record through, recognising now most of the tracks I've heard booming out their message from the studies at all hours of day and night. No, quite definitely this is *not* my cup of tea, although I have a sneaking liking for Blackbird

Song. Quite a catchy little tune, that one, with some good lyrics too.

Blackbird singing in the dead of night
Take these broken wings and learn to fly.
All your life
You were only waiting for this moment to arrive.

Imagine my horror and confusion when sometime later I discovered that in an editorial *The Times* had described the Beatles as being on a par with Schubert when it came to the art of writing songs and lyrics. Be that as it may, give me Franz any time.

With all packed up and the car ready to go, I pay my respects to the housemaster, wish him a happy holiday and somehow manage to turn down the now customary offer of drinks and lunch. No, I say to myself, if I set foot in there now we'll be chewing the cud until all hours and I'll certainly be in no fit state to be driving off to South Devon and home. So I leave him sitting there in his study in solitary splendour.

Long journeys alone in a car can be productive, I find. Sorting out matters past, present and future. Attempting to analyse the status quo, working out the next steps. Inevitably, my thoughts now turn back over the past year. How have I done? Is this for me? What do others think of me? No crystal-clear answers to these questions, of course. Better turn one's thoughts to the future, I think, as I near my destination.

In my breast pocket I have the address of a young Frenchman, Pierre Lemercier, from Le Morbihan, Brittany. He had been hitch-hiking in England and had been given a lift by Dr Wright, a colleague, who had kindly invited him to set up his tent in his garden and stay for a few days. It was here that Pierre and I met for the first time. I liked him and had invited him into my classes to tell us a little about Brittany, its history and culture. Before I knew it he was pressing me to visit him and his wife, Danielle, and stay – for as long as I liked – in their little flat above the little primary school (where they both taught) in the little village of Kerfourn, inland rural Brittany. I already knew parts of coastal Brittany through past family holidays, but the idea of penetrating the wild interior way off the beaten tourist track appealed to me. Yes, I would ring Pierre on arrival home, fix a date with him, take the Plymouth to Roscoff night ferry and then set off towards Kerfourn on foot, my knapsack on my back. A fine antidote to a year spent within the gilded portals of Marlborough College, a revisiting of the freedoms once offered by those still not too distant student days, a shaking-off of the class-room chalk dust and the restrictions of a life at school.

A relaxing week at the Vicarage with my parents – both clearly relieved to see me emerge seemingly unscathed from this first year in my new role in life – then a lift to the docks, Plymouth to take the boat for a three-week stay *chez* Pierre. This is going to be good for my spoken French and I relish the thought. Happy to return home again in August for the Dartington Hall Summer School of Music – a wonderful setting for both professional and gifted amateur musicians to make and perform high quality music of a wide variety. A place, too, to rub shoulders with well-known names (I've already been in the company of the likes of George Malcolm (harpsichord), Julian Bream (guitar and lute), Vlado Perlemuter (piano) among others – who next, I wonder?)

With these projects in mind it is no surprise I arrive home in buoyant mood. Travel and music – two healthy strands on which to build over a lifetime, perhaps?

Chapter 15

Weldon and the Wenches

If teachers ever tell you they're not in the game for the holidays, don't necessarily believe them. No other job I can think of will allow you almost one-third of the year off with next to no strings attached. I speak for myself, of course, the ordinary humble beak, and not for those of my colleagues who have already begun to climb the professional career ladder. These people are without doubt attached by strings and do have their holiday time eaten into by administrative responsibilities. For example, Heads of Department drawing up policies and priorities, Housemasters having to cut short the summer break to deal with 'A' level and Oxbridge entry results. And what about the Master, sitting right at the top of the tree? Is he *ever* able to shake off the weight of the burden he has chosen to shoulder? Will he ever know anything like the sense of release and freedom I've been enjoying over the past eight weeks? A *dépaysement total*, first in Brittany, then at Dartington Hall. Bathing in the rustic delights of rural France – *la France profonde* –and then immersed in the finest of masterclasses and concerts that the summer school of music has to offer. The former is good for my spoken French, the latter both meat and drink to the soul.

So, much refreshed, I now find myself returning for a second year relaxed and in a state of eager anticipation of what the following months are to hold in store. A far cry indeed from the anxious 'new boy' of twelve months previous not knowing whether or how he was going to cope with the new challenges to be faced. I now have friends in Common Room (among the pupils too – Giles has sent me a card from Ireland, where he's been mackerel fishing), also a more than comfortable existence in Turner House and I already feel I've gone some way in learning the ropes of the job.

I find Hugh Weldon not in his study but in the house library watching the six o'clock news perched precariously on an old plastic chair. (Why he doesn't plump for one of the armchairs goodness knows – certainly more comfortable even if somewhat faded and dusty). Having secured a welcome invitation to drinks (will it mean supper too?), I first have Andrews, the houseman, take my luggage up to my rooms before sprinting off down to Common Room to collect my mail. It was naive of me to have been surprised, alarmed indeed, on seeing the sheer quantity of bumph that had accumulated over the past two months. My bin is crammed full of papers of all sorts, shapes and sizes and indeed overflowing with them on all sides. I stop dead in my tracks at the very sight. God knows the time I'm going to have to spend sorting out all this little lot and satisfying the demands doubtless contained in it.

I dive in, grasp the contents, clasp the unwieldy pile to my chest and, now more than a little dispirited, wend my way back to my rooms. Question. Do I attempt to start to plough my way through this veritable mountain now, or do I forget it all till tomorrow and make a dash for Weldon's study and the strong drink(s) I feel I now need? The answer is, of course, clear, but not before I've thrown a quick glance over the paper at the top of the pile – a request for immediate payment of an overdue CR bill. And the paper under it. This is another request – namely that I again offer my services to the glorious cause of Junior House rugby refereeing, but this year devoting *three* afternoons a week to the pursuit rather than the two I'd been previously apportioned. *Merde!*

Once safely ensconced in *my* great chair and in the womb-like snuggery that is Weldon's study, all again becomes well with the world. The thought of Junior House rugby pales as the gin takes hold and smooths the path towards relaxation, benign conversation and not a little laughter.

Elizabeth, ensconced in her own chair, wielding both gin and cigarette simultaneously as usual, gives us the run-down on her holidays. (Delicious smells emanating from the kitchen show she's today very much back in the culinary saddle again). Weldon is listening (Yes, he's a good listener too) and pouring another round of drinks. As night follows day, so dinner follows drinks, all washed down with a fine claret. Both dinner and drink are now conspiring to bring on that much to be desired state of gentle mellowness which subtly but surely follows in the wake of good wines and fine dining.

All the more strange therefore that my deep sense of well-being should abruptly and cruelly be shattered just as I'm on the point of helping myself to a deliciously over-ripe slice of *brie de Meaux* which is beginning to 'swim' on the board just as it should. I'm all of a sudden consumed by the thought that somewhere lurking within my monumental pile of bumph is my new timetable for the year. I go hot all over and shudder at the thought of what it might contain. How on earth did I forget to winkle it out from the pile before setting off for drinks?

The dinner draws to its close with my mind elsewhere. I decline a brandy, pleading travel-tiredness, and race back to my rooms and desk. The one and all-consuming question on my mind – had my head of department entrusted me this year with a public examination set ('O' or 'A' level) or had he not? If not, the implications are clear and devastating. It simply means that on the basis of my last year's efforts I'm not considered to be up to the standard required to see pupils successfully through their important public examination years, be it 'O' or 'A' level.

Imagine my delight when, having teased out the vital piece of paper, I read that I'm to teach *both* an 'O' level French set *and* an 'A' level French set. Imagine the severe blow to self-esteem and self-confidence had this not been the case. *Que le bon Dieu soit loué!*

Tired but mightily relieved, well fed and watered, it's hardly surprising that I fall into a deep sleep the moment my head hits the pillow.

The following morning holds no surprises – same speakers at same meetings – with one exception, namely the Master is announcing the imminent arrival of the school's first girls ever. Marlborough College is today going co-educational. Not that this in itself should cause much surprise, since the whole matter had been first mooted then decided upon more than a year previously. Nevertheless the imminence of the transformation appears to catch the meeting on the hop, at least in some quarters. The Master carefully outlines the scheme and the provisions made for the girls – only fifteen 'A' level students – emphasizing the fact that they had been hand-picked not only for their academic abilities but also for their social skills, skills that were clearly going to be tested to the utmost if they were to integrate successfully into the community. Fifteen girls versus over eight hundred pubescent boys? Wow, I think to myself, hardly knowing whether to pity these brave few or envy them.

Questions follow the Master's introduction à gogo. Are the girls to be treated exactly like the boys? In class? Outside the classroom? What allowances are to be made vis-à-vis the school rules? And what about punishments? Surely a girl cannot be beaten? (Corporal punishment was still in operation well into the seventies). No one asks the obvious one – how close should a boy be allowed to get to a girl? Time will tell.

All these questions and others are skilfully batted back by the Master who, as a firm believer in co-education, had from the outset been one of the main instigators of the whole scheme. I can sense division in Common Room over the matter. The hard-line conservative traditionalists (Hugh Weldon very much one of them) detest the whole idea, but are perhaps somewhat mollified by the insignificance in number of this unwelcome intake. The progressives, however, are delighted, and see the initial modest number of girls as merely the thin end of the wedge, hoping that numbers will increase year by year, thus one day enabling the school properly to call itself co-educational.

As for myself, I'm strangely indifferent to the matter. Never having taught girls, I'm loath to pronounce either way, except to say that I won't really mind should one or two of them wind up in my 'A' level French set, if only to see whether they alter the class dynamics or not.

"Well, Housemaster, what do you make of all that then?"

We're crossing Court on the way back to house after the meeting and I'm asking a question the answer to which I already know. Just a little tease.

"What, pray, do I make of *what?*"

"Well, you know. The new intake."

"If by that you mean the wenches – a lot of piffle and bunkum."

"Yes, the girls or…er, the wenches. Don't you think they'll make the place more natural?"

"Natural? Poppycock. I'm sorry but what on earth is natural about parachuting a handful of pubescent girls into a mob of testosterone-fuelled pubescent youths, then herding them together within closed walls in rural Wiltshire and telling them to get on with it? I don't call that natural. It's no better than the zoo, placing the meat between the bars of the cage and then telling the lions they may smell it but not touch. Pure piffle, and dangerous too, mark you my words."

By the time we've reached Turner House Weldon has donned his anthropological hat (He teaches Anthropology as well as Latin) and is regaling me with the practices of the West African Ibo and Yoriba tribes with regard to the bringing up of the opposite sexes. Namely that they should be brought together only when they are considered to be of marriageable age and ready to start a family.

"Be that as it may. Let us now go fortify ourselves with a glass of sherry wine so better to face the onslaught of our worthy parents and their delightful spawn."

That evening I opt for Common Room dinner, but not before a beer in the Sun Inn where I run into several of the new beaks, who are also knocking back the pints, doubtless to help steady their nerves. I'm happy to bump into two who, like me, hail from Trinity College Dublin. With Gerald 'Monkey' Murray that now makes four of us and surely a quorum for future St. Patrick's Day celebrations.

Afterwards at dinner I find myself seated next to yet another of the new intake, this time a cheery, chatty young fellow who already appears to be very much in his element and also very much at the centre of the conversation. Amusing too, he is. The subject of conversation is the appointment of the school's first woman teacher. Yes, this was clearly designed to coincide with the admission of the first girls, and a sensible idea it is too. However the all-powerful Common Room committee (Weldon is vice president) has had to make a few awkward decisions in the light of this ground-breaking appointment. Question number one: Should she (Janet) be admitted to full membership of Common Room or should she merely be relegated to the ranks of the ancillary members, these for the most part being peripatetic music teachers and staff on the bursarial side?

It had been leaked that the voting had been close but common sense had eventually prevailed and Janet was rightly admitted to full membership. Question number two: Should she also be granted dining rights in Common Room dining room? Here logic would presuppose the answer 'yes', but both logic and common sense have now been thrown out of the window and Janet has been denied the right to eat with her male counterparts in their dining room. Instead she has to be sent down to the Dames' dining room where she will be taking her meals in the company of the redoubtable and awesome House Dames – keepers of the boy's linen and clothing, supervisors of the bevvies of seamstresses who mend, darn and sew their way through the months of mountains of college-laundered laundry.

The illogicality of the decisions appears at least odd, even if opinions on the subject seem to vary. I feel myself being pulled in two directions. Has not my own whole upbringing been almost exclusively male-orientated? (So too my father's and his father's). Have I not for ever been dining in exclusively male company? At prep school, at Cranleigh (that *minor* public school, as the pompous Digby-Jones delights in pointing out), even at TCD where evening Commons was barred to women undergraduates. (One once did try to infiltrate by cross-dressing but was discovered by a porter, who sharply bundled her out by the scruff of her neck). Is it not understandable that I should therefore consider all-male dining as the norm? And what about the worthy members of White's, Boodle's and all those other prestigious West End London clubs which only grudgingly hold the occasional Ladies Night? Would they not have been in total accord with CR committee's highly contentious decision? Surely, yes.

It's only on leaving the room that the light suddenly dawns on me. This is ridiculous. No way should Janet as a full member of CR be banned from eating with her fellow colleagues. It is not only totally illogical but also sexist, reactionary thinking and, worse still, deeply insulting. I'm at once feeling ashamed and pondering on the suddenness of this my uncharacteristic damascene conversion, when a voice calls out from behind me.

"John, isn't it? Would you care to come up to my rooms for a coffee? We could have a chat and pass matters in review."

It is none other than Martin Evans, my cheery and amusing companion from the table we've just left. He, like me, is a resident house tutor, but unlike me lives in Court and right in the centre of the College. A most conveniently placed set of rooms, I think to myself while climbing the stairs, for those in search of a momentary perch, a coffee, a chat or more.

"Hi, sir!"

"Sir, will you be in later?"

"Evening, sir."

"Oh, sir, I've invited the Housemaster round for coffee after Assembly. Would you like to come too?"

"Sir, I've got you for History. What period are we going to be doing?"

"Good night, sir."

This last greeting from a younger member of the house. In pyjamas and dressing-gown, he's already off to his dormitory and bed. The invitation to coffee, I learn, is from the Head of House. Goodness, I think to myself as I settle into a comfortable armchair, here's a fellow who's lost no time in getting to know his house. Barely twenty-four hours into the job and he already seems to be fully and effortlessly integrated. Conversation flows freely and it becomes clear that we've much in common. I learn too that he was President of the Union during his time at Durham which surely goes far in accounting for his persuasive conversational skills. Also the humour and quick repartee. These qualities are all going to stand him in good stead, I muse, as he recounts a hilarious account of his experiences on teaching practice in an inner-city Liverpool comprehensive. Mimicry of the language of the Scouser he has at his fingertips. He's a born storyteller, and this one has me in fits of hysterics. I've a feeling he has plenty more of these up his sleeve and that I'm going to be hearing them in future sessions of 'passing matters in review', as he puts it.

I leave him and his rooms as he potters down the corridor to coffee with Head of House and Housemaster. Perhaps I've now just found another haven to equal that of Hugh Weldon's snug study. That would indeed be fortunate.

The following day sees routine swing into action in a big way – in at the deep end with a full seven classes to face. Ouch! But it's a welcome surprise to find two pretty young girls trotting in with my Lower Sixth French 'A' level set. Since I'm already in the room before they enter I'm able to direct each and every one of them to their places at random, thereby forestalling the attempts of any of the more adventurous boys forming happy little cliques around the girl of their choice. A clever move on my part – well done – aimed at ensuring that *I'm* to be the centre of attraction, not the girls.

That evening I'm at my desk sorting the remainder of the bumph (not as bad as I'd feared) when there comes a bold knock at the door. Giles, of course, come to pay his customary beginning of term respects, to recount his holidays, to share in the customary glass or two.

"You know what? I've brought my motorbike back."

"You've *what*? You've brought that infernal machine back? Are you mad? Don't you know it's highly illegal? If it gets found out you're really going to be for the high jump!"

"Yep, I know, but don't you dare tell anybody. Dave the plumber is hiding it in his garden shed for me. Good, isn't it?"

"*Good*? No, it is most definitely not! Besides don't you realise you're now in your 'A' level year and you're here to work your guts out and not be gallivanting all over the Wiltshire Downs on a death-machine risking life and limb to yourself and all and sundry? Do your parents know?

"No." A wink and a smile.

What can I do? What *should* I do? The Janus image immediately raises its ugly two-faced head. Here am I again on the one hand wielding the stick of authority and on the other hand conniving with the breaking of the law. Hunting with the hounds and running with the hare – at times exhilarating, at times nerve-racking. But I must admit I *do* like the idea of playing off the one against the other. Good schoolmastering? I hardly think so.

"Have you heard what happened in Weldon's 'A' level Latin set this morning? Toby told me. It's hilarious."

Hugh had seemingly been confronted with a girl in his set. Without the slightest acknowledgement of her presence and without batting an eyelid he immediately, as was his wont, called for the roll of those present. Names were duly given to be recorded into his mark-book. Woodroffe, Heywood, Conyers-Baker, Crighton, de Cordova, Philbrick, Elizabeth Clough...whereupon Weldon raises an eye to enquire.

"Madame, you *did* say Elizabeth Clough, did you not?"

"Yes, sir." (blushing)

"Then, Madame, be so good as to tell me whether the name is hyphenated or not."

Suppressed laughter from all, deeper blushes from Miss Clough. Typical Weldon. Amusing but mischievous – and naughty. One shouldn't get into the habit of belittling a pupil – be it boy or girl – just for the sake of a cheap laugh. This is not the way to go. I heard later that he continued in his naughtiness by from time to time referring to the 'thorn between two roses', thereby not only causing embarassment (at least initially) to the nice Miss Clough but also to the two (presumably) attractive boys sitting on either side of her. I'm told that by the end of the term they'd come to see the funny side of it all. Resilient, these young Marlburiennes certainly are.

Weldon, that archetypal old school bachelor, rarely ventured into the town. There was simply no need – all was provided on campus. A story has it that another middle-aged bachelor Housemaster eventually decided to take the plunge and get married, but only on the condition that he could remain living in his bachelor College flat. He set his wife up in the town and 'went out unto her' only during the holidays. (Weldon's crony Raymond James Foxwell Cook, too, had happily remained a confirmed bachelor living in College rooms until well into middle age, when he unexpectedly announced that he would get married, but only to a fully qualified nurse and a *cordon bleu* cook – which he did.) Happily times have changed and we no longer live the cloistered existence of our predecessors. Opportunities now abound for those of us who are keen to step outside the sometimes claustrophobic 'hothouse' atmosphere of life in the 'gilded cage' in search of the fresher air of Wiltshire and the world beyond.

Accompanying teams on away fixtures is perhaps the most common form of escape. Coaches are constantly leaving for destinations far and wide carrying the élite of our games players representing almost any sport one cares to mention – the three major ones, of course (rugby, hockey, cricket – no football, thank you), but also squash, fencing, Rugby fives, Eton fives, tennis, racquets, shooting and beagling among others. Understandably (luckily, too), being only at best a lukewarm games player my services are only rarely required on these sorties.

Beaks accompanying teams on away fixtures have it easy. All they have to do is sit on a coach, then stand out in the cold for a couple of hours (if it's a rugby match, for example) bawling their lungs out on a touchline often peppered with Marlborough parent supporters, also bawling their lungs out to their embattled, panting and puffing offspring with exhortations to tackle, pass, ruck, kick, heel, attack and (more than once from a demented father) "Go for him, Rupert, go! Kill! Kill!" ("Go, Marlborough, go! 'brah! brah' go!" or "Ra! Ra! Radley!" – traditional enemies – from the opposing touch-line.) They then troop off to tea, crumpets and cake in the opposing camp's Common Room before boarding the homeward coach, exhilarated or dejected depending on which of the two teams has been the more successful in slugging it out in a sea of mud, blood (often) and sweat. Never mind the broken bones (sometimes).

I personally tend to go with the person who said that once rugby players have succeeded in getting their boots on the right feet, the mental challenge of the game is largely over, but I certainly wouldn't dream of telling colleagues that. Competitive games are still too much of a sacred cow in these parts, even if excelling in them will now no longer automatically secure a place at Oxbridge. (John Betjeman will be pleased – together with his fellow aesthetes in 1920s Marlborough, when he railed so fervently against the preponderance of bat and ball, his 'greatest dread, the dread of games'.)

Beaks accompanying theatre trips and the like, however, can easily and unwittingly fall into all sorts of potential pitfalls unknown to my sports-orientated colleagues, as I can already vouch, to my own very considerable cost. My first venture last year was a trip to the Bristol Old Vic to see a performance of Bizet's *Carmen*. I'd fed my Lower Sixth French set a selection of Mérimée *contes,* so they were already acquainted with the storyline. My suggestion that we see the opera version went down surprisingly well, and all fifteen members of the set signed up. Little did I realise that before even boarding the coach I'd created a problem for myself. That morning after class James had been deputed by common consent to approach me with a small request. (Why James? Well, simply because they well knew that he was the one most likely to secure the favourable response – how right they were.)

"Please, sir, do you think we could leave a little bit early for a quick drink before the performance?"

"Yes, James, I don't see why not" (idiot). "What time were you thinking?"

"Well, sir, we were thinking four o'clock would be a good time. Yes?"

"Yes, OK, then four o'clock it is."

Which of course meant I'd already fallen into the trap. By leaving at four they'd correctly calculated the time of arrival in Bristol at six at the latest – opening time. With the performance due to start at seven-thirty I suddenly realised too late what had been meant by a 'quick drink'. With the prospect of over an hour in the pub, clearly the adjective was the wrong one and the noun should have been in the plural. Too late.

Come seven-fifteen, and several pints later I managed somehow to herd a somewhat wobbly group of adolescents across the road to the theatre. However, since our seats were dotted all over the place I'd no sure way of knowing whether I'd arrived with a full complement or not. Judging from the number of pit-stops the poor driver was asked to make on the return journey ("Please, sir, can you ask the driver to stop. It's urgent, sir") I would judge that almost certainly two of the group, if not more, never actually made it to the theatre at all. What should I do about it? Don't know. What *do* I do about it? Nothing – except have the coach stop at regular intervals ("Please, sir, it's really urgent again.") so that Chris and Hugh could empty their little bladders of God knows how many pints they'd managed to down.

The tolerant driver's only comment? "Well, sir, boys will be boys, won't they?"

"Yes, I suppose they will."

Lesson learnt. So when a few months later a similar request was made. I was well prepared.

"Sir, they're doing *Le Mariage de Figaro* at the Oxford Playhouse next week. Don't you think it'd be a good idea to go?"

"Yes, I do, Kevin. A very good idea."

It was indeed a good idea, since we'd just finished studying the text in class.

"Sir, if we could just leave a little bit early so...."

"No, Kevin. No, I'm sorry we can't. I've got work to do. (Lie). The performance is at seven-thirty you tell me, so we'll leave at six-fifteen. OK?"

"OK."

He instinctively knew I wasn't for playing ball – there was no point in insisting. But they were again right in their choice of spokesman. Kevin Maxwell was a natural linguist – his mother was French – and as such a valuable member of the class.

I knew the road to Oxford and timed our arrival to a nicety. No question of a 'quick drink' this time thankfully. However, during the interval Kevin approached me with another of his good ideas.

"Sir, my mother has invited us back for a light supper after the performance. Just soup and cheese in the kitchen. Don't you think that would be a good idea?"

I thought about it, couldn't see any obvious pitfalls and consented. Of course it meant a pretty late arrival back in Marlborough, also perhaps angering the odd Housemaster or two. Too bad. But it was only once back behind the wheel of the minibus and en route for Headington Hill Hall that I found myself thinking about Kevin's father whom we would surely be meeting. Hadn't I read in the press that here was a man larger than life who led a rumbustious lifestyle, didn't suffer fools gladly and was very definitely not to be approached by the faint-hearted? A shiver went down my spine.

"Er, Kevin, do you think your father's likely to be there?"

"No, don't worry, sir, he's out canvassing. It's just my mum. You'll like her."

We duly arrive at the imposing mansion set in its spacious grounds and were given a warm welcome by Madame Maxwell. Seated round a large kitchen table with soup, cheese and wine set before us, all this was indeed turning out to be a good idea, when suddenly and without warning the door was thrown open and there stood none other than the imposing figure of Robert Maxwell, MC MP (Buckingham).

"What's going on?" he boomed. "Who are these people?"

The atmosphere changed instantly and we all froze as the big man, his questions answered, drew up a chair to the table.

"Well, Kevin, what have you been talking about?"

For reasons best known to himself Kevin was in the middle of a discussion about the American Bill of Rights.

"American Bill of Rights, dad."

"Go on then."

Whereupon Kevin, now nervous, attempted to resume the thread of his thoughts on the matter, failed to do so, floundered and juddered to an ignominious halt.

"Kevin!" (still booming) "You've not the slightest idea what you're talking about, have you? You're an 'A' level History student, aren't you? What do you think I pay expensive school fees for? First give me the definition. What *is* a Bill of Rights?"

Silence.

"You don't know? *You* then!"

The inquisition had begun in earnest and an aggressive, jabbing finger was working its way inexorably round the table, moving closer and closer to where I was sitting.

"*You! You! You!*"

I had no doubt whatsoever that I was to be included in the interrogation (the teacher to be *doubly* shamed in front of his pupils) and now knew just what it must feel to be awaiting execution, head on the block.

Merciful God! Saved in the nick of time by the ringing of a 'phone from an adjoining room. He was immediately up and out. We, too, after having thanked our charming hostess. Up and out, only thankful to have had the torture so unexpectedly curtailed.

"Sir, do *you* know the definition of a Bill of Rights?"

"Yes, Kevin, of course. Now kindly don't distract the driver."

One would have thought that by now I would have had enough of theatre trips, but no. Shortly after the Headington Hill Hall fiasco, Malcolm, Head of House, came to me with a request I could hardly refuse. Would I like to organise a Turner House outing to see *Equus*, a play by Peter Shaffer, showing in the West End? Good reviews, he assured me, so I booked both seats and coach and thought no more of it till the day of the performance arrived and we all set out one wet Saturday afternoon for London town in a mass exodus. I was with no fewer than forty-five Turner House youths, ranging from thirteen to seventeen in age, all of us happy to be leaving a soggy Wiltshire for the bright lights of the Metropolis. No question of a 'quick drink'. Straight to Shaftesbury Avenue and in.

So far so good. But on arrival at the theatre I was somewhat taken aback to see a giant poster advertising the play and showing a naked youth fondling the head of a horse. Of course I had realised the play must have something to do with horses, but I was totally unprepared for what I was about to witness. No sooner was the curtain up than we were introduced to young Alan, a deeply disturbed youth with a pathological and quasi-religious fascination with horses. The play shows his fixation to be both erotic and sexual, made all too clear as he mounts his animal bare-back and stark naked. In the confusion of his mind he worships the sacred animal as his God and his only chance of rediscovering his sanity is through Jill, the young stable girl working by his side with the horses, who endeavours to seduce Alan in an attempt to save him. There followed a scene of wild, unbridled sex with total frontal nudity, both male and female, paraded before us on stage. The play ended with Alan, now totally deranged, plunging a metal stake into the eyes of his horse/God in a scene of horrifying and sickening violence.

The final curtain, now thankfully and safely down, found me somewhat shaken by this unexpected and brutal assault on my sensibility.

"Well, Malcolm, what did you make of all that then? I just hope that the little ones don't get a sleepless night as a result of it all."

"Well, sir, I just hope they're not going to be traumatised and scarred by it for the rest of their lives! Even I found it hard to take. Lord knows what they made of it."

An uneasy silence descended on the coach as we headed westwards back to Wiltshire and the safety of our beds and ordered lives.

Having plunged straight back into the daily routine of affairs and with all going well, I was suddenly taken short a few days later by a call from the Master's secretary.

"John, the Master would like to see you in his study tomorrow after lunch at one-thirty."

"Oh! Do you happen to know what it's about?"

"No, I don't. Sorry."

Phone down. True to form I immediately crash. In come the doubts, fears, anxieties and that all too familiar pit in the stomach. What have I done now? What's he going to do to me? I rack my brains. No answer.

I didn't have long to wait. The Master's very first question showed me exactly from where the attack was going to come.

"John, am I right in thinking you took Turner House on a theatre outing last weekend?"

The penny dropped immediately. It seemed I was going to have to answer a letter of complaint the Master had received from one of the Turner House parents. Yes, that must be it. The letter lay there on the desk before him and I went hot all over at the thought of its probable contents, imagining the lurid light that had doubtless been cast over the event.

Dear Master,

I am writing to you to complain about a theatre trip my son went on organised by Mr Wilkinson, House Tutor in Turner House. I'm led to believe by my son that the play chosen for him to see was a most unsuitable one, full of not only smutty, sexual innuendo but also explicit sex on stage. I'm told that two of the characters appeared on stage totally naked. I shudder to think what they were doing. I gather too that scenes of gratuitous violence and cruelty to animals were shown. A horse, it appears, is somehow involved in the whole ghastly show. Can I count on you to take up the matter with Mr Wilkinson? He has to learn to act more responsibly on such occasions.

   May I also add that my son is barely fourteen years old and that my wife is every bit as concerned as I am.

Yours sincerely,
James Higginbotham.

Chastened and subdued, head hung low, I slunk back to my rooms to lick my wounds. En route I decided to look in to Weldon's, tell him of my plight and see what take he had on it.

   "Pure piffle! Just what these boys need – a bit of reality in the raw. All this pampering and mollycoddling – I just can't be doing with it."

   Comforted by his words of reassurance (also by a welcome large gin) I left for my rooms and the rugby pitches in a much more buoyant frame of mind.

   It was only shortly after this, my third theatre outing fiasco, that I received a call from my friend Liz Scott. We had met at the

Department of Education, Cambridge, where we had both been studying for the Diploma of Education – we had also briefly 'gone out' together. I was nevertheless somewhat surprised to hear from her.

"Hi, John. I'm ringing from Heathfield, Ascot where I've had my sixth form girls badgering me to arrange a dance fixture for them. I immediately thought of you and wondered whether you'd like to bring a group of those delightful young Marlburians with you for a Saturday evening gig here."

Having already been bitten by no less than three outings, I was in no mood for rushing headlong into yet another one without considering carefully all the potential and unsuspected snares. I told Liz to let me think it over, spoke to Malcolm of the idea – he thought it was great, of course – and said to him I'd be prepared to take a small group of fourteen (minibus) but only on condition that he and I could agree on who was to take part. We decided to limit it to school prefects and House captains, thereby hopefully taking on only pupils who were in positions of responsibility.

Applicants came there thick and fast and the poor Malcolm was put under severe pressure by his peers. Eventually a group to my liking was selected. A group to be proud of, I thought, as I surveyed the list. To a man they were worthy citizens, intelligent, personable and good-looking. What could possibly go wrong?

Excitement was in the air as we sped along the A4 bound for the long-awaited tryst. Clearly the smell of the chase was already in the nostrils. Rather them than me, I thought, recalling vivid memories of the hell of the dancing classes I'd had to endure at their age. Waltzes, foxtrots, tangos and, worst of all, endless Scottish reels. Dancing with some of the partners foisted on me had been rather like trying to move a piano and I now called to mind the German poet who'd said that British women danced as though they were riding on donkeys. With the boys doubtless conjuring up erotic images of the ravishing princesses who were to be theirs and me thinking of pianos and donkeys, we soon arrived at our destination, to be met not only by Liz but the Headmistress herself. The latter took it upon herself to take the boys in to meet her brave girls (blessed relief – I wouldn't have to witness the embarrassment of the initial breaking of the ice while the two opposing teams eyed each other up before finding the courage to plunge in) leaving Liz and I to go our own way.

There followed a nice quiet supper in a cosy flat, memories of our Cambridge year together tumbling out. When out of the blue there came a rattling at the door and in burst a breathless, distraught-looking girl sent with a message.

"Please, Miss, can you both come quickly? There's trouble at the dance."

God, I thought, what is it now? We raced along corridors and into the dance hall. Who's disgraced himself? How? No sign of the Headmistress – she'd seemingly been long gone on urgent business elsewhere – just two huddled groups, girls at one end of the room, boys at the other. Tension in the air. It was only on approaching that we could see that each group was clustered around one of its number and both were holding them down and restraining them, amid much shouting from both ends of the room. Malcolm drew me aside and in a whisper spat out the sorry saga.

"All was going well, sir. Dancing OK. Supper OK and not too much drink, when all of a sudden in the middle of a dance Hisham started yelling at his partner, spat at her and gave her a great wallop in the face which sent her flying across the floor. Pandemonium broke out as you can imagine, and we're now just trying to keep them both from getting at each other's throats."

Hisham, he went on to explain in over-excited tones, an Egyptian and the son of a prominent diplomat from Cairo, had discovered that he was dancing with none other than the daughter of an Israeli cabinet minister. He had simply exploded and rounded on the girl, giving vent to the deadly and venomous hatred of the Arab people towards their Israeli neighbours.

"You do realise, sir, the six-day war is still very much in their minds. Hardly surprising they're daggers drawn, is it?"

I was in no mood to discuss the ins and outs of this most recent of the Arab/Israeli conflicts and certainly not there and then. A fast exit was the order of the day. A hurried thank you and apologies to a bemused Liz – still no sign of a headmistress – and we were out and off.

Hopes that we were in for a peaceful journey home were dashed from the start. Hisham Abdel Azim Fahmi hadn't yet finished, and he treated us to a prolonged outburst of Arab indignation at the Israeli invasions during those six dramatic days in June1967. Had those Israeli dogs not destroyed the Egyptian air force in a totally unprovoked attack? Had they not caused the army to suffer heavy losses during its chaotic and disorganised retreat? Had they not then invaded and captured the Gaza Strip and Sinai Peninsular from Egypt? And the West Bank from Jordan? *And* the Golan heights from Syria?

A captive audience, we could only but listen, impressed both by Hisham's grasp of the facts and by the ferocity of his attack on the 'enemy'. Pity the girl can't be with us, I thought to myself, to give the other side of the picture. I immediately thought better of it. Clearly, with Hisham on his present high horse, dialogue was out of the question. We returned to base wiser and sadder, having witnessed at first hand the strength of feeling now running in the troubled lands of the Middle East. Where would it all end up?

Taking the lads on day outings is all very well, but it certainly now seemed to me there was a price to pay. Amongst it all two large-scale continental holiday outings also chanced to come my way – both of them surprisingly problem free. Andrew, colleague and fellow linguist, and I set off in our two cars, a small group of six boys (Giles and his brother included) on board, on a one-week youth hostel tour of Holland. Only on arrival did I realise why Andrew had been so keen to visit Holland. It was not to practise his fluent German on the Dutch (thankfully – they would have understandably hated it) but to visit two small towns, Alkmaar and Zwolle, to show us two of the finest baroque organs in Europe. Having somehow managed to wheedle the keys out of the authorities, he then proceeded to play –to us and others visiting these fine churches – on these finest of instruments. J.S. Bach he chose, and he couldn't have chosen better.

I too had my reasons to favour Holland and on our last night I stayed with my Dutch aunt on her houseboat south of Amsterdam.

My bedroom was below water level and had portholes through which I could count the fish swimming by. Turning to a flickering black and white television, I saw to my surprise an American walking on the moon. Fish trying to get in on one side of the room, a man on the moon on the other. This really is bizarre, I thought to myself. Surreal.

My second continental outing the following year, an altogether much more ambitious affair, was with a larger group of boys studying for 'A' level Russian on their two-week visit to Moscow and Saint Petersburg. A train rattling through the night and West Germany, East Germany and Poland, finally delivering us up to the care and attention of Galia, our charming if tight-lipped state-appointed official guide who showed us what she thought we ought to see and no more. Then on to the glories of Saint Petersburg before travelling back to Tilbury by sea on the *Alexander Pushkin*, and a boat better equipped with giant saunas I can't imagine.

They say that if you're happy, time flies. If you're not, it drags. I must have been happy. Time positively flew. Now four years into the job, I suddenly found myself considering the prospect of life without Giles. His last term had arrived and he was up to his neck in biology, physics and chemistry. His relaxation time included hair-raising sorties on the motorbike and more sedate ones with me out to the White Hart at Hampstead Marshall. He really had taken a liking to the Krug '64 they had in stock there.

It's the last night of term and Giles is at the leaver's dance. I'm waiting in my rooms for him to come up for a last drink after it's over. A knock at the door. But it's Toby (we've since made it up after my earlier and unfortunate ordering him off the Turner House premises for no apparent good reason).

"He said me to meet him here after the dance."

"That's fine, Toby. Come in and sit down."

"But I'm not sure he's going to make it. You see, he's gone and fallen for this kitchen serving girl and says he's going to try his luck tonight."

Nothing for it but to sit it out and wait, we decide, comforting ourselves with champagne and Dvorak. Wait we did, till very late, and until it became clear we'd both lost out to the girl. Toby tottered off and into the night, leaving me with a sombre thought. If one's going to befriend one's pupils one is going to have to learn to accept the inevitable – that sooner rather than later they are going to shoot off on their own trajectory, never to be seen again.

And to think it will have taken me four years to learn this salutary lesson. Or have I already learnt it?

"Fret not. You'll be seeing him again when he's up at Oxford as sure as eggs is eggs."

"That's if he gets in."

"He will, mark my words."

Weldon's words of encouragement proved correct. Giles did get into Oxford, and we continued to meet frequently during his time there. Indeed he took as quickly to the best Oxford restaurants – the Elizabeth, the Bleu, Blanc, Rouge, the Quatre Saisons – as he had to Krug'64 in Hampstead Marshall.

Within the year another departure had been announced which was also to affect me, albeit in a somewhat different way. John Christopher Dancy, the Master who had appointed me, was on his way to become Principal of St. Luke's College, Exeter. During his eleven-year mastership he had introduced changes and reform which had radically altered the nature of the school. Girls had been successfully introduced, the pioneering 'A' level Business Studies course and the SMP Maths project had both been born at Marlborough. Russian and Chinese had joined the Modern Languages Department. The compulsory attendance of Chapel on both weekdays and Sundays had been relaxed, so too the compulsory training of boys in their second year with the Combined Cadet Force. Beatings by prefects were abolished and there'd been a general loosening of discipline in favour of trust (Betjeman would approve). Dialogues, regular meetings between pupils and staff to iron out the various problems of the day, had been instituted.

The fact that these liberalising reforms were successfully (for the most part) introduced with the student revolts of the Swinging Sixties as a backcloth bears testament to the steadiness of the hand on the tiller. Liberalisation, however, was certainly no call to licence.

There had to be limits, even if it meant having to sell the idea to long-haired seventeen-year-old fans of Mick Jagger and his like that a boy's hair should no longer cover the ears or overlap the collar –by no means an easy task.

A fine administrator, a respected voice in the world of educational reform, an intellectual with several erudite publications to his name (A Commentary on Maccabees 1 – Maccabees? To my shame I had had to ask what it was), here was a man respected and held in awe by boys and beaks alike. Feared, too, particularly by the younger beaks like myself.

I personally got off to a bad start in an interview for the job when I was asked if I'd read Proust. No, was the answer. The Master later told me that he'd phoned my TCD tutor – a referee – on a crackling line to Ireland.

"I gather Mr Wilkinson is no Proustian."

"On the contrary, Mr Dancy, he's a good Christian."

Had my sporadic chapel attendances perhaps retrieved the situation and got me the job?

A sticky interview was promptly followed by a sticky lunch, during which I found myself seated at the high table in the dining hall surrounded by the Master and his fifteen prefects. Since most of the conversation was in-talk, I felt excluded. Clearly I was there to show that I could compete – which I couldn't.

Then there'd been the smoking on the canal episode followed by the *Equus* débâcle, both of which had been the cause of adverse comment. But worse, far worse, was to come.

Sunday lunches at the Master's lodge were regular affairs. The composition of the guest lists tended not to vary that much. The principal guest would almost invariably be the preacher, a bishop maybe with wife in tow, others would include a housemaster and wife, a prefect or two, a couple of girls and more often than not a new beak. Me on this occasion. The party kicked off well enough and I was relieved to have been seated next to Angela Dancy with the Master at a safe distance holding the conversation at the far end of the table. Angela was proving not too difficult to talk to and I was beginning to loosen up when suddenly I heard my name called out from the other end of the table. It was the Master, and I froze.

"John. We're a bit stuck down here. I wonder if you could enlighten us. We're discussing the existentialist doctrine on salvation. Would you in a nutshell be able to tell us what Sartre, for example, has to say on the matter?"

Would that the earth had opened there and then and swallowed me up. But no, there I was well and truly caught like a rabbit in the headlights. The fact that I'd been in the middle of chewing my way through a lamb chop when the bombshell landed on me didn't exactly help, even if allowed me a few seconds to think. Neither did it help to have the whole table suddenly fall silent, all eyes swivelling onto me, as I was hastily swallowing the lamb, half choking, trying to figure out how I was going to get off the hook. Had I had the wit I would have surely come up with some flippant remark which might have caused amusement and saved me. But again no, and I was reduced to blathering my way through hardly knowing what I was saying, such was the terror welling up within me. By the time I eventually petered out, the Master had had the answer to his question – no, I most certainly couldn't enlighten him, neither in a nutshell nor in any other kind of shell he might care to mention.

I left the lodge that Sunday both ashamed and angry. Ashamed that I'd been shown to be unequal to the challenge, angry that while having been appointed as a linguist I was now being asked to perform as a philosopher. Sartre! I muttered angrily to myself en route back to Turner House. Existentialists! Curse the lot of them! Curse their doctrines and their works! And if anyone thinks I'm now going to go off and study Sartre's *Being and Nothingness and the origin of negation* they'd better have another thought.

It was of course Weldon who bravely bore the brunt of my shame and anger later in the evening. He knew what to do – fill me with gin and let me talk it through. It worked, and I later left in a calmer frame of mind.

However, if I thought I'd plumbed the depths of my relationship with my employer on that disastrous Sunday, I had another thought coming. On that day I'd had a bombshell land on me. Now I was about to face far worse – a veritable thunderbolt hurled down at me from the heavens.

The day in question was the very last day of the school year, 1972. The last bell had rung on that beautiful July morning and I was busily packing the car hoping to be off within the hour (Weldon, being without car had 'employed' me as chauffeur to drive him to Paris where he had 'affairs to see to' (suitably mysterious) when suddenly my name was called from behind. It was a breathless senior prefect with a message.

"Mr Wilkinson, sir. It's the Master. He'd like to see you."

"When?"

"Now, sir."

"Now?"

"Yes, sir. Right now in his study."

Sudden mood swings I've known, but nothing quite to equal this one. Yet again I find within me the terrified eight-year-old, summoned by the headmaster, knowing he's about to be caned.

The interview opens with a specific charge.

"John, I've been told by your head of department that you've been going into class smelling of alcohol. Is this so?"

Yes, it was probably indeed so. No point in denying it. Weldon and I had got into the habit of taking lunch at the Savernake Forest Hotel. Long liquid lunches they were too, meaning that more often than not I was arriving back just in the nick of time to take a five o'clock early evening class.

Further specific charges were followed by those of a more general nature. Was I not living the life of Riley in Turner House? (True.) Was it not detrimental to my teaching in general? (probably). Most of what was said had the ring of truth about it and there was not much I could offer in my defence.

"Well, John, I would simply say that had I been staying on here as Master I would have recommended that you seek employment elsewhere."

End of interview. Almost sacked, but not quite.

The senior prefect, whose path I crossed as I dejectedly plodded my way back to Turner House, clearly saw that all was not well.

"Don't worry, sir. Just think about the eight-week holiday in front of you. You'll have forgotten about it all by the time you get back."

I wasn't going to argue the toss with him, no more so tell him that there are times – bad times – in life which simply cannot be erased from the memory. This latest brush with authority was, I was sure, going to stay with me for a long, long time, if not a lifetime.

"Anyway, sir, if you want cheering up just let me tell you what happened to Mr Evans last night."

"Martin Evans? What on earth happened to him then?"

"Well, sir, he went to bed last night as usual only to find this morning that he'd been bricked into his rooms."

"Bricked in?"

"Yes, the leavers had got hold of a load of breeze blocks and cemented them in between his outer and inner door. Hilarious, don't you think? So when he'd opened his door he found he'd been entombed alive as it were. (A hearty gust of laughter.) But they'd been kind to him and built a little recess into the wall, leaving in it a book for him to read during the hols. And do you know what the book was? (Further gales of laughter). It was a copy of Edgar Allan Poe's Tales of the Macabre – a great choice, don't you think? Especially as he's for ever telling stories about prisons, the death sentence, the gallows and the like. Anyway the Works Department spent most of this morning demolishing the wall and they finally got him out."

I left the senior prefect chuckling to himself and couldn't help but be amused by the story myself and particularly by the choice of reading matter supplied. Clearly Martin had been putting his natural skills as a raconteur to good use and the boys, like myself, were being treated to his rich collection of gruesome stories of crimes, prisons and punishments. Stories, too, about his chance encounter with Albert Pierrepoint, England's last official hangman, who by the time of his retirement in 1956 had dispatched some four hundred condemned men to the next world. Martin had worked next to him at the Southport GPO where both of them (Martin as a student) were engaged in making extra pocket-money by sorting and delivering the Christmas mail. Leg-pulling was endemic ("Hey, Albert, stop hanging around, will yer?" or "Albert, just shut yer trap!") and Martin's already vivid imagination had been clearly set afire by this most unusual experience.

Martin's stories and 'imprisonment' not only amuse me. They allow me momentarily to focus on him rather than on myself. Introspective, destructive thoughts of self-doubt are briefly set aside as I consider the impact he's made in these first years of his schoolmastering career. Charismatic, amusing, extrovert, he had clearly made a good start. He had taken to life in the golden cage like a duck to water. He had found a path to follow. And myself? Not sure. Maybe there were better paths for me to follow where I'd feel less like a square peg in a round hole. Time would tell.

We leave shortly for Lydd Airport, where both car and ourselves board the plane bound for Le Touquet. From there to Paris and the faded grandeur of the Hotel de la Gare d'Orsay. The next day sees drinks with Marlburian parents in their exquisite apartment behind the Opéra, followed by dinner Chez Maxim, high temple of Parisian gastronomy, in the Rue Royale. Weldon is talking to me about housemastering. He seems to be saying that I should be making this an aim in life. But I'm not really listening. I'm rather listening to an inner and much more beguiling voice telling me what I half know already. Namely that here I am in France, here I feel good, here could be a real life for me in the *real* world. An exciting thought. Time will tell.

Chapter 16

Acting Housemaster

Things started off more or less all right under the new regime, even if the new Master, Roger Wykeham Ellis (already with one head-mastership to his credit), had the unenviable task of summoning me within his first week to say that my file and record did not make for good reading. Understatement. This he somehow managed to do uncensoriously and in such a way that I left the study relieved rather than downcast and with the distinct impression that I was being given the chance to turn over a new leaf. I instinctively liked the man – as did we all – and was determined to plunge into my activities, both academic and extra-curricular, with renewed vigour. I was now feeling more and more at ease in the classroom, my re-sults continued to be good and self-confidence grew accordingly. I soon realised I was creating an image for myself – a French one – by smoking untipped Gauloises, driving an old second-hand Citroen Diane, playing Brassens, Brel and Ferry at anyone who would listen, sloshing out wines – French wines, of course – to those happy to follow me on the road to all things French. As President of *Le Cercle Français* it fell to me to arrange talks, films, musical and literary evenings. Cheese and wine parties, too, and indeed anything likely to promote the cause of French culture and civilization.

As master i/c the Toulouse Exchange I found myself in the enviable situation of abandoning the College in mid-term and flying off with my class to the warmer and pleasant climes of *la ville rose* on the Garonne. Here for three weeks at a time I turned myself into a teacher of English and unwittingly laid the foundations of what was to become a post-Marlborough chapter to be lived out in France. Closer contact with country, language and people meant that my French – spoken French especially – was improving by leaps and bounds. Unlike some of my colleagues, I now felt able to confront with equanimity my top 'A' level French sets and the clusters of bilingual pupils they inevitably contained. My knowledge of French *argot* is now thankfully every bit as good as theirs. Life outside the classroom was generally pretty good too. Weldon, not content with fine wining and dining me both in Turner House and in the county now took it upon himself to invite me as a guest to the dinners of the Marlborough Dining Club, of which he was a founder member. Before I knew it he'd proposed me for membership (seconded by Dr Hunter, also a founder member), proposal accepted nem. con. The club had been founded in the '50s and had from the first modelled itself on the classic gentlemen's clubs of a more leisurely age when gentlemen schoolmasters of a social disposition asked for nothing more than to while away the evening hours eating and drinking in congenial company, with the proceedings often prolonged into the early hours by the passing of the port and madeira, the reading of the minutes, the drinking of toasts ("Gentlemen, please be upstanding for the loyal toast. The Queen. God bless her. You may now smoke"), the smoking of cigars and all this interspersed by speeches – the witty, the controversial, the slurred – by any such member who felt the urge to express himself. ('Himself', please note – no question of women membership in those distant days.) Membership was limited to forty – twenty to be selected from Common Room, twenty from the county. (The latter numbered among them the landed gentry and the professional classes – doctors, solicitors, barristers and the like.) A system of blackballing was in operation. My joining such a club understandably did not go without comment, particularly from some of my contemporaries in Common Room who at best regarded it as an unwanted relic of some distant past and at worst as divisive, this latter view expressed possibly by the person(s) unlucky enough to have suffered the indignity of having been blackballed. Suffice it to say that I was the youngest member by a long chalk, and not content with that I found myself within the year happily replacing Tommy Hunter as club secretary. In for a penny, in for a pound.

My comfortable life in Turner House as resident house tutor, however, was suddenly and unexpectedly disrupted. Weldon suffered a minor heart attack and took sick leave of absence for the remainder of the academic year. Almost before the penny had dropped I'd accepted the Master's invitation to fill the place as acting Housemaster, and was initially most happy to do so. After all, what was there to prevent him from parachuting in someone else from outside to hold the fort, a more experienced colleague, for example, and one with a better proven record than mine? Not hard to find. Initially all seemed to run smoothly enough even if from the outset I felt as if I was sitting on a volcano. What with one or more of the sixty boys under my charge busily stoking the fires – or so I imagined – who was to tell where and when the eruption would occur?

As the weeks and months passed I began to realise that house-mastering was no bed of roses. Far from seeing myself as the 'father' of an extended 'family', I felt more like the bobby on the beat sent out on a damage-limitation exercise, a cat-and-mouse game with the mice outnumbering the cat at sixty to one. Besieged on all sides, boys reported to one for having broken school rules, others for having failed in their work, yet others for showing disrespect to one's colleagues. Continually harassed by all and sundry with requests that one 'deal' with this boy or that for this misdemeanour or that. It was endless, doubtless made worse for me due to the fact that the 'rogue' element, some of whom I liked very much (amiable rogues they were), were there to try and test us, to see how much they could get away with now that this novice was at the helm. I felt uneasy at sanctioning those found drinking and smoking – of course I did, being a prime offender myself. Less so for intervening over matters academic when even the idlest of youths would have to recognise that at the end of the day he was primarily at a school to work and not at a holiday camp to horse around as he pleased.

Rustication is high on the list of punishments available to a Housemaster. It involves sending a boy home for a week or more for either having repeatedly broken some school rule or other or for simply having been a general pain in the neck to authority in general. Thankfully, only once did I have to ring a parent and summon him to take his son away home for a one-week cooling-off period. The parent in question, a retired naval captain, without even giving me the chance to present him with the charges levelled against his son, slammed the phone down and was on the Turner House doorstep within the hour. "Well, Wilkinson, what is it? Buggery or worse?"

Somewhat taken aback by this opening gambit I hesitated with my reply, my thoughts being more than a little taken up with wondering what on earth the man would consider as being a misdemeanour worse than buggery. "Er... no, not buggery. Persistent drinking and being drunk and disorderly after several warnings. After a last warning he was found in his study last night incapacitated having consumed a bottle of sherry."

"Sherry?"

"Yes, sherry."

"What kind of sherry?"

"South African sherry."

"*What! South African* sherry?" (Rising anger and turning to his son.)" Are you completely out of your mind, boy? You know full well I won't have the filthy stuff in the house and here you are now poisoning yourself with it. When will you learn to be more discriminating in your drinking habits? Had you stuck to decent *Spanish* sherry as I keep saying you'd doubtless not be in the pickle you now are. Would he, Mr Wilkinson?"

"Er... well, no, perhaps not." I just hoped and prayed that my own bottle of South African sherry was well and truly hidden from view amongst the many other bottles in the drinks cabinet. Phew!

Clearly of the opinion that the punishment fitted the crime, he marched the poor boy out of the study, informing me in no uncertain manner that he personally considered crimes of bullying, cheating and lying to be far, far more serious than any sexual peccadillos his son might or might not have engaged in. "Anyway, just think of the navy – all rum, bum and the lash as they say." he chuckled on leaving. Encounters with parents can be tricky. Relieved, I turned to the cabinet, found a bottle well hidden from view at the back and poured myself a glass... of cheap South African sherry.

After giving me a somewhat bumpy ride, the term thankfully drew to its end and the Master nicely gave his verdict. "Well, John. If you didn't manage to quench all the fires you at least were able to give most of them a good dowsing down. Well done!"

Weldon's return the following term saw a welcome return to the former status quo with me back in my house tutor's flat at the other end of the corridor and once again comfortably out of the direct firing line. But if I wanted an example from an experienced Housemaster of how to deal with recalcitrant parents, Weldon soon provided me with one. One day shortly after his return we were both in the study before lunch partaking of a preprandial drink when there was a loud knocking at the door. "'trez!"

In flounced a large lady, well-endowed in all respects, skirts billowing. "Oh! Mr Weldon, how good it is of you to give up your valuable time to allow me a few words with you. And no, Mr Wilkinson, please don't leave on my account. My son has told me so much about you." (Horrors! What?) Having thrown her not inconsiderable self into the chair proffered and crossed her legs with a flourish, she then leaned well forward to fix Weldon firmly in her gaze while starting to deliver herself of what was clearly to be a forceful and well-rehearsed diatribe with her dear son as the *causae belli*. Why were his biology reports suddenly so poor, she asked? He was finding maths too easy – should he not be put up a set? And what about his bassoon lessons? Should he not be encouraged to do more practice? Had he been entered for the Associated Examining Board's Grade Five Theory? If not, why not? Would he be made a house captain next term? If not, why not? And what about his Oxbridge prospects? Did we realise his grandfather had had a double first from Balliol?

The onslaught of evermore pressing questions continued unabated for just under the hour. A mother in full-blooded pursuit of her son's best interests. And Weldon? His performance throughout was a magnificent example of the art of the evasive answer. Never once a direct answer to a direct question. Sympathetic noises, yes, ("Oh, my dear, how right you are.") but nifty side-stepping of the issues in hand, qualified statements only at best, followed by stalling tactics and deliberate attempts at deviation from the topic under discussion. Nevertheless, and in spite of Weldon's superb demonstration of the art of prevarication, our mother eventually left the battlefield reassured and seemingly totally satisfied, fortified by three large glasses of La Ina.

Clearly baffled and not a little discombobulated by the experience, Weldon turned to me for elucidation. "Well, well, house tutor, whatever next? Do tell me who on earth that was?" An uncontrollable fit of laughter overtook me as I had to admit that I did not have the vaguest inkling of the identity of our unexpected visitor either. It was comforting to know that even powerful housemasters have feet of clay.

A further by-product for me of Weldon's heart attack was that I was asked to take over as Common Room cellarer, Dr Hunter having told Weldon that he was to stop humping around cases of wine. The appointment suited me fine as it doubled up with being Hon. Sec. of the Marlborough Dining Club. I was then taking orders not only for my colleagues' day-to-day drinking but for Dining club functions. Our suppliers were Christopher & Co., the highly respectable wine merchants from Ormond Yard, Jermyn Street. Apart from providing for a select private clientèle, they also looked after the cellars of many an Oxbridge college, where they frequently held tastings to which Weldon and I were regularly invited. Since these were invariably held at midday our departures for Oxford were inevitably scheduled for the beginning of the mid-morning break, and this in turn meant that I usually had a problem somehow 'getting rid of' a class or two –less of a problem for Weldon, who was on a reduced housemaster's timetable.

It was old Raymond Cook's cue I took when the problem arose in conversation one evening after he had joined Weldon for drinks and was slurping back his huge tumblers of whiskey and ginger. "Look here, Wilkinson, nothing simpler. If it's a Lower School set, find a prefect to sit in for you. If it's an Upper School set, tell them to take a study period. If it's during the first half of term tell them to prepare, if the last half tell them to revise. Nothing simpler." (Slurp.) "And whatever happens make sure the little devils never put pen to paper." True. Nothing could be much simpler, and the tactic generally worked.

Very occasionally one was invited to Jermyn Street for a full-blown wine merchant's lunch, an invitation if at all possible not to be turned down, even if it meant missing one's early evening classes as well as the morning ones. Wine merchant's lunches tend to be both liquid and long. This one was to be no exception. Superb clarets and Burgundies were finely matched to each course. Weldon and I finally left the table at five-thirty and made for a nearby tea shop where I downed two strong black coffees before making off down Piccadilly in a car filled to the roof with cases of wines, spirits and liqueurs bound for the Marlborough cellars.

We go down into the depths of the Piccadilly underpass, traffic buzzing all around. An impatient biker dangerously overtakes both me and the car in front, only suddenly to lose control. He and the bike part company, the bike smashing headlong into a reinforced concrete pillar, leaving the biker spread-eagled on the tarmac. The car in front brakes hard enough to avoid hitting the prostrate biker by a matter of inches. I too brake hard, but not in time to avoid clipping the back of the car in front, thereby demolishing my offside front wing, which spectacularly buckles into the tyre. Nobody hurt. Not a single bottle broken. Just a mammoth tail-back in the underpass leading to total gridlock above, radiating out from Hyde Park Corner to Piccadilly, Knightsbridge, Buckingham Palace Road, Park Lane. All of this at the height of the London evening rush-hour.

The police, eventually the breakdown services and finally Paddington and the train back to Marlborough. Time during which to share my concerns with a surprisingly up-beat Weldon – perhaps he likes the element of the 'adventure' of it all. "You know, housemaster, whenever I organise and go on an outing it either ends in near disaster or total disaster. I think I must have been jinxed."

The weeks following the Piccadilly fiasco were quiet ones. Back to routine. Settling comfortably back into routine can be pleasant – a break from it equally so. How fortunate I am to be in a job offering both one and the other.

The following Monday afternoon brought with it the usual stint on the rugby field, and I was in my rooms unenthusiastically getting kitted out when there came a knock at the door. Surprise upon surprise, it was none other than my brother Mark from Ely, Cambridgeshire – he taught at the King's School there – on half-term and on his way through to South Devon. Knowing well my aversion to running around aimlessly refereeing in the rain, he did the decent thing, grabbed my whistle and headed upfield with me in tow. Little did my rag, tag and bobtail bunch of boys know what was about to hit them. Suffice it to say they were drilled, trained, exercised and coached for well over the hour, at the end of which they emerged transformed. Gone the idling and loafing around. Here now were two teams recognisably playing rugby in a way I had not imagined possible.

Indeed the impossible did happen and in front of my very eyes – Freydown Nikpour from Teheran, with a flying tackle, brought down none other than the Bulldozer himself. Unheard of. Soon others were following suit. The final whistle and two teams leave the field, exhausted, yes, but with the sure satisfaction of knowing time had been well spent. The message to me is plain. Schools are best served by people like my brother – good in the classroom, good on the games fields. People like me are firing only on two cylinders. There's no denying it, games *are* still important, whether one likes it or not. (As if to reinforce the point I find myself selected to play for Common Room against the 2nd. XV the following weekend – myself on the left wing, Martin Evans on the right wing. Horrors!)

I was able to persuade Mark to partake of a Common Room tea before he continued on his journey to the Vicarage and home. Still somewhat in awe of his prowess on the rugby field, I was doubtless subjectively looking for ways to turn the tables. It was now my turn to impress him, and what better way than to start off with a slap-up tea – toasted crumpets, muffins, sandwiches of all sorts, cakes and cream buns. So far so good, and when the conversation turned to the King's School, Ely, I immediately grasped a further chance to impress.

"Well, brother, King's Ely doesn't exactly have the history and kudos of a school like Marlborough, you'll have to admit."

"I'm not sure about the history. You'll have to tell me when Marlborough was founded."

"1843," I reply proudly.

"Oh, yes, I see. A bit like schools like Rugby – you're Victorian railway schools. No, I think as regards history Ely can do better than that. Its origins are in the religious house founded by St. Etheldreda in 673 AD, which 300 years later turned itself into today's school, founded in 970 AD."

I swallow hard. Love fifteen to brother. Damn. "Ah, yes, well... but I bet you haven't any alumni to equal ours." I know the impressive list almost by heart – it starts with William Morris in the 1840s – having learnt it to impress my father among others.

Mark listened attentively, as did others round the table, as the household names came tumbling out. That'll keep him quiet, I thought to myself, at last scenting victory.

"Not bad, especially for a railway school. However, I notice you have neither a king nor a saint among your numbers. Saint Edward the Confessor, last of the Saxon English kings, educated at Ely under St. Etheldreda in the early 11th century."

Double damnation. More swallowing and now love-thirty to my younger brother, who sits back soaking up the interest shown round the table. Just as well bells were beginning to ring for afternoon school – any more of this and it was going to be game, set and match to Ely.

I crossed Court en route for my classroom somewhat ill at ease. It was only upon reflection that I began to realise why. I had been out-manoeuvred in my defence of Marlborough College, and this I had taken personally and to heart. Careful, an inner voice seemed to be saying, don't get things out of proportion. This is just one school among thousands where you for the moment choose to have a job.

The school therefore has certain rights to your time and energy, but not exclusively. It has no rights whatsoever to your emotions, heart and soul. Beware of burying your head in the Marlborough sand and cling on like billy-o to the wider picture. (The inner voice becomes more insistent.) Look around you and you'll see what can happen if you're not careful – boy at Marlborough, Senior Prefect at Marlborough, Teacher at Marlborough, Housemaster at Marlborough. There are those who've given their *all* for such a life in a gilded cage. No! Keep a reasonable distance from it all. Keep your eyes above the parapets. Does it *really* matter that Marlborough wasn't founded in 673 AD, or that it produced neither king nor saint?

"Sir, Sir! Was that your brother? Can he come and take the game again next week?"

"No, he can't, Rupert. He's got his own team to coach in his own school."

"Which school, sir?"

"Rupert, you'll never have heard of it. Some tinpot school in the Cambridgeshire fenlands. You'd call it a 'minor' public school, what what, Rupert. Definitely not up to the standards of Marlborough, what, what!" (Don't worry, I'm telling my inner voice, I'm just joking.)

"Right. More subjunctives this evening, gentlemen. Books out and let's look chirpy."

"Oh, no, sir! Please, sir, not subjunctives *again*."

Chapter 17

Secrets and Sexuality

"Oops! Steady we go, John. That's it. Just come and sit down here."

It's a Saturday evening. I've just left a great drinks party at Martin Evans' (having perhaps had one too many) and am now bound for Ben Trimble's study, where I've been invited to have supper. Late, I take the three flights of stairs at a run, arrive at his door puffed out and trip on the carpet, more or less landing in his outstretched arms before being guided to the only armchair in his tiny attic room. His study companion is clearly out for the evening and the little coffee table is set for two. Glasses are produced, the wine brought out of secret storage and before long we're both turning our thoughts back to those now dim and distant days – a full five years ago – when our paths first crossed. The gentle and well-mannered thirteen-year-old Ben of my first-ever Shell French set, embarrassed and blushing having to explain his gym shoe had been flushed down the loo. A gentle soul, unsure of himself. And now the more composed seventeen-and-a-half-year-old, a handsome young man indeed, yet with those same pale blue eyes, that same winsome smile, the flowing, golden locks. And the gentleness still intact. He remains as attractive to me now as ever, and he knows it. I don't mind. I had regretted not seeing him again in my classroom, but that hadn't really mattered.

The contact had remained. Coffees here, coffees there. Talks and the occasional walk. Oh yes, and the regular Sunday singing in the chapel choir. There was never any doubting when he was carried away by a favourite hymn, anthem or voluntary thundering out from the organ – pure joy which we regularly communicated to each other from our respective sides of the chapel as the music soared and we were both swept away by the beauty and power of it all. And here we were now near the end of his last term to take a last supper together. I had no doubt this was to be the farewell. How kind. But there was more in store for me for which I was totally unprepared.

"John" (He'd been in the habit of using my first name ever since Giles had left.) "I just wanted to tell you something before leaving. Something I've been wanting to tell you for some time. Something I've never told anyone else."

"Oh, yes. Well, go on, Ben, tell me then."

"I'm gay."

Silence. A prolonged silence, which he finally breaks. (I'm momentarily struck dumb by this bolt from the blue.) Once launched, there's no stopping him and it's with a sense of relief that I realise he needs to talk, to share his inner feelings, to unburden himself. I'm there merely as a sounding-board, not as provider of answers to a problem. I have no answers. There's no teacher's manual entitled 'What to do when a pupil tells you he's gay.' At least if there is one the Department of Education, Cambridge didn't seem to know about it. I'm simply not into castigating, congratulating, condoning or condemning. I can merely listen and commend dear Ben on his courage. His honesty, too, both with himself and with me.

As I listen, I'm aware that his story is largely mine. I too, at prep school, had admired boys from afar. I too, at Cranleigh, had engaged in same-sex relationships – no choice. Trinity, Dublin had produced for me both girlfriends and boyfriends – the best or the worst of all possible worlds? Who's to know? Not me. And yet here and now is a pupil of mine, over twelve years younger than I, showing all the signs of having sorted out his sexuality in a way I have as yet found either impossible or undesirable.

"John, you know, those girls you sometimes have over for the weekends, the ones you sometimes bring to chapel, are they your girlfriends?"

"Well, Ben, to be quite honest with you, not exactly. Mostly merely ornaments. Good for the image perhaps. Smokescreens, some might say."

Without thinking I'm now at last repaying honesty with honesty. Ben listens intently as I confide in him my own doubts and worries for the future. By the end of a long evening of much unburdening I can sense that we've both gained from each other – generous sharing and understanding has drawn us closer together, and I leave feeling I've been a good friend to him as well as, rightly or wrongly, a good schoolmaster.

"You know, John, I think I'll remember this evening for a long time – maybe for ever."

"I, too, dear Ben – yes, maybe for ever." Telling Ben about my so-called 'girlfriends' was one thing. Having to admit to myself my poor track record in the whole matter was something else. Already in my thirties and hardly a conquest to boast about, Heather of my student days being the nearest I'd come to a meaningful long-term relationship – and that had hardly set the Liffey on fire. Since then a succession of 'ships in the night' – Sophie from Nancy where I'd done my year as *assistant d'anglais* after TCD (she'd ended the year and our brief relationship by throwing herself under a train). Liz from my year at Cambridge, Eleanor from London and my teaching practice at St. Paul's, Hammersmith, and a brace of female colleagues from the college. All of them fleeting affairs, and I couldn't say I minded.

There remained Kate, a primary school teacher in London who played the guitar rather sweetly. If I thought I had the time and felt the need, I'd sometimes take the train on a Sunday afternoon, stay the night with her and dash back early on Monday morning just in time to be in my classroom at 9 am. Only on the one occasion did I miss the early train back and knew full well I was not going to make classes in time. I was sprinting through the Swindon station underpass, shirt-tails flying, tie awry, when as luck would have it I rounded the corner and ran slap into the Master (doubtless on his way to a London College Council meeting). "Oh! Good morning, Master." "And a good morning to you too, John." (Without so much as batting an eyelid, just a sparkle in the eye and the faintest trace of a kindly smile.)

It was at about this time that I realised I was getting away from the college more frequently and on my own terms. There were now younger colleagues, and it was they who were having to accompany the coach loads to the various organised outings around and about. Quite right too. It was good to be able to accept invitations to meetings of the House of Lords Noblemen and Gentlemen's Catch Club (for the singing of Glees and Madrigals) which took place from time to time either in the Lords dining room or in the medieval dining hall of Westminster school. Invitations reached me through none other than my dear old TCD friend and mentor Carl Henrik Bonaventura Harald Bontoft, Vicomte de Saint Quentin. What a surprise it had been to see him striding across court one day. "Bon! What on *earth* are you doing here?" "Visiting old haunts, silly. What did you expect?"

Only then did I realise he was an Old Marlburian and did he realise that I was teaching at his *alma mater*. Bon himself was now teaching too – also modern languages – at the City of London school. No Saturday classes there, lucky things, which meant he would from time to time be found weekending in Wiltshire, seeing those beaks with whom he'd kept in close contact (Weldon included) and not infrequently taking a German class in my place. He loved it, being able to show off outrageously and with impunity. The boys too loved it, soaking up the *double entendre*, the improper, the suggestive, the *risqué*, the Rabelaisian – Bon had clearly lost none of his powers to shock and delight.

My periodic forays into the world of the Lord's Catch Club became doubly attractive to me. Firstly it allowed me to keep in contact with Bon, secondly it meant I caught up with a long-lost friend from my Cranleigh days. Rodney Williams had started life as a chorister at King's College, Cambridge in the good old days of Boris Ord (he'd once been given the solo to sing in Once In Royal David's City at the carol service), had then gone on to Cranleigh as a music scholar and after that wound up singing as a lay clerk at Westminster Abbey. This latter post had brought with it the Secretaryship of the Lord's Catch Club.

We had much to talk about; I wanted to know all about his musical career, he wanted to reminisce on our 'naughty' days at Cranleigh. Conversation bounced from one topic to the other happily enough, interspersed by the singing of Morley, Wilby and Weekes inter alia.

Equally welcome was the arrival one day of a beautifully embossed invitation to dinner at St. James's Palace, courtesy of David, former head of Turner House. He was now an officer in the Household Division (Coldstream Guards), as I already knew, and explained in an accompanying letter that he and his fellow officers had decided to each invite a beak of their choosing from the schools they had attended to a regimental guest night to be held in the officer's mess at the Palace. Would I like to be his guest? Would I? I most certainly would – even if it meant putting into operation the technique of yet again 'getting rid' of two Friday evening classes. (If ever I felt professional qualms at deserting ship I only had to look around me to see colleagues playing the same game – some of them on an industrial scale. No names, no pack-drill.)

The day arrived and I set off (black tie) with expectations high on yet another jaunt. I was not to be disappointed. Parking provided in the Palace precincts, pre-dinner drinks served on a terrace adjoining the mess with commanding views over the Palace roofs and beyond. David welcomed me warmly and explained the procedure. Drinks to be attended by the Colonel, six young officers, their girlfriends and former teachers. The girlfriends would then be (politely) asked to leave (of course) when the men and officers would repair to the mess and settle down to the serious business of working their way through a substantial five-course dinner, wines from the regimental cellars accompanying each course. The surroundings were a pure delight – an oak-panelled room, full-length portraits on all four walls, a fine table groaning under the Georgian regimental silver. The company too was a pure delight: an Etonian, a Harrovian, a Wykehamist, a Stoic, a Radleian and David, my Marlburian. What a fine breed of young men, decked out as they were in their fine scarlet mess dresses.

Once at table, matters proceeded with decorum, the Colonel very much steering the conversation. But with the passing of time and the wine, with dusk falling, with the lighting of the candles in the heavy chandeliers and of the portraits on the walls, tongues were soon loosened and conversation was effortlessly blossoming out from all four corners of the table. "Oh, do tell me, that fine portrait over there..." I'm talking to the Etonian seated to my right. "Yes, the most impressive one in the room – the one hanging in place of honour over the fireplace. Who is he?"

"Oh, that. That's an ancestor of mine. Clive of India."

Clive of India! My God! I always realised that the top British army regiments prided themselves on their long histories, fine traditions and close family associations, but this takes the biscuit, I think to myself while searching for the family likeness in the face beside me. I was sitting next to the Hon. George Windsor-Clive, a direct descendant of Clive of India.

The conversation takes a sharp turn and we're now firmly in the world of history books as I'm given a two-hundred-year bird's-eye view of the Clive family story. Fascinating. The Loyal Toast, the passing of the port and madeira, the leaving of the colonel, and the evening, now well advanced, takes on a new turn. Brandies are served, the table forsaken for the handsome, comfortable leather sofas and armchairs, where talk rapidly turns to tales out of school. Hilarious accounts of schoolboy escapades and brushes with the authorities, to which David and I generously contribute. David has some classic Weldon stories to tell and the evening eventually comes to a close in the mutual agreement that schooldays were indeed the best days in a life – *Floreat Etona!* et cetera.

It was high time to leave the Palace, but not before I'd been flagged down by a Lifeguard at the gates requesting a lift to Whitehall. A full six foot tall – add another foot and a half for the gleaming helmet and its sharp spike – wearing his spurred boots which reached up to the very top of his legs, he was in full ceremonial dress, sword clanking at his side. It was a major operation squeezing it all into the car. Once at the Whitehall gates to the Parade I was invited by my 'hitch-hiker' to accompany him on 'inspection'. A discreet bell was rung, gates swung open and I immediately found myself in what can only be described as a farmyard. Imagine my surprise. Farmyard smells and noises – straw and hay for the nostrils, the neighing and clatter of hooves for the ear. Horses aplenty, ostlers and grooms busy at work preparing these magnificent animals for duties later in the day.

I left them to it, mindful of my own day ahead, and headed west for the now well-familiar M4. Gone were the days when one was pushed off it and onto the A4 at Maidenhead. With the Maidenhead-Swindon section at last complete, we at Marlborough were now very much in reach of the bright lights of the West End. A lifeline – to me at any rate.

The Marlborough Dining Club was another source of away fixture dinners. The MCC club dining room at Lord's cricket ground, Leander's at Henley, a combined dinner in Oxford with our sister dining club, the Trimmers of Shrewsbury school among others.

Perhaps the most memorable of all was a dinner given by Sir Frank Bowden (Dining Club member) at Thame Park, to which he most kindly invited Martin Evans and myself. We'd not exactly realised what we were in for, until the impressive gates loomed up ahead and we were bounding down the long avenue – acres and acres of landscaped parkland on either side – at the end of which stood the hundred-room Oxfordshire home of Sir Frank, previously a Cistercian monastery before the Reformation.

Drinks before dinner took the form of a private viewing of one of the largest and most eclectic private collections of Japanese swords and armour to be found anywhere in the world. A magnificent display, and clearly Sir Frank's pride and joy. The following dinner for fourteen, too, was unforgettable – not only for the splendour of the surroundings and the table but also for the fact that each of us had a footman behind his chair throughout the meal. Not any old footman, one in full livery made out of the finest of cloths – a delight to behold. I had to pinch myself to make sure we were still in the 1970s and hadn't all suddenly been transported into the 18th century.

Equally splendid and another surprise awaiting us after dinner was the sudden (terrifying) appearance of a fully grown Kenyan cheetah, which proceeded to circle the table, as if to check up on the guests. This was Chui, Sir Frank's tame (?) pet cheetah, to which he was devoted. Most of us present froze as the prowling continued (I noticed Martin kept his hands together and firmly under the table as a sensible precaution). But all was well. Chui, with a purr like windscreen-wipers, was in a good mood and we all relaxed. (He could run at the speed of a bullet and a BBC TV filming crew had been disappointed that their van dragging a rabbit as bait could not go fast enough to stretch him fully).

Further agreeable sorties came courtesy of both Weldon and Gerald 'Monkey' Murray – neither of them possessed cars, Weldon having way back sold his Rolls Royce after it had eventually given up the ghost having been used as an MC Beagle pack transport carrier over the years, and I was only too happy to play chauffeur if there was an interesting outing on offer.

One such was a trip to the Salisbury Playhouse to see Micheal MacLiammoir performing in his one-man show *The Importance Of Being Oscar*, a *tour de force* based on the telling of Wilde's tumultuous life story. Murray knew I would appreciate the Irish in both performer and subject. I certainly did and I'd already seen MacLiammoir on the Dublin stage during my Trinity days. But, in true Murray style, this was to be more than a mere theatre trip. 'Mummy' (Old Miss Rogers of the town, spinster and Murray's devoted housekeeper) had prepared for us a pre-theatre picnic of Edwardian proportions – she'd been in service before the war in her younger days and knew how to do things in style. Nothing was left to chance – the large wicker picnic hamper with its heavy leather straps, a fine old tartan rug on which to sit, a small collapsible table and two chairs, and then the contents of the hamper itself. What a feast! Sandwiches, a pork pie, sausage rolls, pâtés, cheeses, straw-berries and clotted Devonshire cream – all washed down with the help of a Château Margaux and then a sweet white wine from the Sauternes. Perfect.

And the setting for this gargantuan feast? None other than Old

Sarum – the site of a Norman cathedral, motte and bailey castle and, later, royal palace – with its commanding views over today's Salisbury and its 'new' cathedral and imposing spire, now bathed in the gentle sunlight of a classic English summer day. Perfect, too.

Mac Liammoir's performance was superb. It was punctuated only by Murray's guffaws of laughter throughout the first half, then heavy, successive snorts and snores as he snoozed his way through the whole of the second half. All I could do was administer the occasional prod in an attempt to stem the worst of the snoring, otherwise just sit tight and be embarrassed by the voluble antics of my kind, elderly Irish friend.

Our next outing was to visit and have tea at the Watts Gallery, near Guildford, invited by the Curator and friend of Murray, Wilfrid Blunt. On the drive over Murray was able to tell me all about George Watts, 19th century English painter and sculptor (He had briefly been married to the actress Ellen Terry). Also all about his friend Wilfrid Blunt, who had been the art master at Haileybury, then Eton over many years. I suddenly realised I was about to meet the first of the Blunt brothers. The second I already knew, Christopher, was the most influential figure in British numismatics of the century – also a member of my Dining Club. The third, Anthony, we can no longer talk about since he was exposed as a Soviet spy. Suffice it to say that the three brothers were brought up in a country vicarage and that all three were educated at Marlborough.

Gerald Murray was as good value on his home turf as he was on his outings. Many an evening did I spend with him in Dundrum, his bungalow close by the Master's Lodge gates. There he would dispense both colourful conversation and fine wines ("Wilkinson, kindly get another bottle of Madeira if you would, dear boy – in the bedroom in the sock drawer of the chest of drawers. Top left"). The topics could vary, but in the end generally came round to his beloved Ireland, its history, culture and literature. Fascinating.

With me he was, of course, preaching to the converted. My four years in Dublin had taught me at least the names and a little about the likes of Wolfe Tone, Charles Parnell, James Conolly, Patrick Pearse – intrepid fighters in the name of Irish independence – but

Murray was so good at putting the flesh on the bones and bringing these names to life, seasoning his remarks with apt anecdotes and personal reflections. His take on the great Irish literary figures – Joyce, Yeats, O'Casey, Syng inter alia – was also revealing. He would read me extracts, and he read well, with emotion and an enthusiasm that was all the more remarkable when one knew that his family, like many another Protestant family, had lost all during and after the 1916 Easter Rising. He would become particularly animated when holding forth on his two revolutionary heroines – Constance Countess Markievicz and Maud Gonne, both of whom fought fiercely for Irish independence, for the cause of the suffragettes and socialism. Both, too, were actresses and very much at the centre of Dublin theatrical life, with Maud Gonne becoming the lifelong 'muse' of W. B. Yates.

I would sit and mostly listen, contributing when and where I could. I told him I'd known old Captain Alexander Henry, who remembered meeting and greeting the old Queen, Victoria, arriving at Kingstown (Dun Laoghaire) on her last State Visit to Ireland in 1900. I told him my tutor at TCD had been Owen O'Sheehy Skeffington, son of Francis, the pacifist and best-known victim of the 1916 insurrection. I told him, too, that I'd spent many an evening in The Bailey knocking back the Guinness with an inebriated Brendan Behan. He liked that.

At times conversation turned to Marlborough College of the 'good old days', with amusing stories of past Common Room 'characters'. One was old Leslie Coggin ('Cogs'), who was famously absent-minded. One evening he drove his car to London for dinner at the Reform Club, took the last train back to Marlborough, and unable to find the car outside the station, reported its theft to the local police. The latter eventually traced it – parked outside the Reform Club – and the next day 'Cogs' was back at the station ticket office asking a confused employee for a 'third person singular' to Paddington to retrieve the 'stolen' vehicle.

His pupils didn't take long to size him up either. They had a tape recording made of the school bell and would play it sometimes only fifteen minutes into the class. "The bell's ringing, sir. Can we please go?" "The bell? Surely not. Already? I can't...." "Yes, sir. Can't you hear it? (volume turned up) We've got to go or else we'll be late for Latin." And off they would scamper, leaving a bemused Cogs standing at the door of his classroom, wondering why none of the other classes had been let out. On one such occasion he was sheltering in the doorway of his classroom – it was pouring with rain – pondering over the early disappearance of his class (yet again) when a younger colleague bounded up to take shelter beside him. "Oh, Mr Coggin, I see you have an umbrella. You're not by any chance going over to Common Room, are you?" "Well, yes. I seem to have mislaid my class so I might as well. Do take shelter under my umbrella with me." They both stepped out into the pelting rain, proceeded to cross court at a leisurely pace and eventually arrived in Common Room – both soaked to the skin. Cogs had indeed raised his umbrella, but had forgotten to open it. It had remained furled. Cogs was cocooned in a world of his own and blissfully unaware of the elements, and the younger man preferred to suffer in silence.

And then Lionel ('Wiggy') Gough. 'Wiggy' because he wore a wig – a bright flaming red one – which wasn't exactly what might be called a tight fit. On occasion it caused him problems. To wit on days out hunting with the Tidworth, when on more than one occasion he and wig parted company as he and his horse failed to swerve and avoid the lower branches of an oncoming oak tree. Since he wasn't the most competent of horsemen, to put it mildly, it sometimes took him a full ten minutes or so before he'd managed to bring his fiery steed under control, whereupon a wig search party would be sent back to try and locate the offending hairpiece, leaving a wigless Wiggy doubtless feeling somewhat exposed. The article, bedraggled (on rainy days) and now looking more like a dead stoat, would be returned to grateful owner who would in turn proudly return it to its rightful place. The hunt could continue.

Not content with riding horses – dangerous at both ends and un-comfortable in the middle – Wiggy also had a penchant for bicycle riding, at which he was no more competent than horse riding. His bicycle he generally parked in his classroom, and it was every pupil's prayer that he would be moved to mount his boneshaker during the lesson and wend his wobbly way around the classroom and in between the desks. This he would do, to much cheering and encouragement from his audience, but only if in a really good mood. This could be induced, so they learnt, when a really good piece of work had been produced (Wiggy was a teacher of English) or when a boy had excelled himself in class debate. Then he would excitedly rise from his dais, jump onto the bike and set off on his erratic course. The louder the applause the faster the performance, with increased danger to both boy and beak alike. Often the inevitable happened, and both beak and bike ended up unceremoniously on the floor, much to the delight of the boys. Their good work had been fully rewarded. Good old days indeed, and where are the like of these 'characters' today, I ask myself? In shorter supply, it would seem.

We once got on to the Marlborough Literary Society, which Gerald had founded decades previously and now continued to run as President. This was an élite group drawn from the most talented of the literati the College had to offer. Poets in the making perhaps, destined to follow in the steps of their predecessors – MacNeice, Sassoon, Sorley, Betjeman. Who knows? The high-powered meetings would generally consist of either a talk given by a distinguished outside speaker or a paper read by a member aimed at leading to an open discussion on whatever the topic chosen. "Wilkinson, you old bugger (a favourite form of address made in jest, no harm meant, no offence taken), since I'm clearly not going to get rid of you till the early hours of the morning – have another Madeira, m'dear – I might as well show you an example of the kind of work Lit. Soc. members have produced over the years." (Here he walks – no, dances in a jig-like fashion – over to the dining table stacked high with papers, folders, books and stuff, forages around and eventually fishes out a single sheet of A4 paper.) "I'll just read you a poem – or would you like to read yourself? *Can* you read? (Gurgling laughter.) It's by a boy who was a member of the Lit. Soc. in the late '50s, it's a sonnet à la Shakespeare and it gave rise to a discussion centring around the ideas of Love and Lust. Isn't that just great?"

He reads the poem. Beautifully. I listen in rapt attention. He finishes, tears rolling down from his eyes. Here is a poem with which he clearly identifies, a poem he knows will also ring true to me. The poem of a seventeen-year-old Marlburian boy's love for another Marlburian boy. Here it is:

SONNET
When I remember how at night we lay,
Exulting in a passion that now seems
Only the fire of angry, writhing flesh,
Lit in the tortured darkness of our dreams;
And how in sorrow I would lie awake
To watch your sleeping figure, and to mourn
This bitter lust, pale mockery of love,
Pale as the ghostly shadows of the dawn
That wash the early sky; when I recall
Your sensual satisfaction in this art
The melancholy sadness of it all
Cuts through the savage ardour of my heart.
There is no pity in the path of fate:
From impure love to lust, from lust to hate.

All this from a mere seventeen-year-old, think I, returning late to Turner House that night, poem in hand. And so much already understood and at such a tender age.

My fairly frequent gallivanting around might predispose one to think that I was neglecting my work in the classroom. Not the case. The fact was that after now ten years in the job I was feeling on top of the teaching and totally at ease in the classroom. Gone the fear and general lack of confidence. Gone the need to prepare for every eventuality in every lesson. With both 'O' and 'A' level syllabuses largely repetitive year after year, with better planning and organisation on my part, now knowing exactly where I was going and where the difficulties were likely to appear, I was now simply in a position to spend less time on the academic side of the work. Added to which I encouraged brevity in the writing of essays, quality not quantity, thereby cutting down on marking time. In this I was much inspired by the story of a 16-year-old boy from Hampshire who won the World's Shortest Essay competition. Competitors were asked to write a concise essay containing the following elements: 1) Religion 2) Royalty 3) Physical Disability 4) Racism 5) Homosexuality. The prize-winner wrote: "My God," cried the Queen. "That one-legged nigger is a poof." The quality of my lessons seemingly remained high. Results continued to be good. Added to that, my extra-curricular activities – house tutoring, running the Toulouse French exchange, presiding over the *Cercle Français*, playing games (ugh!), running the Common Room cellar and Marlborough Dining Club – were not only largely pleasurable ones but also ones which could hardly be described as onerous.

So invitations out to play continued to arrive and I invariably continued to accept. The Beaufort Hunt Ball at Badminton House, dinner with the Bishop of Bath and Wells (Turner House parent) at the Bishop's Palace, Wells, a mega-eighteenth birthday party for Ginny (pupil) for which a full fairground had been hired, a Green Jackets Regimental dinner at Tidworth, not to mention a plethora of London parties.

Let it not be thought for a moment, however, that I was the only one on the loose. Martin Evans, for example, was out and about every bit as much as I was, if not more so, and he was certainly not one to accept any old invitation. His tended to come from the upper echelons of society, and when we compared notes he almost always won on the prestige scale. "Wilks, there's the test match on at Lord's next week – England playing the West Indies. Would you like to come?" An odd suggestion, I thought, since Martin well knew my views on games in general and cricket in particular – dead boring.

Only twice can I remember ever having been amused by anything to do with the game. Once on hearing Richie Benaud referring to a streaker at Lord's – "There was a slight interruption there for athletics" – and then John Arlott delivering his classic – "The bowler's Holding; the batsman's Willey". It was only once in the car driving up that Martin let on he'd just been elected a member of the MCC – no mean achievement, since many an applicant is turned down, at least initially. Clearly his proposer and seconder had been men of weight and consequence.

However, any idea I had that I was bound for the members' pavilion, with its plush boxes, bars and restaurants, was to be short-lived. At the entrance gates the sheep were divided from the goats. The latter, together with myself in the midst of a heaving and jostling crowd, were herded into the arena and then eventually to our places – seats with no protection whatever from the heat of the summer sun now beating down upon us. The heat was one thing, the noise another. I found myself penned in and surrounded by a vast multitude of West Indians who, at the slightest movement from the crease, burst into jabbering, hollering, dancing and singing, ably supported by a Jamaican steel band pumping out the calypsos at full volume and at a distance no further than ten yards from my left ear-drum. There was clearly nothing for it other than sit it out, following the dreary procession of batsmen arriving and then departing at irregular intervals.

In trying to take my mind off the whole ghastly experience, I rehearsed to myself a definition of cricket I had given to my Breton friend, Pierre: "Pierre, you have two sides, one out in the field and one in. Each man that's in the side that's in goes out, and when he's out he comes in and the next man goes in until he's out. When they are all out, the side that's out comes in and the side that's been in goes out and tries to get those coming in out." Blank bafflement and bewilderment from the Frenchman, feelings with which I could well sympathize. I left the hallowed turf later that day, half-deaf, vowing never to set foot on it again.

It was only shortly after my Marylebone nightmare that Martin, with the coveted MCC membership already in the bag, came up with yet a second triumph. The team he sent from his Debating Society to compete in the Observer Schools Mace – the annual, national debating tournament for secondary schools in the UK – won the competition in great style and returned bearing the magnificent Silver Mace, a fine feather, indeed, in the College's cap. So it was really no surprise when shortly after the following notice went up: 'I have appointed M. C. W. E. to be Housemaster of A2 as from September. R. W. Ellis.' Richly deserved, and Martin was now on the bottom rung of the schoolmaster's career ladder. Since A2 was a

Junior House (for first year boys) his next jump up would normally take him to a senior housemastership. And then a headmastership? Time would tell.

At about the same time I too was summoned to the Master's study, to be told that, although I was in line, I was not to be appointed Head of Modern Languages. This dubious privilege was to be reserved for a colleague junior to me in the department. I didn't go as far as actually thanking the Master for his wise decision, but I left the room more than relieved. The poisoned chalice had been spared me. For another the delights of paper-pushing, drawing up lists, chairing meetings, tracking examining boards, correlating, standardizing, formulating and setting departmental policy, following the national educational trends in modern languages and more and more and more...Let me never forget, I came into teaching to teach in a classroom, not to be an administrator in an office.

With the relief, however, there did come the realisation that here was an avenue being closed to me – the departing head of department had been appointed Rector of Glasgow Academy. Open to me still was the possibility (remote?) of a housemastership. But was that what I really wanted? My term replacing Weldon hadn't exactly been a bed of roses, and the thought of the standard fifteen-year stint of more of the same sent a shudder down my spine. Ten years into Marlborough already, I thought to myself, as the summer term 1977 drew to its close. While Martin Evans contemplated his move across Court to more spacious accommodation, I contemplated my move across the Channel and back to *La belle France* – again – and this time for a one-month stay with my friend Gérard to help out in his Hotel Restaurant Le Postillon in the little town of Draguignan, set in the hills behind the delights of the Côte d'Azur. After that came a flight to Crete for a hike through the Samaria Gorge, solo, then along the unspoilt south coast.

Martin was sticking his colours very firmly to the Marlborough mast – quite right too. After all, not only did he now sport the distinctive MCC tie but he was also a member of the Royal Birkdale Club. Cricket and golf – what better combination could you possibly have to fit the housemasterly image? Perfect. (The thought of golf appals me every bit as much as cricket, having only once in my life wielded a club in anger and then almost knocking the brains out of my best friends at school.)

I too was sticking my colours to the Marlborough mast, albeit perhaps less firmly than Martin. But I surprised myself for the first time by turning down an offer from Weldon of a holiday in Turkey. How many such kind offers had I gratefully accepted over the ten years? Holidays in Cumbria, Paris, Venice, Provence, Sicily, Morocco and more besides. However I had learnt that a holiday with Weldon was, at least in part, a holiday with Marlborough College, and that was now not what I wanted or needed. I wanted and needed to breathe new air, meet new people, discover new lands. Only then would I be able to return to MC refreshed, and indeed glad to give yet another year in a job I was lucky to have in this great school.

Chapter 18

Rest and Recuperation

My second decade at MC started satisfactorily enough with the usual mixed-bag timetable, the usual extra-curricular activities. With regard to the former, I continued to relish the challenge. Give me the dimmest and slowest boys in a Shell French set 6 or the brightest linguists of a top 'A' level set and I will know how best to advance their causes. I at last felt entirely on top of my game.

Martin Evans, too, was at this stage feeling on top of his game. He had made a fine start to his housemastering career and was clearly enjoying every moment of it. That is to say apart from a moment when, as he later told me, he had narrowly escaped major embarrassment. He had arranged with the Registrar to see prospective parents at nine in the morning and was in the process of getting dressed when at eight-fifty, ten minutes early, there was a knock at the door. Only half-dressed, he had managed to make a dive for his desk and was sitting firmly behind it as both Registrar ("Sorry if we're a little early, Martin") and parents entered. All would at first seem to be in order with the Housemaster, clean white shirt, MCC tie, sitting behind his impressive housemasterly desk. However, all was far from well. Martin was simply unable to stand and welcome. Reason? He had no trousers on. Sitting trapped behind his desk, he did what he could with a welcome which at best must have seemed odd, and odder still when he attempted with covert glances to impart to John, the Registrar, the nature of his predicament. John, not being at his sharpest in the mornings, failed to get the message, and an unusual meeting between two bemused parents and a trouserless and vulnerable Housemaster creakily got under way.

"John, wouldn't you like to take them over to the far window for a moment? A fine view over Court." (This'll give me the five seconds I need, thought Martin, to slip into the bedroom and get the trousers on. Good thinking.)

"Oh, no, Martin. Not necessary. I've already shown them round Court."

And so the meeting ended as it started – creakily – with the Housemaster bidding his farewells still firmly anchored to his protective desk. His performance at interview must have been better than he had feared. The parents' son duly entered the House the following year and both mother and father were much amused – reassured too, doubtless– on hearing Martin relate the event later in the year.

The following year Hugh Weldon took a sabbatical, and I was yet again asked to hold the fort in Turner house as Acting Housemaster during his term of absence. Having once already endured the experience I was, of course, this time not as alarmed, although hardly enamoured of the prospect. But it was an offer I could not really refuse. The scenario was roughly similar with me, hosepipe in hand, desperately trying to 'douse down the flames, dampen the fires' (as the Master had so graphically put it) of student excesses. However, this time round Housemaster's meetings turned out to be more enjoyable – Martin Evans was, of course, beginning to make his voice heard. On one occasion Housemasters were told that yet again the date for the start of the Michaelmas Term was to be brought back to even earlier in September.

"But, Master, I've just worked out that if this trend continues, by 1990 we'll be returning for the following term on 24th December. In which case can you ensure that Housemasters be issued with full Father Christmas outfits on expenses, so that when parents are told to send all Christmas presents to the school, the Housemasters, suitably attired, will then be able to distribute them on Christmas Day *in loco parentis?*"

On another occasion Housemasters were informed that canings were no longer to be allowed as a form of punishment. Corporal punishment was henceforth out.

"But, Master, I've always thought it was one of the perks of the job."

Martin was at his best when in mischievous mode.

Having completed my second acting-Housemaster term I'd expected things to return to normal. They didn't. Rather, initially they did, in that the following term I again took up my normal full timetable, but half way through that term I found myself facing a particularly gruelling week ahead with a heavy load of extra internal exam marking and wondered whether I'd ever see it through to the relative oasis of the weekend. Saturday seemed an unconscionably long time in coming and when it eventually did – marking completed, processed and sent in on time but with only the greatest of effort and difficulty – I found myself limping back to Turner House, exhausted and anxious, to regain the safety of my rooms – a wounded soldier crawling back on hostile ground to the doubtful security of the trenches. Once arrived, I slumped into the armchair, sat motionless, head bent forward, gazing vacantly at the patterned carpet beneath my feet for what could have been an eternity. Hours it most certainly was, for daylight was soon giving way to dusk. And there I sat, lifeless, arid, empty and seemingly drained of my last ounce of the life blood.

If I somehow eventually managed to haul myself out of the chair and drag myself off to bed, not having eaten since midday, it was in the fervent hope that after a good night's sleep I would awake next morning with vigour and vitality restored. Forlorn hope. There followed a sleepless night of tossing and turning with growing anxiety at the thought of another day that had to be faced and fought through. Fighting was clearly out of the question. The act of getting out of bed was in itself almost more than I felt equal to. I struggled to shave, to dress, to face the ordeal of Common Room breakfast – please God that I be the first to arrive and get out before the others.

"Good morning, Mr Wilky. And how are you this morning?"

"Fine, thank you, Joe. Fine."

Only to be followed by the ordeal of choir practice and chapel. Then a further afternoon of self-imposed exile, this time punctured by bouts of sheer panic as I contemplated yet another Monday now just over the horizon together with the piles of exercise books staring reproachfully from my desk and waiting to be marked. Marked they were not. Monday morning, following on from yet another sleepless night, found me zombie-like plodding off to my classroom, with nothing prepared and nothing to say, empty, isolated and worthless. It must have been as if a subconscious truce had been established between me and 'them' – we'll leave you alone if you leave us alone – and I duly emerged mid-morning without suffering the mauling I had so feared and expected. Common Room coffee break did nothing to relieve the dread of what was yet to come – a double sixth-form French lesson – and I found myself fighting back the tears as, admitting defeat to myself, I dismissed the class with a curt 'please continue preparing' and fled back to my rooms.

By the end of the day the doctor had been summoned, a diagnosis given – endogenous depression – and my mother sent for. The remedy? A fistful of pills, plus two to three weeks away with lots of long walks in the fresh country air. It worked. After two weeks I was beginning to feel better by the day and after three weeks I was positively straining at the leash to get back to work, well away from my mother's long walks in the fresh country air.

Endogenous depression: a major depressive disorder. Individuals with this disorder experience hopelessness, helplessness, guilt or self-hate. Other symptoms include fatigue and lack of energy, difficulty in concentrating, social isolation and insomnia. This was indeed me and the doctor rightly put me on guard by pointing out that these 'black dog' bouts would in all likelihood be recurrent. Correct. They were to become annual – sometimes biannual – occurrences. Sometimes I held them down, sometimes they defeated me and I would have to withdraw hurt and licking my wounds, only to bound back again with renewed energy, rediscovered enthusiasm. Oh what joy in the rebounding! Life reaffirmed! Appetite regained!

But recovery came with change; a change in outlook and attitude. It was as if my view on life had had to change to take account of this unwanted incursion. From now on I would subconsciously have to prepare for the worst – future breakdowns. Within the year I had resigned my resident housetutorship and bought a small town house nearby (a surer retreat in times of need). Likewise I shortly later turned down the offer of a senior housemastership. Although glad to have received it – a great morale-booster – I realised full well that having to control a rambunctious pack of teenagers – sixty or so of them – when I was unable to control my own health was totally out of the question.

Other opportunities for retreats from life on campus also helpfully presented themselves at this time. Firstly I was already running a French Exchange with a prestigious Jesuit school in Toulouse, so I was able to continue with frequent trips to Le Caousou with a group of Marlburians, teaching English classes there while they struggled with maths, physics and the like taught to them in French, poor things, but a breath of fresh air for me. Secondly I was appointed Oral Examiner in French by the Associated Examining Board. This was a summer term activity which saw me rocketing around Wiltshire swooping down on comprehensive (mostly) schools to listen to their 'O' and 'A' level students murdering (mostly) the French language.

Admittedly these visits were mixed blessings. Firstly, to get to where I needed to be at the required time I often had to juggle with my timetable, to give 'study' periods to free up an afternoon. (I suspect my Head of Department suspected. He said nothing. I supplemented my income.) Secondly, having to travel sometimes considerable distances, sometimes losing my way, I more often than not arrived tired and bad-tempered before even confronting the first of sometimes up to thirty candidates.

You square up to the first combatant, a trembling waif who can scarcely hold the reading passage still for long enough to read a sentence. (Mark well the reading passage: you will hear it over and over and over and over.)

"Très bien," you say encouragingly and you ask him his age. He claims to be six (sometimes it's sixty), though he could be taken for sixteen. To check, you demand his date of birth: May 1942, he says confidently. A young-looking forty, you muse.

"Avez-vous des frères?" you enquire. To this he replies: "Oh, oui. J'avez (or possibly j'avais) trois frères." This poses a problem. Either he has (grammatically incorrectly) repeated the part of the verb you have just used, or else he has used the past tense (correctly) – in which case the brothers have fairly recently been wiped out in some awful cataclysm which is best left unexplored. Moreover, his answer has also blocked other lines of enquiry. Holidays, for instance, having a high rating for cataclysms, are now a no-go area.

"Quel est votre sport préféré?" you continue, hoping that a change of tack will enable the candidate to sail into smoother water. "Je joue le crick." This "crick" is said with particular emphasis. Could he mean cricket? If so, he is in trouble. French may be the language of diplomacy but it lacks the vocabulary for a decent conversation about the game of crick.

"Décrivez votre maison," you say in a kindly voice. The waif has prepared for this. You can tell by the expression of relief in his manically working features. His house has 6/16/60 rooms – any of which might be true. "Devant ma maison," he adds eagerly, "mon père cultive des vegetables et mon mère cultive des fleurs dans la derrière!" This statement invites disbelief on anatomical grounds. Though you can dock him for the "mon mère" and "vegetables", this insight into his domestic circumstances is linguistically unassailable. Who knows, his mother might have been the original young lady of Leeds (who swallowed a packet of seeds). Yours not to reason what he meant to say, yours only to judge his French.

It's time to glance at your watch lest, absorbed in the conversation, you run over. Time drags. Yet the painful exchanges go on and on and on, candidate after candidate.

"Quels programmes aimez-vous regarder à la télévision?" An unwise question to ask, you realise too late, since alert candidates can make a meal of this one. All they need is "j'aime" and "et" and they will stretch the answer to eternity if allowed. "J'aime Grandstand et Sportsnight et Top of the Pops, etc, etc." Sometimes they say it with a French accent, sometimes they say it in French (Coronation Rue, Bleu Pierre) – a ploy also adopted when giving their name. James Green will announce himself as Jacques Vert and you can spend twenty minutes looking for J. Vert on your list.

And as yet another candidate appears ("Je m'appelle Michel Mange" – Michael Eaton, perhaps?), you square up to him.

"Quelle heure est-il?" you ask, as though you didn't know. "Non," he replies conversationally.

Thirty candidates later, you emerge into the daylight unsure of the gender of "homme" and wondering if you'll ever be the same again. Is it really 1882, as most of them said? Are there really 300 pupils in every class? Does that lad with pimples really spend Saturday nights in a "maison publique"?

Don't get me wrong. I was always nice to candidates. I rejoiced with the strong and felt for the weak. But while they were being marked for French, I was being marked for life.

The doctor was right. As with the passing of the seasons, so too my depressions came and went. Endogenous (resulting not from external factors, but rather from a chemical imbalance in the brain) they may well have been, but they in no way spared one from also being affected by the very real causes for sadness which at times appeared in one's path in a steady, mournful trickle, forcing one out of the College cocoon to face the raw facts of reality, of life and death.

The assassination by the IRA of two well-known, well-loved Marlburians and Marlborough parents within a month of each other came as a very real shock to the community. Professor Gordon Hamilton-Fairley (First Professor of Oncology in the UK and a pioneer in the field of immunotherapy) was killed by a car bomb meant for his neighbour, Tory MP Sir Hugh Fraser. Ross McWhirter (Co-founder of the Guinness Book of Records) was shot dead on his own front doorstep after announcing a £50,000 reward for the capture of Hamilton-Fairley's killers. Five years later Ian Gow MP, also a Marlburian parent, was to join this sad list, killed by an IRA car bomb for his close relationship with Prime Minister Thatcher and because of his role in developing British policy in Northern Ireland.

Death then struck elsewhere and closer to home. Gerald 'Monkey' Murray, friend and mentor, central pillar of the *ancien régime*, passed away, his demise almost certainly brought on by a mugging he had suffered at the hands of a gang of *ragazzi* ragamuffins when visiting Italy with the faithful Miss Rogers ('Mummy'), his housekeeper and cook. He was a giant among schoolmasters, a 'renaissance' man of multiple skills and interests, whose infectious spirit enriched the lives of many, mine included. Rare indeed are the schoolmasters granted a full obituary in *The Times*. ('A pioneer and polymath amongst schoolmasters...a leader in the movement which transformed PT (Physical Training) to PE (Physical Education) with the emphasis now on circuit training and remedial gymnastics... war service in the RAF... a fascinating and much-loved teacher of English literature... Has there been another head of PE who was President of the Literary Society and who became the school's librarian? ...an enthusiastic horticulturalist skilfully tending the College gardens, a prodigious memory, generous in his hospitality and an impish sense of humour.)

The sense of humour remained with him until the very end. By now confined to bed, within days of his passing he received a visit from the Master: "Ah!" (a twinkle in the eye and a chuckle) "The Chinese Ambassador, I presume."

If the death of Gerald Murray seemed to herald the end of an era, so too did that of Hugh de Weltden Weldon, 'my' Housemaster, also friend and mentor. His was the Edwardian world of the country house, of the gentleman-schoolmaster (*à la* E. Waugh), of drinks and dinners, of clubs and croquet. Charismatic, eloquent but enigmatic too (Did he ever *really* have a wife?), he stood tall both as a pillar of his time – the arch-conservative – and a relic of a bygone age. Gone the rewarding interchanges with a conversationalist *par excellence*. Gone, too, the stylish dinners and the fabulous annual Feasts given to honour the memory of his 17th century ancestor sir Anthony Weldon, knighted in 1617 by James 1 ("the wisest foole in Christendome").

Gone, too, within the year, Dr Peter Carter, a Head of the History Department without equal, of whose intellect, knowledge and teaching skills we all, pupils and beaks alike, stood in awe. Where now are the schoolmasters to replace these giants? Will we ever see the likes of them again?

Given the above, I might have supposed that I should have been suitably prepared by then for the unexpected 'phone call from my father saying that my mother had not survived her second operation for cancer. Can one ever be sufficiently prepared for the death of a mother? No. One can only be thankful that the ordeal has to be faced only once in a lifetime. Quite enough for anyone.

Just as night gives way to day, so too were days of gloom and despondency dispersed as if miraculously, to allow in yet again the sunlight of the good days of the past. To remain impervious to the ubiquitous boisterousness of youth encircling one at all times of day and night is not an option. Such exuberance is contagious, and it is nigh impossible not to be swept into the prevailing fever. Yes, life here in the hothouse was largely lived at fever pitch and day after day unexpected situations and challenges continued to pop up all over the place.

For example, the day when I find myself at Salisbury Theological College with a group preparing for Confirmation. We are attending Divine Service in the college chapel. It is Candlemas and we've all been issued with a candle. Simon, who is sitting in front of me and who wears his hair – 'thatch' I call it – brushed well forward over his forehead à la Trump, is holding his lit candle dangerously close. Disaster is waiting to happen. And sure enough, at the most solemn moment of the service, the little flame leaps up, instantly setting alight the curly ends of the protruding thatch above. A crackle, crackle – the distinctive sound of burning – breaks the silent solemnity of the moment, followed by the unmistakable acrid smell of singed hair. Total conflagration is only avoided by quick thinking. Simon makes a dive for his pocket and extracts a handkerchief which he instantly applies to the sizzling sound, thereby extinguishing the fire. Convulsive fits of giggling, suppressed only with the greatest of difficulty, ripple through the pews. A dozen kneeling bodies shake silently, mine too, desperately fighting down the uncontrollable laughter welling up within. I have known similar situations since, but none quite like this one for sheer intensity.

Like the day when I wander into the Memorial Hall to look in on the dress rehearsal of a Modern Language Department production of Jean Anouilh's play *Antigone*, starring Kevin Maxwell as Créon, the king. Sitting in the back row of the darkened auditorium sits a large man behind a large Havana cigar. I stop dead in my tracks when, eyes by now accustomed to the dark, I see who it is I have before me. Horrors! My retreat is momentarily cut off by Gerald, the producer.

"John, can you go and tell whoever it is that smoking is not permitted in here?"

"No, Gerald, sorry, I can't."

"What?"

"Sorry, I can't and I won't."

"Why on earth not?"

"Do it yourself. Go and see for yourself."

He does, immediately decides discretion is the better part of valour and joins me in beating a hasty retreat. Robert Maxwell MC MP is allowed to puff on contentedly unhindered.

The buying of Number 41 George Lane was turning out to be a good thing. It gave me the privacy I had lacked in Turner House. Close enough to the College for colleagues and pupils alike to continue to drop in – drinks and supper parties for the lucky few – it also opened up new horizons in the town. My new circle of town friends I found refreshing and dinner parties with them contrasted favourably with those with College colleagues, where conversation too easily descended into loose talk about factions within the narrow confines of life on campus. Talking shop was more often than not the norm. However, playing the Town card had to be done with certain care and the College was always going to demand its pound of flesh – rightly so – especially where bachelors were concerned. What with my increased town connections, together with the fact that I was having fun (and spending some considerable time) building a brick garden wall of some considerable proportions as well as creating a back garden, I realised that I was sailing somewhat close to the wind. It doesn't take the authorities long to detect a beak who is not fully pulling his weight. He'll soon be found some suitably unpleasant extra-curricular post to fill, such as Master i/c Bicycles – one of the worst – involving vandalism, theft ("Sir, it was one of the town boys!" "How do you know, Gadsby?" "Well, sir, he talked like a town boy.") and often the police. So I continued to play my part in the life of the College, even if my heart was now finding satisfaction elsewhere.

France, too, was moving centre stage in my mind. Frequent term-time visits with my exchange class to Toulouse – *la ville rose* – meant that not only was I beginning to know and love that city but also that I was making for myself a new circle of friends – *mes nouveaux amis gascons* – among whom were the Thomas family from a village to the west of Toulouse, St. Paul-sur-Save, who lived in the château, farmed their land and ran a successful *Centre Equestre* on it. It meant I was no longer obliged to spend my weekends cooped up in school and living on a corridor surrounded by a bevy of Jesuit priests. Instead I could choose my mount, Hippy, and spend happy hours cantering over the hills and through the valleys, discovering charming little villages as I did so. One such village, Le Castéra, particularly took my fancy. Situated on top of a hill, it gave magnificent panoramic views of the distant Pyrénées ("*Si vous les voyez, Monsieur, il va pleuvoir.*"). Added to which the main street contained a veritable Aladdin's cave of an antique shop and the little village square a Café-Bar whose *patronne,* Betty, would always give me the warmest of welcomes. Was it really surprising that I found myself spending holiday time too in this *petit paradis gascon,* unencumbered by a gaggle of feisty Marlburians?

Other opportunities for 'escape' also presented themselves. Off the ferry and bounding through the early morning Normandy mists with the promise of a beautiful spring day to come, a college minibus filled with the keenest of French 'A' level candidates and driver, me, hell bent for Paris and on the trail of Honoré de Balzac and his Parisian haunts. What exalted company, I thought to myself as I reeled off the names of my passengers – Paul Clément de L'Epine, Anna Horsbrugh-Porter, Mark Groves-Raines, Julius Landale-Mills, etc. Such mellifluous-sounding double-barrelled *merveilles* – how could

I, John Wilkinson, with my *petit bourgeois* name, ever hold a candle to these beauties? To talk to them merely emphasizes the divide.

"Julius, if you weren't on this trip where would you be now?"

"In Devon with my aged grand-mother. She's such a bore, sir."

"A bore about what?"

"Oh, about Saint Petersburg when she was young. She was an English governess in the Tsar's palace – the Winter Palace she calls it – and she goes on and on about some half-mad, bearded monk whom they all ganged up on and murdered."

"What? Rasputin?"

"Yeah, something like that. Anyway, she seems to have been totally besotted by him. On and on she goes."

Well she might, I muse to myself, and more's the pity that such fascinating first-hand recollections are totally wasted on the ears of young Julius.

The delights of Paris, however, were far from wasted on this delightful group of young Francophiles. The Maison Balzac in Passy whetted their literary appetites, giving context to the novels already studied. It was in this very house that the greater part of the *Comédie Humaine* had been written, and the museum was full of fascinating memorabilia.

Culture done and the Marlburian being the highly sociable animal that he is, we were soon speeding along the road to Vincennes and dinner chez M. and Mme. Clément de L'Epine – generous Marlburian parent hosts who saw to it that we left them at the end of the evening well-fed and well-watered. Marlburians in their element.

The following evening's entertainment was my idea. All those years ago in my student days – oh, dear! Yes, now a full twenty years ago – I had been a regular visitor to the little, inexpensive Latin Quarter bistro Les Assassins, in the heart of Saint Germain on the left bank. It was a favourite haunt and stamping ground for students, and we had been attracted there by the nightly cabaret which accompanied dinner well into the early hours. A talented young guitarist sang songs he described – accurately – as *cabaresques, croustillantes et humoristicoquines* (cheeky, spicy and saucy). Was the restaurant still there? Yes, it was. Was there still the young guitarist singing his naughty songs? Yes there was, only, like me, he was now of course in his forties.

The table was duly booked and I was eagerly looking forward to an evening of risqué double-entendre which I was sure would appeal to the Marlburian sense of fun and humour. That is until I had a late call from M. and Mme. Clémant de L'Epine asking if they might join the party. To refuse the request was unthinkable, especially after the warm hospitality we had received at their hands the previous evening. But how would they react to the 'entertainment' set before them? Smut, pure smut and totally unsuited to a school audience!

With scars from the disastrous Equus theatre outing débâcle still with me, I immediately found myself having to consider the very real prospect of yet another letter of parental complaint winging its way to the Master's Lodge. "Dear Master, My wife and I are writing to complain most vigorously about Mr Wilkinson's choice of 'entertainment' for the party of Marlburians he is presently leading here in Paris...blah, blah, blah...Yours disgusted, A. Parent. "

Seated comfortably at our table, M. and Mme. C. were bathed in the warmth of the ambience, and with the wine starting to flow, I awaited nervously the appearance of our entertainer, comforting myself with the thought that twenty years on he had in all probability 'cooled off' and accordingly toned down the songs. Such was not to be the case, and from the singing of the very first words of the very first song I immediately realised to my horror that we were in for one hell of a roller-coaster of an evening. The *salle* loved it –a plethora of raunchy songs, all of them peppered liberally with suggestive sexual innuendo. Thunderous applause and the banging of cutlery. The Marlburians loved it, I loved it and M. and Mme. C? They too loved it. *Ouf!* All was well and I was let off yet another hook.

"Well, John, thank you so much for having organised this evening for Paul and the others. And also or allowing us to muscle in on it. We all thoroughly enjoyed it and Marlborough is lucky to have teachers like you prepared to spend holiday time on trips like this. You seem to love France and its way of life. Have you yet taken a sabbatical term? No? Oh, well, I'm sure by now you must be due one, aren't you? You should take it here in Paris on the Left

Bank – you'd love it!"

How right she is. Yes, I'm coming to love France, of course, Toulouse and the *grand sud-ouest* in particular. And, yes, maybe she's right, too, in thinking I must by now be due for a sabbatical term.

No sooner said than done, *sitôt dit, sitôt fait.* Within the year I had not only secured my sabbatical (not a term but a full two years off, my job held for my return) but had also bought the house in Le Castéra, the hilltop village set in the Gascon countryside to the West of Toulouse – a half-timbered 17th century village house which I had already set my heart on, situated on the central little village square and, conveniently, opposite the village café-bar. The house was in need of total renovation and presented a challenge which would occupy me fully for the two-year break now staring me in the face. The idea of replacing life in the classroom with life in the cement-mixer was an exciting one.

The last term before my impending two-year departure, a summer term and my seventeenth, flashed by at the speed of lightning. I was determined to make it one to remember. No fear of a depression – they struck only in the autumn and spring – and the light at the end of the tunnel was growing brighter every day. I went about my college business with renewed enthusiasm, both in the classroom and at the extra-curricular activities. Social invitations from pupils, too, poured in from all directions, be it a beer in a House bar, drinks in the Prefects Parlour or dinner with the Parthians (Dining Club) and at these I often found myself rubbing shoulders with Martin Evans. ("Let's invite Farty Marty and Silky Wilky.") On one such occasion he and I found ourselves invited to attend Cullum's seventeenth birthday party to be held on a river boat on the Thames. Martin, by now a Senior Housemaster, nevertheless jumped at the chance of what was clearly going to be a fun night on the town, as did I.

We duly presented ourselves at Westminster Pier, boarded the luxurious river boat and set off upstream towards Greenwich with thirty or so Marlburian party-goers, music, champagne and dinner on board. The result was a foregone conclusion. The boat returned to Westminster towards midnight and disgorged itself of thirty or so high-spirited, well-oiled Marlburians, who were scooped up by a waiting coach and whisked off back to Marlborough, while Martin and I tottered over to Westminster Abbey to await the colleague and car sent to fetch us.

While waiting in front of the perimeter railings, I cast an eye over the attached notice board announcing the month's preachers.

"Oh, look, Marty. The Right Reverend David Loveday, Bishop of Dorchester (hic). He's my old headmaster."

"Oh is he, Wilks?" (Hic.) "Well, it doesn't say so."

Whereupon Martin reaches into his breast pocket, produces a black felt-tipped pen and proceeds to add to the Bishop's credentials – 'Wilky's old headmaster', in bold, thick lettering. Still admiring his fine handywork, Martin is then suddenly brought back to reality with a sharp shock as a heavy hand comes crashing down onto his right shoulder from behind.

"Hullo, hullo, hullo. And what 'ave we got 'ere then?" He immediately swivels round to find himself confronting a burly Metropolitan police officer of an impressive height who is training his torch on the amended notice.

"Oh… well, officer, I was j-just amending the n-notice."

"Amending? And who, may I ask, is Wilky?"

"I'm Wilky," I manage to squeak in a strangulated tone.

"Well, sir, may I put it to you that you were not amending the aforesaid notice but that you were defacing it. Defacing a notice on private property is an offence, sir."

"Yes, officer. Sorry, officer."

"And not only is it an offence, it is in this case a serious offence. Westminster and its grounds, sir, is a Royal Peculiar, sir, which means, if you don't already know, sir, that it belongs to Her Majesty the Queen. You have therefore committed an offence against Her Majesty by defacing her poster, sir."

"Yes, officer, terribly sorry. It won't happen again, officer."

"Well, gentlemen, since you don't appear to be the vandal sort, I'm prepared this time to turn a blind eye. I suggest to you gentlemen that you return to your homes quietly and without causing further damage to property public or private."

"Thank you, officer. Thank you (hic). Good night, officer."

Inevitably news of the episode found its way to the ears of the Master, who the following morning summoned Martin to his study, seizing the occasion for a good leg-pull. ("You do realise, Martin, that we are a Church of England foundation?") The joke was shared and we were left thankful that we had a Master with a sense of humour.

Term was now fast moving to its close, with the last lessons largely taken up with exam handbacks and end-of-term admin. I entered my classroom in a buoyant mood – one last lesson, Shell French, followed by end of term lists for the whole school before the clear, cloudless skies of the long summer holidays ahead and, for me, the prospect of a two-year sabbatical immersion in the life of a Gascon hill-top village.

On entering the room I was met with an uncharacteristic silence, not the usual rowdy running-around I'd come to expect from this boisterous group of thirteen-year-olds. Instead each boy was in his place, eyes down, seemingly in a state of anticipation. I soon realised why. Staring at me from the blackboard at the other end of the room and written in bold lettering were the four words 'Silky Wilky is Gay'.

I had only seconds in which to work out how I was going to square up to this one. How quickly to diffuse potential embarrassment all round? I sauntered up to the blackboard – keep cool at all costs! – took a piece of chalk and added a question mark to the four-worded statement. Then, turning to face my accusers– or had someone else crept in during Break to write the dastardly words? – I spread both hands wide in front of me, head slightly tilted, a note of enquiry in my eyes and a slow, gentle smile gradually spreading over my lips.

"Well then, gentlemen, let's now try the interrogative form, shall we? Charles, translate!"

"Sir, I don't know the French for 'gay'."

"*Gay. C'est le même mot.*"

"Er...*est-ce que Silky Wilky est gay?*"

"Correct. Freddy, now give me the shortened form of the inter-rogative."

"*Silky Wilky est-il gay?*"

And from there to the negative forms and eventually the collo-quial synonyms. Here they were able to shine and hands shot up. Their list was a long one – queer, poof, poofter, bent, camp, pansy, bender, fagot, queen, fairy. Mine was shorter –*pédé, tapette, pédale, vieille tante, tantouze.* By mutual consent the prize went to Piers, the class geek. "Cupcake!" he squeaked from the back row. "Shirtlift-er!" The latter brought the roof down with a burst of laughter from all, myself included. I then declared synonyms over for fear of worse to come, marvelling at the width and breadth of vocabulary from those as yet so young.

"Sir, how do you say 'He's as bent as a Swiss scenic railway' in French, sir?"

Having explained for the umpteenth time that word-for-word translations are by no means always the best, I manage to come up with a French equivalent. (*Il est pédé comme un phoque,* although why on earth seals should have been singled out for this particular affliction God – or a marine biologist – only knows.)

By the time the bell finally rings a happy band of boys take leave cheerily, chattering amongst themselves happily like monkeys. (*"T'es pédé." "Non! Lui c'est une tapette." "Vieille tante, toi!" "Sale vieux phoque, toi!"*) Hardly standard GCSE vocabulary, I muse to myself, much relieved at having clearly turned a potentially embarrassing encounter to my own advantage. Not many a dull moment in the life of a classroom teacher. In fact I'm now starting to think I might even miss them over the next two years, the little rascals.

"Shall I rub the board, sir?"

"No, James, don't bother. Add another question mark if you like."

A wink from me, and a cheeky smile from him says it all.

I join the stream of excited youth crossing Court, dodging parents, their Volvos and labradors already beginning to arrive, en route for the Mem. Hall and the Master's end of term lists. Little do I realise that he, the Master, like me stepping into my classroom, is on the point of unsuspectingly stepping into his own lion's den.

All is going well, prizes have been awarded, the following term's advanced notices given, when suddenly and just when the meeting was about to come to a close, the heavy stage curtains behind the Master's podium part at the middle and out pops an almost totally naked young lady. Within a split second she has homed in on her target and snuggled up to his side, somehow enveloping herself into the folds of his gown, and now proceeds to deliver the naughty nuzzle for which, as a 'kiss-a-gram', she had been paid. Well paid, probably. It is only now that the assembled company, initially stunned by the sight of this totally unexpected apparition, finds its voice and roars its approval at the untimely intervention. The Master, wisely, refrains from attempting to struggle free from the unwanted embrace and awaits help, which is at hand, while the whistles and catcalls continue unabated. Master and girl are at last prised apart, the latter then being bundled off the stage unceremoniously to applause from the hall. The Master dusts himself down, then, choosing his moment, raises a hand. Silence falls.

"Well, ladies and gentlemen. (Pause) I think we can agree on one thing. (Pause) We've all seen better than *that!*"

Thunderous applause. Quick thinking, and he'd turned the tables. The experienced schoolmaster who instinctively knows how to sail the troubled waters. The job keeps you on your toes. I find myself thinking back over my seventeen Marlborough years, times good and less good. All in all, challenging times and – fun. Now the prospect of a clean two-year break. A much-needed change. For the better?

Chapter 19

The Great Escape

The raw rough-and-tumble of village life in Le Castéra did indeed prove to be a change for the better. More than that – it was a powerful antidote to the refined and rarefied atmosphere of life within the walls of Marlborough College. I threw myself into day-to-day village life with gusto, and so too into the rebuilding of the 17th century ruin I'd acquired. I did the work of a labourer, I spoke the language of a labourer. I went 'native'. No longer for me the sophistication of the language of Corneille, Molière and Racine. I wallowed in the grass-roots of the language, the vernacular, the colloquial, the common parlance, jargon, slang (*argot*) and dialect (*patois*). I laid on the twang of the local gascon accent with a trowel. *Ce matin j'ai acheté du pain, du vin et du boursin* became *ce matang j'ai acheté du pang, du vang et du boursang.* I became a fair expert in the use of the expletive – *putain de merde de connerie de mes couilles!* (best left untranslated). It amused me to imagine the reaction of my Modern Languages Department colleagues were they to hear me prostituting a language the purity of which they revered, a purity nurtured and propagated by the likes of the highly respectable Académie Française. Tut tut! they would say, looking down their noses. *Tant pis*, I told myself, mine is the French of the real world.

Real world or not, time flew and I was soon facing the very real prospect of my return to academia and linguistic rigour. There was no choice. I'd not been earning for nearly two years and finances were low. So it was with a heavy heart I left my cement-mixer and building site, my village and new friends, and headed north to *le perfide Albion* with its grey skies and cold climes. It was hardly ever going to be a homecoming. I had no home to go to, and had to make do with a soulless college flat on the Bath Road some distance off the campus. I felt isolated.

Repeated moves from one set of rooms to another over the following seven years caused an almost permanent feeling of restlessness which I was unable to shake off. I felt rudderless. Depressions continued to loom large. Nor was the school I was rejoining the school I'd left two years previously. There was a new Master at the helm with a new agenda. Chief among his instructions from the College Council was that he should steer policy towards admitting girls, not only at the sixth form level but throughout. The college was to become totally co-educational. I should have sensed we were heading for a bumpy ride.

My teaching and classes, however, remained much as they had always been, even if I soon detected that one was no longer automatically being given the *carte blanche* to conduct one's classroom business more or less as one liked. Pressure was being applied from above. During my absence senior management had burgeoned and now included a Master i/c Teacher Development, whose job it was to see to the appraisal and assessment of a teacher's performance in the classroom (Big Brother is watching you). Countless hours of countless meetings were now spent on the discussion of new teaching methods (don't teach an old dog like me new tricks, please), so too on discussing who would be best qualified to assess a teacher's classroom performance. Should it be the Head of Department, the Master, the Master i/c Teacher Development, or even an experienced teacher from another school? Round and round in circles we went. My one contribution to the debate was that the pupils themselves were clearly the best qualified to judge a teacher's performance – in my experience they would always unerringly distinguish between the good, the indifferent and the bad teacher. Needless to say, the idea was considered impractical and I was able to slump back into the state of sullen resentment which now characterised my attendance at such meetings.

Resentment only increased when I was forced to teach an Upper School minor studies course on 'French for Business'. French for Business, English for Business, the very mention of the word Business – what could they possibly dig up calculated to inspire me less? So too was I not best pleased being asked to spend one period per week in the computer centre with my Shell French set.

"Why?" I bluntly asked.

"Well, the pupils need all the practice they can get on computers."

"Why need they be taken from my French classes?"

"Well, they're taken from other classes too, you know."

"What do you expect me to do with them in a computer room?"

"Well...anything. They could write something."

"No, they can't. Your English keyboards don't show French accents."

"Well...does that really matter?"

"Yes, it bloody well does!"

Such encounters inevitably left me questioning not only the stance I'd chosen to adopt when confronting them but also the validity of the move I'd made in the first place by returning to the pastures of the past – pastures once fresh, rich and green and now appearing less fresh, poorer and colourless. How to recapture the enthusiasm of those earlier days?

Enthusiasm, if not felt, certainly had to be feigned during teacher-parent meetings, which seemed to have proliferated beyond belief during my two-year absence. No exeat, no half-term, no well-earned holiday was not preceded by protracted jousting with phalanxes of anxious parents bent on getting the best for their money. A solid three hours or more of ten-minute slots. Exhausting. Worrying, too, when one couldn't always put a face to a pupil whose progress (or lack of) one was supposedly discussing.

"You will understand, Mr Wilkinson, that Luke does respond to encouragement. If only you could give him a little more encouragement I'm sure you'd see the results."

Yes, Mrs Popplewell, you feel like saying, but I have twenty-four other little Lukes in the class so yours will receive just one twenty-fifth of my encouragement, no more, no less. (Wondering at the same time whether L. Popplewell is indeed the great lump slumped in the back row never paying the slightest attention to proceedings – OK, let him just wait and I'll give the great oaf an overdose of my encouragement which he's unlikely to forget.)

So enthusiasm for life in the classroom was waning, that much I had to admit to myself, even if, given the right circumstances and a class I liked, good work was still done, high standards maintained and all reaped the rewards as ever. However, given less than the right circumstances and a class with which, for whatever reasons, I felt less in sympathy, the prospects were not so rosy. Too often now, I lost patience. If for a moment I thought I saw in a pupil that highly provocative (I still think so) mix of arrogance and ignorance, I would more often than not fly into a rage. Dumb insolence, too, would rile me beyond measure.

On one occasion, when in full flight admonishing some poor youth for idleness, ignorance, arrogance, subversion and anything else I could think of, I suddenly became aware that I was being observed from a window at the back of the classroom. A window-cleaner had been peacefully cleaning his window when, without warning I had suddenly launched my attack, volume turned up full. Managing not to fall off his ladder, the poor man had nevertheless been taken totally by surprise and froze, sponge stopped dead on window-pane, mouth opened wide in disbelief, as he witnessed a ferocious attack of the 'toff' teacher on the 'toff' pupil. His disbelief was doubtless doubled by a string of expletives and a coarseness in the language employed, which he would most likely have associated with a Battersea barrow boy or a Billingsgate fishwife– certainly not with a Marlborough College beak.

It was mildly comforting to know that I was not the only one to lose control from time to time. Martin Evans, by now well into his senior housemastership was in most respects very well-suited to the job, but he was certainly not unacquainted with its stresses and strains. At times much bellowing would be heard emanating from the study. ("What! What!! What do you fiddling mean, boy? Get out of my house! You're about as effective as a fiddling fart in a force nine!)

"Oh, don't worry, sir. He's just throwing an epi."

"Throwing a what?" I asked.

"An epi, sir. Short for an epinephrine, or adrenaline, if you like. It gets pumped into the bloodstream, causing the heart to beat faster and sudden bursts of anger. An epi, a wobbly, a temper tantrum. It won't last long, sir."

Clearly a boy who not only knew his medicine but his Housemaster too. He knew the storm would blow itself out and peace would be restored. The ineffective offender would overnight be forgiven his offence. ("Henry, you are bliss and rapture unconfined. You are *la crème de la crème*, dear boy. What are you?")

If Martin's boys from time to time irked him, they also well knew how to please him. The College woke on the morning of one Prize Day to find the flagpole flying not the College flag, but a large, white bedsheet with scrawled on it in large capital letters the words 'MAR-TY FOR MASTER'. John, the porter, was quickly there offering to climb up into the roof to lower the offending flag.

"Thank you, John, but don't you think we could perhaps leave it up there till lunchtime?" purred a happy Housemaster, knowing full well that pupils, beaks, parents, the Master himself (ha ha!) Members of Council (ah, yes!) and all would be passing by to see this most welcome, if unexpected, publicity which could only enhance his growing reputation as a Housemaster of weight and consequence. After all, the next rung on the ladder was a headmastership, was it not?

Personally, having turned down a housemastership, headmasterships were the last thing in the world to be concerning me – it would be digging myself deeper into the system when I was beginning to wonder how best to dig myself out of it. Attempts at doing this continued to see me spending as much time as possible in town circles – town not gown – and Marlborough town offered much in terms of alternative entertainment. As a former major 18th century staging post for the London to Bath coaches the town boasted a multitude of former coaching inns still functioning as hotels, pubs and bars. The Ailesbury Arms, with its genial landlord John Fleming and quirky barman Chappie, became a favourite watering-hole of mine, as it did with a small but regular band of College colleagues. Chappie had become a legend in his lifetime. ("Oh, Mr Wilkinson. You here again? Don't you College masters ever do any teaching? We've just had Mr Fogg and Mr Kwiatkowski in and they had a young Mr Richards with them...I wondered if I'd ever get rid of them.")

When not in the Ailesbury Arms or the Sun Inn (the 'Common Room pub') I would often be found in Mildenhall (pronounced Mi-nal for some reason) an attractive village a five-minute drive to the east of Marlborough. Here I had befriended the Wickham family, Mark and Sophie, recently divorced, and their two little daughters, Phoebe and Louise. Mark I already knew as Head of the Art Department at the College and through him I'd met Sophie – dear Sophie, who'd at once seemed to have sensed that I was in need of a retreat, a haven. How right she was. And what a cultural haven it was too. There were anecdotes from the life of Mark's grandmother, Mabel Lucie Attwell, the British illustrator known for her cute, chubby cheeked, nostalgic drawings of children, based on her daughter, Peggy, Mark's mother. Stories too about actress Peggy Ashcroft, Sophie's aunt. So no. 28 Mildenhall became a home, the girls there to provide light relief, supper on hand – lentil pie was my favourite – and a bed from time to time when it was decided I should drive the girls to school the following morning. This is more like a 'normal' life, I thought to myself, as I raced back to College and to my gilded cage, often only just in time to hear the bell ringing in period one. (Summoned by Bells – and I know I'm following in the path of the poor boy Betjeman. Fear of being late.)

My time off-campus, my ever more frequent sorties into the life of the town and beyond, while making life vaguely tolerable were certainly not going unnoticed by the powers-that-be, the authorities, Senior Management – those employed to see each member of the team was pulling his weight. Added to which it was noticed that since my return from sabbatical I was no longer singing in the Chapel Choir nor in the Choral Society, and no longer playing clarinet in the brass band. I had also long since ceased to function as Master i/c Squash and Master i/c College Beagles, having abandoned both to those more qualified than I. Now no longer a Resident House Tutor, too, I was clearly, and rightly, perceived to be distinctly underperforming on the extra-curricular activities side.

It was therefore not long before I was being found unenviable jobs – job offers which could not be refused – which were to last me off and on to the end of my final term. Jobs normally of an administrative nature requiring time and effort. Jobs which, if not undertaken efficiently, brought with them untold opportunities for multiple cock-ups capable of resulting in either severe embarrassment for oneself or serious retribution. Master i/c Post 'A' Level Time Activities. Designed to keep leavers occupied and 'out of trouble' after their last paper till the end of term. Activities included Cookery Classes (Common Room wives to be recruited, kitchens found, equipped and stocked – a nightmare.), Typing Classes (typewriters to be assembled, repaired, ribbons replaced – a nightmare.), Individual Projects (pupil chooses his Project and 'friendly' beak to 'supervise' and nothing gets done (OK by pupil and his 'friendly' beak who already has quite enough on his plate without supervising and marking Projects) – less of a nightmare by far for me, since pupil escapes the system while I have less cooks and typists to hound into their classes, fewer irate Common Room wives to placate. ("Oh, John, who are these dreadful people you've sent me? They're just not taking their cookery seriously. Why should I bother to give of my valuable when all they can do is…" and so on.)

Master i/c Charities, another admin job. Each House to select a Rep, the Rep to join my Charities Committee. So far, so good. Attendance at meetings good – beer and sandwiches on offer. Charities to support chosen – radically opposing views over animal charities often expressed. Reps. then with unenviable task of raising money in Houses. Not easy. Efforts met with a level of indifference. Hardly for me to criticize. What about my own level of indifference? Where is my own burning desire to dedicate maximum time and effort to charitable giving? Why can I not find it in me to send out my reps inspired and with fire in their bellies to convert their peers to the cause of charity? I can't. Nor, too, can I summon up enthusiasm for organising Red Nose Days or 30-mile charity walks, the administration of both of which is again a nightmare.

If these two appointments – Master i/c Post 'A' Level Activities and Master i/c Charities – were hardly to my liking, there was even worse to come: Master i/c Norwood Hall. The Norwood Hall, named after Sir Cyril Norwood, a previous Master of Marlborough, was the central feeding outlet (self-service) where well over a thousand meals were regularly churned out per day and a place where the standard of pupil behaviour had recently been reported to be deteriorating, particularly during the evening meal when the pupils ate alone, unlike at midday when lunch was served to pupils, Common Room and administrative staff alike. Hence the brilliant idea to appoint a Master i/c Norwood Hall – me – to control and patrol the place at supper times.

By now knowing myself well, and realising full well that I far preferred running with the hare to hunting with the hounds, it took me no time to see that this was to be a policing operation which I was very definitely not going to enjoy. Here was the beak (Jason the Two-Faced) dishing out the impositions and punishments when all and sundry knew him better for pouring out the chardonnays and sauvignons. Caught between the pillar and the post, a rock and a hard place. The punishable misdemeanours were frequent and varied. Bread rolls, sometimes worse, flung from table to table, rudeness to members of the staff, the multiple banging of cutlery on trays and tables as a form of public protest, the singling out of specific girls as they entered the Hall – the lion's den – for prolonged catcalls and wolf-whistles.

Poor girls; they well knew that they were simultaneously being judged and marked on a scale of one to ten on their various physical attributes as they braved their way between the tables and through the turbulent throng towards their scant reward of a bowl of thin gruel and sometimes not much more. Would this lack of respect shown by the boys continue to dog the girls through their lives after school, through their student days and thereafter into the work-place? Have children and youth been being cruel to each other since time immemorial? What hope for the future? I would muse on this as I patrolled my way up and down, attempting to nip the worst excesses in the bud. But what irked me every bit as much as having to witness this almost daily exhibition of poor behaviour was the fact that the job was seriously eating into my *apéritif*-drinking time, my time in the Sun Inn downing a well-deserved evening pint of Wadworth's 6X or three with colleagues.

Decidedly the halcyon days were at an end – although not en-tirely. Good teaching did still continue to come my way, and gifted pupils continued to inspire me to give of my best. Good times, too, spent on extra-curricular activities, even if in my case these involved forays well beyond the walls of the college. Driving a minibus full of post-GCSE pupils to Normandy for a tour of the beaches and sites of the Allied Normandy Landings was a very real plea-sure. Just me, Dominique Priour (our extremely attractive young *assistante française*) and ten hand-picked boys – all the makings of a fun end-of-year *sortie*. And fun it was. Cross-Channel ferry Portsmouth-Cherbourg, *Auberge de Jeunesse* at Issigny-sur-mer, visits to the Bayeux Tapestry, Le Mont Saint Michel, the Allied Landings museum at Arromanches, a France-Angleterre football match against the local school, swimming in the sea and improvised Allied Landing re-enactments on Omaha beach led by Charles Rob-in Huebner, who then purely by chance stumbled on the memorial to his near-namesake C. R. Huebner – Lt. Gen. Clarence Ralph Huebner, in overall command of the American assault on Omaha Beach by the US 29th& 1st Infantry divisions. A relative of his? We left him to puzzle that one out before returning home to plunge into his family archives.

A further foray into France took place during the summer holi-days of 1987, when I was able to organise a Marlborough College Chapel Choir tour of south-west France. Months of pre-planning was required, much of it in conjunction with friends and acquain-tances I'd made over my two-year sabbatical. Hence concerts in the cathedrals in Auch, Albi and Lombez, a concert and Sunday sung

High Mass in the Basilica Saint Sernin, Toulouse, an open-air Serenade concert in the central courtyard of the château de Caumont, country seat to my new friend M. le Vicomte Jean de Castelbajac. Another well-placed Toulouse Airbus contact of mine was able to secure the services of both coach and driver throughout the length of the tour, paid for by L'Association English 31 and British Aerospace.

It was a group of almost forty strong, including singers, Director of Music, College Organist, singing colleagues and a sprinkling of camp-following parents, that finally embarked on what turned out to be a fairly ambitious programme of events. Spirits were high, so too the quality of the music, and public acclaim was forthcoming. All was going well. Those of us, however, who were well-acquainted with the nature of the Marlborough beast when in 'holiday mode' knew better than to think there wouldn't be the occasional hiccough. Jean de Castelbajac, who kindly laid on a buffet supper after the château concert, was surprised by the number of times he had to descend to the cellars to fetch up yet more bottles of wine. (*"Mais John, c'est les filles aussi!"*) Not so Aimé, our friendly driver, on being told that one of the party had violently vomited on his coach on the way back after the party. Abject apologies from embarrassed colleagues were met with a smile and a gallic shrug of his shoulders.

"Mais ça, ce n'est rien! You have to see the state of the coach after I've returned with the local rugby club after one of their Saturday night *beuveries... oh là là! ça, c'est quelque chose! Ça, alors!"*

The two-week tour finally drew to a close with an impromptu concert held on the last evening in 'my' village, Le Castéra, perched on the top of the hill. The tiny village square, flanked by my house, Madame Dat's house opposite, the Village Hall and the café, was packed with expectant *villageois* and others. The former particularly, having got to know me and my cement-mixer during the period of my sabbatical, were now curious to find out more about the English invasion of their village which I had orchestrated. Would they approve? Perhaps the last time the village had been 'visited' by the English in such numbers had been during the Hundred Years War in the time of Eléanor of Acquitaine. I hardly wanted to revive such memories. In the event all was well. The English sang their hearts out, the Castérois applauded generously. Honour was not lost that day. Added to which M. le Comte Yves de Chiris, another blue-blooded friend I'd recently acquired, arrived to support us on our last evening. He and his wife Kiki came bearing huge baskets filled with bread, cheeses and pâtés – and wine. Having witnessed the Marlburian appetite for such things at the Château de Caumont they knew that quantity was every bit as important as quality. Added to which Yves had been sent to school in England as a boy, to Stowe, and knew well the needs of the English public-school boy when *en fête*. Result? A great send-off party was had by all.

The end of the tour meant I was able both to relax and continue with the renovations of the house during the remaining weeks of the long summer holiday. September soon approached, however, and it found me unwillingly packing up to return to yet another year of Marlborough teaching – my twenty-fifth. Little did I realise at the time that it was to be my last.

The atmosphere back on the campus was not a happy one. The run-up to full co-education with the introduction of girls from the age of thirteen was proving to be more than a little unsettling to the status quo. Disruption of various kinds was inevitable. Buildings had to be either built or adapted to accommodate the new intake. New protective measures and pastoral care policy had now to be put in place to cater for the likely needs of girls of such tender years. Conservative-minded colleagues took umbrage when told that thir-teen-year-old girl pupils were not to be treated as if they were boys. Allowances were going to have to be made. "Tosh and bunkum!" fumed an arch-right-winger. "If the little madams don't pull the line when I say so they'll get the sharp end of my tongue, mark my words, madam or not!"

Indeed, not dissimilar attitudes were to be found in pockets throughout Common Room, where there was a distinct feeling that whereas Marlborough College for boys with a smattering of Sixth Form girls as an adornment was maybe a good thing, a full-blooded co-educational Marlborough College was definitely overstepping the mark. Old Marlburian opinion on the matter was particularly discombobulating. "I mean, for heaven's sake, where on earth do they think they'll get the rugby XVs from if they continue to emasculate the College like this? Lost against Radley? What, again? Not on." Sentiments like these, expressed forcefully and with emotion, reverberated within the walls of the likes of Boodles and Whites. They were sentiments also reflected by pupils themselves – particularly the older ones – who didn't much care for being told to treat the new girls with the respect due to them, preferring to look back to the Golden Age when boys could be boys together and rough it, unconcerned by considerations for the tender sensibilities of the gentle sex. Was life not so much simpler back then in those heady days of yore?

If you were tempted to think that with the eventual arrival of the new Lower School girl intake in September 1989 all would start to settle down and life return to normal, you had another think coming. In fact, things went from bad to worse and a general growing state of unrest soon translated itself into increased numbers of punishments, suspensions and expulsions among them. Boys and girls alike were kicked out variously for drug, drink and sex offences. (A boy found in his bedsit with his girlfriend, both of them in a state of more than half-undress, on being asked by his Housemaster to explain himself, saw fit to reply in all honesty: "Well, sir, it was raining and there wasn't much else to do, so at the time I thought it quite a good idea.")

Inevitably the national press soon got wind of the fact that all was not well. *The Daily Telegraph* and *The Times* tackled the issues at stake objectively and with sensitivity (Times leader: The Unhappiest Days). The tabloids went to town and raked up as much muck as they could find. Banner headlines blazoned abroad salacious titbits for all to see. 'More Shocks Hit School For Scandal,' 'Random Pot Shots at Cannabis College', 'Why I'll Quit My Sex-Row School.' There were lurid stories of girls being expelled for saucy late-night romps or prescribed contraceptive pills, of boys causing criminal damage to a village bus shelter after a drinking spree in a village pub, of random drug tests and urine samples taken without warning and laboratory tested for traces of cannabis, amphetamines, cocaine, heroin and crack. Reporters from London lurked at the gates waylaying pupils in the hope of further twists on the latest gossip. A bunker-like mentality was fast descending on the College, and we were all, Common Room and pupils alike, caught up in it.

Most affected of all by the turmoil, after a tenure dogged by controversy, was clearly the Master himself – the buck stopped there – and nobody was much surprised when the College Council announced it had accepted his resignation for the end of the academic year. ("I believe that by the end of this academic year, I shall have completed the tasks that I saw as being important when I first became Master in 1986, in particular the successful transition of the school to full co-education.") Successful? Could it ever have been anything other than a bumpy ride at best? I hardly think so.

Others equally affected by the successive scandals were the Housemasters, responsible as they were for the discipline within their houses. Some of them were coping with the added pressures better than others. Martin Evans, I thought, seemed to be managing the unsettling times better than most. That was until he chose to throw his next 'epi' – one which seemingly came straight out of the blue but which, to judge from the volume of the expletives emanating from the study, should more accurately be described as a 'mega-epi', and it continued to consume him in anger throughout the day. Late that night, in an attempt to relieve the pressure, he grabbed his felt tip and penned a ferocious letter to the Master. I was a forthright and stinging critique of the abysmal state of the nation, the cause of all his woes and ills. This he posted through the front door of the Master's Lodge at midnight. At two in the morning he woke, sat bolt upright in bed and decided this had been a bad idea. At two fifteen he was kneeling outside the door of the Lodge fishing through the letter box for the fateful document. He was in his pyjamas and had brought with him a cunningly bent wire coat hanger. A faint whimpering carried on the still night air. At two-thirty the letter was retrieved. Martin unsealed and reread the letter and... bravely replaced it.

The ends of terms too, were particularly testing times for House-masters. Traditionally sixth-formers had broken bounds on the last night and got up to all manner of pranks, some of them harmless, others causing damage. Minis had been pushed up the nave of the chapel and deposited on the altar steps. A herd of cows had been found happily grazing in Court on the last morning. Benches from the cricket XI had been used to build a Stonehenge – also in Court. Things being what they were, however, the Master was now having nothing of it and had issued strict orders for all-night patrols with heavy punishments for anyone found out at night.

Needless to say it was then left to Housemasters to deliver the magisterial message to their Houses. Martin Evans sensibly chose to do so during House Assembly after prep. The reaction was predictable – a united groan went up at the idea of yet more restrictions being imposed from above. This reaction was anticipated by the Housemaster, who peremptorily dismissed the House and thought no more about it. That is until later, when he met up with his sixth formers at the nightly Captain's Meeting. Those present unwisely proceeded to give vent to their anger over the proposed draconian end of term measures.

"But, sir, it's unfair."

"Sir, I bet *you* used to get up to end of term pranks when you were at school."

"Anyway sir, it's part of the tradition. They can't take that away from us."

The Housemaster, tired of having to further argue the toss with his querulous boys and ready for bed, surprisingly decided not to throw one of his 'epis' – he could have been forgiven that – but rather to use his not inconsiderable wit to counter the arguments.

"Well, gentlemen, if that's how you feel – go for it! After all you deserve to have fun here, don't you? Your parents pay enough money, don't they? Who am I to stop you wrecking the joint, if that's what you want?"

His remarks, dripping with irony, amused his audience, who immediately recognised the direction the conversation was taking. The Housemaster, also enjoying giving a performance, soon warmed to his theme. "I mean, after all, why don't you all get out there and *really* paint the town red? Just think what you could do! Rip up the geraniums in front of the Master's Lodge, pee into the letter box, murder the cat..."

By now the Housemaster is well into his stride and the possibilities he imagines and goes on to offer are legion. His audience can barely contain themselves for laughter – the wit and the humour they adore, the ironic and sardonic elements they fully understand. With one exception. Rolf, a Dane from Copenhagen, being blessed with a Danish sense of humour (limited), was congenitally unable to detect the irony, even though it was laid on with a trowel. Horrified at hearing his Housemaster countenancing nothing short of mass mutiny in the ranks, he immediately rang his mother to tell all, chapter and verse. His mother, wife of the Danish Ambassador to Thailand, also being blessed with a Danish sense of humour (limited) and therefore equally horrified at what she was hearing, did the very proper thing of warning the Master that he had a maverick Housemaster on his staff intent on bringing the College to its knees. The Master, amused and without difficulty detecting the hand of Martin Evans in the matter, was able rapidly to defuse the cause for concern, leaving a Danish family musing over the vagaries and imponderables of the English sense of humour.

There were no bounds broken that last night and the Housemaster, having had his leg pulled by a sympathetic Master, got a good night's sleep.

It was a Monday at the start of the following term. Just yet another ordinary Monday as far as I was concerned. Except that I had a full timetable and it was raining and I was facing the prospect of having to referee a game of hockey in the rain – all in all, a less than ordinary Monday. A black Monday, for sure. Added to which I'd argued with the beak i/c hockey when he'd approached me, saying that I thought games were for kids and that now at 50 I was past that sort of thing. He'd immediately countered with the obvious reply, saying that if colleagues of ours aged 60 and above were capable of walking up and down a hockey pitch with a whistle for an hour or so, then so was I. *Touché!* But otherwise, yes, just another ordinary Monday to be got through, which saw me trudging through Court and down to the Common Room Bin Room on my way to Common Room dining room breakfast. The sight of my bin did nothing to improve my humour, filled as it was with post and papers all doubtless requiring attention.

My attention, however, was drawn to the Master's notice board, where a new notice had just been posted. I read it and, hardly able to believe my eyes, re-read it:

EARLY RETIREMENT

Any member of Common Room aged 50 and above considering early retirement should see my secretary in the next few days.

"Well, Wilko, what are you going to do?" came a voice from behind me. It was Nick Fogg, head of the RE Department.

"I don't know", I replied, not having immediately digested the implications of the offer. "What are *you* going to do?"

"Grab it and run." came the unwavering reply. Nick, like me, had already for some time been hankering after pastures new and now immediately saw the chance staring him in the face.

'Grab it and run' – the idea dominated my thoughts all morning. Teaching went onto automatic pilot as I played with the concept of a total break with the past and contemplated the start of an exciting new dawn. Black Monday was fast turning into Golden Monday, a Monday during which I could turn my whole life around.

The end of the morning saw me in the Master's secretary's office. By afternoon the rain had stopped and I dutifully took my place on the hockey pitch, bashing the ball about with the best of them, still lost in thoughts of the enticing post-Marlborough world which was now looming so close. Discussions with the Bursar over the following weeks soon made the situation clear. I was being offered a generous package – a lump sum from the College, another lump sum from the Ministry of Education and a college pension in line with the twenty-five years of service given.

With my finances secure, I was now in a position to plan out the future. The plan, in effect, was the one which had been germinating in my mind ever since I'd bought the house in Le Castéra. Now that I had finished work on the first floor – providing my living accommodation – I would turn my attention to the ground floor, which in previous generations had been given over to the animals. Stabling for the statutory two oxen required the ploughing of the modest plot of land owned by successive generations of peasant farmers, a pigsty, hencoops and rabbit hutches, all of which, together with the presence of a huge oak wine vat, a deep well and a brick bread oven, bore witness to the fact that these simple folk were every bit as self-supporting as it was possible to be. Crucial to my plan was André Escande – electrician, plumber and friend – who was in full agreement with my project, namely to convert the whole of this ground floor into a restaurant, complete with bar, kitchens and toilets. With a single phone call I was able to secure his services – a major triumph. We now had a team.

News of my impending departure at the end of the academic year clearly surprised no one, neither colleagues nor pupils. Some of the former told of their surprise when I'd reappeared after my two-year sabbatical.

Nor did my 83-year-old father show surprise when told. "Well, John, I always thought you'd done well to get that job. When I was up at Peterhouse I had among my friends Etonians, Wykehamists and Marlburians. The Etonians? Well, they were generally what you'd expect – Etonians. The Wykehamists? You sometimes wondered if they were walking on another planet. But the Marlburians – ah! delightful. Fully rounded individuals, sociable and always good company. Yes, a good school and they've been good to you too."

A good school, yes, which had certainly been good to me, and I had no grounds to regret the twenty-five years of service I'd given. But a good school now going through difficult times, which surely made my firm decision to leave the easier.

Leaving parties for me and others littered my last summer term. There was also a welcoming party to introduce the incoming new Master to Common Room. I knew no more than that he was the present headmaster of Felsted, until a phone call from Tom, Felsted Housemaster and friend from TCD days, informed me that all I needed to know was his nickname, 'Basher'. It seemed to me just what the College needed – someone fierce to bash it back into shape. I was only relieved that I would be well over the hills and far away when the bashing commenced. Clearly Providence had dictated that this was exactly the right moment to be on my way, carrying with me fond memories of happy past times and having avoided – just – the very real possibility of future teacher burn-out.

Now was a moment to grasp the bigger picture. I was already half a century down my road, the first quarter as boy and student, the second as a beak. And beyond? The third quarter? As an English restaurateur in the hills of Gascony? To leave the teaching profession was one thing, to leave one's country of birth another. Yet both prospects appealed equally – a new life outside the classroom, a new life in France.

Farewells over, all packed and ready to go, the last few days saw me in high spirits. Then I was finally bound for the Channel ports with the last school bell ringing in my ears and the well-known lines from Shakespeare hovering on my lips again: '...for I love France so well that I will not part with a village of it; I will have it all mine...' Henry V, Act V, scene II.

Chapter 20

A Fair Wind for France

Taking the car ferry to France was by no means a new experience, and I was fully acquainted with the procedures. Customs. Roll on, roll off. Customs. Easy. During the seven-hour crossing (Southampton-Le Havre) I had plenty of time to call to memory the first time I had made that crossing. That first time had not been so easy.

The year was1953 and I was 11 years old and still at Carn Brea Preparatory School, Bromley, Kent. The country was still in post-war mode, the economy stagnant, the outlook gloomy. With some of the wartime rationing still in operation, it was hardly surprising that there were those looking for means of escape. Continental holi-daying seemed to offer one such escape, even if there were difficulties to overcome with restrictions still placed on the amount of sterling that could be legally taken out of the country. Cars, too, presented problems. They had to be adapted to continental driving. Yellow bulbs had to be fitted to headlamps and beams had to be adjusted to allow for driving on the right. For some reason tyre numbers had to be recorded and presented at customs. Insurance policies, too, needed to be amended in accordance with the country/countries to be visited. Surely it was enough to put off a good number of potential continental holidaymakers from taking the plunge. Only the intrepid were prepared to see it through.

The excitement of the holiday started at Southampton Docks. The loading of the cars onto the ferry was indeed a sight to behold. Parked on the quayside, they were one by one driven onto a rope net, then, cradled in the net, scooped up by a mammoth crane and hoisted up to dizzy heights before being perilously swung over the ferry and lowered into the belly of its hold, there to remain till the following morning when the same operation was performed in reverse. A night in a cabin on a boat added to the general excitement, so too the first sighting of the coastline of our nearest continental neighbours as we approached Le Havre early in the morning. These were the days before ferry terminals (those soulless, aseptic, sterile concrete constructions – not unlike air terminals, universally alike) when ferries sailed up to and into the old town harbour, there to dock right up against the quayside. Dockings were accompanied by many manoeuvres, much shouting and the throwing and catching of mooring ropes.

Eventually the gangways were swung into place, but not before we had had the chance to survey the harbour scene set before us. Opposite and across the road from the jetty was a row of houses, half of which were cafés, their brightly coloured awnings standing out proudly in the early morning sun, their sturdy marble-topped tables with wicker chairs spilling over onto the pavement in front. Smart waiters dressed to kill – white shirt, black tie, waistcoat and trousers, white full-length apron – were already scurrying around serving the early customers. How attractive, I thought to myself. It was an immediate and hardly surprising impression from one whose only experience in café life had heretofore amounted to not much more than odd visits to stuffy Joe Lyon's Corner Houses.

Brother Mark and I soon realised that Mother and Father were of like mind and were similarly attracted to the scene playing out in front of us below, and within minutes we found ourselves clattering down the gangway ("Hold on to those ropes, boys!") bound for the nearest café and breakfast. If I had expected father to order his customary porridge I was to be much mistaken. We were now on the continent and continental customs were to be adhered to. Four continental breakfasts were accordingly ordered. Much needed explaining to these two young first-timers.

"And you know, boys, the origins of these croissants? Have they taught you the Siege of Vienna yet? No? Well, when the Ottomans laid siege to Vienna in 1683 they had with them their flags and pennants depicting the crescent moon – a symbol of Islam. And when the Christian forces defeated the Ottomans the local bakers and pastry-makers adopted the crescent shape in celebration of victory. And since the Viennese were well-renowned in pastry-making of all sorts, their influence soon spread abroad and particularly to France. Hence the French croissant."

Delicious, we thought. So too the *baguettes* ("Literal meaning, John? A wand") and *petits pains au chocolat* on offer, so too the freshly ground coffee (we being a tea-drinking family) served in large ceramic bowls ideal for the dunking of bread and *pain grillé* alike, a habit brother and I adopted at once, taking our cue from those sitting beside us. A strong aroma of coffee permeated both the café and its *terrasse*.

We caught another aroma, equally strong and pervasive. Cigarettes?

"Yes, darling, they're called Gauloises. You know Gaul? Roman France. So, French cigarettes, very strong, made with dark tobaccos from Syria and Turkey. Look over there! There's a packet of Disque Blue. Same thing. Unfiltered too."

"And Mum, what are they drinking here? And over there?"

"Here they're drinking red wine and over there pastis – it's an aniseed-flavoured spirit. Strong, too, darling;"

"But, Mum, Dad always says we don't start drinking *apéritifs* till midday and it's only eight-thirty."

"I know, dear. But we're in France now……"

So this was France, and I was discovering it. I liked it. I liked the differences – *Vive la différence!* Perhaps this was to be a holiday with a sharp learning curve. Anyway it was a change from the usual holidays on the Devon beaches. We didn't leave that friendly little café until I'd also understood the principles of the *jeton* – that chunky little metal disk to be bought at the counter if one wanted to use the public phone – and the dangers of the French/Turkish toilets. Forewarned is forearmed. These tricky toilets come in the form of a slab of porcelain with a hole in the middle and two foot imprints on which to stand/crouch/teeter while performing one's business. Keeping one's balance and aiming straight are the challenge. Once finished, don't flush till you're ready to make a quick exit – these toilets have a nasty habit of spraying lots of water over a much larger area than just the toilet, meaning that you risk wet feet – if not worse – unless you're quick enough to escape the oncoming deluge. I wasn't and returned to the table with socks and sandals soaked, much to the amusement of all.

A leisurely drive westwards took us to Brittany and Sables d'Or-les-Pins, where we were shown to the holiday let we'd booked for the fortnight. That first evening we ate in the local restaurant. Further lessons to learn. Namely on entering a French restaurant, be sure to greet all present with a friendly *bonsoir* and a cheery smile – it matters not that you're amongst total strangers. Be not surprised when a tureen of soup turns up on your table when you haven't ordered it. A welcoming gesture from *Madame la Patronne*, the tureen will remain with you while you help yourselves then passed on to further clients as and when they arrive. Friendly places, these French restaurants, I thought to myself, while observing those surrounding us happily engaged in the serious business of eating and drinking.

Happy days they were, spent swimming in clear blue waters, playing on beaches of golden sand, riding on bicycles, enjoying picnics, visiting medieval fortresses, frequenting the cafés and engaging with the locals wherever possible. Indeed, we were much encouraged to engage with the locals. ("Well, boys, if you really want more ice creams you can go and buy them yourselves. *Une glace, s'il vous plaît, Monsieur* or *Madame. Au vanille, au chocolat. Merci, Monsieur* or *Madame.* And don't forget the *Monsieur/Madame* bit.")

And so there followed a succession of summer holidays in a similar vein, always in France but each year venturing further and further south. Batz-sur-Mer in the Loire Atlantique, then Vieux Boucou in the Landes, then finally twice Banyuls-sur-Mer. Ah, Banyuls! Like the others, a village on the coast but not on the Atlantic. This time on the Mediterranean, on the Côte Vermeille to be precise, close by the border with Spain. Why exactly Banyuls made such an immediate impact, why it seemed 'different' from the France we had already experienced, I was at the time unable to explain. It just felt different. It looked, smelt, sounded different.

It was only later I learnt why. Prior to the seventeenth century the southern half of France (Le Midi) had been largely independent of Paris and the north. It was politically governed either as a single entity or controlled variously by the powerful lords of the region – the Dukes of Aquitaine, the Counts of Toulouse and Foix. A region known as L'Occitanie, boasting its own history, culture, literature and language, it was very different from those of Paris and the north. The roots of the language of the south (l'occitan or la langue d'Oc) owed nothing to that of the north (la langue d'Oil). Their literature and music were the making of the medieval troubadours, with their fine lyrical poems in praise of chivalry and courtly romances. Their climate and culinary traditions were also distinctive. All in all it was a rich and powerful heritage, aspects of which had filtered through to the present. Its power seemed to permeate even down to the Banyuls of the 1950s. That was what made one feel one was in a different country. One only had to bathe oneself in the warmth of the southern climate and waters, to behold the sudden profusion of vineyards, olive groves and orchards, to open one's ears to the twang of the spoken word, of the Occitan dialect still spoken by the old folks and indeed to the sounds of the beguiling music of the Sardane – that stately Catalan dance beloved by all in these parts.

All this and more gave another meaning to the concept of the word France – a southern, gentler, milder, richer and more beguiling version of the northern counterpart. And the traditional Mediterranean diet, the provençal gastronomy? What delights to be found there with the emphasis on olive oil, vegetables (tomatoes especially, garlic, onions, cucumbers, mushrooms, peppers and salads), fish and seafood, meat (sheep, goat, chicken, duck – beef not so much) and herbs (rosemary, basil, dill, fennel, oregano). A healthy diet too (not for the southerner the butter, the dollops of cream, the rich, heavy sauces associated with French *cuisine* in Normandy and elsewhere). And what about a bottle of local wine with which to wash it all down – a cheeky little Bouquet de Provence (rosé) or a Saint Chinian (red) perhaps? Also good for the health, they'll tell you – *avec modération, bien sûr!*

Little did I then realise that I was hardly the first to discover the delights of the Mediterranean culture. A whole generation, the nineteenth-century Romantics, fell for it in a big way. When I first read Goethe's poem *Kennst du das Land wo die Citronen blühen?* – Mignon's song from Wilhelm Meister's Apprenticeship – I knew exactly what he meant.

You know that land where lemon orchards bloom,
Its golden oranges in gloom,
That land of soft wind blowing from blue sky,
Where myrtle hushes and the laurel's high?
You know that land?
That way? That way
I'd go with you, my love, and go today.

Proximity to Spain was an added attraction to the Banyuls holidays. On the second of the two I'd spotted a poster advertising a bullfight in Figueras, a Spanish town just over the border. Can we go, I asked? No we can't, came the firm reply, followed by a lecture on cruelty to animals. I persevered, flexing my still far from fully developed sixteen-year-old muscles in a brave bid for adolescent independence.

"Well, dear, *we're* not going. *You* go if you like."

Retreat was not an option, and the next day saw me beetling off down to the station to catch the train, equipped with a minimal amount of money, an 'O' level in French and a fair measure of apprehension. The journey presented no problems, and once in Figueras all I had to do was follow the flow – a whole population seemingly out to make the most of the local *fiesta* on a perfect summer's Sunday afternoon. Whole families were out in their best *corrida* clothes, the women in broad-brimmed summer hats and long, billowing light summer dresses, their fans swinging from their wrists, all exuding an impression of eager anticipation of the afternoon's entertainment to follow.

The arena was soon full to bursting. Thousands of excitable Spaniards were being 'warmed up' by brass bands who clearly knew how to do it. The temperature rose, the noise level too, with clapping, singing and dancing on the benches, and by the time the gates opened and the spectacle started the crowd was more than 'warmed up'; rather the lid had been blown off a boiling cauldron. Wild applause greeted the proud actors as they paraded round the arena in a lap of honour, saluting to the presiding dignitary sitting in the central box seats.

Once in place they solemnly turned to the gates, which were swung open yet again to the strident sound of trumpets blazoning forth a fanfare to welcome the principal guest to the party – a 600-kilo bull which burst in on the scene like a ball out of a 24-pounder Howitzer. The atmosphere was electric as the ballet-like dance sequences commenced. One could not help but be swept up into the general elation. Act II started with the arrival of the picadors, both of them mounted on heavily padded horses. It was they with their long lances stabbing at the neck of the bull who were the cause of the spilling of the first blood. I winced at each stab. The crowd roared approval. Bull repeatedly charged horse, repeatedly to be re-pulsed by further well-aimed stabbings, resulting in the trickles now turning into a steady stream of blood gushing out of the tormented animal's neck.

It was at this stage – the stage when I was consciously averting my gaze from the scene of torture – that someone must have decided enough was enough. Off with the horses, onto Act III with the ban-derillos – three men armed with well-sharpened barbed sticks with which they danced around the already-weakened animal, throwing darts with deadly accuracy into the pre-determined choice parts of their moving target, now sufficiently weakened through loss of blood to be considered ready to face Act IV and his final tormentor, the matador, face to face.

At this stage I was praying the man would dispatch the animal with immediate effect to put an end to the suffering. It was not to be. This final act was what the crowd had come to see, man pitted against monster. The matador's skill was now on show to the adoring, admiring fans, who urged on their hero to further feats of daring. Dicing ever closer with danger and death, he was at last able to lead the highly ritualised *danse à deux* to its ultimate conclusion – a once brave, proud and noble animal finally brought to a total standstill in front of its tormentor, scarcely able to remain standing through heavy loss of blood and now resigned, facing death. The matador was poised perfectly on the toes of his feet, his sword poised equally perfectly for its final downward thrust. The bull, head lowered, presented an easy target for that sword, which now plunged down and sliced into the flesh between the shoulder blades as a knife into butter...

I saw none of this. My face was hidden behind my hands, my face and hands buried between my legs. When I was eventually able to look up again it was to witness the undignified sight of that great carcass being dragged off by two strong dray-horses – off to the butcher's doubtless. It was only then that I realised that the horrors had barely started. Five further bulls were presented, five further killings to stomach. Needless to say I left that arena drained of emotion. Sickened, a sadder person, and wiser too, perhaps.

"Well, how was it, darling?"

"Fine, Mum. A great experience. Wouldn't have missed it for anything," I lied. No more was ever said of the matter.

Over the years I've met and talked with many Spaniards. I lead the conversation so that it always ends up with them attempting to justify their national 'sport' by saying it's a Spanish tradition. Whereupon I reply that so too was the burning of witches an English tradition, but it was a bad one, and England, being a civilised country, has long since banned it as barbaric. Needless to say I have not made many Spanish friends. Not to be confused with the Catalans, who not only refused to participate in the worst aspects of the Spanish Inquisition but have also now banned the *corrida*. Bravo! For that alone they deserve their independence.

As predicted, family holidays came to a halt after Banyuls. Further visits to *la belle France* resumed during those golden years as a student at Trinity College, Dublin. There was that trip to Paris with my good friend and fellow-student Michael de Larrabeiti to work for Clarkson & Co. as tourist guides during a summer vacation. A further visit the following year, alone this time, with Orwell's *Down and out in Paris* in my pocket saw me eventually finding a job selling the *New York Times* on the Champs-Elysées – publicity for the paper, any sales takings straight into my pocket. Americans there certainly were on the Champs-Elysées but not many of them were interested in news from back home. There were just enough, however, to enable me to pay the rent on the seedy, stuffy hostel bedroom I'd taken on the Left Bank. Any remaining francs went on *baguettes,* sandwiches and beer.

Then suddenly on the 6th of August 1962, luck came my way. Already in situ, I'd opened my bundle of papers and had immediately focused on the headlines. Momentarily overcome at what I'd read and without thinking, I cried out the stunning, sad news to all and sundry – 'MARILYN MONROE DEAD' – and within seconds I had clients clamouring. Sales rocketed, and twice I had to return to the office for extra supplies. That evening we ate and drank like kings – restaurant, champagne. We toasted our benefactor, Marilyn, with the warmest gratitude from three hungry, thirsty down-at-heel students who now, through her, had been fully restored to the land of the living. Dinner was followed by a visit to the bars, clubs and jazz cellars of the Rue de la Huchette, one of the oldest streets on the Left Bank, followed in turn by a nocturnal tour of Les Halles, the Central Market ('The Belly of Paris', said Zola),which was now coming to life in the early hours of the morning. A traditional *soupe à l'oignon* while viewing the traders buying and selling their wares – meat, fish, vegetables, fruit – bargaining, laughing, shouting, gesticulating. It was a scene surely not much changed since the original market opened there in the twelfth century, we mused.

Sundays, our day off, were spent largely in Shakespeare and Company, the well-known new, second-hand and antiquarian bookshop opened by the American George Whitman in 1951, a haven for all with a love of books and literature, writers and readers alike. It was a free reading room for all who cared to drop in – stay ten minutes, stay the day, it mattered not. Coffee and tea were on tap at all hours of day – just help yourselves. Beds were tucked between bookshelves for those happy to lend a hand in the shop. Chessboards for those interested. Reading and talking in the window seats – views over the Seine and with Notre Dame de Paris directly opposite. Were we not lucky to be in this most beautiful of cities in this most beautiful of countries?

Lucky, indeed, to be a student and so to have the long holiday times in which to travel and explore. With my fourth and final year at TCD now fast ebbing away, I instinctively turned my mind to finding a way to prolong the student life. It was not long in coming and no sooner had I graduated than I found myself entering the Ecole Normale D'Instituteurs of Nancy, Lorraine, as an *Assistant d'Anglais*. I had a place kept for me at St. John's College Cambridge, where I was to study at the Department of Education the following year. Four years of the student life now become six – not bad, I thought to myself. Even if Nancy had appeared nowhere on the list of towns I was expecting to be offered, it at least had the advantage of being within striking distance of Strasbourg, a town with much to recommend it and the gateway to Germany, where I spent a holiday hitch-hiking through the Black Forest and discovering the delights of the old university towns of Freiburg, Tübingen and Heidelberg. Was I right to be putting so many of my eggs in the French basket? Should I not be spending more time in Germany? Would I eventually have to choose between the two?

These questions remained unanswered throughout the following year, which saw me at St John's, Cambridge and sitting in the University Department of Education training to become a teacher. Once there, the questions were of a different nature. What was I doing there? Did I really want to become a teacher? The year got off to a gloomy start, the boring lectures seemingly irrelevant. The importance of the 1944 Education Act. Health and safety requirements in the designing and building of new schools. How to write on the blackboard without turning your back on the class. Hardly inspiring topics. The second term, however, offered brighter prospects. I was sent on teaching practice to St. Paul's school, Hammersmith, a school with an awesome academic record. Although happy to associate myself with such a fine establishment, I was nevertheless plagued by doubt, fears and sleepless nights. Would I be up to it? Would they land me with the top scholarship class, where I would surely flounder? Luckily the worst imagined scenarios were not played out, and by the end of the term I was reasonably happy that on most occasions I'd risen to the challenges set before me. Phew!

On accepting the post at Marlborough College the following September, I imagined I'd finally come to the end of my student days. Oh what sadness! What an irretrievable loss! I had imagined that on walking onto that campus for the very first time the portals would have immediately slammed shut behind me, leaving me imprisoned in a Wiltshire ivory tower for an eternity. Gone the foot-loose, fancy-free trampings through foreign parts, gone the freedom. Here to stay an institution with its high walls, its curfews, its cells complete with adolescent inmates, backboards and chalk dust.

Imagine my joy when, within a mere six months of taking the job, I realised that my gloomy predictions were totally without foundation. Why? I had simply failed to account for the holiday factor. A wise schoolmaster will not run around shouting to all and sundry that the best part of the job is the long holidays which go with it, although he may well think to himself that to be the case. Up to a third of the year on holiday on full pay. Well, I thought to myself, what a bonus! Let us continue with our lifestyle much as it was. And so I did. No sooner had the last bell rung than I was up and off, usually bound for the Channel ports. Sometimes I headed for the north of France, sometimes the south, sometimes elsewhere on the Continent.

A favourite destination was Brittany – not the tourist Brittany of Mont St. Michel and the beaches, but rather the deep interior, still very much off the beaten track. I would stay in the little village of Kerfourn near Pontivy with my friends Pierre and Danielle, both of them primary school teachers at the village school. They lived in the tiniest of flats above the two classrooms, and pretty basic it was. Electricity, yes, but only one water tap – the cold one – in the kitchen. For the loo one had to go downstairs and cross the playground to a rickety *cabanon* with its ubiquitous Turkish porcelain hole-in-the-ground affair. For a shower there was nothing for it but to drive into Pontivy to the *douches municipales* and join the queue with others similarly deprived of washing facilities in their own homes.

The pupils, with ages ranging between three and eleven, were clearly from deprived backgrounds. The state paid for their schooling, so too for their midday meal. This was produced from a Nissen hut-type construction tacked on to one of the classrooms and serving as both kitchen and dining-room. An elderly biddy from the village would arrive shortly after the start of classes and could be heard clanking around toiling over heavy cauldrons of soup, which at midday would be sloshed out to all and sundry (myself included) to be followed by a meat dish and a fruit. After lunch all hell would break loose when the children were released into the playground for half an hour. Whatever games were played, they were invariably accompanied by much rushing around and shrill shrieking.

Fairly average general chaos would momentarily be brought to order on the arrival of the local priest, *M. Le Curé*, looking somewhat forbidding in his black cassock, who would scoop up a small group of boys and girls and lead them off to the village church across the road for their weekly dose of Catholic doctrine. The Catechism. The Curé, who turned out to be a friendly old cove, saw no reason why I should not tag along with them, which I did on occasion, at first not knowing quite what to expect. I soon realised that the Catechism is really no more than a series of questions and answers, the questions asked and the answers given by the Curé, the answers then to be learnt by the children. A classic example of rote learning – knowledge gained by repetition. There were standard questions on doctrine to which standard answers were to be given, parrot-like inevitably. No room here for individual input from the child, no room for debate. Indoctrination, I thought to myself, but then I remembered how I myself at the age of fifteen had had to rote-learn the Lord's Prayer, the Creed and the General Confession and repeat it word-perfect and indeed parrot-like in front of the Housemaster. 'Just learn it and don't ask any questions' seemed to be the mantra.

It was with Pierre that I was able to discuss the implications of the 1905 Law on the Separation of the Churches and the State. How since then religious teaching in France had been removed from the state schools, how state school teachers were generally non-believers and how they were more often than not left-wing in their political views. I learnt from him too that generally speaking relations between village primary school teachers and their Curé were not good and that the genuine friendship between himself and M. le Curé de Kerfourn was very much the exception to the rule.

Rural Brittany held its appeal, but so too did the South of France, and it was to Provence I headed during the long summer holidays. Staying with friends in the Var, I was well-placed to discover both the Riviera coastline and the fleshpots of St. Tropez, as well as the charming hilltop villages of the hinterland – Bargemon, Claviers, Callas among others. My base was sometimes in Draguignan, *chef lieu* of the Var, where my friends the Audumarès family ran the family hotel Le Postillon in the centre of town. The arrangement was I had a free room in the hotel and gave a hand in the kitchens and dining room when needed. Ideal. When not needed I was up into the hills off to some summer weekend village *fête* or other which would see us playing *pétanque* with the locals, then taking a *vin d'honneur* with M. le Maire before making it to the restaurants in the village square there to dine, wine, sing and dance our way through the evening into the small hours of the morning.

Sunday mornings would bring further attractions, notably in the charming and picturesque village of Bargemon, whose *fête* always included the Sunday lunch 'aioli'. *Ah! Un bon aioli – magnifique!* This was Provence's glorious garlic-based answer to the ubiquitous mayonnaise. Great buckets of it were prepared in the homes of *les bonnes femmes du village* and borne out together with the accompanying boiled eggs, vegetables and fish to be placed on the trestle tables set up on the little square. A good aioli begins not in the blender but with a mortar and pestle and a generous quantity of garlic. When the garlic is pounded to a paste, it's whisked into the traditional preparation of egg yolk, lemon juice, mustard and olive oil. *Et voilà... délicieux!* When one has once tasted a true provençal aioli, it is difficult to go back to Hellman's.

There were lazy summer Sunday afternoons sitting in a provençal hill-top village square and at tables with the villagers both old and young – toothless old grannies in black, babes in arms – in the shade of the age-old plane trees with a gentle breeze occasionally stirring their broad leaves, *apéritifs* littering the table (yes, mostly Pernod and Ricard, of course), so too bottles of rosé (what a lovely delicate, pale colour), so too basket-loads of freshly home-baked country bread (and how good is that dipped into the aioli!) The gateaux, the coffee, the *digestifs* (brandy or liqueurs) were all set aside awaiting their turn to be put before this happy band of *fêtards (Vive la fête!* we all cry out loud). Was it any wonder, I asked myself, that I was falling in love with life in *la belle France?* A simple lunch, yes, but bliss!

And as if this wasn't enough, further entertainment was often available in the evening. That is if we were lucky and Elizabeth was at home. Elizabeth Collins' magnificent home was Le Château de Bargemon, set right in the middle of the village. I was given to understand that she had inherited Coty perfume and Sutton's seeds. Be that as it may, she certainly knew how to entertain.

Then there were other days when I was free and would head not for the hills but for the coast. Downhill to Saint Maxime, turn right and off on the road to Saint Tropez. A wander round the little port there would always fascinate. The yachts of the wealthy, moored side by side, each one vying with the other for pride of place – which one could boast the finest teak decking? Who had the most grandiose gladioli display on deck for all to admire? Or indeed the prettiest girls? Sometimes we would make for the beaches instead – Tahiti beach or Pamplonne. Once, on my way to Saint Tropez, I decided to visit Christopher, Old Marlburian and former pupil, who had told me he lived outside Cavalière. Having been given directions I soon found myself in Cavalière and fighting my way through a camping site of impressive proportions with caravans, camping-cars and tents galore, getting lost in the chaos of it all and on the point of turning back mission unaccomplished. Who would ever want to live amidst all this, I thought to myself. But then suddenly gates appeared before me and within no time I'd left the seething world of campers for the peace and quiet of a drive which gently wound up into the hills above Saint Tropez. There were heavily scented pines and lush vegetation on either side with only the buzzing of the cicadas in the heat of a hot summer to break the silence.

At the end of the drive I came to two separate manors, Domaine du Paradou and Domaine de la Sauvagère, secluded Provence-style houses set in a large country estate of some twenty-five acres. The estate had been bought and the houses built in the 1900s by Christopher's grandfather, Sir Antonin Besse, a successful businessman with interests in Aden and the Middle East and founder of St. Anthony's College, Oxford. There it still stood, untouched and undiscovered, effortlessly recalling a bygone age when the Riviera was becoming the chic holiday destination of the cognoscenti: Coco Chanel had a home here, as did Pablo Picasso and Somerset Maugham. Sir Winston and Clementine Churchill visited regularly, Clementine having been a close friend of Christopher's grandmother. I was regaled with stories of Resistance activities here during World War II and eventually left imbued with a sense of the history of this special place, marvelling at the fact that it should have remained intact and unspoiled within the same family for so long while so much all around had been developed and despoiled. Not for the first time did it strike me that Marlburians seemed to possess the enviable knack of arranging to have the finest of nests to return to.

Such holiday flirtations with Provence lasted well into my Marlborough years. Only with my appointment as i/c Toulouse French Exchange in 1977 did my attention and affections turn to South West France – *le grand sud-ouest* – and Gascony. Goodbye Provence – with thanks. Hello Gascony – with hopes.

Having taken early retirement from Marlborough, crossing the Channel this time was very different. I was no longer merely going on holiday, but was to take up permanent residence in what had till now been only a holiday home, but was now to become not only my *résidence principale* but the village restaurant, which was to provide a living for me as well as a welcome addition, I hoped, to the life of the village. Not that the prospect was as alarming as it might have been. After all I'd got to know Toulouse well during numerous Marlborough College exchange visits, so too 'my' village, Le Castéra, after a two-year sabbatical spent there. But still I was anxious and wondering whether I would not come to regret my bold mid-life change of direction. The only question – how well in the long term would I manage to integrate within this rural Gascon community, with simple country folk of similar backgrounds so different from mine? Would I cope?

Driving southwards through the Dordogne, my thoughts dwelling on such matters, I was reminded of a fine Englishman whom I knew and whose ability to integrate fully into a French rural community had greatly impressed me. Hal Milner-Gulland had bought his French property near Montignac in the early 1960s. One of the first of a long line of Brits to 'adopt' the Dordogne, he was a pioneer indeed. The two 'ruins' on the property – 26 hectares – he resurrected with the greatest of attention to the local building practices, beautifully restoring the roofs using the old traditional Dordogne stone roof slates.

Several years back I'd once stayed overnight. I had arrived mid-afternoon and had tracked Hal down to the local restaurant, where he was entertaining the village to lunch. Thirty or so happy *paysans* sat at a long table under the trees with Hal, sporting a *béret basque* amongst them relishing the excited exchange of banter and local gossip. Behind him the wild boar snorting and snuffling around in their pens, possibly wondering when it was to be their turn to be served up as the *civet de sanglier* the like of which the assembled company had just demolished with evident relish. Hal's rapport with his neighbours was clearly a close one, and so was that of his wife, Nan – no doubt about that. Of the two she was the great communicator – outgoing, fun-loving and at one with all and sundry. Hal, on the other hand, as I discovered later in the evening, professed an interest in the region which went somewhat deeper. He'd unearthed a local, almost forgotten 19th century novelist, Eugène Le Roy, whose novel, *Jacquou Le Croquant*, he was busily translating. His scholarly work was later recognised and, at a *vin d'honneur* given in the Montignac town hall in his honour, he was awarded the medal of the Eugène Le Roy Society.

A casual glance through the visitor's book the following morning showed that I was but one of many to have received kind hospitality in that charming little Valojoulx farmhouse. I found the names of countless 12-year-old scholars from Cumnor House Preparatory School invited out by Hal, their scholarly and inspiring headmaster, to immerse themselves in the history, indeed pre-history, of a region with so much to offer. Notably there were visits to the nearby Lascaux caves to view and study the animal cave drawings of the Upper Palaeolithic period, which would have done much to light up the imaginations in those young, fertile minds – hardly surprising that they were going on to gain the scholarships at the major public schools. Indeed, turning the pages, the name of the Headmaster of one such school (Marlborough College, none less) appeared too in the book – John Dancy, Hal's friend and fellow classicist, who doubtless, like me, had allowed himself to be lulled by the aura of simplicity and scholarship permeating the walls of this lovely home.

The Latin inscription engraved into the lintel above the open fireplace left no doubt that here was Hal's own little paradise.

Ille terrarum mihi praeter omnes angulus ridet. (Horace): "This nook of the world has charms for me beyond all else." Or "*Ce coin de terre me sourit plus que tous les autres.*"

Would I, like Hal, manage to create a Gascon home for myself which I, too, would want to proclaim as my very own little paradise? I could only hope so. Time alone will tell, I told myself, as I drove up the last hill and into the village of Le Castéra to begin a new chapter in life – a life beyond Marlborough College.

View of Le Castéra with the Pyrenées.

Rue de l'Eglise with Le Manoir on the left and Le Bacchus, café-bar, on the right.

Le Bacchus with entertainment from Joseph, the village accordéoniste.

Life inside the bar with 'la jeunesse dorée castéroise.'

Jeannot ('Colombo'), le patron. Not always easy to handle.

Drinks in the village hall – or 'getting to know the village'.

One of the many convivial meals held in the village square.

Supporting the village pétanque team.

Further gentle exercise on Hippy.

Making sure I'm warm in the winter. 'Celui qui coupe son bois se chauffe deux fois.'

Chai John. The stable block to be transformed into a restaurant.

Aimé Arucat ('Totosh'), the local builder's labourer.
A packet of Gauloises always at hand.

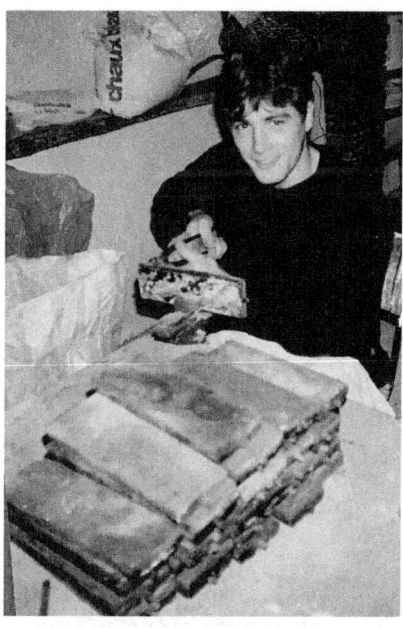

Another shot of Totosh, who cost me as much in beer as in labouring costs.

Thierry prising staples out of mahogany parquet flooring blocks.

Learning the trade.

André Escande – master electrician and plumber.

André shedding the light and spreading the good news.

Sanding the mahogany parquet flooring – pride and joy of Chai John.

André, prouder of his fireplace than his electricity and plumbing.

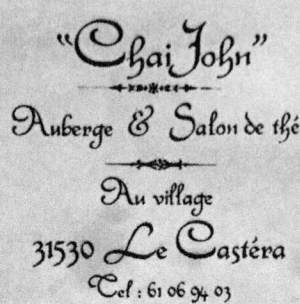

"Chai John"

Auberge & Salon de thé

Au village
31530 Le Castéra
Tel : 61 06 94 03

Dans un beau village ◦ cadre rustique ◦ vue panoramique ◦ terrasse ombragée ◦ ambiance chaleureuse ◦ musique ◦ cuisine soignée ◦ menu à partir de 95 f ◦ ouvert du vendredi soir au dimanche soir ◦

English spoken, of course !

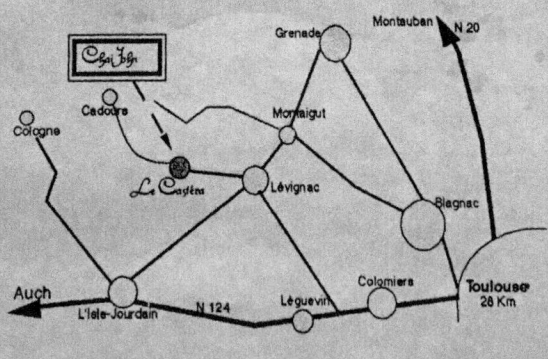

The first Chai John flier – Roll up! Roll up!

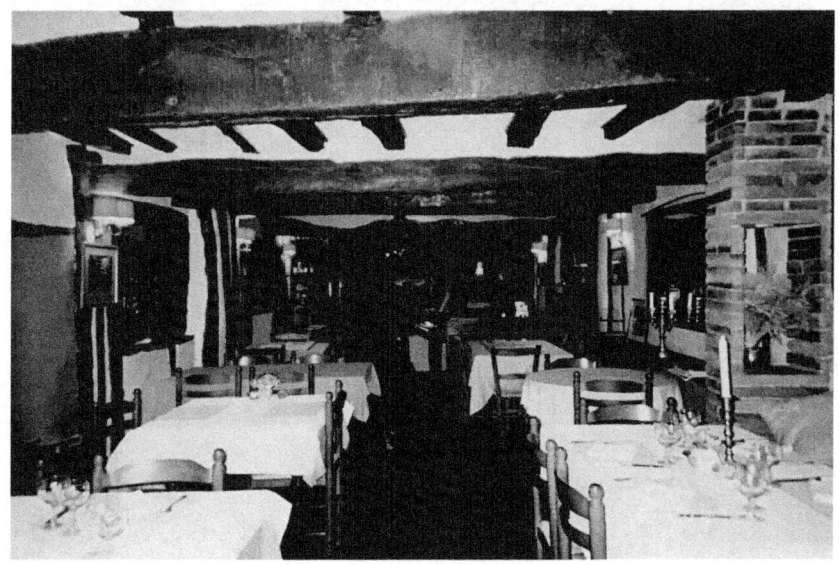

Chai John – open for business in October 1993.

Dining room – seating for 55.

André's fireplace in operation.

Le patron, Marie-Thérèse and Fred Burdick (private pilot to the Sultan of Brunei).

Soirée musicale – a swing group this time.

A summer supper on Le Manoir terrace.

Le Manoir terrace with 'parc' beyond.

An O.C. (Old Cranleighan) getting to grips with the washing up.

An O.E. (Old Etonian) preferring to operate from behind the bar.

An O.M. (Old Marlburian) and angle-grinder preferring to work outside in the fresh air.

The 'Bradder's Steps – the result of much angle-grinding.

Le Manoir south face before renovation.

A renovated south face.

Le parc du Manoir.

Chefchaouen, nestling in the Rif Mountains, northern Morocco.

Chapter 21

"Achète-la!"

My leaving England for France in 1992, aged fifty and already a retired schoolmaster after a mere twenty-five years in harness, might to many have seemed more of a leap in the dark than it actually was. Certainly friends were solicitous and father made muttering noises ("Will you have enough to live on?"), but I continued to remain unconcerned with the practicalities. Making the move was the all-important decision to have made – of that I was never in doubt. The rest would somehow follow. And after all, had not good work during my two-year Marlborough sabbatical seen a once tumbledown wreck of a house now already well over halfway towards full restoration? The upstairs living accommodation was more or less ready for me to move into immediately, both water and electricity having been connected to the mains in my absence. Further work there was indeed yet to be done – the creation of a separate dining-room and opening up of a terrace with views over the valleys below, the Pyrenees looming up impressively all along the distant horizon – but at least I already had sufficient space for myself and furniture from which to operate comfortably while I worked towards the completion of the renovation.

From the start my attention focused primarily on the ground floor

– a surface area of no less than 130 square metres, stretching the full length of the house from front to back. What on earth to do with it? It had formerly been stabling and home to a variety of domestic animals – a pair of oxen (the rack still ran along the wall), pigs (two sties still standing), rabbits and poultry (hutches and coops dotted around everywhere). What indeed to do with a thirty-metre-deep well (beautifully brick-lined, bucket and pulley still operational), a brick-built bread oven, a huge oak wine vat (standing two metres high with a capacity for hundreds of litres) and four or five two-metre-deep brick-lined silos set here and there in the ground for the safe storage of grain? (Safe, I was told, because these silos would then be hidden from view by straw spread throughout the stable and consequently their contents not declared for taxation – crafty indeed they were, those *paysans* of days gone by.) These questions troubled me not because I didn't have the answers – I did – but because I hadn't yet tested them on other people to get their opinions, and the person whose opinion I now most needed was a certain M. André Escande. André (a Ronnie Corbett look-alike), who had already much helped me with the house when on sabbatical, was not merely a talented plumber/electrician but now also a friend. A man of imagination too – he writes poetry – and one whose counsels I had come to respect. It was his support I most needed for my untested idea. So it was when I faced him with the direct question: "André, what about converting the stabling downstairs into a little restaurant? *Une bonne idée? Qu'est-ce que tu penses?"*

I awaited his answer with bated breath. He looked me full in the face, his little blue eyes twinkling behind his heavy glasses, and in tones brimming with enthusiasm, he replied *"Ah, oui, mais oui! Quelle bonne idée!"* With that he was gone for the week to work out his ideas and costing for the project, leaving me – together with Aimé Arucat (alias 'Totosh' to all and sundry), the local self-employed builder's labourer – to consider the prospect of consolidating 110 square metres of crumbling cob walls. The original 17th century walls were made from compressed earth and clay reinforced with wooden laths and straw, also known as daub and wattle. These over the following months I was to come to know intimately. I passed over every square centimetre of them six times in all – firstly to replace and consolidate crumbling daub *(torchis),* then to cover all in wire netting, then to apply a coat of cement to bind all together, followed by a coat of lime to smoothen the surface on which finally to apply two coats of paint. *Ouf!* Weeks of solid, hard work, rewarding yet demanding.

The following week saw André back brimming over with his plans and proposals, all of which I liked, not least because they cleverly incorporated the various historic features –bread oven, well and the like. One problem – finding sufficient space for the kitchens was going to reduce the dining area drastically. Too much. We needed more space. But where? André, undaunted as ever, had the answer.

"Well, what about the house next door – *Le Manoir?*"

"What about it?"

"It's uninhabited."

"*Et alors?*"

"Well – buy it! *Achète-la!*"

It took some while to recover from this bolt from the blue. Buy it? What? With what? From whom? The first question was clearly a matter for the bank manager, the second, I reckoned, for M. Jean Jacquemin, incumbent of *Le Bacchus,* the village café-bar across the square not twenty yards from my front door which was the ultimate source of wisdom relating to almost every matter concerning village life.

First things first – to find out from him more about *Le Manoir* next door, the most impressive big house (*maison de maître*) in the village – the Château apart – with its twenty-five-metre frontage standing opposite *Le Bacchus* and with an arcaded sunny southern side looking out over an attractive small *parc* (vines, a fig tree and two fine Lebanese cedars) and the rolling hills and valleys beyond. A fine property indeed, I thought to myself, peering over the walls of *le parc,* but all I want is a kitchen. What on earth to do with the rest of the vast space available? A question for another day, I decided, crossing the square bound for the café not only for the daily well-earned after-work *apéritif* or two but this time also on a *Manoir* fact-finding mission.

From the very start I'd been a regular visitor to *Le Bacchus* – it was both a handy watering-hole and a good place to launch my Integration-Of-The-English-Into-The-Life-Of-A-Gascon-Village programme – a pet project which I soon realised wasn't after all going to be the walk-over I'd initially imagined. Was I not the first Englishman ever to have bought a property in Le Castéra? Was I therefore not in some minds a creature from another planet, someone to be distrusted? And what about *Le Perfide Albion*? And Jeanne d'Arc? And Napoleon? And Churchill's ordering the British bombing of the French fleet at Mers-El-Kébir in 1940? The list of historical grievances was a long one and some of my neighbours – the older ones generally – were determined to make a meal of it. And not only was I heavily engaged defending the British take on historical but also on contemporary events. Mme. Thatcher – *la dame de fer* – had only to open her mouth and I was immediately held responsible. The French seemed spellbound by the British Prime Minister and even their President had succumbed. He'd seen a certain ambiguity in her character. "*Elle a la bouche de Marilyn, le regard de Caligula,*" remarked François Mitterrand.

So I knew to be careful, initially at any rate, about what I said in the café. My words were being weighed and measured, often twisted and misinterpreted. The friendly remarks I would make were taken as hypocritical. What did *L'Anglais* – my adopted name – *really* think of France and the French? Was he not merely disguising his typically English, arrogant and superior disregard for all things and people 'foreign'? I was learning fast that French feeling ran deep when it came to arguing the toss over matters French and English – not exactly surprising when the two countries had been jockeying for hegemony in some form or another for over a thousand years.

My *Manoir* question, therefore, was delivered as casually as I could so as not to raise suspicions.

"*Excusez-moi, Jean-Claude*" (Jean-Claude – alias *Le Gros Bouchon*, goodness knows why – a beefy, burly, beer-swilling garlic farmer)"But do you happen to know who owns *Le Manoir*?"

"*Pourquoi?* I suppose you want to buy it."

I saw at once my bluff had been called and was immediately

subjected to a twenty-minute lecture on the ten reasons why there was no possible chance of my ever buying the property. First and foremost Mme. Lachaze, the owner, was a cantankerous old witch who had quarrelled with the village but had no intention of selling. Secondly she had already led countless prospective buyers – Airbus pilots included – up the garden path only to ditch them at the last moment. Thirdly, she detested the English (so he said) – and so on.

Somewhat dejected, I crossed back over the square and told André the bad news. He at once put my mind at rest, saying that firstly I shouldn't be listening to loose bar talk from a semi-sozzled garlic farmer and secondly I should go forthwith to *La Mairie* and the mayor to get an address and telephone number for the redoubtable Mme. Lachaze. This done, the following Monday saw me downing trowel and mortarboard, putting on a clean set of clothes and driving down to Toulouse for the rendezvous I'd without difficulty secured. Mme. Lachaze's town house stood in the old quarter of Toulouse, tucked away peacefully behind the cathedral. It was large but somewhat in need of tender loving care. The family had perhaps fallen on hard times.

Mme. Lachaze, cantankerous though she might have been, nevertheless received me with civility while remaining evasive over matters concerning the sale of her house in Le Castéra. She would have to discuss the matter with her daughter and family. I left, but not without discovering that in fact she had nothing against the English and was clearly very much in favour of the Scots – the Auld Alliance, an alliance made in 1295 between the kingdoms of France and Scotland and seemingly by some still not forgotten. Good.

I left after securing a second rendezvous. It was André's idea that for this I should arrive bearing gifts of the finest Scottish shortbread and malt whisky. Whether this was the determining factor in Mme. Lachaze's eventual willingness to sell or not we shall never know. Suffice it to say that the bank manager was placated, the sale was completed within two months, *Le Gros Bouchon* was left with egg on his face and work on the kitchens could proceed.

André immediately proceeded to break through to *Le Manoir* to create the kitchens, and Totosh and I continued to work on the walls.

Hard work, but with time off for relaxation. Totosh indeed needed time off to roll his Gauloises cigarettes – he was a chain-smoker – a *mégot* permanently drooping from his lips. He needed time off also to hydrate, especially when temperatures rose, hence frequent visits across the square to the café in search of Pastis, Ricard, 51 or whatever. An *apéritif* break for a Pastis became more often than not a lengthy Pastis session, thus doubling my costs for his labour.

Not that I didn't visit the bar/café out of working hours and without Totosh. I did, and frequently. M. Jean Jacquemin – Jeannot or Colombo to his friends – had had his aged father create a *salle de restauration* on the first floor above the bar and it is there that they would serve the *menu du jour/repas ouvrier* at midday during the week. And what a feast that was! For a modest sum – 45 francs – one would be confronted by a table groaning with *les entrées* self-service – *soupes, salades, charcuteries, pâtés* – to be followed by a choice of main course – *steacks, magrets de canard, volailles, poissons* – and rounded off with a second table, also groaning, with cheeses and desserts, also self-service – *fromages, gâteaux, tartes, salades de fruits*. And all that accompanied with as much table wine as you wanted – *du vin à volonté*. It was truly gargantuan in scale. There I would be rubbing shoulders with men working on the roads (*La* SCREG), men working for the EDF (*Electricité de France*), builders, plumbers, electricians working round and about (no women present) – all of them in the best of humour tucking into the monumental good thing of a full two-hour lunch break and before somehow attempting to get back to an afternoon's work. Inevitably for me it was often too much of a good thing and I would more often than not wobble back home across the square not to work and to the cement-mixer but to feet up in the armchair for sometimes many more than forty winks.

If I wasn't over-eating at *Le Bacchus* at midday – I managed to resist the temptation most days – then I would surely clock in there in the evening after work. Here was a very different scene. *La jeunesse dorée* (if it can be termed as such) of Le Castéra would then congregate for the *apéritif du soir* – a moveable feast some-times stretching into the early hours of the morning involving the swilling of countless rounds of bitter beer (*vin blanc* for me) and accompanied by excitable adolescent chatter and banter. Initially at any rate I remained somewhat the 'outsider' – *L'Anglais du Castéra*, the first to have invaded this tightly-knit village community and a bit of a mystery. But gradually I found myself being swept into the general flow of the conversation – with its constant leg-pulling and boisterous bombast of half-baked adolescent Gascon opinion ("*Hé! L'Anglais! La Thatcher, c'est une conasse, une mal baisée!* (best left untranslated) *Les Anglais c'est tous des pédés!* The vulgarity of the opinions expressed was rivalled only by the coarseness of the language used. If I was to participate effectively I was clearly going to have to adopt a similar linguistic register myself. My command of the vernacular and vulgar colloquialisms thus increased exponentially, so too my knowledge of the vocabulary of insults – *les gros mots*. ("*Abruti! Andouille! Arsouille! Bourrique! Branleur! Vieux con! Pauvre con! Crétin! Crotte! Débile! Dégonflé! Enculé! Enfoiré!* – and so on through the alphabet. A vocabulary scraping the very bottom of the linguistic barrel.) Added to which and caught up in the heat of the moment and argument I would slip effortlessly into the local accent – the Toulouse twang – thus adding to the impression that I, *L'Anglais* from another planet, was fast beginning to act and sound like the local Castérois lad (the imitation game).

Thus was I gradually assimilated into *Le Club des Jeunes du Castéra*, partly due to the fact, I presumed, that I'd showed and proved myself willing and able to adapt my game to theirs, partly too, I soon realised, as a potential source of a free round of drinks – or two – from time to time. To this end young Freddo, not unpleasing to the eye, was chosen to 'keep me happy'. A good choice, I had to admit, and his chat-up technique certainly improved over the weeks and months, ensuring more often than not that yet another round – or two – of drinks was safely secured through his good offices.

Entering this little world meant entering the world of local jargon and the nicknames dished out to all and sundry. If I was 'L'Anglais', I was rubbing shoulders with the likes of Toto, Goupil, Petit Clou, Titi, Gros Bouchon (the garlic farmer), Petit Bouchon (his younger brother), Balou, Criquet, Le Colonel, Menou, to mention but a few of the names, the origins of which remain a mystery to me to this day. M. Jean Jacquemin, *le patron du Bacchus,* also had a nickname – Colombo, taken from the TV series of that name. Jacquemin had simply bought and was wearing the exact replica of the iconic mackintosh as worn by Colombo, the Los Angeles homicide detective. Colombo, himself a confirmed bachelor, was equally well integrated into the lives of his young clientèle, entering fully into the cut and thrust of debate. Any idea that a *patron* should perhaps keep his distance and maintain a certain level of discretion vis à vis his clients was here thrown straight out of the window. Colombo was forever at the heart of the debate, a big, solid man raising the volume of his big, booming voice to well beyond the level of all others, laying down the law, passing judgement on all the world and its wife for us all to hear. Highly indiscreet talk, I thought to myself, thinking the consequences might well one day come back to bite him.

My frequent visits to *Le Bacchus* across the square did in fact fulfil a purpose. They gave welcome relief from the cement-mixer, paint brush and manual work generally, while at the same time they got me a foot in the door vis à vis the life of the locals. In this later respect and in the early days the village had anyway precious little else to offer me. It was hardly as if my neighbours were going to shower me with invitations to meals – just as well, since I was not yet in a position to repay such hospitality.

Apart from the bar, my other brief *sorties* in the village were restricted to the *épicerie* next door to the bar, also run by Colombo and his aged parents – useful if one had forgotten to buy the salt or other such basic requirement, to the antique shop *(brocante)* at the bottom of the street where I rummaged around for likely items with which to decorate the restaurant, and to the church next door where the mass was said once a month – a small congregation which swelled tenfold when the church bell tolled the knell sending the entire population to its knees in the pews (women on the one side of the church, the men on the other) to mourn the passing of family or friend. Deaths outnumbered weddings and christenings and the population, as in the rural communities throughout France, was diminishing (*L'exode rurale*). It meant that people, the young especially, were drifting to the towns where the work was to be found. In fact I was surprised Le Castéra still had its little primary school – two classes, CM 1, CM 2 – but for how long?

"*Ah, oui*", said M. Auriol, the mayor, one day when passing by. "How different things here were before the war. Maybe we were some of the last to have electricity, water not until 1972, but at least we had a baker and a butcher in the village. A blacksmith too, and *le père* Bégué, who owned the bar and was also a horse dealer (*maquignan*) and would also sit people down on a barrel and cut their hair...*eh, oui, c'était comme ça...* and we had Auguste Saintes too, he and Mimi lived in your house, *eh, oui, Monsieur* John, he was the village carpenter. (Ah! I thought to myself, so that's why there are so many lovely oak planks lying around just waiting to be made into bookshelves.) Auguste also, like others, had a few *hectares* to cultivate with his pair of oxen. "*Oui, Monsieur* John, *mais à l'époque tout le monde ici travaillait avec les boeufs. Les Américains, eux, ils avaient leurs tracteurs – nous, non!*"

Chatting up the local youth in the bar was one thing and it was at times amusing, but listening to the likes of old M. Auriol, the mayor, musing on the war years and after was perhaps more instructive. Did I realise that the local farmers would once a week load up their carts with produce, harness the horses and set off on the twenty-five mile trip to the Toulouse markets, leaving Le Castéra at four o'clock in the morning? Men of grit and determination, I thought to myself. Other such stories from the post-war years came from Charlotte, Austrian and mother of Jean-Claude Ransan (*Gros Bouchon*), the garlic farmer, Betty and Bernard (*Petit Bouchon*). *Le Père* Ransan, stationed in Austria with the French army after the war had scooped up Charlotte there, married her and afterwards returned with her as his wife to Le Castéra. Once installed there, like me forty-five years later, she found herself very much the 'outsider'. Known by most as The Austrian (*L'Autricienne*) but by the more unkindly members of the community as *L'autre chienne* (the other bitch), she well knew what it was like to be ostracized. Post-war anti-German/Austrian feeling ran high in Le Castéra as doubtless in a thousand other similar villages in France. (Others later to pick up equally vulgar nicknames were Manfred and Edith Kühl, a German couple living in Le Castéra and working with Airbus in Toulouse. Manfred became Jean Kühl (*J'encule* = I sodomize/bugger) and Edith became Testy Kühl (*testicule* = testicle.) Other such stories of Le Castéra's past I wheedled out of Mme. Martres and Mme. Carbonnel, both of who had been bright-eyed local young girls during the war and were only able to marry when those unsettling years had become a thing of the past. Mme. Carbonnel *née* Bégué and daughter of François Bégué, owner of the Café-Bar, married the young M. Carbonnel on his return from post-war service in Germany.

Mme. Lachaze and *Le Manoir* too, I discovered, harboured a Le Castéra war story. I found a small bedroom in *Le Manoir* in which a frieze had been hand-painted around the top of the four walls. Underneath and in a corner had been written 'Painted by George Soulé.' On questioning Mme. Carbonnel I was eventually able to find out who George Soulé was. He was a nephew of Mme. Lachaze who had spent his youth in pre-war Le Castéra, attending the village school with the other local children of his generation. Having left school and towards the end of the war, at a time when German troops were occupying south-west France, he suddenly disappeared from Le Castéra, only to be spotted by chance in Toulouse one day by one of his former classmates. Here was a 'gentrified' Georges dressed in a fine set of new clothes, driving a fast new car with a pretty brunette at his side. Further enquiries soon revealed the shocking truth – namely that he was working for the *Milice*, that much-hated political paramilitary organisation created by the wartime Vichy régime to help fight against the French Resistance. It participated in summary executions and assassinations, helping to round up Jews and *résistants* in France for deportation using torture to extract information from those interrogated. The French Resistance considered the *Milice* more dangerous than the Gestapo and SS because they were native Frenchmen – the likes of Georges Soulé – who understood local dialects fluently, had extensive knowledge of the towns and countryside, and knew the local people and informants.

Come the end of the war and with the time of the settling of scores (*règlements de comptes*) the fate of the *Miliciens* was sealed. Either they fled (mostly to Germany), they were imprisoned for treason, they were executed following courts-martial or they were murdered by vengeful *résistants* and civilians. The latter was the fate of Georges Soulé when his former classmates from Le Castéra banded together, went down into Toulouse one day, found him on the canal and promptly shot him through the head. Such killings were taking place throughout France in their thousands with thousands of villages tracking down their Georges Soulés, creating divisions within their communities which had still not healed fifty years after the devastating events of the Occupation. Small wonder that Mme. Lachaze hated Le Castéra and its inhabitants, small wonder Le Castéra and its inhabitants hated Mme. Lachaze and her family.

The more I scratched the surface, the more I was discovering divisions within my small community, many of them dating from those harrowing days of the Occupation – a time for each family to decide whether to resist or whether to collaborate. Georges Soulé chose to collaborate. (His rewards? A fat pay packet and eventually a bullet to the head). So too did the French girl who chose to sleep with the German officer. (Her rewards? Fine dining and wining and eventually the shame of being stripped, tarred and feathered by vengeful friends and family alike.) But the French farmer's wife selling six eggs to the German soldier, she too was 'collaborating'. Her rewards? A few francs for her six eggs and eventually a sullied family reputation for evermore. So was Le Castéra, a village like many another, torn asunder by indelible memories of its occupation.

How will I, an Englishman, ever really understand the French wartime experiences when we, the English, have not had to suffer the boots of the likes of a Napoleon or a Hitler for over a thousand years? Yet perhaps I *do* begin to understand, to sympathize. And perhaps that's why I'm feeling I'm beginning to like France and the French more and more. They've had an awful lot to put up with over the last century – thrice defeated, thrice invaded – any village war memorial will bear witness to the enormity of the sacrifice and price paid.

Meantime work on the restaurant was going well. André, alias Ronnie Corbett, was placing plugs and pulling wires everywhere (I had seriously underestimated the cost of the electrics), and Totosh was continuing to smoke like a chimney *(fumer comme un pompier)* and drink like a fish *(boire comme un trou)*. The walls were at last finished and the ceiling could be started (with polystyrene wedged between the oak beams).

Life off-site in Le Castéra, too, was continuing to keep me occupied. Chatting up both the local *jeunesse* – how different from young Marlburians in their attitudes and values! – as well as the oldies for their memories of the past gave me much food for thought. However, I could also look outside the village for further recreational purposes. Jean-Paul and Thérèse Thomas, the friends I'd made when on exchange in Toulouse with my class of Marlburians, were as welcoming as ever and a five-minute drive would often over a weekend see me in Saint Paul sur Save at their *centre équestre* where Hippy – 'my' horse – would be awaiting me. A country trackway leading back up to Le Castéra was ideal for an exhilarating twenty-minute canter/gallop. Arriving in the village after one such ride M. Lorenzo, farmer and the largest land-owner in the village, kindly offered to tether the horses while we went for a drink at Le Bacchus. On returning we found them contentedly drinking from the pails of water he had kindly set beside them. Such was my first meeting with Christian and Marie-France Lorenzo. What nice friends they would make, I thought to myself riding back down the hill.

Other friends I'd made during my two-year sabbatical I also continued to see. These were the 'upmarket' ones, sophisticated people and necessary antidotes to the village youth. Jean and Michèle de Castelbajac, M. le Vicomte and Mme. la Vicomtesse, when not in Paris were on their country estate at the Château de Caumont where the Marlborough College chapel choir had performed on the Gascony Tour of 1987. They were fondly remembered both for having sung beautifully and for then having drunk the wine cellars dry to celebrate the event appropriately. Jean and Michèle continued to issue me with their kind invitations – swimming in their pool in the heat of summer afternoons, dining at their table at formal dinner parties where I was clearly *le représentant anglais* and expected to sing for my supper. Not difficult in these circles once one had understood that the French aristocrat is a confirmed anglophile and a fervent admirer of the House of Windsor, and his/her great delight it is to listen to tales of the English Royal Family. These I was able to provide in quantity, with embellishments if required.

While propagating all things English on these august occasions I had to be careful to abide by the etiquette required and practised. For example *le baisemain*, the kissing of the hand, is *de rigueur* in such circles. And certainly not any old slobbering kiss. One's lips should touch as lightly as possible (*effleurer*) the proffered hand. Be careful, too, with your use of *vous* and *tu* – in other words, never use the familiar *tu* form in such company. Hide your carefully cultivated twangy Gascon accent. Remember the exalted language of Corneille, Molière and Racine. Pretend to be *le Milord anglais* and all will be well.

If these plucky remnants of the *Ancien Régime* managed somehow to keep up both their appearances and their châteaux it doesn't mean the bank accounts are bulging. Often the châteaux are crumbling and shabby chic is the order of the day. They remind me of those I'd visited of the remaining protestant Irish ascendancy, another example of a social phenomenon living on borrowed time. But family ties remain strong and ennobled families continue to cling together for mutual support. Even the young generation is keen to uphold the family name. Parties (*les rallyes*) are organised for them during the season by their doting parents, ever anxious that their progeny should mix with the right people and in the right fashionable circles. A Marquise who succeeds in marrying her daughter to the son of a Vicomte will indeed be well pleased. One might as well be turning the pages of a Balzac novel, to all intents and purposes.

Living close by to the de Castelbajacs are my other aristocratic friends, Yves and Kiki de Chiris, M. le Comte et Mme. la Comtesse, whose acquaintance I had also made during the Marlborough College chapel choir Gascon tour. They had attended the final concert and farewell party in Le Castéra, arriving with basket loads of bread, pâtés, cheeses and wines. They too continued to shower me with generous hospitality, due doubtless in part to the fact that Yves, having been to school at Stowe and being bilingual, liked nothing better than a good after-dinner conversation in English and about the English. This I was more than happy to provide, encouraged and assisted by liberal quantities of the finest Armagnacs *hors d'âge*.

Inevitably there soon came the time for the repayment of hospitality and with my house now more or less up and going I timidly was able to start inviting friends to drinks and meals. To one such *apéritif* I had invited both Jean and Michèle de Castelbajac and Yves and Kiki de Chiris. Safe, I naively thought, knowing that they already knew each other. What I failed to appreciate was the social divide that set these two families at loggerheads, the de Castelbajac title having been granted during the *ancien régime* under the Bourbons, whereas the de Chiris title came only later during the Napoleonic era, an era despised by the *ancien régime* nobility, who considered Napoleon no more than a foreign usurper to the French throne. This clearly accounted for the frostiness I detected between the Vicomtesse and the Comtesse. I was later told of a conversation between the two which had been overheard:

La Vicomtesse: "Tell me, my dear, is your husband working? What does he do?"

La Comtesse: "You know very well, my dear. He's working in the perfume industry."

La Vicomtesse: "Really? I had no idea – he might as well have been selling umbrellas for all I know."

A bit rich coming from the Vicomtesse, herself having been an air hostess before marrying Jean de Castelbajac. Yves de Chiris was indeed working in the perfume industry, his ancestor Antoine Chiris having opened one of the first *parfumeries* in Grasse in 1768. Generations of the Chiris family followed generation. Léon had the honour of receiving Queen Victoria at the factory and later at dinner in 1891 when she was on one of her Côte d'Azur tours. The British Royal Family's love of France and things French continued under Edward VII, who as Prince of Wales clearly found more to amuse him in Paris than he did in London. Later as king he did much to encourage the signing of the *Entente Cordiale* in 1904, and since then the loyal little band of French monarchists has more or less adopted the Windsors as their own royal family. Not that they have forgotten the Bourbons. In most French towns of any size there will be a church which will on 21ˢᵗ of January solemnly celebrate a requiem mass for the repose of the soul of Louis XVI, declared a 'royal martyr' by the Catholic Church shortly after his death by the guillotine.

Back on site, all was continuing to go well. André had sufficiently advanced in his electricity and plumbing for us to be able to order the tanker-lorry with the concrete to finally pour the screed on which to lay the mahogany parquet blocks – my pride and joy. These blocks I had found stacked in plastic sacks behind Marlborough College's Barton Farm. They had been dumped there open to the elements after being ripped out of several classrooms ear-marked for 'modernization', and upon closer examination they turned out to be interlocking and of high-quality mahogany from India having first been laid at Marlborough in the 1840s. I was round to see the Estates Bursar like a dose of salts and there and then secured the purchase of the entirety for a modest sum (£100). I was later told by one who knew that I'd had a very real bargain.

It was only on laying them now that I realised how lucky I'd been. Easy to lay on heated tar – one only had to be sure to get the first row right and the rest followed – and wonderful to behold once the industrial sander had smoothed out any irregularities. The full beauty however was revealed only after wood stain had been applied and the mellow, rich and dark-honeyed colours first showed themselves. A final coat of vitrification sealed those colours in for all time and a gentle buffing up with the polisher completed the task.

"*Mon Dieu! Quelle beauté!*" said André, admiring the finished result. He told me what I already half suspected, that there was nothing like it in the region.

"*John, ça c'est plutôt pour les châteaux de la Loire, tu vois!*"

I was glad of course that André approved and that he was putting me up on a pedestal with the châteaux on the Loire – high praise indeed. Also that he reflected a general approval from those who popped in to check up on the latest developments. There were of course exceptions, not least among them Colombo of *Le Bacchus*, who was perhaps wondering about his clientèle. Would my opening affect him and his trade? Little did he realise that I was having similar thoughts. What about *my* clientèle? Where was that going to come from?

"Oh! I wouldn't worry about that," said Monsieur Auriol, the mayor, one day. "That'll sort itself out. It depends on what you're offering as to who comes along. At any rate with what you've got here you won't be attracting the same clientèle as Monsieur Jacquemin at *Le Bacchus*. Of that you can both be sure."

Further advances were being made. Kitchen appliances were being installed, so too electric radiators and a sound system which I hoped would provide the kind of music to help with inducing that feeling of well-being so important to any restaurant dining experience. This consideration also dictated the colours I chose to put on the walls – warm and cosy ones calculated to further comfort the senses, the visual ones this time. Never forget, I repeated to myself, that the primary sense to be satisfied is that of the palate. If the taste of what is in the plate in front of the client is not up to standard, nothing else will compensate.

With these somewhat sobering thoughts my attention was turning to cooks and menus. Where was I to find the perfect cook? What was to be on the menus? Even before starting I realised that there was inevitably bound to be a large element of trial and error here, given my total lack of experience in the matter. I was clearly going to need practical advice.

Consulting with friends wasn't always that helpful. Some thought I should go upmarket and aim high to attract the Toulouse gourmet gastronomes. Some thought I should keep it simple with an emphasis on regional dishes. Others thought I should be unashamedly English – fish and chips, the Sunday roast with trimmings, muffins, crumpets and scones for tea. Almost all were of the opinion that I should first find my '*créneau*' – that personal and individual 'niche' that would distinguish me from all the other restaurants of the region. The only place in South West France that serves a good haggis, for example, is at John's restaurant in Le Castéra. Not that I was ever thinking of haggis as my distinguishing signature dish. But a dish or a concept that stood out from all others, that is what would be required if I was going to make my mark. To decide either way would be difficult without first having secured the cook. This now was becoming a priority. So too the securing of a waiter or a waitress. Where was he or she to come from?

It was with these thoughts swirling around in my mind that I was now spending more time in Toulouse in the Chambre de Commerce and other such offices busying myself with securing the necessary licences and authorizations needed to open a restaurant. I also had to acquaint myself with the employment regulations, and arrange for the various inspections to be carried out on the premises to ensure that all was *'dans les normes'* – visits from the hygiene authorities, the fire brigade and the police, all accompanied by the mayor. Nothing like the French for red tape, as I was fast discovering.

By this stage the summer days were now arriving and my little team, André, Totosh and myself, had been at work for almost a year. The end was in sight. Totosh continued to smoke and drink himself into an early grave, not that that gave him the slightest concern. For ever jovial in demeanour, exuding *bonhomie* while whistling and humming his way through the day, he continued to amuse us, especially when on occasion he would burst into song, singing in the local *patois*, the regional Occitan dialect. He once told me that he had been traumatized at the tender age of five when he had been first packed off to walk the ten kilometres to the nearest village school. When he arrived he was totally lost – they were speaking French, not a word of which he understood. A word of *patois* from him at school would earn him a severe rap on the knuckles from the mistress. André also continued to amaze me with his inventiveness and skills. On his own initiative he had decided to build me a brick-faced fireplace which involved taking the chimney through my bedroom upstairs – nothing was too much trouble for him. So now I would have an open log fire in the restaurant, a bonus indeed. André even managed to come up with the name of the restaurant.

"'Chez John', André? That sounds a bit naff, doesn't it?" I said.

"*Non, John. Pas 'Chez John' mais 'Chai John'*" (same pronunciation) he replied, delighted with the play on words he'd conjured up. (*Chai* is the Gascon word for *cave* – the wine cellar where vats and bottles are kept.)

I, for my part, found the solution to the waiter/waitress problem. I wrote and sent off twenty or so letters to the foremost public schools in the UK addressed to the Modern Language Departments offering a job to gap-year students wanting to perfect their French helping in a hilltop Gascon village restaurant. I had no idea what the response would be. There now remained not much more than to secure the services of a cook, decide on an opening date and publicise the same.

My thoughts along these lines were brutally interrupted when one morning Fred suddenly burst in from Bellegarde, the next village.

"John, you need a holiday. It's two weeks in Thailand and it's a freebie. How about it?"

Fred Burdick, formerly of British Caledonian and Freddie Laker, was now working and flying for Airbus. Also, like me, he was restoring the wreck of an old farmhouse and we always had much to discuss about our projects, particularly on Thursdays when he would come to Le Castéra and meet with fellow pilots at *Le Bacchus* for lunch. A *bon viveur* and a great conversationalist, he would regale us all with his jokes and shaggy dog tales – they were endless.

His sense of fun was further demonstrated when one day he invited me to his daughter's birthday lunch, saying I was to be there at midday on the dot and not a minute later if I wanted to see the 'show'. Intrigued, I arrived a few minutes before time and was led into the garden. I had hardly raised a glass to my lips when a deep-throated rumbling could be heard coming from Toulouse. The noise rapidly gathered in volume and within the wag of a duck's tail an Airbus A320 was upon us, having narrowly missed the village church spire, so low was it flying. The sound was deafening as it skimmed over the garden only then to regain height, turn and fast disappear again in the direction of Toulouse from whence it had come.

When Fred was not wowing his daughter with highly illegal birthday party flyovers he was mostly to be found either in the simulator training pilots to fly or in Brunei where one of his jobs was to teach the Sultan to fly the two A320s he had just acquired. The Sultan was a good pupil but a demanding customer, insisting that one of the planes be returned to Hamburg to iron out problems with a cut-glass chandelier in the dining room which 'clinked' when the plane attained cruising speeds. Shoddy work indeed! Tut! tut!

Fred's offer to me of a two-week free holiday in Thailand co-incided with his completion of a Thai Airlines training course for the pilots and crew of the Airbus they were to fly from Toulouse to Bangkok on its delivery flight. Fred was to sit in the cockpit seeing that all went well at the controls. I was to occupy business class as the sole passenger on board, there so that the stewards and stewardesses could practise the serving of both the liquid – champagne – and the solid sustenance needed to see me through the fifteen-hour flight.

This was clearly an offer that was too good to refuse. My initial hesitations were convincingly countered.

"But, John, it's all up and ready to go. Look, the pictures and curtains are hung, the tablecloths are on the tables, the glasses and carafes behind the bar. What more do you need to do? Give yourself a break and open a bit later when people are back from holiday and school has started."

Good thinking. Decided. Let's get off to Thailand and forget all about restaurants and openings for a fortnight.

No sooner said than done. The flight fully lived up to expecta-tions, so too the reception at Bangkok Airport where Fred and I were treated to garlands and the red carpet in the presence of the Thai Minister of Transport. Then to be whisked off to Fred's base for the next two weeks – a plush hotel in central Bangkok. He was scheduled to be working with his pilots during the day, and I was free to organise my own time as I best saw fit. With Fred having introduced me to the dubious delights of the Patpong Road on the first evening, I decided next day I'd spend my two weeks travelling outside Bangkok, first heading south by coach to Pattaya and the coast, then north by rail to Chiang Mai and the hill tribes on the Burmese border. The contrast between Pattaya and Chiang Mai could hardly have been greater. The former basked in its reputation as Thailand's answer to Sodom and Gomorrah – a reputation it certainly seemed to be living up to – while the latter was rich in culture with its 300 Buddhist temples, the oldest dating from the 13th Century.

Having made the most of what these two fascinating destinations had to offer, I was preparing to return to Bangkok by train when Fred rang.

"Where are you? Chiang Mai? Good. Get yourself to the airport and we'll come up and collect you."

The one and only time in my life I've been collected by a chauffeur-driven aircraft. VIP treatment to be sure.

My return to Le Castéra was as sudden as had been my departure. The Thai leap into the unknown was now abruptly followed by a return to reality with a bump, though the bump was somewhat cushioned by the good response to my circular offering jobs to *serveurs/serveuses*, with applicants from Etonians, Wykehamists, Harrovians and Marlburians amongst others. I decided to take the Etonian as my first appointee – probably for all the wrong reasons – with others following on through the year.

André too had good news. He had found me Thierry, a young cook, who was looking for weekend work and ready to start at once. He seemed pleasant enough, although having discussed menus with him I had a feeling it would be unwise to ask too much of him. We would stick to traditional menus, initially at any rate. It was decided that the last weekend in November was to see us open, up and going, leaving me a full six weeks of nail-biting and worrying about what I could have possibly forgotten to do in preparation for the big day. Why, indeed, had I ever conceived of the whole project when I had not even the slightest scrap of experience in the matter? The answer to this was clear – I had simply wanted to disprove George Bernard Shaw's dictum "He who can, does. He who can't, teaches." At the same time I wanted to prove to myself that I was perfectly capable of doing something other than teaching. Now I was not so sure.

Last minute doubts were momentarily dispelled when an article appeared in the local press publicising the imminent opening of *Chai*

John. The headline ran '*Chai John – un Charme Exquis*'. The doubts reasserted themselves on the unexpected arrival one afternoon of Xavier, friend and owner/chef of the highly successful restaurant *Au Canard Gourmand* in Samatan. He had known of my project from the beginning and had done his best to dissuade me.

"Try a wine bar, John, it would be far simpler. Far less red tape, paperwork and regulations," he had advised. Here he was now seeing I'd ignored his advice and set up a full-blown restaurant.

"Ah well – good luck, John," he said with a smile. "I hope at least you've got a good accountant."

An accountant? It hadn't even crossed my mind. *Merde!* An accountant. Yes, of course, I was going to need an accountant. *Zut!* How naïve can one get! What an omission!

"Very important, John, in the workings of any business. Examining of financial records, ensuring their accuracy, preparing the annual financial reports showing profits and losses, seeing relevant taxes are paid and sent in on time…"And so on and so on. The more Xavier expounded on the role of the accountant, the need for the careful keeping of the books, the skills required for the management of a successful business concern, the more I felt my enthusiasm for the whole project draining away. This was all going to be too much and certainly not the fun I'd envisaged. Me in management? I think not. (A fail in 'O' level Elementary Maths first time round would hardly qualify me).

So with feelings of apprehension and self-doubt, similar to what I'd experienced on returning to Marlborough College after the long summer vacations, I was now steering myself straight into the lion's den and towards Friday 26th November – the opening of the doors of *Chai John*. No turning back now. Deep breath.

Chapter 22

Chai John

From professional schoolmaster to amateur restaurateur. From chalk to cheese some might say, though it soon struck me that techniques I had used in the classroom I was now deploying in my restaurant. After all, in both places I was a salesman, in the one selling the delights of French and German grammar, syntax and literature and in the other the contents of plates and glasses. Admittedly the clientèle was different. Then it was a question of English middle and upper-class adolescent boys and girls, seasoned with a sprinkling of foreign intake, now it was a matter of opening up to all and sundry. But the question remains the same for both categories – how best to sell one's product to the general satisfaction of all? If perforce in the school context it had to be with a combination of the stick and the carrot, in a restaurant context there can only be room for the carrot. Carrots galore. A fitting temperament and personality are called upon, a sunny disposition towards the client at all times, be he/ she surly, uncooperative, provocative and at times downright rude. What is needed is *l'esprit commerçant*, in other words to be open, welcoming and friendly with all so as better to sell one's wares.

"*John, ne sois pas comme Colombo. Lui, il n'est pas commerçant.*" Good advice from André, who had observed Colombo operate, Colombo from the café *Le Bacchus* opposite and now my competitor in trade. Indeed, the latter, somewhat volatile by nature, would at times give vent to his feelings – raw ones often – in front of his customers, feelings it would have been better to have kept to himself. Anger, scorn, mockery directed at whoever happened to be his *bête noire* of the moment. Not good for trade.

Almost certainly my Marlborough College clientèle was the easier sell. After all they were a captive audience and didn't have to be wooed into their desks. They were a carefully selected clientèle too, having successfully jumped over the Common Entrance examination hurdle. Neither did they have to pay. Well, of course they did, indirectly, through their parents, but that was the last thing that was ever going to trouble their little minds.

The sell was not so easy in a restaurant context, as I was soon to discover. The clients would come only of their own volition – no question of dragooning them as schoolboys into a classroom – added to which they were having to pay good, hard-earned money and the central issue was clearly always going to be the question of *le rapport qualité-prix* – was one getting good value for one's money? If I at first thought the answer to this lay with the contents of the plate and the glass, I soon learnt otherwise. Yes, of course, the quality of the food and drink served is the very first consideration. If a client leaves gastronomically dissatisfied he is most unlikely ever to reappear. But when it comes to what is meant by a good evening out at a restaurant, there is so much more at stake other than just the quality of the meal. Is the welcome up to the mark? Is the service too slow/fast? Is the music too loud/soft? Is it the right music, or would no music at all be better? Should the heating be turned up/down? The lighting turned up/down? Why can't the child at the next table stop whimpering? Can't the young couple by the fire leave off kissing and cuddling till they get home? And so on, and so on. One will never please everyone all the time. All one can hope is that a prevailing mellow *bonne ambiance* will permeate those present and go some way towards creating an agreeable atmosphere of toleration and cosiness.

If a lot of my time and effort was spent on attempting to keep customers happy. so too was it spent on looking after my employees, even if these amounted to no more than two – the cook and the gap-year student. Cooks can be tricky, that much I had already learned from friends. They will often have prima donna tendencies, will need handling with kid gloves and will take kindly neither to advice nor criticism. Young Thierry, my first cook – and there were to be several to follow – was indeed pleasant enough, initially at any rate. However, any ideas I might have entertained that he might one day blossom into a latter-day Escoffier were soon quashed. He was just a mediocre cook and would ever more continue to be such.

I soon realised that for as long as I offered only weekend work I would never attract the good cooks. Good cooks had full-time jobs including weekends, the less good worked in *les collectivités* (schools, etc.) where they would be free at weekends to take supplementary work to boost their incomes. Thierry and the others who followed him did precisely this. They turned up, clocked in the hours, did the work and cleared off as soon as possible with the extra cash in pocket. No sense of commitment, no concern for the establishment they were working for. The less scrupulous both cut corners and skimped on the work, causing me at times much indignation and fret. Those eating out in a restaurant, lulled into a sense of well-being, will not often be aware of the strength of the emotions being felt – expressed, too, sometimes – beyond the green baize door and in the kitchens. Sullenness, sulkiness, resentment, anger as cook and employer wage wars of attrition in attempts to gain the upper hand and assert control. Rarely are these wars fought out in the open. More often not a word is said in anger. Angry inner seethings of discontent will gnaw at the mind – sometimes for hours, sometimes days on end – sparked off by perceived misdemeanours or imagined slights. All of this is most energy-consuming, and especially when one is simultaneously supposed to be putting on a polished performance 'front of house'. Between leaving the kitchens and entering the restaurant the scowl must instantly give way to the beatific smile – all is well with the world, even if it isn't.

At fraught times such as these I would more often than not seek consolation in my gap-year student and James the Etonian, who was always happy to lend a sympathetic ear as I spelt out the difficulties inherent in the cook-employer relationship. That we could discuss these matters sensibly should have been no surprise to me. After all I had much more in common with him than I would ever have with the likes of Thierry the cook. So too was the case with the host of other students who followed in James' footsteps. Not only did I get on with them fine (hardly surprisingly since I'd selected and appointed them in the first place) but so did my customers. So James got off to a good start and was at the receiving end of much kudos when I revealed his Etonian background. Added to which he looked the part – tall and handsome, fair-haired and blue-eyed, elegant in his bearing and agreeable in his manner. No hint of arrogance. A fine ambassador to his country.

Others followed in his mould, even if they weren't all always as level-headed as he was. Some took rather too readily to the bottle and the *Bacchus* bar – much mopping up in the early hours. One in particular, Charles, got involved in a drinking session with fairground folk *(les forains)* who were in Le Castéra for *la fête du village*. Having attempted to out-drink them – unwise – he eventually left the *Bacchus* in the early hours totally sozzled, wended his wobbly way across the square, let himself in through the wrong front door, climbed the stairs, entered the bedroom and only realised his mistake when he found young Bruno, my neighbour, already in bed and soundly asleep. The latter awoke when Charles finally hit the floor with a crash. Needless to say the village heard all about the unexpected and indeed unwanted intrusion the very next day, and were much amused.

From that day hence Charles lived with the reputation of a night prowler and Bruno adopted the wise habit of locking his front door at night. Poor Bruno! It was not as if this was the first time he'd faced problems emanating from his neighbour, *L'Anglais*. Only months previously I'd been drilling our party wall – using a mighty Makita drill with a 50-centimetre bit attached – intending to make a hole to the half-way mark and no further. Inexplicably the Makita seemed to take on a life of its own and within seconds I'd broken right through to the other side, from whence there issued a piercing cry. I'd broken through into Bruno's loo, just to the side of the loo itself and dangerously close to Bruno himself, who had happened to have been sitting on it at that very moment. To have been threatened by the sudden arrival of a fierce king-sized drill bit aimed at his un-protected nether regions when he was least expecting it must indeed have been unsettling to say the least. My attempts to minimize the matter with talk of 'a miss is as good as a mile' didn't go down very well. Understandably enough. I did better by standing him drinks at *Le Bacchus* until good relations had been restored.

Henry from Radley College was the gap student who eventually replaced Charles. He was certainly no night-prowler and knew how to take his drink. Not that he didn't spend time in *Le Bacchus*. He did and was encouraged to be there by Colombo who liked him around because he played the guitar (but almost certainly for other reasons too!) The cry would go up *"Henri de Navarre et sa guitare – au bar ce soir!"* and he would regularly attract a good audience.

Ben from Sherborne, too, was good value and integrated well with all. I'd received his application one day just before setting off to the UK to see my aged father in Dorset, and a small detour took me to Sherborne and the school's porter's lodge, where I was able to call for Ben. A satisfactory impromptu interview was carried out there and then and I'd bagged yet another highly personable young man. It was only on leaving that I remembered what we'd always said of Sherborne at Marlborough, namely that they hadn't yet heard that the Archduke had been assassinated. Oh dear! Would Ben therefore turn out to be a cross between a dinosaur and an ostrich?

In the event he didn't. Far from it. In fact he had such a good time that he ended up crashing the *Chai John* delivery van beyond repair. The impending arrival of his parents to visit their son gave me an ideal opportunity to vent my anger in front of them. However, by the time they were knocking at the front door sweet reason had prevailed. In what way would involving the parents improve the situation? All was purring and smiling and they left happy in the knowledge that their Ben was doing such a good job, demolition not included. All was forgiven, much to Ben's relief.

All in all my English gap-year students were far less of a problem to me than were my cooks. They also helped keep me in touch with the UK. So too did ex-colleagues who frequently dropped in on their way through to Spain and ex-pupils who would invite themselves to stay in return for their labour. The Hon. John built a fine flight of brick steps, Charles laid a pavement of bricks and pebble stones from the Garonne, Richard spent months as a carpenter installing built-in cupboards and a mezzanine. Was I for ever going to gravitate within the Marlborough orbit? In a way I hoped so, even if it felt a little like having one's cake and eating it. Life in Le Castéra was nevertheless now to be my primary preoccupation and it was suiting me – even if by no means matching up to the level of sophistication of a Marlborough life.

The seasons came and went. So too the traditional village gatherings. The first weekend in May always saw the staging of *La Fête du Village* – four full days of merriment. The fairground, with dodgems, coconut shies, rifle-stands, tombolas and *buvettes*. *Pétanque* competitions and fishing in the Mayor's lake for prizes. Four days of music-making, eating and drinking with *Le Bacchus* working overtime into the early hours of the morning. A festal high mass in the church on the Sunday morning, followed by an *apéritif* – *un verre d'amitié* – in the village hall offered by *M. le Maire*. Each day ended with dancing in the village hall to music of all kinds, the final Sunday evening being reserved for the traditional *Bal Musette*, popular music written for the accordion and thus appealing to the French of all generations. At one moment I'd find myself dancing with granny, the next moment with her six-year-old granddaughter.

Once the *fête du village* was over, the village would settle back into its habitual sedentary ways, that is until the next events of the 'season' once again set the wheels turning. The 14th of July, Bastille Day and a cause for much rejoicing, the 11th of November, Armistice Day and a cause for much reflection at a ceremony in the cemetery when the Mayor solemnly reads out the names inscribed on the war memorial of those young villagers who fell in the Great War – 15 of them – "*Mort pour la France*" the congregation intones after the reading out of each name. Moving indeed. This is followed shortly after by the celebrations of the third Thursday in November – the day of the releasing for sale of the *Beaujolais nouveau* and a good excuse for downing great quantities of this light red wine together with the freshly roasted chestnuts considered to act as blotting paper. December then sees the year out with the *Repas du 3e Age* – a free pre-Christmas lunch offered by the Mayor to all aged 65 and over.

Added to the above are the annual *Assemblés Générales* of the various *Associations* in the village – the AGMs of *La Pétanque Castéraise, Le Cycloclub Castérois, L'A.C.C.A.*(hunting and shooting) among others, these meetings being summarily dispatched so as members joined by their guests might then turn their attention to the more important matters of eating and drinking. Renowned as the most enthusiastic eaters and drinkers in the region are *les chasseurs,* whose Saturday morning shoots in the season produce quantities of rabbit, hare and partridge. For their annual dinner – not to be missed – they not only shoot the roe deer and wild boar, but butcher them, prepare, cook and then serve them up to eager, hungry supporters. Although by no means a natural fan of blood sports – my one and only encounter with bull-fighting saw to that – I nevertheless find it hard to say no to a beautifully cooked plate of venison when placed before me. These gatherings, as with those others peppering the annual village calendar, are generally most convivial; the company is good, the occasions festive, sociable and lively.

It was hardly surprising then that after three or four years working in the village I was beginning to feel very much part of the furniture, even if Colombo pointedly continued to refer to me – not always in flattering terms – as *L'Anglais,* as if to say that no matter how hard I tried I would never be one of them. Try hard I most certainly did and to the extent of joining Colombo whenever (frequently) we were invited by *la jeunesse dorée* to join in celebrating birthdays in the *Gazou,* the village clubhouse set aside for such occasions. And there we would stay, both of us now middle-aged, till the early hours of the morning surrounded by *les jeunes,* some of them half our age, propping up the bar knocking back the beer with them, rocking and rolling on the dance floor with them. However, more often than not I would find myself leaving such revelries with mixed feelings. On the one hand it was flattering to be invited, on the other hand I never really felt in my element, pretend as I might, both to myself and to those present. Gyrating and whirling around in a smoke-filled room to music – no, to loud heavy metal noise which was so loud you couldn't hear yourself speak – this is hardly my 'scene'. Better stay at home reading and listening to Bach cantatas – quality time. So, correct, they were right and I would never really be like them, try as I might. Eventually the penny dropped – I should try less hard and allow events to take their natural course. So be it.

It was that same natural course of events which allowed my friendship with Christian and Marie-France Lorenzo to grow and blossom – Christian who on that first day's canter to Le Castéra had spontaneously offered to tether and water the horses while friends and I took time off at the *Bacchus*. Now we were firm friends and I was soon 'adopted' by their three children as *Tonton* (Uncle) John. Their door was always open for both *apéritifs* and meals, and with only the square separating us I was a regular visitor.

It was during one such visit – one of Marie-France's renowned couscous evenings – that conversation turned to *Le Manoir*. Now that I had firmly established myself in the tower – *Chai John* kitchens on the ground floor, my study first floor, spare bedroom second floor – had I plans for the remaining 75% surface area of the building which remained unoccupied? If so, what plans? I had to admit I had none and that my thoughts during the length of my waking hours had been almost exclusively focused on the running of *Chai John*. It was then that the idea of converting the building into flats was sown in my mind. An interesting idea, I thought, before asking the two pertinent questions which immediately sprang to mind. Firstly, who was to pay for the conversion and how much? Secondly, was there a demand, and where were the potential tenants to come from?

Thinking about the idea with Christian and Marie-France I soon realised that the latter question was by far the easier to answer. Toulouse was the answer. It was rapidly becoming a wealthy city with a bright future ahead, owing largely to the formation of Airbus Industrie GIE in 1970. Ever since then the aeronautics and aerospace industries comprising hundreds of companies and tens of thousands of employees had been steadily growing, hence the demand for suitable accommodation. Employees were drawn too from the other European countries which had joined the Airbus consortium – the UK, Germany and Spain principally – and engineers from these countries with Airbus/British Aerospace contracts were now pouring into Toulouse. The coming into service of Concorde in 1973 and the birth of the A320 in 1987 both gave the Toulouse-based industry a further boost, placing it in direct competition with Seattle and the mighty Boeing empire.

Le Castéra, too, was well placed with regard to all this – just 20 minutes to the west of Toulouse and on the right side for easy access to both the airport and the Airbus/Aerospace complex. Transport links had been upgraded and were now fit for purpose. I had to agree with Christian and Marie-France that there was a potentially bright future here for my dilapidated *Manoir*. But where to find the money? Subsidies, grants and bank loans, came the answer, and I left the Lorenzos that evening with the hint of a suggestion from them that they might one day be interested in investing in such a project with me. The thought was a heartening one, partly because Marie-France was endowed with a good business sense (she already managed her husband's 300-hectare farm) and partly because in no way could I imagine myself undertaking such a vast project on my own. So, once again, here was a case of allowing time for the natural course of events to play themselves out. Patience.

Having my thoughts turned towards the future of *Le Manoir* couldn't have come at a better time. The Mayor had already begun making muttering noises about the state of the building. An unsightly pile right in the middle of the village, he said, and what was I planning to do about it? I had mostly managed to fend him off with evasive answers but clearly this could not continue for long. I decided to take the bull – the Mayor – by the horns, invite him, his wife and a few village worthies to supper, then reveal to them my plans for the conversion of *Le Manoir* into flats, hoping that would keep him quiet until the Lorenzos came up, hopefully, with a concrete proposal.

The evening started agreeably enough with me sloshing out the *pousse rapière* – the local *apéritif* with its Armagnac liqueur base topped up with a sparkling white (this could be the local *vin sauvage* from Château Monluc or a *Blanquette de Limoux*, or indeed a champagne, if you're feeling rich.) We then sat down to a traditional French supper – no point in foisting quaint English culinary delights upon them, I thought to myself, since they just wouldn't appreciate them. (I was slowly learning.) *Soupe à l'oignon, daube de boeuf,* (It was winter) *plateau de fromages,* (<u>before</u> the dessert) *tarte aux pommes* – how much more traditional can you get?

The evening was still going well with the wine glasses filled and filled again. It was over the coffee and liqueurs I eventually saw fit to reveal my plans for the future of *Le Manoir.* These appeared to meet with the general approval, to the extent that the Mayor rose to his feet to propose a toast to my health. He started by saying how pleased he was I had come to Le Castéra. (*"Monsieur John, je suis content que vous soyez venu au Castéra."*) Immediately, instinctively, unwisely and without thinking, I jumped to my feet to correct what I'd just heard.

"Non, M. le Maire. Non, on n'est pas venu au Castéra – on est REvenu au Castéra."

There followed a deathly silence which clearly showed the assembled company was with difficulty digesting what I'd just said – "No, Mister Mayor, we (the English) have not come to Le Castéra – we've come BACK to Le Castéra!" All understood at once what I'd so unwisely chosen to point out – namely that the English had already occupied the whole region for a period of hundreds of years ever since the day Eleanor of Aquitaine, the most powerful woman of her times, had had her marriage to French king Louis VII annulled and had then married the English King Henry II, bringing with her to the English crown a vast dowry including the Duchies of Aquitaine and Poitou. (A huge area and not much less than one third of the size of modern-day France), Henry, already Duke of Normandy, thus became every bit as powerful in France as the French king himself – if not more so.

Voilà! I'd put my foot right in it and committed the cardinal sin. Never speak of such matters – the Hundred Years War, Joan of Arc, Napoleon – lightly in front of French people you don't know well enough. They don't take kindly to talk of what might be considered as English 'superiority' being forced down their throats. That is not to say that these matters cannot be aired among friends. Such spirited conversations are indeed to be had, imbued with much banter and amusement on both sides with my French friends counter-attacking England *(Le Perfide Albion)* and the English *(Les Rosbifs)* with equal vigour. Good for them!

M. le Maire was thus not best pleased, understandably enough. If I was having a bit of a bumpy ride with him it wasn't to matter too much since he was drawing to the end of his term of office. I simply made a note to be more circumspect with his successor, Monsieur Sacareau. Colombo from *Le Bacchus,* too, was seemingly giving me a hard time, although he was civil enough to me in front of my face. I was hearing through the village grapevine that he'd taken to the habit of speaking ill of *Chai John* in front of his customers, spreading unfounded rumours about low standards and poor returns for one's money. Doubtless all villages have their gossipmongers, people who delight in indulging in idle talk, groundless rumour, petty tittle-tattle – more often than not malicious. But if the gossipmonger is also the one who runs the village café-bar one can be sure that the poisonous rumours he spreads about will travel fast, far and wide. Such was the case here. Those at the bar with ears to hear also had tongues to wag, and it wasn't long before such incriminations came to the ears of those whose names were being besmirched, as it was in my case.

Worse was to come. One day I received an unexpected visit from the hygiene authorities, who wanted to carry out an inspection of the *Chai John* kitchens to satisfy themselves that the correct standards were being adhered to there. Thankfully all was well and I was given a clean bill of health. However, the very next day I heard – again through the village grapevine – that I'd been denounced by Colombo and that it was he who had telephoned anonymously to inform the authorities and request they carry out an inspection on the grounds of insalubrity. True or not true? I shall never know. All I do know is that invaded occupied France during the war was plagued by informers *(dénonciateurs)*, people prepared to deliver their own countrymen into the hands of the enemy for personal gain.

Also that the practice of denouncement is still alive and kicking in post-war France in a way that it is not in the UK, a country which kept the Invader at bay, thus the informers largely, too.

It was also at about this time that I had a major spat with my next-door neighbour, with whom I'd never really felt able to identify. The feeling was mutual. Christian had married Françoise, one of the daughters of Mme Lubespère, the owner of the *brocante* (antique shop) as well as several other properties in the village. It was generally thought the family considered itself 'top drawer', the 'cat's whiskers' *(le haut du panier)* with the village a lesser breed – *L'Anglais* doubtless included. Christian and Françoise had a 16-year-old son, Stéphan, with whom from the start I had at least one thing in common – neither of us got on too well with his parents. Consequently he would spend a considerable time during weekends and holidays *chez moi* lending a useful hand here and there, sometimes chain-saw wielding, sometimes fiddling with the electrics, about which he already knew a considerable amount.

It was just before Stephan's birthday that I had a deputation from two of his young friends. They wanted to give him a surprise birthday party. Would I let them give it at *Chai John*? There would be thirty of them and they'd like to take the restaurant for the whole evening. Agreed. The day arrived, they arrived and all was going well – eating, drinking, music, dancing – when just before midnight I was asked to open the terrace doors. They seemingly had yet another surprise for Stephan, so we were all then and there bidden out onto the terrace and into the *parc*. No sooner were we there than the most almighty burst of bangs broke out into the peace of the midnight air as firework after firework rose into the dark skies above. There was much amusement and laughter as the five-minute 'surprise' played itself out to the delight of all – myself included.

The next morning was another story. Once out of the front door I was immediately set upon from my right – Françoise, Stephan's mother, gave me both barrels. She and her husband had both been awakened by the 'explosions', had first thought their boiler had exploded, and then had had a sleepless night. What disgraceful behaviour from a neighbour. I should be ashamed of myself, and so on and so on. I had neither time to apologize, nor to explain that the firework display had been as much a surprise to me as it had to Stephan. She had retreated, slamming the door behind her. Still reeling from the unwarranted and brutal onslaught, I was then immediately confronted by shrill screaming from my left. None other than Mme. Lubespère, mother of Françoise, who was yelling obscenities at the top of her voice from outside her shop.

"*Connard!* (stupid bastard!)" she shrilled. "*Connard! Connard!*" echoing down the full length of the street. Curtains twitched. Doors opened ajar.

"*Connasse!*" (silly bitch!) I screamed back, furious. "*Vieille connasse! Vieille connasse!*" Here again no chance to apologize, to explain, but I later congratulated myself for at least having had the presence of mind to have added the adjective, thus not only having put the knife in but having twisted it to maximum effect. I was later told that she too had been awakened by the 'explosions', had thought that the Arabs were invading the village and had had a sleepless night fearing she was about to have her throat cut or worse in her own bed.

While in general village life continued to amuse me in a Rabelaisian sort of way and was a welcome distraction from the worries of running a restaurant, I certainly didn't want to join with any of the conflicting factions from whence emanated so much of the gossip-mongering. Doubtless it was all part of what Prosper Mérimée would call *couleur locale*, but I nevertheless felt better for keeping out of the fray and viewing the scuffles and skirmishes from the sidelines. *On va essayer de garder ses distances.* Let's keep a little distance from it all, while calling to mind Clochemerle – a 1930s satirical novel set in a fictional French village called Clochemerle relating the bickering and in-fighting between Catholics and Republicans over the plans to install a new public *pissoir* in the village square. All quite amusing yet distinctly parochial.

Time was flying by and I was already five years into my new job and well into the groove. Weekends generally speaking found me pretty well occupied – I was busy keeping the *Chai John* wheels turning, all the while asking myself whether they could/should be turning faster and more smoothly. There were the good days and the less good, happy clients and the less happy ones. Mondays would find me in introspective mode – self-questionings, self-doubt –also with time on my hands wondering how best to avoid falling into the trap of taking sides in the various village feuds always simmering gently, at times on the point of boiling over.

And so, on one such Monday in the middle of the summer, it came as a very welcome surprise when Peter Tosney came to see me in Le Castéra with the offer of a job I could not refuse. Peter I had first known in the Marlborough days when i/c the French Exchange – he had arrived with his French class in tow and had taken over my timetable while I had skipped to Toulouse with my Marlburians to take on his English teaching there. Here he was now with the offer of a job teaching English to post-Baccalauréat students on a two-year course in *les Classes Préparatoires* to gain entry to *Les Grandes Ecoles*. Only those with the top Baccalauréat grades can be considered for the '*Classes Prépas*' where they will prepare for the competitive exam for *Les Grandes Ecoles* – higher education establishments for the academically élite founded by Napoleon.

The students I was to be given were studying the sciences and higher mathematics, and all of them were gifted and highly motivated in their subjects. English was obligatory for all and certainly difficult for those who were not necessarily linguistically gifted. Without a good *note* in English the path ahead was barred. I was appointed as a *khôlleur* – a teacher concerned with developing comprehension skills and the use of the spoken word. This was largely to be done through the studying of articles on topical subjects taken from the British/American press. The classes were conducted exclusively in English and involved the rehearsal of regular mock-oral examinations. Almost immediately I realised that here was a job I would take to like a duck to water. Precious little preparation required, totally at ease in one's native language, never any marking to take home at the end of the day, no exams to set, no end of term reports to write. I simply walked into my classes, taught and left. Job done with none of the chores attached which had totally absorbed me during the Marlborough days. No house tutorial duties to perform, no school rules and dress codes to enforce, no parental meetings, no departmental meetings. No games to referee/umpire, no theatre trips to organise, no proctorial rounds to perform, no nannying, mollycoddling, spoon-feeding, policing, punishing, placating. Certainly no longer *in loco parentis* – just the Englishman teaching the language he knows best and loves most. Rubbing shoulders with students of an older age-group, too, suited me well – no longer fearful of upsetting thirteen-year-old girls – and, while knowing them less well, they proved every bit as cooperative as the average Marlburian.

One day when meeting and talking to Jeremy Nichols, retired Headmaster of Stowe, I was trying to compare and contrast my Toulouse students with previous Marlburian pupils.

"Well, here in Toulouse they somehow appear to be generally more normal, more natural," I said.

"Oh yes," he replied. "I know exactly what you mean – less peacocking!"

He knew exactly what I meant. The public-school boy at his worst – ostentatious and strutting like the peacock. How lucky I had been that Marlborough had produced comparatively few of such specimens. May God preserve us all from that particular brand.

I soon fell into the new routine and without difficulties. Weekdays happily teaching in Toulouse, weekends anxiously nursing *Chai John*, that dear little restaurant to which I had so enthusiastically – and perhaps not a little unwisely – given birth. It was a good balance and meant my hands were now full and I was more easily able to avoid descending into the murky world of village gossip and hearsay.

Not that I was cutting all my links with the village. Far from it. There were now several doors open to me and I continued to enter them with gratitude. Not least among them was the Lorenzo door – always wide open for a drink and/or a meal. It was during one such meal that they broached the subject of *Le Manoir*. Yes, they said, they had long considered the matter and would be happy to enter into a partnership with me as co-owners of *Le Manoir* with a view to developing the property into flats. What a relief! The idea of undertaking such a project on my own was unthinkable and Marie-France had a training in book-keeping and management which I very definitely lacked. Both she and Christian seemed to possess those qualities which would bind us together and see the project to a successful conclusion. Both were straight-talking, level-headed in negotiation, practical in financial matters, hard-working – qualities I soon learned to connect with their origins and backgrounds. Both were *d'origine pied-noir*, meaning they originated from those French families which had settled in Algeria from 1830 when the French had first taken possession of that country. Christian and his family had known the worst of times when the Algerian war of independence had broken out in 1954, accounting for the most horrific atrocities on both sides with those dead numbering some 300,000 when the cease-fire was finally ordered on the 19th of March 1962. By the time independence had been declared on the 3rd of July Christian, aged 19, his whole family and over one million *pieds-noirs* had been told to leave the country (*la valise ou le cercueil* – pack your bags or make your coffin). They left for exile (mostly in France), leaving all behind save the clothes they stood in and the suitcases they could carry. Those who were not quick enough in departing received a chilling warning with the Massacres of Oran on 5th of July when 700 *pieds-noirs* were brutally slaughtered in cold blood.

Understandably men and women who have suffered the trials and tribulations of war and exile will bear the weight of the bitter memories for a lifetime. Families uprooted from their homes and land – some had been there for more than four generations – and banished to a country which they had every reason to distrust now felt, and were made to feel, totally alienated in exile. De Gaulle, who had come to power on the *Algérie Française* ticket, had then done a U-turn, granted independence to Algeria and had thus betrayed the French *colons* who had trusted him to defend their interests and livelihoods.

In Christian and Marie-France I saw and understood that streak of distrust – trust was to be hard-earned with them. They, like me but for different reasons, saw themselves as 'outsiders', wary and circumspect with strangers. Their circle of friends, often *pieds-noirs*, was a close-knit one. But once a friend, always a friend and their loyalty to both friends and family was fierce. Politically right-wing – very definitely – and better not bandy around any loose left-wing talk about the benefits of immigration with them. Feelings go deep. A strong sense of right and wrong, justice and injustice.

My days were now full juggling with my classes in Toulouse and my restaurant in Le Castéra and in between setting up the *Manoir* project with Christian and Marie-France. The latter involved frequent visits to Toulouse with applications for grants available for the restoration of listed buildings and later on for meetings with architects. On-site meetings, too, and most importantly visits to banks to beg for the huge loan required to finance the whole affair. Never in my life had I borrowed such a large sum of money. It was to be paid back monthly over a period of fifteen years. The repayments would be covered by the rents from the four flats, but only on the assumption that all four of them were occupied for pretty much the whole of the fifteen-year period. What chance of that, I wondered. Worrying. Nothing for it now but to trust the Lorenzos and their faith in the whole project. The best way to find out if you can trust somebody is to trust them, said Hemingway.

So planning for the project continued over the following months and we were already well within sight of the day when the builders would move in. A fitting time, I thought to myself. The year was 1999 and here I was embarking on a new project for the new millennium. With its coming, one's thoughts turned naturally enough to the future. Would the 21st century continue to see me ensconced in Le Castéra and at the helm of *Chai John*? For how long? Or were there yet pastures new to be discovered? Just as life had taken me beyond Marlborough College, was I now about to be taken beyond Le Castéra? If these thoughts were preoccupying me, they were imprecise, and I had not an inkling where the next chapter of my life was about to be played out.

Had anyone suggested that I was bound for Morocco, I would have heartily laughed them out of court.

Uta el Hammam – the central square

A mosque in my quarter, the 'Blessed Quarter', so named for being on the east end of town, therefore that much nearer to Mecca.

A typical Chaoueni door – blue

Goats clattering by as they do daily

Dar John – my front door

The living room

A neighbour drops in for a piano lesson

Count Randal MacDonnell for supper

View from the terrace

St. Andrew's Anglican church with me,
the peripatetic organ-grinder

The terrace – the ideal venue for eating, drinking, sleeping, reading...
or simply sitting and thinking

The 'Olympic' swimming pool – a great place to wallow and keep cool

Randal with an aperitif on a
Tangier terrace

Randal trying on a hat in the Minzah hotel

ST ANDREW'S CHURCH, TANGIER

RANDAL MacDONNELL
18th August 1950 – 24th November 2019

A MEMORIAL PRAYER

TUESDAY, 18th FEBRUARY 2020
11 am

Randal's departure. RIP.

Chapter 23

The Road to Morocco

It was around Easter, as usual, that I was summoned by my accountant to Toulouse for the annual audit of the accounts and books of *Chai John*. As usual, I was in a state of some trepidation. The results were never very encouraging and this year less than most.

"*Monsieur John*, you're not actually losing money yet, but getting closer to it each year," he said.

What was I going to do? Would I continue doggedly hoping for an eventual upturn, or would it be better to abandon ship before matters took a turn for the worse?

It was with these questions in my mind that I returned home determined to resolve the issue rapidly one way or the other. To abandon ship would bring a certain relief from worry. It would also allow time for other things. More time to devote to the conversion of *Le Manoir* into flats – a big job, scheduled to take a year or two to completion. More time, too, to devote to my friends. However many invitations to meals, weekend breaks and sometimes holidays had I had to turn down over the years owing to the demands of *Chai John*? Was now not the time to be thinking of liberating myself from its shackles?

Not that I'd reached a state of terminal disillusionment with my pet project. Far from it. I still enjoyed the contact with clients – most of them – and I particularly relished setting up the regular *soirées musicales*. These were much varied in content but always well attended. Groups playing blues, swing, boogie and jazz, an accordionist with a programme of *Chansons Françaises*, a guitarist playing flamenco, evenings of Irish and Brazilian music. Classical music too, sometimes a violinist, sometimes a piano trio. Once a young Marlburian music scholar from Singapore played Lizst's piano sonata in B minor – no mean achievement.

There were good times, too, on Sunday afternoons when people would make their way up from Toulouse to browse in the antique shop. They would then drop in to *Chai John* and while away the time over tea, muffins and scones – in summer on the terrace in the sun, in winter inside in front of a warming open fire. Times of relative relaxation and cheerful chatter.

My decision was not long in coming. To stay with *Chai John* was merely to offer myself more of the same at best – I was certainly not going to be able to transform the place into a Michelin 3-star no matter how long I gave myself. So better draw stumps now while the going was good and rather in the manner I'd closed the Marlborough chapter of my life. After twenty-five years at Marlborough I felt I'd 'done' teaching. So too after seven years with *Chai John* I felt I'd 'done' being a restaurateur. To continue would merely be to repeat, adding nothing to the experience I'd already gained. Better therefore to turn another page and wait and see what new venture the future would bring.

To close on the 31st December 1999, the last day of the millennium, appealed to my sense of history. It would be a good opportunity for a mega-party. Such turned out to be the case, and I spent the last months happily working towards the Grand Finale. This once over and now seen safely into the second millennium, I yet again found myself in the familiar waters of school terms and the long holidays which followed on. During the latter I was not long in renewing past friendships principally from the UK and some dating back to the Trinity College, Dublin days. The Dieppe-Newhaven crossing soon became a favourite.

It was just before one such school holiday – the Easter holiday, 2001 – that I found myself invited to a wake in Toulouse held in the memory of a friend of Canadian and Irish descent who had unexpectedly passed away. His wake was held in his second-hand bookshop where he had made himself a multitude of friends – myself included – by dispensing free cups of coffee and glasses of wine to all and sundry entering his premises and grateful for his warm hospitality. Those present on that day to drink to his memory did so with gusto and in the best of traditions much alcohol was consumed. Somewhat incoherent speeches were made, most mawkish, some silly, and it wasn't long before James, the recent Oxford graduate to whom I was speaking, and I decided to withdraw from the semi-sozzled assembly to take a quiet nightcap at the bar round the corner. It was here that he told me he'd just returned from a holiday in Morocco.

"Oh, Morocco, know it well. Been through the country when I was not much older than you. Fez, Marrakesh, Essaouira and so on – know them all."

"What did you make of Chefchaouen?" he asks.

"Where? What? Chefchaouen? Never heard of it. What is it?"

"What!" he answers. "You say you know Morocco and haven't even heard of Chaouen, one of its most beautiful jewels?"

He then proceeded to deliver a lengthy lecture on the delights of this walled town set high up in the Rif mountains. Clearly the place had made a deep impression, and I listened intently. The more I listened the more my own distant memories of Morocco began to re-emerge, and I found myself wondering how it was that for now over twenty years I'd given hardly a thought to that fascinating country. Surely it was time to revisit.

By the time James had finished his eulogising, I had already made up my mind. Spurred on by his graphic account, I would use my impending two-week Easter holiday to drive to Morocco, there to re-acquaint myself with its charms and culture and finally discover Chefchaouen for myself. Thoughts of a return visit after so long now reminded me of the heady excitement I'd experienced on first entering that country in the early 1970s.

It was the Easter holidays, 1972, and I was shortly to turn thirty. Perhaps it was this unhappy fact that led me to decide on a hitch-hiking holiday to the South of France – one last throw of the student dice. It was the end of a cold and wet March and I was kitted out appropriately – stout walking boots, heavy woollen pullovers, a water-proof combat jacket with headgear to match. A sturdy stick in my hand and a handsome haversack on my back completed the picture. In my pocket I carried Robert Louis Stevenson's *Travels with a Donkey in the Cévennes*, my aim being to follow Stevenson's 12-day, 200 km hike through the sparsely populated and impoverished areas of the Cévennes in south-central France, a venture he undertook in 1878. Modestine, a stubborn and manipulative donkey, was his travelling companion. I would travel solo.

"For my part I travel not to go anywhere but to go. I travel for travel's sake." So said Stevenson, and I liked his thinking.

I was soon back in my student hitch-hiking mode. There were not many competitors on the road and I used my old trick of displaying an impressive Union Jack, reckoning that those with an affinity for the country, indeed those wishing to practise their English, would be more likely to stop and take me on board on seeing it. It worked again and I was soon speeding south through France.

It was south of Limoges that a car stopped with a young couple heading for a skiing holiday in the Pyrenees. They were a fun couple and it wasn't long before they'd somehow persuaded me to postpone my Cévennes plans with an offer to spend a few days skiing with them and in the chalet they'd rented. It seemed a good idea at the time, less so on arrival when I realised I was going to have to hire boots and skis at some expense, and also remembered that I was not exactly a natural on the slopes. Announcing my departure the following morning was easy, finding a lift out of the remote Pyrenean resort where I found myself, less so. I eventually tracked down a car leaving for Spain and Barcelona and took it, realising I was heading south as opposed to north but reasoning that once in Barcelona I would at least be on a major road network and well placed to head north again into France and on roads eventually leading directly to Montpellier, close to the Cévennes.

I asked to be left in central Barcelona in front of the railway station and close to the one-night cheap hotels. Rather than first find myself a hotel for the night, I chose to take a peep into the station, goodness knows why. There I found the overnight sleeper about to depart for Andalusia and the south. The mere sight of the word 'Andalusia' immediately summoned up the names of those magical cities Granada, Cordoba and Seville, about which about I'd already heard so much said in praise.

I must have then taken leave of my senses. Any thoughts of the Cévennes paled into insignificance, and within half an hour I'd bought my ticket, boarded the train, dropped onto my couchette and felt myself slowly moving out of the station and into the night. Deep sleep was not long in coming, and I awoke as we were pulling into Malaga. Glimpses of the deep blue of the Mediterranean whetted the appetite and an early sun was already rising into a cloudless, pale blue sky.

Within four hours we were approaching our destination – Algeciras. The name meant nothing to me and it was only on leaving the station that I realised exactly where I was. To the left rose the great Rock of Gibraltar, ahead the Straits of Gibraltar with Africa looming and beckoning in the misty distance. Yet again I must have taken leave of my senses. Andalusia I would leave till another day. Africa, a whole new continent set out before my eyes, was now suddenly my new goal and within the hour I was on a ferry heading across the waters and into the unknown.

No sooner was I aboard than I realised that the temperature had risen considerably. Here we were in the heat of the midday sun and there was I still wrapped in warm, heavy winter clothing destined for the chill of the Cévennes. My rucksack was soon bulging with unwanted garments – only my heavy walking boots could I not jettison. I also soon realised that I'd been wrong in assuming we were heading straight for Morocco. It was explained to me that we would be docking in Ceuta, an enclave (together with Melilla nearer the Algerian frontier) the Spanish had retained after Spain and France had granted independence to Morocco in 1956. Strange,

I thought to myself, that the Spanish should kick up so rough about British 'colonialism' in Gibraltar when they themselves were guilty of exactly the same sins in Morocco.

So it was after an hour's boat ride that we landed in Africa, but still in Spain, not yet in Morocco. Clearly the latter was now my new goal, not that I had any idea where I was going, and I soon came upon a dilapidated bus heading along the short distance towards the frontier with its customs post and then on into Morocco. The bus stopped a few times to take on more passengers, and close to approaching the frontier we were already a seething mass of humanity of all shapes and sizes on board with myself glaringly the only non-Moroccan.

There were principally the elderly and less elderly – no children – returning home, I assumed, after a day's work for the Spanish in Ceuta, nearly all of them wearing the traditional djellabas, the women with their headscarves, the men sporting turbans of various descriptions. Most of them, the women particularly, were burdened down with bundles and packets of varying sizes containing goodness knows what. Some of these packets – the smaller ones – were surreptitiously offloaded onto me and pushed under my seat shortly before the arrival of the customs and boarder police – both Spanish then Moroccan – to check the contents of the bus. And check they did – documents were examined, pockets emptied out and bundles torn open. Nobody came near me, the startled young Englishman with heaven knows what contraband concealed under his seat. A general sigh of relief when the whole ordeal was eventually over and with the bus at last on Moroccan soil I received multiple slaps on the back and conniving winks from those who now gratefully retrieved their precious packets.

The bus chugged on along bumpy, pot-holed roads and through poorly-lit villages till it finally limped into its final destination, Tetouan, where all and sundry spilled out into the central bus station – a latter-day Black Hole of Calcutta if ever there was one. Built into the rock-face and as the cavernous basement of a modern high-rise block it sucked in buses from all over Morocco – buses spewing out their evil noxious fumes and battered human cargoes into the gloom and stench of a hell-hole littered with would-be passengers, old and young alike, awaiting an eventual deliverance, some standing, others squatting, crouching, kneeling, lying – all submersed in vast quantities of baggage – cases, bundles, boxes, bottles and bags of all manner of descriptions.

My first thoughts were flight – flight from the stench and noise of both buses manoeuvring and crowds thronging. Once out into the fresh and balmy evening air and with a star-studded sky stretched out above, I was on the point of considering my next move when a sudden tap on the shoulder and the whispered words "Amigo! Amigo!" found me confronting a couple of local youths who immediately took it upon themselves to help me consider just that – my next move. Did I want somewhere to stay? To eat? Did I want to go to the cinema? Slightly fazed by this unexpected burst of questions, I paused before answering, only to find myself facing a second batch. Did I want alcohol? *Cerveza*? *Bière*? The conversation was clearly going to be part Spanish, part French. A smoke? Then, in a deeper whisper, did I want a girl? A boy?

First things first, I thought. Somewhere to sleep. I was on my guard, of course, since this was my first foray into countries non-European, but since my interlocutors appeared neither menacing nor malevolent and first impressions were not unfavourable I ventured to ask where I might spend the night. Follow us, came the answer. It was thus, on my first day in Morocco that I learnt how easy it was for a European to 'pick up' Moroccans. I had yet to learn how difficult it could then be to shed them.

A five-minute walk took us towards the centre of *La ville nouvelle* and on towards the medina – the walled old town. There, close by one of the medina gates, I was shown to a house with an open door above which was scribbled the word 'Hostal' – otherwise nothing to show that it was a hotel. Nothing much inside either – just a gnarled old woman with a battered old register, a rickety old staircase up to room number 6 which could only be described as basic. A bed – old iron bedstead – a blanket, a pillow, a light bulb swinging from the ceiling, a cracked washbasin with a wonky tap out of which feebly dribbled brownish, cold water. No more, no less. A loo of sorts somewhere down an unlit corridor. None of this mattered and, having checked the bed for fleas and bed bugs I fell onto it and slept like a log on this, my first night on a new continent.

Next morning I wasn't that surprised to see my self-appointed guides awaiting me on the doorstep. Since I'd not had the money to pay for their services in finding me a hotel they were now clearly more than anxious to show me the nearest bureau de change where I might exchange traveller's cheques into dirhams. This done, it was suggested that I might like a tour of the medina, and I was steered back towards Bab Tut, one of the seven 15th century gates built into the crenellated rampart walls of the old town.

Once through the gate I could hardly believe my eyes and had to pinch myself to be sure I wasn't dreaming. It was if the clock had suddenly been set back to Biblical times and I had been transported into another world, a world of totally unfamiliar sights, sounds and smells – vibrant colours of fabrics and clothes, strange wailing sounds emanating from the mosques with their frequent calls to prayer (*muezzin*), pungent scents of exotic fragrances and eastern spices. All in all a full, frontal assault on all the senses, the like of which I'd never, ever experienced before. I allowed myself to be fully swept up into the exoticism of it all.

Weaving one's way down narrow, cobbled alleyways, competing for space with donkey-driven carts and sheep and goats being led off to market, admiring the carpenters, blacksmiths and weavers at work as one passed on by – it was all like a dream. There were cafés and restaurants on all sides – no more than upturned shoeboxes with a bare wooden table and chairs inside – shops (also shoeboxes) crammed to the gunnels with anything and everything for sale, the owner somehow sandwiched in amongst it all, lively street markets in the hidden little squares with their pretty tiled fountains babbling. No sign of a tourist, a European, a car – nothing to break the magic spell of the moment as we drifted through the Andalusian, Berber and Jewish quarters, past the mosques, the hammams, the tanneries, the bread ovens, finally plunging into a restaurant/ shoebox known to Mohamed and Mustapha, my guardian angels, and offering kefta (meat balls) and mint tea by way of sustenance.

My 'guardian angels' were in fact illegal tourist guides (*faux guides*). This I realised when on leaving after lunch we found ourselves approaching two policemen. Mohamed and Mustapha instantly melted from my sides to merge into the swirling crowds, only to reappear once the danger was past. I could imagine the punishment could be worse than a slap on the wrists. And so we wandered on past further souks and sights eventually to re-emerge back into the 20th century through a gate just to the side of the king's palace – a magnificent building with its high, dazzling whitewashed walls, sitting squarely between the medina and the new town. Heavily guarded too it was, with armed soldiers in their sentry-boxes and court officials in all manner of dress clustering around the main ceremonial gateway. Above the high walls there peeped the tops of palms and cedars hinting at the fabulous gardens within. Without, and kept at a distance, was I, surrounded by the impoverished masses, the beggars on the streets. The essence of the Third World, I thought to myself. An all-powerful ruler with his clique on the one hand and mass poverty on the other, with precious little between. "*Pourvu que ça dure*" said the wizened little old Corsican, Napoleon's mother, on hearing of yet another of his military victories. "Provided that it lasts." Can it last? Should it last? When will come that great Deluge which will sweep all away? Not yet, surely, I reassured myself, as Mohamed and Mustapha began plotting their next move.

Would I like to go to the beach? "The beach?" I queried, trying to figure out the geography. "Yes", came the answer. "It's not far and we could get a taxi," said Mustapha, already propelling me towards the nearest taxi-rank. Well, I thought, in for a penny in for a pound. At least I had the good sense to ask the driver the cost before stepping aboard and within thirty minutes we'd reached the sea and the beach – a beautiful, sandy beach with precious few people about. Would I like to visit their friend, a Dutchman, who lived in a cabin he'd built in the dunes where we could listen to music? In for a penny...

We approached the cabin as the sun was setting. Music could indeed be heard – the Rolling Stones (not exactly my kind of music) – together with the sound of talk and laughter. I was at once introduced to the assembled company – a dozen or so youths/young men, all friends of my two guides, who were clearly already well into a beer-drinking session. A bottle was thrust into my hand by the Dutchman, a genial, long-haired hippy who, when he discovered my mother too was Dutch, clearly thought Christmas had come and plied me – and Mohamed and Mustapha at my expense, I correctly supposed – with bottle after bottle until I was really getting into the party mode.

It was then that the cigarettes were produced – at least I thought they were simply cigarettes. It turned out we were smoking *Kif*, the local marijuana cultivated in great quantities in the Rif mountains. The effect on me, a total newcomer to such delights, was immediate. The world was within minutes totally transformed. The Dutchman at once became my best friend, related surely to my mother's family from Breda, the music suddenly took on a depth of meaning I would never have suspected and I found myself effortlessly moving from bar to dance-floor – old wooden planks tacked together with sand seeping through the seams – where I was welcomed with open arms by Mustapha and where we danced our way through several more beers and, I suppose, well into the early hours of the morning. Mustapha, who by now had become my Prince Charming and the sexiest dancing partner I'd ever known.

When and how the evening ended I shall never really know. Suffice it to say I awoke the following morning in the dunes, most of my clothes scattered to the four winds with Mustapha, now clearly my 'Guardian Angel' No.1, at my side. It took little time putting two and two together and realising that this was certainly an evening to remember for ever, like it or not. I set about pulling myself together while taking much comfort in a saying attributed to Sir Arnold Bax, the composer. "Try everything once in life, except incest and English country dancing." Whatever had taken place among the dunes in the early hours it certainly wasn't incest – phew! And whatever the antics on the dance-floor they were a million miles removed from the stately English Morris dancing I'd once witnessed at a vicarage tea party and village fête in Oxfordshire. Phew! again – Sir Arnold would thus surely not entirely disapprove.

"Plans for today will be mine and mine alone," I repeated to myself as I plodded back to the cabin, Mustapha in tow, in search of a much-needed coffee. A seedy establishment indeed, I couldn't help but notice in the sober light of day, the music still playing – ghastly music – with the Dutchman –seedy too – collecting up empty beer bottles strewn all over the floor. He broke off to relieve me of a sizable wad of dirhams – had we really drunk that much beer? No way of telling. We left after I'd told Mustapha of my plans to take the taxi back, to retrieve my rucksack from the hotel and to take the next bus out of town.

Conveniently enough, Mohamed chose to appear just as we were boarding the taxi. His appeals for me to stay another day went un-answered, and it was reassuring to feel that I was now taking back control. Reassuring, too, to know how much the taxi was going to cost. Less reassuring was the fact that I had no idea whatsoever how much to give Mohamed and Mustapha for their 'services' rendered.

My first feeble attempts at haggling and price-bargaining took place in that taxi back to Tetouan. They had me over a barrel. I was no match for them and surely paid over and above the going rates, if there was indeed such a thing. I vowed there and then never to put myself in a similar position again. Haggling and bargaining should always take place before, not after. Good to have learnt at least that lesson for future reference.

Goodbye to my 'guides' and thank you to them too when, later, I was told that Tetouan was a nest of vipers with a bad reputation for uncouth youths carrying knives and ready to use them on their selected victims. I'd been lucky with Mohamed and Mustapha and should henceforth take all sensible precautions.

Early afternoon saw me back at the Hole of Calcutta and on a bus bound south to Fez. Fez, together with Cairo and Damascus, one of the three largest medinas in the world, one of the oldest (8th/9th century) and today still totally intact. I now knew roughly what to expect – Tetouan and a lot more in addition. I was not to be disappointed. The bus trundled in after a spectacular six-hour drive and left me outside the Bab Bou Jeloud, one of the main gates into the medina. I now made an immediate dive for the nearest one-night cheap hotel, firmly fending off countless would-be guides and now knowing the prices I'd be asked for a room.

The following morning, armed with a small pocket guide-book, I set off on my own to discover the delights of Morocco's cultural, spiritual and intellectual heartland. Far from resembling an aspic-preserved museum, the Fez medina remained a living, earthy (yet car-free) town. Apart from electricity and improved plumbing little had changed. Venturing through its main horseshoe gateways was an immersive and almost bewildering foray into a labyrinthine knot of narrow streets, lanes and alleys punctuated with dead-end squares. Thoroughfares twist and turn, rise and fall among warrens of homes that meld with shared walls and rooftops.

There's a romantic, almost child-like, pleasure in getting lost in this low-rise urban tangle. The challenge lies in seeking out its monuments – ancient mosques and elaborate madrasas (religious colleges) with stunning decorative courtyards, tomb-shrines or discreet hammams and crumbling fondouks (caravanserais – inns where merchants, pilgrims and their horses and camels may rest). In the middle of it all is the 11th century tannery, one of the oldest in the world and still fully operational – a sight to be seen and a pungent smell never to be forgotten. Above all the Al-Kairaouine, one of Africa's oldest and largest mosques also the oldest existing continually operating university in the world according to UNESCO and Guinness World Records, founded in 859 AD. One wonders what was happening in Oxford and Cambridge in that year. Not much: nothing significant would stir there for 400 years.

After a full week spent within the walls of this magnificent medina, overawed by the beauty of what I was seeing, it was not long before I understood what people meant when they talked about the Islamic Golden Age – that period of cultural, economic and scientific flourishing in the Arab world between the 9th and 15th centuries. Education played a major part in that society when scholars and students gathered together in the pursuit of knowledge. Studies ranged from Law, Theology, Philosophy and Metaphysics to Algebra, Geometry, Trigonometry and Calculus to Astronomy, Physics, Chemistry, Biology and more besides, for example the study and practice of poetry and music. A Golden Age indeed.

The end of the week saw me on the return journey north and homewards. Part bus, part train, part hitch-hiking, avoiding Tetouan, saluting in passing Andalusia, where the Islamic Golden Age had reached its zenith, ignoring the Cevennes, I sped back to the UK in time for another summer term at Marlborough.

Such was my first visit to Morocco – an inspiration. Colleagues expecting to hear about the Cévennes were instead regaled with stories about the beach of Tetouan. Hugh de Weltdon Weldon, the housemaster, soon heard about my exploits and at once informed me that his great friend Chris Oliver, from Peterhouse, Cambridge had just been appointed to the faculty of languages at the university of Marrakech. Hugh had been invited by Chris to spend the summer holidays in Marrakech. Would I like to go too?

Indeed I would, and it was only a few months later that I found myself with Hugh jet-bound to Marrakech for the summer. Marrakech was awash with celebrities and Chris, charismatic and highly sociable, was in the middle of it all. The ex-pat social scene was humming, with Yves Saint Laurent presiding at its apex, and with invitations to drinks, dinners and parties raining down on us daily – hardly time to visit the wonders of the Medina.

Chris' entourage included the likes of Robert Carrier, the restaurateur, who with the opening of his restaurant, Carrier's in Camden Passage, Islington, had spearheaded the 1960s cult of the bistro, and his book *Great Dishes of the World* had become a best-seller. To be invited at a later date to his magnificent riad for a slap-up Christmas lunch was indeed an unforgettable experience. If I thought Moroccan dishes would be the order of the day I was much mistaken – turkey and trimmings followed by Christmas pudding. Delicious, needless to say.

Billy Willis, the inspirational American interior decorator, was also a great party-giver, with extravagant gatherings of extravagant people in his extravagant Dar Noujoum, a rambling riad which was once a royal harem. Angus McBean, the Scottish portrait photographer and theatre set designer, was also on the party circuit. So too the likes of John Shepherd and Christopher Wanklyn, the Canadian painter, both friends of Paul and Jane Bowles, the literary gurus from Tangiers.

When not party-going we'd often sit in the Café Renaissance, Gueliz, with the elderly Sir Claude Auchinleck – the Auk – the World War II Field Marshal and British Supreme Army Commander. There on the terrace we would all eye up the passing local 'trade' – lithe, handsome young Moroccan men doing the rounds. It was hardly surprising that Chris had fallen straight into the Moroccan gay world – these were the people who had set Marrakech alight with their louche, hedonistic lifestyles and their pursuit of *la dolce vita*. An outwardly attractive lifestyle, I had to admit, but perhaps on closer acquaintance it was not always quite up to what it was often cracked up to be.

Be that as it may, my second Moroccan experience was every bit as intriguing as my first, and over the years several more were to follow. Most of them were Marrakech based. Chris was a welcoming host and I would arrive, sometimes alone, sometimes with a friend or friends, and use his base as a *point de départ* for travels around southern Morocco. There were trips into the High Atlas, to the historic towns of Taroudant and Ouarzazate, to Essouira on the coast and down the valley of the Draa to Zagora. Zagora, on the southern border with its sign stating Tombouctou 52 days, the time taken to get to Timbuktu, Mali, on foot or camel. It was in Zagora that Martin Evans, my Marlborough Housemaster friend, took the hired car out into the desert for a night spin and got himself tangled up in a Moroccan army night exercise – tanks, search lights and flares. How he managed to extricate himself and return to the hotel in the early hours shaken, yes, but otherwise unscathed, I shall never understand.

All that was over twenty years past and I'd scarcely given the country a thought since. Perhaps it was because of my mid-life 'crisis' – my move from Marlborough to Le Castéra. I was totally preoccupied by it. But here I was now all those years later in 2001, having heard James eulogizing about a town called Chefchaouen about which I knew nothing, ready and eager to plunge back down memory lane and to Morocco, the country that had captivated me all those years ago.

Chefchaouen here I come.

Chapter 24

Chefchaouen

I took my breakfast that morning on the terrace while observing the Pyrenees rising up in the distance, their snow-capped summits glinting in the early morning spring sun. I imagined they were beckoning me. Look, we're here, they seemed to be saying, just come on over and you're already in Spain. Morocco is the next stop down. No problem.

Problem or not, I'd done my homework and knew I had a good 1500 kms to cover before reaching my Moroccan destination – Chefchaouen. As luck would have it, Mme. Bordes' son Alain ('Titi'), having heard that I was Morocco bound, arrived on the doorstep on the eve of my departure to tell me about the route, which he knew well, being an addict of all things Moroccan. Avoid at all costs, he said, the coast road via Barcelona as heavy traffic and heavy tolls double the cost of the journey. Rather take the motorway through central Spain – cheaper and quieter.

No sooner said than done. I left early, just as dawn was breaking. A two-hour drive on the deserted roads of Gascony took me to the foot of the Pyrenees. A further hour zigzagging my way up, through the ski resort of Saint Lary, up and up to the giddy heights of the Bielsa tunnel – surely one of the smallest of its kind giving access to

Spain. Ten minutes through the tunnel, not another vehicle in sight, and then out onto the Spanish southern slopes, bathed in morning sun, with its monasteries perched perilously high overlooking the sparkling turquoise lakes which filled many a valley.

From here I began the short drive to Huesca and the toll-free *autovia* that was to take me the full way to Algeciras and its ferries over to Morocco. The arid country surrounding Huesca set me thinking of George Orwell's *Homage to Catalonia*, in which he vividly describes the hardships he suffered here while fighting Franco and the Fascists during the Civil War.

Saragossa by lunchtime and then the long three-hour haul on the plateau to Madrid and its nightmare ring roads and spaghetti junctions. To come through all that for the first time unscathed and then find myself on the right road to Grenada and Malaga I counted as a major achievement.

It was with dusk falling and 1100kms. on the clock that I found myself approaching Jaèn, a town nestling high in the lap of two fine mountain peaks. I wound my way up the hill and found an imposing central hotel, the Hotel Xauen, where I asked for a room for the night, saying I would be travelling on the following day to Morocco and Chefchaouen. At the mention of the name Chefchaouen the woman at the reception desk suddenly perked up and asked if I knew the connection between the hotel's name, the Xauen, and Chefchaouen, or Chaouen as it was formerly known. She explained in her halting English that Xauen was simply the old Castillian spelling for Chaouen – they were one and the same place. She then went on to tell of the historical connection between Jaèn and Chaouen – the two names are clearly close, etymologically speaking.

It was in 1492 with the Fall of Grenada that the Muslims' 800-year occupation of much of the Iberian peninsula finally came to an end. With the arrival of King Ferdinand and Queen Isabella and their conquering Catholic armies those Muslims, Jews too, who chose to flee headed for the most part back to Morocco, from whence they had originally come. Those fleeing from Jaèn sought in their Moroccan exile a place to settle that would remind them of their beloved Jaèn.

"And you will see tomorrow, sir, they found exactly that," said my kindly receptionist. "Chaouen, like Jaèn, nestles neatly in the lap of its two fine mountains. It had been founded only some twenty years previously with the construction of its first building, the Kasbah, built with the idea of keeping marauding Portuguese pirates at bay. So the influx of those Andalusian Muslims and Jews after the Spanish Reconquista did much to boost Chaouen's population in its infancy."

I left early the following morning, spurred on by what I had just learnt and anxious to find out more about this old walled town set high in the Rif Mountains, a welcome haven and home to those poor fleeing refugees from all those years past. But first Grenada, where I stopped off to visit and admire the Alhambra – palace, fortress and citadel and one of the finest of the surviving edifices of the Islamic Golden Age. A true wonder to behold. And then down to Malaga and the Mediterranean coast – the *Costa del Sol* – spinning past the fleshpots of Torremolinos, Marbella, Estepone and the like with their pot-bellied Brits basking like bloated whales on the beaches before knocking back the beers in bars serving the Full English Breakfast day and night. Each to their own, I mused, speeding on towards Algeciras and my ferry. Early afternoon saw me safely aboard and sailing past Gibraltar, that reassuring, towering rock of past empire.

"Do you know the origin of the name Gibraltar?" asked the young Moroccan standing on the deck by my side. "Jebel Tariq," he continued. "Jebel meaning mountain in Arabic and Tariq ibn Ziyad being the name of the commander of the first of the Muslim armies to invade the Iberian Peninsula in 711AD."

What I didn't need to be told was that the ferry was taking us to Spanish Ceuta, that enclave which, like Melilla and a smattering of offshore rocks and islands, Spain had retained after recognising the independence of Morocco in 1956. That much I remembered from my first unscheduled visit some thirty years past. The road to the border and frontier post, too, brought back the memories of the bumpy bus ride, with standing room only. The customs post was as chaotic as I remembered it – Moroccans don't queue, they merely push and shove, cars inching forward from all sides, nosing and nudging, horns blaring in general frustration.

I was prepared too for the Morocco I was now entering for a second time – poorly-lit streets, sub-standard road surfaces, the buildings generally in need of a facelift. Here we were back in the Third World, and I reminded myself that allowances were going to have to be made if disappointment was to be avoided. Avoid comparisons and relish the contrasts, I advised myself.

The road to Chaouen passed through Tetouan, or rather round it, since a bypass had since been built and then up and up into the Rif mountains. After an hour's drive I rounded a bend in the road to find Chaouen and my destination set up on high on the slopes of the mountain opposite – a fine setting indeed. The last five kilometres were one long zig-zag, up and up still further, leading one firstly through the outskirts of the town, already half-tumbling down the mountainside, then on towards the little walled Old Town (medina). To reach the medina, Chaouen's jewel, I found myself driving down the main boulevard of the Spanish New Town (Ville Nouvelle). The Spanish, having arrived in 1920 to create a Spanish Protectorate in the north of the country, wisely followed the example of the French, who had established their own Protectorate in the south. Neither occupying power had wanted to interfere with the old medinas – they simply left them as they were and merely tacked on their modern 'quartiers' outside the medina walls. Chaouen is a perfect example of this practice. The main boulevard, Bd. Hassan II – a mini-Champs Elysées – leads straight up to the main medina gate. Broad and tree-lined, it is home to the banks, the post office, Maroc Telecom and upmarket cafés. At one end the formal gardens of the Place Mohamed V – a mini-Place de l'Etoile – Charles de Gaulle designed by the Spanish painter Juan Miro – grouped around it the Governor's house, the Catholic church and the army officers' club-house. At the other end the army barracks (now a school) backed up right onto the medina walls and were therefore well-placed to keep a watchful eye on the native population.

Now on foot I made straight for the main medina gate, Bab el Ain, squeezed in through, thereby leaving behind me the 20th century with its tarmac, traffic and fumes, its harsh noises and stress and finding in front of me a little world of another era – gentler, friendlier, more intimate. It was a pure delight to walk its narrow higgledy-piggledy cobbled streets with its little shops on either side, their contents on display and spilling over onto the streets – goods of all manner of descriptions to be either bought or bartered for by the jostling crowds of both locals and tourists alike. Local leatherwork, ceramics from Fez, locally woven woollen clothing, carpets and copper, djellabas and babouches, inlayed marquetry trinket boxes of Moroccan cedarwood, spices, scents and fragrances galore and so much more besides – a feast for the eyes wherever one turned.

It was a pure delight, too, to open my ears to the unfamiliar sound of the *muezzin*, the call to prayer, issuing forth from a mosque around every corner. The sound of the braying of donkeys as they transport gas bottles and crates of soft drinks to and fro, the sound of the bleating of the goats as they clattered past on their way up to their mountain pastures – all was music to the ear. Unfamiliar smells, too, abounded – freshly-cut mint on a stall, bread baking in the local bakehouse. Leather goods hanging in the streets, cedar being cut by the carpenter in his doorway – these smells too beguiled as they wafted in the clear mountain air. And was that the hint of a puff of marijuana – known as *kif* to the locals – as I passed by that tumbledown café?

It wasn't long before I emerged into the main central square, La Place Uta el Hammam, with narrow little alleyways running off it in every direction. Here was clearly the beating heart of the medina with the hotels, restaurants and cafés vying with each other for the prime locations opposite the Grand Mosque and the Kasbah, the impressive fortified citadel built in 1472 to keep plundering Portuguese pirates at bay.

Just a three-minute walk off this bustling central square I found the hotel, L'Hôtel Cordoba, for my first night in Chaouen. There too I made my first Chaoueni friends – Hakim with his little grocery store opposite the hotel and his brother Mouad, a carpenter. My first evening spent with them told me much of the town which their family had inhabited for generations, and certainly enough to keep me sightseeing and discovering its secrets for the whole of the following day. I visited Ras el Maa where the river cascaded down, drawing the women folk to the wash-houses through which the river flowed. There they chattered away, scrubbing and scrubbing carpets, rugs, clothes, linen sheets all jumbled, piled high at their sides and waiting to be washed and then dried in the sun. I climbed up to the Spanish mosque at the end of the day for the view and to capture the sun setting over the town and turning all to a subtle shade of amber, the 'golden hour' indeed. I discovered the Mellah, the quarter where the Jews were allowed to live. I found the best carpet-seller in town, the best restaurant and, of course, the one and only bar.

It was only at the end of the day that I found the answers to the questions I'd asked myself at the beginning of the day. Namely, why does this little Chaoueni medina appear so different from the Moroccan medinas I already knew (Marrakech, Fez, Meknès, etc)? Where lie the differences? It was only when I remembered the origins of the first inhabitants of Chaouen, in exile in Morocco, that the penny dropped. Here, indeed, was a town with much more in common with many a mountain village and town set back in the Andalusian interior than with other Moroccan towns. It was first conceived as an Andalusian town and remains to this day Andalusian in looks, feel and flavour. The dominant white and blue limewash of facades and courtyards, the blues (both Oxford and Cambridge) of doors and woodwork and the pretty wrought ironwork surrounding windows are all distinctly southern Spanish in character. Chaouen doesn't set out to impress. It sets out to charm and I returned to the hotel and the brothers that evening entirely captivated by the delights of this friendly little town set high in the Rif mountains, *la perle du Rif*.

"Hakim", said I that evening, "can you take me to a house agent tomorrow?"

"No", came the immediate answer. "There aren't any. If you want to buy a house just go down to the square, sit in the cafés and tell everybody what you're looking for. Then just sit back and wait."

This I did, and spent the two following days being shown everything from ruins to riads. Everyone seemingly had a house to sell – 'seemingly' being the operative word – and the foreigner expressing the desire to buy property comes wearing a halo with flashing dollar signs and thereby attracting the attention of all and sundry, local rogues and riff-raff included. So one's first job is to try to detect and deter the latter, who will attempt to sell you houses which either don't exist or which they don't own, or only partly. Then locate the serious offers – easier said than done, and several fail at this early stage, to their own later cost.

Then one needs to know fairly precisely what one is hoping to find. In my case a house a) in the medina b) low price range (£6,000 – £10,000), small and to be renovated and extended if possible, c) with a terrace and views, d) with its own independent entry. This last feature is not necessarily all that easy to come by, with many medina houses served by a communal 'rat run' leading into a communal courtyard. Not that one is anti-neighbours, just that one doesn't want to be living in their pockets. In a medina one is inevitably going to be living cheek by jowl, but the ideal is to find the maximum privacy amongst it all.

It didn't take me long to find a property that ticked all the boxes. I was lucky on several scores. Firstly the owner's son, Abdelmalek (who was to become a close friend), was a teacher of English in the top lycée, so there was no scope for misunderstandings and negotiations through the solicitor could proceed quickly and smoothly. Secondly, the Municipal Architect, whose permission was required to add an extra floor to give not only more space but also an enhanced view of the encircling mountains, turned out to be Abdelmalik's uncle. Permission granted. Thirdly, Abdelmalik took me straight to Ghali, the honest builder I needed, a builder who, unusually for Chaouen, came with his own plumber, electrician and carpenter in tow. This made life much simpler and it wasn't long before the building plans and costs had been knocked into shape – usually in Gali's café and on the back of an envelope – including the transport of bricks, sand and cement on donkey-back. I discovered later that Gali had been surprised that I hadn't haggled over his estimate, which is usually to be expected in such circumstances. I simply forgot. But I too was surprised – surprised that such a large extension which doubled the surface area of the house could be done at such low cost. I was even more surprised when it was explained to me that the 50 dirhams (£3) I was paying the builder's labourer was not the hourly rate – it was for a full eight-hour working day.

Yes, indeed, I'd been lucky. Added to which I managed to hit it off with the neighbours, who were mostly Abdelmalik's extended family, from the start. Building work was finished in eight months, on time and on budget. Lucky me, I thought, whenever I was later to hear of sorry stories of foreigners encountering difficulties – rogue builders, dodgy finances, angry neighbours… and worse.

When Fouad of 'my' café on the Place Uta el Hammam, the central square, later heard I'd bought in the Quartier Autiwi he said I had been blessed.

"But why blessed, Fouad?" I asked.

"Because Autiwi is on the east side of the medina," he replied.

"And so?"

"So you're that little bit nearer Mecca. You are indeed blessed, Monsieur John."

Nearly twenty years have now elapsed since I bought Dar John (John's house) in Autiui, the 'blessed' quartier of Chaouen, and it has indeed turned out to be a blessing. No longer tied to Le Castéra and my restaurant, Chai John, I was now free to live out my Moroccan dream whenever school holidays permitted – winter, spring and summer. Equipping and furnishing Dar John was my first preoccupation. From the outset I decided on an English interior – not for me the Moroccan zellige tiles with their elaborate Islamic geometric patterns. An English interior designed for comfort and to cater for the whims of a middle-aged Englishman – the open wood fire (wood free courtesy Mohamed of the Forestry Commission), my books, my piano, air-conditioning, wifi, broadband, BBC TV and radio, hot water bottles, slippers. (Pipe? No. No pipe yet – just the odd draw on the kif-pipe. Most relaxing and giggle-inducing.) Not forgetting the 'Olympic' (irony) swimming pool on the terrace. Ah! My terrace! *Mon petit paradis!* It all goes on up there…eating, drinking, bathing, gardening, sunning, sleeping, and more…recollecting, dreaming, planning, too. The next move? (Mauritania here I come?)

And all this under the impassive, majestic gaze of that mighty mountain looming all-encompassing above. Oh that mountain! Black and threatening, green and fertile, brown and parched, amber and gentle, depending on time and season. I will look up unto the hills, so says the psalmist, from whence cometh my help. Help? Maybe not. Inspiration? Certainly, yes, as I sit there peacefully passing the time of day and night. Not much to disturb me up there, especially now that I've disconnected the doorbell, the cheeky ringing of which was starting to become a silly-little-girl-game, much to the disapproval of the (sensible) little boys. ("Holà, Monsieur John – it's not us. It's the girls.") The varied sounds drifting up from the alley below are gentle ones for the most part, punctured from time to time by something more arresting.

Sounds. Yes, here surely lies a dichotomy, an incongruity between 'their' sounds and 'my' sounds. Incoming sounds. Outgoing sounds. Among the former the five times daily ¼ tone wail of the Muezzin (Call to Prayer), the shriek of kids playing in the alley below (47% of Chaouenis under 15yrs old), the clank of gas bottles being unloaded from donkey backs, the piercing calls of the street vendors, the pleading mother-to-child cries of "Agi! Ali! Agi!" ("Come 'ere! Ali! Come 'ere!), the twice daily clatter of goat's hooves as a herd of twenty or so charges up off to, then back down from grazing-grounds on the mountain sides. A veritable mini-Charge of the Light Brigade with pungent cheese smells accompanying...

All this in stark contrast to 'my' sounds – those sounds for the most part which are unfamiliar to Arab ears and drifting down to them from on high and at any time of day or night. John Humphries harrying a politician on BBC Radio 4's Today, Jeremy Paxman barking on BBC 2, the BBC Proms with myself and other likeminded Brits singing along on the Last Night, me staggering through/ murdering a Bach Prelude and Fugue, a Schubert Sonata, Debussy's Clair de Lune depending on mood and moment... goodness knows what they make of it all. Not much probably. Certainly Mehdi, my teenage neighbour and most frequent visitor, seems to take it all in his Muslim stride, even if he could no more spot a Bach Fugue than fly through the air. (He persists in telling me that the prophet

Mohamed (peace be with him) used to fly in the air on a horse with golden wings. *("Oui, Monsieur John, c'est vrai! C'est vrai!")* Who am I to tell him otherwise? He'll frequently drop in and cook us delicious kefta tagines, seemingly impervious to the strange sounds emanating from all around, although he did surprise me one day by asking "Monsieur John, why is it called a Prom?" No, not surprising really since we've been watching and listening to them for some years now.

When it comes to the battle of the sounds, however, I have to concede defeat. It was the start of Ramadan and nobody had warned me. I was awoken from my slumbers at around three in the morning by the distant beating of a drum, the intensity and volume of which grew as the bass drummer drew closer and closer to my house, marching down my alleyway, past the bedroom and within inches of my tender ear, by now burning with apprehension and awe and wonder at the indescribably complex syncopation of the beat (the kids, though, manage perfectly to imitate it on their plastic bottles). It was the mother of all drumming of all time to awaken the sleeping faithful (not to mention the dead) to get up and eat before sunrise. What a penance, I repeat to myself. And so, so unfair! I, a poor Anglican, made to suffer this nightly assault on my fragile person through the full length of the Holy Month of Ramadan! (Talk about the English townie 'gone rustic', whingeing on about the village church clock-chimes and the dawn cock-crows – he's heard nothing to compare with the ferocity of the nightly Ramadan drum).

Not that I spend all my time cocooned at home, content though I am there in my little nest surrounded by my toys. I'm indeed equally happy to stride out beyond the blue front door and into the very different world of the medina and beyond.

"But, John, what do you actually DO up in Chaouen all the time?" asked an English ex-pat 'chattering class' friend living in Tangiers. What he actually meant was what do I do *buried* up in Chaouen all the time. He clearly wanted to know who gives the cocktail parties and who is invited. To such people I'm sometimes tempted to reply, Winnie the Pooh-like, "Sometimes I sits and thinks. Sometimes I just sits." To tell the truth there are no cocktail parties and I don't in the slightest way feel 'buried'.

My daily routine is a simple one and varies little. Mid-morning sees me leave the house to take any one of a number of alleyways downhill towards the central square. A gentle stroll punctured by cheerful greetings from old and young alike ("Holà, Monsieur John!") as that rare species the Englishman in Chaouen slowly winds his way down towards the Plaza Uta el Hammam. Now is the chance to drop in to see the artisans and others who've done work for me and whose little workshops line the way down. Workers in leather and wrought-iron, the carpenter, the upholsterer, Mohamed the teacher and part-time calligrapher, Mustapha with his bric-à-brac emporium and Hatim the hairdresser, amongst others.

Late morning and it is now time to make tracts for Chez Fouad – 'my' café opposite the Kasbah and Grande Mosque and a great place for both people-meeting and people-watching. The Plaza becomes opera-set and stage, the people passing through actors. The school-children running, playing, swinging their satchels at each other, the little old lady always dressed in green severely handicapped and having slowly to propel herself forwards on all fours, small gaggles of wide-eyed tourists, a pair of policemen escorting a handcuffed youth towards the town prison, the two old town 'musicians' (if one can call them such), one thumping on a beaten up old drum, the other scratching on the remains of a violin, the local collection of dotty, dippy, scatty crackpots who in another country would have been confined to a psychiatric unit but who here are allowed to wander harmlessly the streets unmolested.

On occasions I will spot the unmistakable – the English public-school boy back-packer on his gap year. Many are the coffees I've shared with these young students-to-be and vivid reminders of my own public school past – once, indeed, with an Old Marlburian who found so much to say when comparing notes with me about the life and times at Marlborough College that he ended up by staying on with me for several days.

High drama too can be met with sitting in that beautiful square. On more than a few occasions disputes have broken out between neighbouring competing café owners resulting in verbal abuse, punch-ups and the general throwing around of both tables and chairs. Clients will automatically jump to their feet, wrestle with the assailants and eventually separate them. An uneasy truce will be established. The most dramatic of events I've witnessed there occurred one day when I heard a roar emitted from the far end of the Plaza from whence there emerged a youth, knife in hand, running for his life and pursued by a second youth wielding a rock, yes, a veritable rock, which he eventually and just in front of me, flung with full force at the fleeing knife-holder. The rock missed its target, the fleeing man's head, by inches. Had the aim been spot-on I guess I'd have had a dead man at my feet.

Other days will be less dramatic – days when I'll simply read my book or chat to Fouad, the café-owner. Fouad has a soft spot for me in so far as I'd been a good friend of Les the Welshman, who had been Fouad's best client and over the years had become a close family friend. Les would arrive regularly every morning on the dot of ten o'clock at the café – he called it the Office, as I now do – take the same seat, drink the same number of coffees (three), sniff the same number of pinches of snuff (number unknown), talk politics with one if one wanted (he'd been a left-wing sociologist), then leave on the dot of midday. I never once saw him pay and was only told why several years after his untimely death. Fouad had been told by the local fortune-teller that there was considerable treasure buried under his house, so he persuaded Les to go to London, buy a metal detector to bring back and smuggle through the customs into Morocco. This was duly done. Since Fouad couldn't afford to pay for the metal detector it was agreed that Les should have credit for two thousand cups of coffee. The outcome was that Fouad found no treasure and Les died with almost one thousand cups of coffee still owing to him.

Maybe Fouad has a conscience. Several years having passed I am now one of the few remembering Les and the only one still paying five dirhams for my glass of tea when the price has since doubled. Not that I really gain much by this since Fouad's tea, Lipton, I don't like and end up bringing my own supply of Earl Grey with me. My five dirhams simply pays for the hot water and a cloud of milk.

I'll then usually leave the 'Office' at around one o'clock, wandering further down through the medina to Bab el Ain and coming out into the Ville Nouvelle and the 21st century. Here the banks, the post office, the meat and fish market, the fruit and vegetable stalls await me. The shopping once done, I'll walk down further to the taxi rank and take a ride back up to Bab Mahruk at the top of the medina, from where I can walk – downhill – back to base.

Afternoons are usually lazy affairs. A light lunch on the terrace, followed by a snooze, reading, listening to music, playing the piano. Early evening might see me keeping a rendezvous at the one and only bar in town. Then back home often to prepare drinks/supper for friends and neighbours. Here young Mehdi plays an increasingly important part. Not only does he cook but he has become a general factotum, seeing to it that the house is well stocked and wanting for nothing.

With house guests staying we'll often take the car for an outing. Tetouan and Ouazzane are an hour away. Neither caters for the tourist trade –yet – and their medinas have a much more genuine feel about them for that very reason. With the arrival of the warmer days come trips to Oued Laou, the closest fishing village on the Mediterranean coast, a spectacular forty-minute drive away through the Rif mountains. Sometimes there's a day trip with swimming and a fish tagine at midday, sometimes driving east further along the coast road, as yet totally unspoilt with arresting sea and mountain views on either side. Here is what the Côte d'Azur would have looked like in the 1900s, I imagine. A two-hour drive takes one to El Jebbah, a charming if somewhat scruffy village spilling into the sea with its little harbour brimming with fishing boats bobbing in the gentle breeze. Old men mend their nets, young boys dive off the jetty. The distant chugging of a boat out at sea, seagulls calling. Otherwise almost total peace and quiet as the population dozes in the warmth of the afternoon sun.

We have an evening meal here in the one and only restaurant, an overnight stay in the one and only hotel, then the following day back to Chaouen, striking inland this time and returning on the Rif mountain road, one of the most scenic routes in Morocco.

So my Tangier English ex-pat 'chattering-class' friends should have no cause to worry about my being bored sat up in my Chaoue-ni mountain eerie. There's quite enough to do when and if I want to do it. As for Tangier – ah! Well, that's another matter. Tangier and Chaouen – as different as chalk from cheese. *Vive la différence!*

Chapter 25

Tangier Tales

Like most of the Mediterranean ports Tangier has a long history, due largely to its location, strategically positioned at the entrance of the Mediterranean. Both Greeks and Phoenicians used it as a trading post and the Romans then made it the capital (Tingis) of the province Mauritania Tingitana. Further invasions followed by the Vandals, the Byzantines and then in 705 AD the Arabs from the East, who set about suppressing the native Berber tribes. It was from here that the Arabs launched their first assault into Europe. remaining the main power in the Iberian Peninsula right until 1492, when they were finally pushed back into Africa by the Catholic armies of Ferdinand and Isabella of Spain. The Portuguese had captured the city in 1471, only to hand it over to the British 200 years later as part of the dowry of Catherine of Braganza, wife to Charles II. Morocco regained control under Sultan Moulay Ismail in 1679 and retained it until the mid-19th century, when North Africa once again began to interest the European powers. By 1912 Morocco had become two Protectorates with the Spanish in the North and the French in the South. Ensuing disagreements between Spain, France and the British over Tangier saw its transformation into an International Zone in 1924 governed by the major European powers and the USA. The

Zone rapidly gained a reputation for tolerance, diversity of culture and religion, and bohemianism, attracting visitors from far and wide.

The first literary giant to arrive was the American author, composer and translator Paul Bowles. Immediately inspired by the multiplicity of the city's culture and customs, he settled in 1947 and lived there for 52 years, to the end of his life. Hotly in pursuit followed the Beat Generation – the post-World War Two American counter-culture movement, attracted by Tangier's permissive and decadent atmosphere and the free access to drugs and sex to cater for all tastes. Jack Kerouac, Allen Ginsberg, Truman Capote, William Burroughs, Tennessee Williams – the list is endless.

Artists, too, had been beguiled – Delacroix and Matisse in the past and latterly Francis Bacon. Others seeking to exchange the gloom and rationing of post-war Europe for the total sense of exotic *dépaysement* Tangier had to offer were quick to jump on the bandwagon – Joe Orton, his lover Kenneth Halliwell, Kenneth Williams and the Rolling Stones among others were frequent visitors.

Traces of Tangier's grimy literary history can still be found – the seedy hotels and bars where they lived, overindulged on drink and drugs, touted for sex and generally abandoned themselves to the louche lifestyle which often was seriously to undermine their state of health, both physical and mental.

The city also attracted those on the run from the law, jail-breakers, money-launderers, sex-offenders, drug-dealers, anyone wanting to leave behind a murky past to carve out a new identity for himself on a new continent. Indeed, Tangier's history is littered with the names of those who would reinvent themselves. There was Barbara Hutton, The American debutante, socialite and heiress ('the poor little rich girl') in Sidi Hosni, her palace near the Kasbah, queening it when presiding over lavish parties attended by camels, snake-charmers, belly-dancers and the 'blue men' all brought in from the high Atlas. There was The Hon. David Herbert, second son of the 15th Earl of Pembroke, interior decorator, portraitist, cabaret singer, writer, aesthete and international party-goer (particularly the latter). He attempted to out-socialise everyone else by holding daily lunch and dinner parties for fellow aristocrats, the rich and the famous. His house on the Mountain, exquisitely furnished and bulging with family china, silver and portraits from the family home, Wilton House, was the mecca and an almost compulsory port of call for the aspiring social climber. Here for almost 50 years he lived out a pampered existence, a ruthless snob for some, for others a charismatic charmer. Then there was Terence MacCarthy, self-styled Tadhg V, The MacCarthy Mor, Prince of Desmond and Lord of Kerslawny, who had had the Irish Genealogical Office mistakenly confer on him the title of the Chief of the MacCarthy clan, allowing him to set up quasi-chivalric orders and then to confer (sell!) titles of nobility to his supporters, making him considerable sums of money on the American heritage tourism market of the time. Only after several years did it transpire that MacCarthy was a colossal hoaxer and that his claims were based on falsely fabricated documentation. His ancestors were in fact ordinary Belfast working people, with the surname of his paternal grandfather listed on his birth certificate as MacCartney.

Hutton, Herbert and MacCarthy – just three names plucked at random from a long list of Tangier oddballs, rogues and imposters whose extravagant personae and exploits were still the talk of the town when I first set foot there in 2002. Here is a place living on its past reputation, I thought to myself, remembering that the Dublin I'd known as a student had also lived on its rich literary heritage. Dublin of the 1960s and Tangier now at the dawn of a new century, both down at heel and with no signs of future investment, I concluded.

It was early on a Sunday morning that I left Chaouen and drove the two hours into central Tangier to St. Andrew's Church and the 11 am Sunday service, a good place to start out on my quest for like-minded ex-pats, I thought. They were there all right, even if more than outnumbered by an impressive posse of sub-Saharan African Anglicans, temporarily holed up in Tangier and waiting, I was told, for the propitious moment to slip into Europe undetected via the Straits of Gibraltar.

Hassan 1, Sultan of Morocco, had donated land to the British community to build an Anglican church. An attractive design, it is notably Moorish in style with a bell-tower shaped like a minaret, and is surrounded by a well-tended church yard and cemetery – a haven of peace in a busy city. It is here I first met the churchwarden and administrator of all things St. Andrew's.

"Oh! You know he not only runs St. Andrew's. He's also very much the doyen of the British ex-pats here", says Mickey Raymond, member of the congregation and former interior decorator from London.

"Oh! You do know he's not only the doyen of the ex-pats here, he's also very much THE icon of London's Swinging Sixties," says Jonathan Dawson, the prince of Tangier party-throwers.

And so he was. Christopher Gibbs, British antiques dealer and collector, was also a highly influential figure in men's fashion (the first man to wear flared trousers in 1961? The first to be ordering flower print shirts by 1964?) and much in demand as an interior designer. And oh so much more! The Old Etonian (he was asked to leave early, he later told me!) 'King of Chelsea' and inventor of 'Swinging London', rubbing shoulders with Mick Jagger, Marianne Faithful and the like. His interest in all things Moroccan had come early in life and by the time I first set foot in Tangier he'd already been coming and going to and from England for many years and living in some style on the Old Mountain with his partner, Peter Hinwood of The Rocky Horror Show fame.

Meeting and getting to know Christopher meant the doors of St. Andrew's were immediately open to me, and it was only shortly afterwards that I found myself from time to time deputising for the organist, bashing out the hymns and throwing in a few voluntaries for good measure. Nothing too serious. And since the St. Andrew's crowd were also the party-going crowd, I soon found myself swept up into drinks and lunches and suppers, studiously avoiding, however, the bridge parties. An interesting party circuit it was by and large, with people well acquainted with Tangier and its colourful past. Eccentric local ex-pat artists, sculptors, interior decorators, bohemians and *bons vivants* mixed happily with others passing through. Those I chanced upon varied from Lebanese princes, genuine or not, to Carol Thatcher, Suzy Burton (fourth wife to Richard Burton) and Lord Montagu of Beaulieu among others. His Lordship showed interest in a day in Chaouen with lunch chez moi. The latter proved impossible, his invalid chair being unequal to the sharp incline of the narrow cobbled streets. A high-profile lunch in the main square was the best we could do.

It was at an embassy party in the Continental Hotel that I first met Georgina Butler, British Consul in Tangier, and Haydon Warren-Gash, British Ambassador to Morocco and world-renowned lepidopterist with several species of butterflies named after him. Conversation warmed up instantly when I let slip that I had 'done' twenty-five years at Marlborough. Warren-Gash, an Old Marlburian himself, had had a son and nephew there, and Georgina Butler two daughters, all of whom I knew. It was perhaps unfortunate that Georgina should there and then choose to reveal my Marlborough nickname – Silky Wilky – to the amusement of all present, even if it didn't deter the Ambassador from appointing me as British Consular Warden in Chefchaouen shortly afterwards.

"Consular Warden? What does that actually involve?"

"Nothing much really. Just a Brit. pair of ears and eyes in situ, that's all. Oh, and invitations to the Queen's Birthday Party at the Embassy in Rabat."

The Rt. Hon. The Lord Mark Malloch-Brown KCMG, PC, one-time United Nations Deputy Secretary-General and Minister of State at the Foreign and Commonwealth Office (*and* Old Marlburian), seemingly got news of my appointment through the Marlborough grapevine.

"Consular Warden? Silky Wilky? Really? Jolly good, he's now on the bottom rung of the FCO. But he'd better get a hell of a move on if he ever wants to be an ambassador!"

The Rubis Bar, in the centre of town and only a short walk from St. Andrew's, is a favourite Sunday watering-hole for those of us who having taken spiritual sustenance from the high altar and are now in search of bodily refreshment in the form of a pre-Sunday lunch apéritif (a 'gargle' or a 'sharpener' in the local vernacular) with tapas to accompany. The Rubis fits the bill because it attracts not only Moroccans – Muslim drinkers looking if not feeling guilty – but also ex-pats and visitors. Many are the times I have been swept up in conversations with others seated at that bar. One Sunday morning I found myself sitting next to a middle-aged Englishman who clearly had a lot to say to the attractive youth at his side. Yarn followed on from yarn with the narrator scarcely drawing breath. Listening more closely, did I not detect a soft Irish lilt in the voice? Yes, surely.

"Dublin?" I boldly interposed.

"Hello. Well, yes and no." came the immediate reply, together with a lengthy and detailed history of the family which had eventually established itself in Ireland, its origins having been in Scotland. MacDonnell was the name and I was speaking to Clan Chief Count Randal MacDonnell of the Glens, Knight of Malta. Here was a man clearly passionately devoted to his family's history, who spoke of it with the authority of the professional genealogist seemingly totally in command of the facts and figures. Generation after generation of MacDonnells were summoned up before me, followed by a concise history of the Order of the Knights of Malta, showing the family connections with that Order. Many hours later I emerged more than a little intoxicated in equal measure on the rich mix of wine and words I had had thrust at me by this loquacious Irishman. I staggered out under the weight of the dates and facts he had plucked from history with such apparent ease. Only later did I discover his Tangier circle had nick-named him Randal MacMonologue.

Such was my first chance meeting with Randal – a well-known Tangier 'character' – and many more encounters were to follow apace. Within the year I found myself with an invitation to stay for a week in Prague – he'd loaned a central flat from a friend. Never could I have wished for a better guide to that fascinating city. Randal knew it all. And never could I have had a better opportunity to find out about his past. From Stonyhurst to Trinity College Dublin to read law. (He never graduated, I later discovered, having preferred the city pubs and clubs to the college lecture halls). He then conveniently came into two substantial family inheritances and promptly took off to see the world. ("John", he would later confide,

"You know, I've never actually had a proper job in my whole life.") Stories of his lengthy stays in California and Hollywood. (Could he really have met all those film stars? Never have I met anyone able to drop so many names in the space of a single breath. Was he really a social secretary to Noel Coward? He could certainly perform a host of his songs at the drop of a hat.) Further stories of travels through the Far East, Australia and the Seychelles were peppered with vivid descriptions of places and people. (All certainly plausible, but embellished and adorned here and there perhaps?)

On returning to Ireland from time to time he would take up with his old friend Gareth Browne (Garech de Brun), the eccentric 'last dandy in Ireland', notable patron of Irish arts, Irish music in particular, and son of Oonagh, a wealthy heiress to the Guinness fortune. (His father, Lord Cranmore and Browne, had had the rare distinction of sitting in the House of Lords for 72 years until his death at the age of 100 without ever once speaking in a debate.) It was to Luggala, a Guinness country house and estate set deep in the Wicklow Mountains, that Gareth would invite Randal to help with the renovation of the house together with the indexing of its library, Randal donning his architectural historian's hat and showing all too rare evidence of a more serious side to him. He had after all, and amongst all the galumphing and prancing around, managed to produce a fine book, *The Lost Houses Of Ireland* (Weidenfeld and Nicolson), an important pictorial record of the demise of 25 Irish country houses and the lives (often eccentric) of those who had lived in them.

In 2008 Luggala saw a major theft of Irish Georgian silver and rare books resulting in a blistering row between the two friends and Randal's escape from what was called the 'silver teapot affair' to Prague. Whatever the truth of the matter, charges were brought, only to be later withdrawn. Thief or not? Suffice it to say that after Prague and with Randal's return to Tangier his funds gradually appeared to dwindle. No longer for him the fine penthouse suites overlooking the Bay of Tangier. Rather a series of rundown medina hostels from which he would emerge on his daily Tangier rounds. These would vary and over the ten years during which I met him when weekending in Tangier (organ-grinding at St. Andrew's on Sunday mornings) I could never be entirely sure where he might not pop up next.

That he was an inveterate trawler of the boulevards was plain for all to see – an already slightly stooped figure shuffling along in a threadbare tweed jacket and baggy trousers, plunging into cafés here and there ever happy to tell another story to anyone willing to listen. And there were many stories and many to listen. Stories about being sent to Gaza to meet Yasser Arafat and the PLO. Stories about the glorious times in Bombay when Gareth Browne was marrying Princess Harshad Purna Devi, times when he was rubbing shoulders with any number of Maharajas and Maharanees you cared to mention – and more besides. The history of Israel from Old Testament times, the history of the European royal dynasties, the multiplicity of discrepancies in the Gospel stories when relating the events of the first Easter morning, the history of the Catholic church, its saints and martyrs – facts and figures tumbled out in profusion from a memory filled to the brim with knowledge gleaned from experiences of a lifetime. A polymath if ever there was one.

On one occasion he was holding forth on antique swords – katana swords, samurai, foils and rapiers – you name it, he knew them. There being only one thing I knew about the world of antique swords, I was determined to put him to the test.

"And where, Randal, does one go to find the best dealer in these matters?"

"Oh, Peter Finer, Duke Street, St. James's – of course." came the instant reply. Correct. Peter Finer's son 'Smudge' had told me just that at Marlborough.

No, Randal was no bullshitter and I learnt it was mostly unwise to take issue with him. Besides, he was an amusing raconteur, provocative too at times. Many the times he earned himself lunches and dinners spinning his yarns. Jonathan Dawson, the prince of party-throwing, would often have him at table to entertain celebrities passing through – the likes of Michael Palin en route south to film his BBC television series *Sahara,* for example. Jonathan and Randal eventually fell out big time, the former considering the latter lacking in sartorial elegance and committing his clothes to the fire. Randal, understandably enough, took exception, the more so having learnt that his Hermes ties had emerged from Jonathan's washing machine strangulated. He latterly took sweet revenge by composing a series of limericks:

> *Some say that our Jonno's a friend of the rich,*
> *While others opine he's a camp Aussie bitch.*
> *But all are agreed who know him, indeed,*
> *That his lifestyle personifies kitsch.*

He would spend time also on more serious matters – hour after hour in 'his' cyber café filling up USB memory sticks for me to store as many hours and days of classical music as I wanted, with the recordings of my preference. At times he would insert 'minor' composers he knew and unknown to me.

"Yes, to be sure, John. Louis Moreau Gottschalk – an American composer and virtuoso pianist living and working in Paris. Knew Chopin, who rated him highly. You'll like him."

Other times he'd be preparing talks to give to the Tangier literati circle – The History of the British in Tangier – while also spending much time and effort in exposing Terence MacCarthy, self-styled Chief of the MacCarthy clan, for the imposter he was eventually proved to be.

Meanwhile however, all was not well with his affairs. Now more or less financially insolvent, he was having to rely on sporadic handouts from an all too absent younger brother, living on the breadline and having to cope with further declining health – he was literally wasting away. Matters were not helped by him being unequal to the task of claiming from both Irish and British authorities the pensions owing to him. He also had a pronounced dislike of 'troubling' doctors with his ailments and steadfastly ignored my advice that he see a doctor ("The body you know, John, cures itself.")

The last months were not easy ones and lung problems made walking difficult. He was more or less limited to Sunday lunches with me, a daily coffee in the Zagora with Philip Ramey, the American composer, who lifted his spirits with talk of the fellow composers Copland, Barber and Bernstein he'd known. Then an evening apéritif with Fouad Menebhi, whose family had played an illustrious part in the history of Tangier and whose great-grandfather, El Mehdi El Menebhi, had been the Minister of War in the 1900s, the only Moroccan ever to have been knighted by a British monarch.

The last Sunday on which I saw him I was bidden to 'his' café – without doubt the seediest in town and known only to the local drop-outs, prostitutes, glue-sniffers and the like. (Yes, Randal's attraction to low-life culture – *la nostalgie de la boue* – had always been obvious to me.) There he was – totally at ease and with a ready audience, regaling all and sundry in his pidgin Arabic.

Thirty minutes and an over-sweet mint tea later we were up and off to the Spanish cathedral, where the Cardinal Archbishop of Rabat was to be introduced to his Tangier flock. No sooner had the Archbishop caught sight of Randal than he took a step forward, clasped him around the neck with both hands and kissed him fervently on both cheeks. He had spotted the pin Randal was wearing in his lapel – the insignia of the Knights of Malta. The two of them were inseparable during the rest of the reception. Randal – open and engaging with all, from the paupers to a prince of the church, and all in the space of a morning.

My constant nagging that he should see a doctor eventually bore fruit. Alas, too late. The following morning a phone call told me he had set out to see Dr Ali, but he had collapsed on the street and was found dead on arrival at the hospital. Kidney failure.

With the passing of Randal a light went out in Tangier. Weekending was never quite the same without him. Who was he? Was he really Clan Chief and the MacDonnell of the Glens? The Earl of Antrim would very definitely say not. It matters little. To those who knew him he was that eccentric Irish fantasist, a man of wit, banter and badinage, sparkling and entertaining in conversation. He died impoverished, but with spirits undimmed.

Shortly afterwards Senator David Norris paid Randal a handsome tribute in the Irish Senate (Seanad Eireann):

"He was a Walter Mitty figure... I remember him parading

himself as Lord of the Isles until I pointed out that that title had been extinguished and absorbed by the title Prince of Wales after the Highland Rebellion of 1745... I remember him parachuting from a helicopter, wearing a kilt and no underwear, into the College Races at College Park, TCD, somewhat to the surprise of Mr Eamon de Valera (President of the Republic). I would like to think Mr de Valera's defective eyesight meant he did not catch a glimpse of the undercarriage as it floated earthwards."

A tribute in the Irish Senate together with practically a half page of an obituary from the *Daily Telegraph* – not bad for someone who'd never had a proper job in his life. RIP.

Home in Le Castéra – the study and birthplace of Boy, Beak and Beyond

Dining room – front right my special friend Simone, aka Madame La Comtesse du Castéra

The terrace. No sign of the Pyrenees today, so no rain tomorrow.

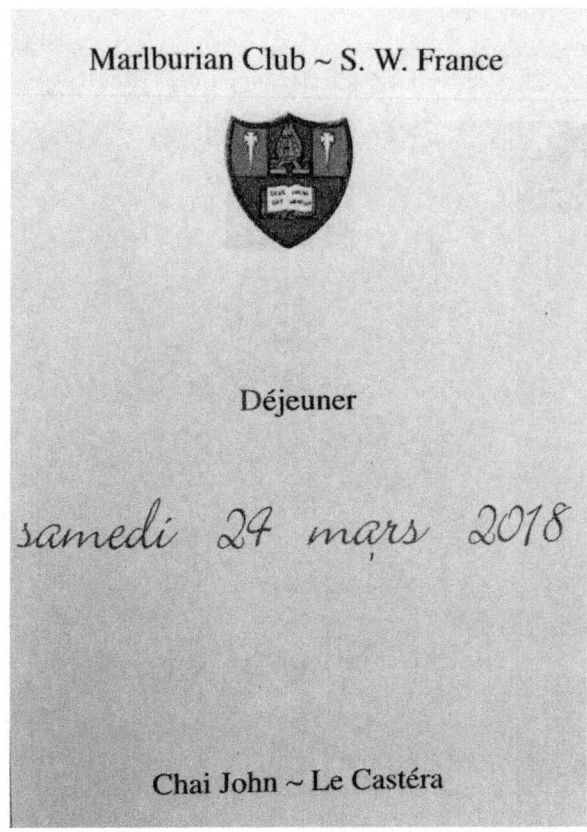

Marlburian Club ~ S. W. France

Déjeuner

samedi 24 mars 2018

Chai John ~ Le Castéra

One of the regular Marlburian Club lunches held at Chai John

Perry Taylor's take on the Master's speech at an M.C. club lunch. Perry is an artist and cartoonist, well known in these parts.

Matéo (21), an apprentice cook unemployed due to Covid 19. Here now as panjandrum and general factotum – cooking for me too, of course.

Simone, looking every inch *la comtesse*

The end of another day

Chapter 26

In Retrospect

Indeed, how wise of Randal, my charismatic and eccentric Irish friend, to have chosen to shuffle off this mortal coil in November 2019, thereby dispensing with the trials and tribulations endured by those of us who are now having to navigate the rough and hostile waters of 2020, the Year of the Plague.

Yesterday is history,
Tomorrow is a mystery
And today is a gift...
That's why they call it the present.

So goes the saying. Today, with the Covid 19 still raging, a gift? A present? A strange one indeed and clearly administered from a poisoned chalice. So no comfort to be gained from writing on the present – a litany of confinements, closures, postponements, cancellations, death and disease. No comfort either to be had casting an eye over the future – a mystery maybe, but now more a litany of uncertainty, doubt, vacillation, hesitation and scepticism.

And so my thoughts in this Year of the Plague have naturally enough directed themselves neither to the present, nor to the future, but rather towards the past. Hence the birth of *Boy, Beak and Beyond*.

Never erase your past, they say. It shapes who you are today and will help you to be the person you'll be tomorrow. Having peeled back the layers of the onion to my boyhood and replaced them layer by layer through youth, adulthood and now old age, I can fully understand those who say one is merely the sum of a myriad of past experiences, good and bad alike. To know me is to know my past. I mirror it. Can we not all say this?

My father, an eloquent example of Edwardian England, used to impart to his children gobbets plucked from the ethos of those times: 'Children should be seen and not heard', 'Cleanliness is next to godliness'. Another was 'Of only three things in life can one ever really be sure – firstly one is born, secondly one dies and thirdly between the two there will be change.' (I have added a fourth – 'there will be taxes too!')

In casting a cursory glance over the past 78 years I can clearly see I've brushed up against and recognised those forces at work for change – change in all directions and at all times. Changes for the better and changes for the worse.

Looking through those old family photo albums I've come across a picture from the 1950s showing the four of us at Stonehenge on a peaceful picnic at the foot of that magical monument. Not a soul in sight. My last visit there in 2018 was a not unexpected disappointment. We fought through the crowds – hundreds of OAPs on a day coach trip and shoals of badly behaved school children – and queued for hours for expensive tickets. No magic there. Very definitely a change for the worse.

Another photo from the 1960s – me frantically cranking my first car (Hillman Minx) trying in vain to get it to start. Now, 60 years later, my car key is a card which unlocks the car from my pocket. The gentle push of a button starts the engine. Very definitely a change for the better.

And so likewise through the decades. Change mostly for the better. But not always. Do whisky-sodden prep school headmasters still thrash and beat ten-year-old boys? I doubt it. In the public schools of the land, do the prefects still take a cane to the younger boys? Surely not. Is physical bullying still the scourge it was? I sincerely hope not. Are these schools not now more civilised for being (mostly) co-educational? Does the alpha games player still rule the roost? Hopefully there are now others too to step into that limelight with their various talents. Room for changes here to be sure.

And the teachers? Those great giants – the Carters, Murrays and Weldons of the Marlborough I knew – do they still stalk the corridors of these great schools? Does the young new French beak still fling that board-rubber (the heavy old-fashioned variety, half wood half felt) at a velocity worthy of a French Exocet guided missile? (Probably not, if only because such board-rubbers no longer exist). Will that new young teacher still be pubbing and clubbing as we did? After-dinner croquet in the summer, port-drinking in the winter as in those halcyon days of yore? Or will they now be toeing a party line which had never really previously existed? Senior management had yet to invent itself, teacher assessments were unknown, teaching methods one's own. I now hear myself saying that there's no longer much room for the amateur who is in the game of teaching partly for the fun of it, partly for the long holidays. Hats off now to the professional and a more 'serious' approach to the job in hand. A change for the better here, do I hear you say?

Life in Le Castéra, that small Gascon village on a hill outside Toulouse, has also seen its fair share of change over the forty years I've known it. Much has been lost. No longer the 14th July fête in the village square with the schoolchildren dressed for the part. No longer the dances in the village hall, gone the communal meals with us all sitting at trestle tables in the square doing justice to the wild boar and venison set before us by the local hunt. Gone the youth who have drifted into the towns (*l'exode rural*) to find employment. And with them gone too the drinking sessions (*les beuveries*) and binges of the Bacchus, the café/bar across the square – now all but surplus to requirement with its *patron* Colombo, forlorn and grumpy, still clinging on waiting for an ever-dwindling clientèle. As a village it is now not much more than a colourless shadow of its former self, giving shelter to me and others of my like – the elderly.

So too has change come to Chefchaouen, Morocco. No longer the goats clattering by below twice daily bound for their pastures. No longer the donkeys plodding by laden with gas bottles and crates of soft drinks. Welcome now to their 21st century replacements – Hondas and Suzukis narrow enough to pass through the medina gates and speeding by unceremoniously. The same too with the cheap imported Chinese motorbikes which are now just about within range of a young Chaoueni's pocket. There goes the local colour – the goats and the donkeys – and here comes 21st century 'progress' – noise and pollution. A bad deal.

The memory of my first visit to Morocco remains undimmed. It amounted to a full-frontal attack on all the senses; the sights, sounds and smells I encountered were all totally unfamiliar. Now that is no longer the case. I now well know the sound of the muezzin, the smells of the spice stalls. Some of the magic has gone. So too past familiar sights are fast disappearing. Chaouenis twenty years ago generally wore the traditional djellabah, both men and boys, the heavy, warm woollen ones in winter, the light cotton versions in summer. Now it's mostly T-shirts, jeans, baseball caps and trainers. Gone the local colour, the exotic.

Visiting tourists are now of another kind. No longer the backpackers and the dirty, dreadlocked Spanish hippies in search of kif. Now it is the Chinese who predominate, who arrive in their droves, staying often only a matter of hours, buying nothing, photographing everything and everyone and eating only in the new Chinese restaurants which have sprung up mushroom-like overnight. The local trades gain little from this yellow invasion and even less so since the Free Trade Agreement signed by China and Morocco in 2016, meaning that cheap Chinese goods have flooded the market, making Moroccan prices more often than not uncompetitive. Many a Chaoueni weaver and leatherworker has felt the impact of this unwelcome intrusion.

However, all is not lost and change for the better there has also been. The medina now boasts dustbins and the vulgar neon street strip lighting has been replaced by pretty Andalusian-style wrought-iron lamps.

An Evensong prayer which has been with me since the age of eight has us ask of Merciful God to protect us through the quiet hours of the night – we who are wearied by the changes and chances of this fleeting world. Wearied? Certainly at times, yes, but equally challenged by them too, perhaps?

To fight against the challenge of changes in life is to invite stresses and strains. To reconcile oneself to change, be it for the better or for the worse, is to go with the flow, serene and composed. A certain measure of serenity and composure I've also found, I now realise as I pen these last lines, by plunging back into my past and retrieving a fund of deep-rooted memories of days long gone by. I have found it is the fond ones which predominate. Boyhood memories of playing on the dazzling white sands of Pentle Bay, Tresco, Isles of Scilly. Youthful memories of the Queen Anne South Devon vicarage with the honeysuckle tumbling down over the front porch. Student memories of four years of passing back and forwards through Front Gate, Trinity College, Dublin, flanked on either side by the imposing bronze statues of Edmund Burke and Oliver Goldsmith. Fond memories of those schoolmastering days at Marlborough College, so too of magical Morocco and finally of Le Castéra, that Gascon village I now long ago found at the top of a hill near Toulouse and have ever since called home.

As John F. Kennedy once said, "Every man has two countries: his own and France." How true. I'll happily settle for that. Fortunate indeed the man who carries both England and France within him. So how can I now possibly ask for more?

Printed in Dunstable, United Kingdom